Civil–Military Entanglements

Civil–Military Entanglements

Anthropological Perspectives

Edited by
Birgitte Refslund Sørensen and Eyal Ben-Ari

berghahn
NEW YORK · OXFORD
www.berghahnbooks.com

First published in 2019 by
Berghahn Books
www.berghahnbooks.com

Library of Congress Cataloging-in-Publication Data

Names: Sørensen, Birgitte Refslund, editor. | Ben-Ari, Eyal, 1953– author.
Title: Civil–Military Entanglements: Anthropological Perspectives / edited by
    Birgitte Refslund Sørensen and Eyal Ben-Ari.
Description: New York: Berghahn Books, 2019. | Includes bibliographical
    references and index.
Identifiers: LCCN 2018056945 (print) | LCCN 2018059262 (ebook) | ISBN
    9781789201963 (ebook) | ISBN 9781789201956 (hardback: alk. paper)
Subjects: LCSH: Civil-military relations—Case studies. | Civil-military
    relations—Cross-cultural studies.
Classification: LCC JF195 (ebook) | LCC JF195 .R475 2019 (print) |
    DDC 322.5—dc23
LC record available at https://lccn.loc.gov/2018056945

British Library Cataloguing in Publication Data

A catalogue record for this book is available from the British Library

ISBN 978-1-78920-195-6 hardback
ISBN 978-1-78920-196-3 ebook

Contents

Acknowledgments

The Entanglement Project received funding from the International Network Programme of the Danish Ministry of Education and Research. The workshop in Copenhagen was supported by the Department of Anthropology, University of Copenhagen, and the workshop in Israel by the Kinneret Center for Society, Security and Peace at Kinneret Academic College and the Open University of Israel through the very welcome support of Prof. Yagil Levy.

Introduction

Rethinking Civil–Military Connections
From Relations to Entanglements

Birgitte Refslund Sørensen and Eyal Ben-Ari

The global security landscape has changed dramatically over the past few decades, altering how military forces are recruited, trained, and deployed globally. As a result, interfaces between armed forces and civilians have been shaped in numerous new ways. Just think of the "wars against terrorism" waged by coalition forces typically headed by a few large military powers but engaging other nations with no, or limited, recent war experience. Think of the increasing deployment of military personnel and technologies to provide "homeland security," and the growing use of troops for "military operations other than war" (MOOTW), including tasks such as border control and provision of security at major public events, as well aiding in humanitarian crises after devastating disasters. Think of the crisis simulations, operational exercises, and live demonstrations of military capacity that take place in public spaces with civilians as audience. Think also of the trend away from large conscripted armies toward smaller voluntary forces, and the concurrent growth of public relations departments within the armed forces (Ben-Ari this volume). Think of the global recirculation and use of militarized human capital, security equipment, and expertise (Grassianni this volume), or of the more subtle presence of "things military" in the commercialized products of the entertainment, technology, and fashion industries or indeed in the landscape. And think of the large number of civilians employed at army bases or who assist veterans, soldiers, and families in need, not to mention military reserves who continuously traverse civilian–military boundaries. Indeed, circumstances under which relations between civilians and militaries are established are many and diverse.

In this volume, we argue that a plethora of critical civil–military encounters demand anthropological attention and necessitate reconceptualizing the field of civil–military relations, which continues to be firmly anchored in the classical debates within political sociology and political science. The basic dilemma that underlies theorizing within these disciplines has centered on the military's potential threat of using the organized means of violence at its disposal to take over political, social, and economic institutions. Hence, previous theorizing has primarily focused on issues concerning appropriate and effective control mechanisms ensuring that military force is used in the interest of society and not against it. This perspective, however, pays little heed to how ordinary civilians encounter and experience military institutions during their everyday lives, nor how civilian life influences the military. We find this line of inquiry critical because it can illuminate how military and civilian domains are tied together, constituting complex entanglements destabilizing the classic civil–military binary and manifesting themselves in unexpected ways. Accordingly, our volume explores the particular perspectives that ethnography and anthropology can contribute to documentations and conceptualizations of, and critical debates about, current civil–military relations. Anthropology is methodologically well suited to capture ongoing transformations and manifestations of civil–military relations from unique empirical positions that go beyond and add to the restricted, nationally framed institutional gaze. Moreover, anthropology can develop innovative theoretical vocabularies enhancing our understanding of the reach and depth of these entanglements.

In what follows, we briefly position the anthropological study of civil–military relations in its wider scholarly background and elaborate on our analytical framework. First, we outline the field's formative sociological legacy and then proceed to discuss some anthropological research trajectories that have clear relevance for the study of civil–military relations but which have only partly or indirectly been conceptualized in those terms. The body of sociological and anthropological literature discussed here is not exhaustive but suggestive of how the scholarly field of civil–military relations has developed. We end by charting out an agenda for an anthropology of contemporary civil–military entanglements building on the limitations and gaps that the ethnographic cases make visible in the existing literature.

The Sociological Legacy

Generally speaking, scholarly studies of the relations between the armed forces and societies are characterized by a broad development that has taken place in political sociology and political science (Lomsky-Feder and Ben-Ari 2000). This movement should be pictured as a number of successive, and cumulative, intellectual waves—each wave characterized by a central theoretical model. All however, proceed from the realization that the central core—the starting point for any analysis—is that the uniqueness of the military (along with the police) lies in the organization of legitimate (if at times contested) state violence (Boene 1990).

The examination of military and society relations in the post–World War II era was launched by scholars focusing on the military as a social institution and on its leadership as a professional and social elite. The emphasis here was on the links between military and civilian sectors of society within a structural-functionalist perspective (Burk 1998; Huntington 1957; Janowitz 1971, 1976; Moskos 1976). These kinds of studies tended to focus on the institutional level, and their *problematique* revolved around the capacity of political systems to balance democratic arrangements with security considerations, the prominence of military elites in decision-making, and allocation of resources to military efforts. The dominant conceptualization within this approach was on how permeable the boundaries were between the civilian and military sectors and the mutual influence of the more extreme orientations of both spheres (Luckham 1971). Because the overwhelming stress within this approach was on institutions and on elites, little was said (or asked) about war as an "autonomous" phenomenon, as an occurrence with a distinctive set of implications for society.

The second wave of research thus investigated the ways in which societies and nations are "made" through preparation for, mobilization toward, and the perpetration of wars. Based in critical sociology, this perspective included "sociological" *and* "cultural" versions. In the more "sociological" vein, war was examined as part of the social order, and especially as an integral part of state institutions as they impact wider society. This was evinced in what may be called the "State, Society, and War" approach: for example, modern war was examined as a primary means by which the state establishes its power within society by mobilizing resources for external conflicts. The most compelling dimension of these studies has been to show how war (or its possibility) works toward centralizing the state and contributes to the institutionalization of the means of violence in a given society (Giddens 1985; Mann 1988; Tilly 1995). Accordingly, while the earlier school focused on the relations between the armed forces and society, this approach concentrated on how war is part of ongoing relations between state and civil society. Such diverging analytical foci were predicated on very different assumptions (Lomsky-Feder and Ben-Ari 2000). First, while the initial (functional-institutional) approach was developed in the heyday of America's success in World War II and was essentially celebratory, the latter (conflict-statist) approach was formulated in the context of the Cold War and the debacle of Vietnam, and was highly critical. Second, the distinct frameworks called attention to different issues: the first to institutional linkages (the structure of a regime) and the second to focal points of power and dissension (in and around the structures of the state). Third, while one asked about the mechanisms by which democracies continued to function in face of the importance of the military, the other asked about how armed struggles figured in the manner by which democratic states were enhanced by certain kinds of militarism.

Studies belonging to the "cultural" approach are allied with the critical sociologists but uncover the manner by which militarism is constructed. This scholarship is concerned neither with the direct study of the military nor with the state, but with patterns of cultural construction since it examines the cultural means by which war is sacralized and constructed in collective memories. Within the social sciences, this broad wave includes such works as those carried out by Kertzer (1988) and Da Matta (1984) on political and military rituals, or by Mosse (1990) on military cemeteries.

The next wave of studies took up many of the macro-level insights of the previous approaches to explore how social construction of the military and war affects individuals' life-worlds. Since the mid-1980s, scholarly investigations began to ask questions about military experiences—in a sense foreshadowing many of the concerns that anthropologists have taken up. For example, the studies in the collection by Segal and Sinaiko (1986) demonstrated the importance of a "bottom-up" approach to analyzing (American) military life and the utility of studying hitherto little explored areas such as socialization into the military, the criteria by which soldiers appraise their own service, or the creation within the armed forces of certain folk images and stereotypes. Other works (Eisenhart 1975; Shatan 1977) suggested the profitability of analyzing military training in symbolic or ritualistic terms. Similarly, Edna Lomsky-Feder (1998) examined how war and military service figure in the personal narratives of Israeli men. In theoretical terms, these studies linked constructions, structures, power, and resources related to the armed forces and war to individual military and civilian experiences.

The Anthropological Entry

With rare exceptions, anthropologists have usually ceded the study of civil–military relations to sociologists and political scientists, perhaps as a consequence of the discipline's historical focus on "exotic others" and "society" rather than the state. Moreover, the proclivity of ethnographers to study the underdog and the marginal has left the study of elites and mainstream (including the military) a relatively understudied subject (Gusterson 1993: 60). Finally, most American anthropologists have viewed the U.S. military in terms of the Vietnam debacle and, since 9/11, through the lens of the occupations of Iraq and Afghanistan. Consequently, the armed forces have often been regarded as somehow morally tainted and therefore not "worthy" of anthropological research, and anthropologists in any way linked to the military have been seen as in some way "polluted" (Ben-Ari 2011; Rubinstein 2012). Indeed, Greenhouse's (1989: 49) suggestions seem to still hold: that because of the common premise pervading our discipline that war is pathological, and because of a professional value orientation that opposes armed aggression, key cultural questions about conflict and the armed forces have been obscured.

While one would expect the armed forces to be a critical site if one wants to understand the contemporary social and cultural significance of armed conflicts (Ben-Ari 2004, 2008), there are relatively few ethnographic studies of the role of armed forces in violent conflicts. As Krohn-Hansen (1994: 367) emphasized, anthropological studies tend to focus on the victim's perspective, often ignoring the perpetrators or the relations between the parties to violence. While it is important to document and consider how wars and armed conflicts impact the everyday lives of ordinary people, the analysis of victims' tribulations does not necessarily tell us much about how relationships between civilians and the armed forces develop and are experienced. In response to this gap, some anthropologists have directed their attention toward perpetrators of violence. However, most of these studies have concerned the emergence and actions of nonstate actors such as vigilante groups, rebels, and guerrilla fighters (Grätz 2007; Hoffman 2011; Nordstrom 1997; Thiranagama 2014; Vigh 2006), positioned on the margins of society and whose use of violence is not legitimized by, but may in fact be directed at, the state. Moreover, many studies in this tradition do not aim to understand relations between perpetrators and victims, but to explore the structural and cultural factors that have pushed or pulled particular groups toward a violent life trajectory.

Military forces, however, have not been entirely absent in anthropological research. A few early contributions included studies of the militaries of authoritarian regimes or majority world countries, but it was only with the critical end of the Cold War that a distinct anthropology of the military began to emerge (McFate 2005). The end of the Cold War resulted in major transformations having dramatic impact on the armed forces. Bickford's (2011) study of how unification of Germany undermined the lives and identities of former East German officers is one example. The initial euphoria following the fall of the Berlin Wall disappeared with the advent of a new kind of abhorrent war, variously termed "asymmetrical wars," "hybrid wars," "postmodern wars," or simply the "new wars" (Hoffman 2007; Kaldor 1999; Münkler 2005), with a heavy involvement of nonstate actors mobilized around "identity politics" and deliberately targeting civilians. While the Global South experienced the lion's share of these wars, they also manifested themselves at the doorstep of Europe and tore the Balkans apart (Cushman 2004; Halpern and Kideckel 2000; Schaüble 2014).

A decade later, the events of 9/11 resulted in a new generation of asymmetrical wars, as armed forces from the United States, the United Kingdom, and other industrial democracies coalesced in "the global war on terror," "peace-building," "counterinsurgencies," or, more benignly, "humanitarian wars" (Masco 2014; Frederic, Rubinstein, and Zoli this volume). Suddenly, it seemed violence that had previously been mostly limited to "out there" came "home," and the areas traditionally studied by anthropologists became connected to the anthropologists' own home countries in new and forceful ways. Civilian urban spaces transformed into "battlespaces" with citizen surveillance (Graham 2009), and troops returning from tours to the more remote zones of prolonged wars also brought war back home. This escalation of transnational military operations reinforced the scholarly interest in the military that had emerged with the end of the Cold War, and a more critical military anthropology was added to the ethnographic descriptions of militaries.

Issues that interested anthropologists from the outset were the armed forces' internal organization or cultural patterns, and how civilians were transformed into soldiers—issues that continue to generate insightful research as armies transform themselves in response to new political conditions and security challenges (Ben-Ari 1998b; Danielsen 2015; Frederic this volume; Hawkins 2001; Holmes-Eber 2014; Kirke 2000; Nørgaard 2004; Simons 1997, 1999; Sion 2004; Winslow 1997). One also finds a growing body of literature on the gendered nature of militaries (Aciksoz 2012; Altinay 2004; Bickford 2003; Duncanson 2013; Enloe 2000; Haaland 2008; Higate 2003; Kilshaw 2009; Kronsell and Svedberg 2012; McSorley 2013; Stachowitsch 2013; Sylvester 2014; Whitworth 2004; Woodward and Jenkings 2013). Another focus area, producing rich ethnographic studies, is military communities around army bases in the United States (Frese 2008; Hawkins 2001; Lutz 2001; MacLeish 2013) and around the world where anti-base movements caught anthropological attention (Altinay and Homes 2009; Fitz-Henry 2011; Inoue 2007; Lutz 2009; McCaffrey 2002; Schober 2016; Vine and Jeffrey 2009). The global military connection was also the core of Gill's (2004) study of the training of other countries' troops in American military schools, and of anthropological studies of the transformation of national armies in former colonies (Agyekum 2016).

The deployment of armed troops from several nations with United Nations or NATO mandates resulted in a series of studies of peacekeepers (Frederic this volume), but also, and very importantly, a revival of studies of war veterans (Gustavsen and Haaland this volume), in vogue in the wake of the two world wars. While earlier studies were the territory of historians occupied with how nations reconciled themselves with the ramifications of "trench warfare" (Mosse 1990; Winter 1995), today studies focus almost exclusively on veterans' experiences of combat-related injuries and suffering. As noted by Hautzinger and Scandlyn (2014), PTSD (Post-Traumatic Stress Disorder), TBI (Traumatic Brain Injury), and depression have been identified as the "signature injuries" of post-9/11 wars, and medical anthropologists are making valuable contributions to this field, challenging psychiatric approaches by emphasizing the social dimensions of these disorders (Finley 2011; Kilshaw 2007, 2009; Messinger 2013; Moss and Prince 2014; Tomforde this volume). While contemporary wars demand fewer casualties, insurgents' frequent use of IED's (Improvised Explosive Devices) repatriate many veterans in need of complicated surgeries and amputation. The body, which anthropological studies of soldiering have demonstrated to be key to the development of the masculine warrior, now threatens to become the source of processes of emasculation (Wool 2012, 2015; MacLeish 2012; Messinger 2009; Wool and Messinger 2012). Other studies have investigated the ties linking armed forces to their societies: Altinay (2004) on the influence of the Turkish armed forces in the country's education system, and Ben-Ari and Frühstück (2003) and Sørensen and Pedersen (2012) on how civilians are exposed to the military as audiences at public events demonstrating military capacities or in ceremonial celebrations of the warrior hero. Each new war requires legitimization, and veterans returning from combat yearn for appropriate social recognition of their efforts, as Gustavsen and Haaland (this volume) show. The cultural understandings and social positioning of veterans, however, are contestable and changeable, and some anthropological works address the dynamic social construction of public images of "the veteran" (Aciksoz 2012; Gustavsen 2016; Sørensen 2015 and forthcoming; Truusa and Kasearu this volume). Moreover, "things military" not only appear in the public sphere, but enter our everyday lives in numerous and subtle ways (Enloe 2000; Lutz 2001, 2002). Building on Der Derian's (2001) work, Gonzalez (2010) shows how the U.S. military markets itself through movies, toys, etc. and infiltrates American families, while Tomforde (this volume) explores how contemporary artists portray the experience of German troops abroad. Sørensen (2015) demonstrates how the Danish military regulates ties between deployed troops and their families. Truusa and Kasearu (this volume) in a like manner underscore how service in the military by Estonian husbands is a central theme in the narratives of their wives.

Military anthropology may still be in its infancy, but it is vibrant and has already demonstrated its relevance to understanding one of the key factors that shape today's world. The authors of the chapters appearing in this volume concur that the military and civil–military relations deserve a central place in contemporary anthropological research, both in terms of ethnographic exploration and conceptual elucidation. In the following section, we trace out our argument for an anthropology of civil–military entanglements as one way to build on existing achievements and what we consider remaining gaps and shortages.

Civil–Military Entanglements

A few key propositions inform the way we rethink civil–military relations from an anthropological perspective in the current global security landscape. Each addresses what we consider two limitations of the sociological legacy: its exclusive focus on Western nation-states and its rather uncritical adoption of the "civil–military" institutional dichotomy. Anthropological writings on processes of economic and cultural globalization have provided us with an alternative source of inspiration, which we find pertinent to the study of contemporary wars and security landscapes. Anthropologists' efforts to capture the complex and dynamic flows and linkages associated with globalization have given rise to a rich and creative analytical vocabulary, including concepts such as "assemblage" (Ong and Collier 2004; Marcus and Saka 2006), "scapes" (Appadurai 1996), "friction" (Tsing 2005), and "entanglement" (Thomas 1991; Hodder 2012). Despite differences in focus and emphasis, scholars are in broad agreement that globalization is marked by contingency, and is inherently open-ended and partly unpredictable, which calls for analytical attention to the specific and local. Hodder (2012: 88), who himself employs the notion of "entanglement," emphasizes that this goes beyond networks simply connecting separate entities, and implies dialectic relationships between productive and enabling "dependence" and constraining and limiting "dependency." Moreover, he contends, entanglements potentially destabilize and reconfigure the constituent parts: "It is not that there are no such divisions, but that the distinctions are effects or outcomes" (Hodder 2012: 91).

We can better understand the nature and dynamics of contemporary civil–military connections, if our attention to entanglements translates into two distinct, but interrelated analytical moves: first, we need to incorporate the views and experiences of nations or groupings with different war trajectories and world order positions, but without losing sight of how these are embedded in wider transnational or global settings; second, we contend that the macro-sociological civil–military dichotomy is one social, cultural *construct* that tends to reduce related phenomena to a simple either/or classification within which one entity or process is "civilian" or "military." Instead of this dichotomous view we suggest directing our analyses toward its disaggregated constitutive elements; the actors, sites, discourses, technologies, objects, etc. that are mobilized and reconfigured in innovative ways and make up particular, sometimes unexpected manifestations of civil–military relations.

Political scientists and sociologists are not alone in focusing their thinking about militaries and their surrounding societies on Western nations. In fact, anthropologists studying the military have mostly focused on the United States, and their works have inadvertently come to constitute the analytical and moral template for exploring civil–military encounters and relations elsewhere, shaping thematic and theoretical orientations and influencing what is considered appropriate or legitimate anthropological lines of inquiry. It is thus largely due to the preoccupation of American colleagues that the military, its army bases, and its communities have emerged as a recognized ethnographic field within anthropology, and inspired anthropologists from elsewhere to scrutinize the role of the military in their own societies. American military anthropology, however, has not only been a source of inspiration, but also a constraining factor or at times even a moral gatekeeper when its heavy preoccupation (sometimes obsession) with the way our discipline has been "subtly moulded by the priorities of national security state and the exigencies of other people's wars" has been projected onto the global community of anthropologists by default (Gusterson 2007: 156; see also Price 2008, 2011a, 2011b: Wax 2003).

But not all anthropologists—and especially those outside the classic and new hegemonic powers—have served such a role, and not all anthropologists are marked by the same kind of disciplinary guilt trip about anthropology's role in colonialism (Ben-Ari 1998a, 2011) and consequently about its role in "serving" the armed forces. By stating this, we do not imply forsaking our discipline's critical potential, but rather insist on anthropology's trademark as a globally and holistically oriented discipline, which calls for an examination of civil–military entanglements from the vantage point of countries with a different "war trajectory and culture" than that of the United States. Lutz (2002) makes a similar point, but whereas she is primarily interested in how different national histories are tied to legitimization and glorification of military action, we propose a broader, more open-ended and comparative exploration of how particular civil–military connections are shaped, negotiated, and entangled in social life in different places. This volume aims to make a modest contribution to a more diversified exploration of contemporary civil–military relations from the vantage points of such cases as Israel or the United States, societies fundamentally ordered in and around armed conflict and internal security concerns, and Japan, Germany, Norway, and Denmark, countries that, each in their way, have long avoided military deployment, but are currently slowly adapting to the new global security landscape and its political agendas, and renegotiating the purpose and mandate of their respective armed forces.

A central concern of American military anthropologists has been with processes of militarization, which entails a complex process where institutions of civilian society are configured in preparation for and conduct of war and violence. Militarization, Lutz argues, "is simultaneously a discursive process involving a shift in societal beliefs and values in ways necessary to legitimate the use of force, the organization of large standing armies and their leaders, and the higher taxes or tribute used to pay for them" (Lutz 2002: 723). Importantly, the mobilization of civilian institutions for war is intimately linked to the creation of hierarchies of race, class, gender, and sexuality, and leaves noticeable as well as more subtle traces in public space and popular culture, as several of the chapters in this volume explicate. For anthropologists, it is in the very everydayness, the taken-for-granted nature, of militarization that makes it such a dominant force since it entails unquestioned ways of organizing societies, groups, and individuals. The countries included in this volume have all embarked on processes involving militarization, but despite remarkable similarities regarding how militarization operates and manifests itself, there are also significant differences, which are rooted in the countries' unique war histories and memories, patterns of social organization and cultural values.

Militarization is never a straightforward process, as Frederic (this volume) shows, since it may be replaced by processes of demilitarization. However, in this respect anthropologists are uniquely situated to study how the armed forces bargain with various civilian entities. At the heart of such bargaining lies the armed forces' autonomy to manage and practice violence, but it extends into negotiations about the entitlements, status, social welfare, and recognition that members of the armed forces should enjoy, as well as struggles over competing discourses and cultural imageries of military, nation, and society, and of veterans, soldiers, and civilians. Uesugi's contribution (this volume) underscores this by showing how Ghurkas who have served in the country's armed forces for generations struggle for inclusion in the citizenship regime of the United Kingdom. In turn, the social position of civilians and soldiers is often intimately linked to the ways in which the military's potential for lethal violence is represented and legitimized or rejected in the cultural imagery. Ben-Ari's contribution (this volume), for instance, charts out the ways in which popular culture is used to soften the images of Japan's Self-Defense Forces and gradually habituate diverse publics to their presence in society and their actions (see also Frühstück 2007). Another example is the perception of recent activist position taken by Denmark in embarking on foreign deployments as a revival of its long-suppressed national identity as a warrior nation (see also Sørensen and Pedersen 2012; Sørensen and Linnet nd.).

The military's potential for violence runs as a thread through much scholarly writing, including anthropology, and with recent developments in the global security landscape there is good reason not to dismiss this focus. However, war and violence do not always take center stage in civil–military relations. Agyekum (2016) provocatively suggests the existence of "positive militarization" when the armed forces utilize their unique resources and competences to support society in times of distress, distributing and coordinating emergency relief without the use of force. Whether the military's role in such "operations other than war" is best perceived as an example of increasing "securitization" of nonmilitary areas (Bajc 2007; Fosher 2008; Tierney and Bevc 2007), or is indeed "civilizing" (or better "civilianizing") the military to consider the use of violence a last resort, as Agyekum suggests, can only be properly answered empirically. In any case, it is important to consider how militaries' benign activities are tied to their potential for violence in their bargaining of relations to civilian populations, whether at home or at sites of operation.

We argue for the inclusion of more "national voices" in exploring present-day civil–military relations and remain critical of the nation-state as a natural analytical framework. That said, it is important to recognize that national militaries are globally entangled. Nordstrom (1997, 2004) forcefully argued that the concept of "local wars" is largely a fiction since they are anything but local, but instead imbricated with much larger systems. Lutz in her work with Nonini (1999) and the essays by Tanaka and Frederic (this volume) demonstrate how transnational economic and political processes have transformed people's livelihood and increased levels of conflict, violence, and warfare. The global entanglement of national armed forces is, for instance, reflected in joint policy making and cooperation through supranational institutions, deployment of multinational coalition forces, exchange of security information, joint training and exercises, and military equipment and expertise purchases, as well as in collaborative efforts to develop postdeployment responses to war veterans' needs and mutual inspiration regarding public display of military powers or public commemoration of fallen soldiers.

Our second proposition concerns the conventional "civil–military" dichotomy itself, inherited from theories in political science and military sociology, which demarcates "military" and "society" as two bounded and opposed entities (Lutz 2001). We contend that it is analytically useful to disaggregate the dichotomy, by which we mean delineating how "civil" and "military" relations occur and are negotiated at multiple levels (macro, meso, micro), involve various actors (ministries, governments, interest organizations, individual soldiers/families, celebrities, media, cultural institutions, the public), and take place in a plethora of domains/sites (parliaments, streets, homes, museums, the internet, or garrisons). Our disaggregation is linked to our understanding of what could possibly be the core issues of the study of civil–military relations. For example, the ties between the military and local governments and communities, economic corporations and subcontractors, the media and lobbies, or humanitarian and human rights movements do not seem to involve only problems of civilian control, the central concern of many writings on civil–military relations. Rather, each kind of link is marked by its own "logic of action" and its unique practices and meanings.

This point is crucial, for it emphasizes anthropology's promise to capture ethnographically the multiple ways in which "things military" (institutions, people, values, symbols, objects, etc.) are entangled with "things civilian" (people, social life, or popular culture). In this sense, anthropology seeks not only to address the classic issues of how societies affect the military, but to explicitly go beyond a focus on states and militaries, beyond law and politics. This point implies directing our analytical gaze toward the mundane, the ordinary, parts of lives and experiences (in homes, museums, schools, companies, associations, etc.) in which the armed forces and various civilian entities negotiate, cooperate, and sometimes conflict.

Seen this way, moreover, we can appreciate how a look beyond formal institutional arrangements and institutional forms reveals that civil–military entanglements are fluid, blurry, contestable, and always negotiable. As Woodward (2004) shows, the very landscape of a territory is something that is constantly created, changing and evolving in interaction with military and security considerations. And as Gustavsen and Haaland (this volume) argue, Norway's historical trajectory reveals how civil–military entanglements may expand and diminish but also become more and less transparent. Tomforde (this volume) shows how different historical periods are marked by diverse entanglements between the military and artistic worlds. In a complementary manner Rubinstein and Zoli (this volume) demonstrate both the tensions between and the blurring of the roles of the military and police via veterans' critiques of militarized policing.

One promising contribution of anthropology to civil–military thinking lies in its ability to trace out the ripples and reverberations of entanglements to areas not usually associated with such ties, but which are significant for how war, violence, and the military shape contemporary societies. The essay by Sørensen and Heiselberg examines the effects deployments abroad of Danish soldiers have on family dynamics and domestic family life, demonstrating the intricate links between global processes and the most intimate kinds of interpersonal ties (see also Heiselberg forthcoming; Sørensen 2013). Moreover, in its attention to everyday situations where soldiers occupy social roles as partners, fathers, and human beings, this study challenges the elusiveness of civil–military relations and undermines the dichotomy between clearly demarcated institutions characterized by more or less permeable boundaries, and points out how such distinctions are always situational and depend on context. Tanaka's study (this volume) shows how such global-intimate ties can be expressed at an even deeper level: he shows how the very bodies and bodily sensations of Okinawan civilians are shaped by the mundane practices of fighter jets taking off and landing at American Air Force bases near their homes. A further move away from the institutional conceptualization of the civil–military complex is exemplified by the studies of Grassiani and Pedersen (this volume), as they demonstrate how notions of "civilian" and "military" assume particular but shifting moral values in relation to wider security and war agendas, and how their attachment to objects, people, and situations becomes one way of creating moral hierarchies. In Grassiani's study, the Israeli security industry's labeling of security solutions marketed to Kenya as "combat proven" is one way to discursively declare their reliability and create obscure entanglements between Palestinian zones and Kenyan citizens. Although such representations are obviously related to how the "reputational content" of the military and of military personnel are promoted or besmirched, their import seems to go beyond the situational. People use talk about "things military" as a medium for discussing or evoking images of themselves and of the societies they live in. Pedersen's study traces how Danish civilians' moral confutation of killing and the armed forces' commitment to casualty aversion interfere with the soldiers' processes of military becoming.

Our approach to "civil–military entanglements" accentuates the methodological questions that have always accompanied anthropology's engagement with war, violence, and the military. These have included reflections on the risks, dangers, and implications of conducting fieldwork under fire (Nordstrom and Robben 1999); cautionary remarks that scholars could be seduced by high ranking informants in the military (Robben 1995); arguments regarding the inevitable political position of any researcher (Frederic 2016; Castro 206; Rubinstein 1998; Weber 2016); and, not least, ethical considerations regarding anthropologists' embedded-ness within military institutions and units (Gusterson 2003, 2007; Gon-zalez 2004a, 2004b; Kelly and Jauregui 2010; Lucas 2009; McFate and Lawrence 2015). Gazit's interrogations (this volume) take us a step away from discussions about fieldwork during times of war and armed vio-lence to questions about fieldwork under conditions of (constant) war preparations and what at present seems to be an ever deeper and subtler penetration of "things military" into ordinary lives. It is also in this light that the collection edited by Rubinstein, Fosher, and Fujimura (2012; also Rubinstein and Zoli this volume) should be seen: as showing the vari-ety of issues and engagements between anthropologists with the military and other parts of the national security state. The most important mes-sage from their collection is that we must be wary of homogenizing the experiences of anthropologists studying civil–military engagements. To this we would add that we should also be constantly alert and imagina-tive in searching out possible empirical manifestations of civil–military entanglements.

The Structure of This Volume

As the chapters of this volume reveal, "things military" and "things civil-ian" meet and get interpreted, negotiated, and entangled at many levels and in many of social contexts. While we acknowledge that civil–mili-tary relations are always framed by the particular security and political environments of nation-states, and that it is important to heed how na-tion-states differently positioned in the global security landscape produce civil–military relations, this volume is not primarily intended to provide an overview of national instantiations. Instead, in order to accentuate the salient point that in our contemporary world, "things civilian" and "things military" do not (only) constitute a macro-level binary, but are indeed intertwined at all levels and take on many disguises, the chap-ters are organized to provide examples from different domains. The first section illustrates how civil–military relations are embedded in everyday lives and intimate relations. The next group of chapters concern public social space, where civilians experience the military as consumers of some sort. Section three is closer to the original aim of civil–military studies, as it directs its focus at how "civilian" and "military" are inscribed in the contract between state and citizens. The next section takes us to the global and international domain. Finally, we recap and integrate the essays in an editorial epilogue.

Birgitte Refslund Sørensen is associate professor at the Department of Anthropology, University of Copenhagen. With her background in conflict studies and political anthropology, Sørensen has been both practitioner and researcher on issues of postconflict reconstruction for the United Nations Research Institute for Social Development and the Danish Refugee Council. She has also been a consultant on veterans' affairs in Denmark. Her latest publications include "Veterans' Homecomings" in *Current Anthropology*; "Public Commemorations of Danish Soldiers" in *Critical Military Studies*, and "Postconflict Reconstruction" in Palgrave MacMillan's interdisciplinary handbooks series on gender.

Eyal Ben-Ari is director of the Center for Society, Security and Peace at Kinneret College on the Sea of Galilee. He has carried out research in Israel, Japan, Singapore, and Hong Kong. His main areas of research are the sociology of the armed forces, early childhood education, and popular culture in Asia. Among his recent books are (with Zev Lehrer, Uzi Ben-Shalom, and Ariel Vainer) *Rethinking the Sociology of Warfare: A Sociological View of the Al-Aqsa Intifada* (2010), (with Nissim Otmazgin) *The State and Popular Culture in East Asia* (2012), (with Jessica Glicken Turnley and Kobi Michael) *Special Operations Forces in the 21st Century: Perspectives from the Social Sciences* (2017), and *Japanese Encounters: The Structure and Dynamics of Cultural Frames* (2018).

References

Aciksoz, Salih Can. 2012. "Sacrificial Limbs of Sovereignty: Disabled Veterans, Masculinity, and Nationalist Politics in Turkey." *Medical Anthropology Quarterly* 26 (1): 4–25.

Agyekum, Humphrey Asamoah. 2016. "From Buga-Buga Soldiers to Officers and Gentlemen. How Notions of Professionalism and Civility Transformed the Ghana Armed Forces." Ph.D. diss., Department of Anthropology, University of Copenhagen.

Altinay, Ayse Gul. 2004. *The Myth of the Military-Nation: Militarism, Gender and Education in Turkey*. New York: Palgrave Macmillan.

Altinay, Ayse Gul, and Amy Holmes. 2009. "Opposition to U.S. Military Presence in Turkey in the Context of the Iraq War." In Catherine Lutz (ed.), *The Bases of Empire*, 270–98. New York: Pluto Press.

Appadurai, Arjun. 1996. *Modernity at Large: Cultural Dimensions of Globalization*. Minneapolis: University of Minnesota Press.

Bajc, Vida. 2007. "Introduction: Debating Surveillance in the Age of Security." *American Behavioral Scientist* 50 (12): 1567–91.

Ben-Ari, Eyal. 1998a. "Colonialism, Anthropology and the Politics of Professionalization: An Argumentative Afterword." In Jan van Bremen and Akitoshi Shimizu (eds.), *An-*

thropology and Colonialism, 384–411. Honolulu: University of Hawaii Press and London: Curzon Press.

———. 1998b. *Mastering Soldiers: Conflict, Emotions and the Enemy in an Israeli Military Unit.* Oxford: Berghahn Books.

———. 2004. "Review Article: The Military and Militarization in the United States." *American Ethnologist* 31 (3): 340–48.

———. 2008. "Review Article: War, the Military and Militarization around the Globe." *Social Anthropology* 16 (1): 90–9.

———. 2011. "Anthropological Research and State Violence: Some Observations of an Israeli Anthropologist." In Laura A. McNamara and Robert A. Rubinstein (eds.), *Dangerous Liaisons: Anthropologists and the National Security State*, 167–84. Santa Fe: School of Advanced Research Press.

Ben-Ari, Eyal, and Efrat El-Ron. 2002. "Blue Helmets and White Armor: Multi-Nationalism and Multi-Culturalism among U.N. Peacekeeping Forces." *City and Society* 13 (2): 271–302.

Ben-Ari, Eyal, and Sabine Fruhstuck. 2003. "The Celebration of Violence: A Live-Fire Demonstration Carried Out by Japan's Contemporary Military." *American Ethnologist* 30 (4): 539–55.

Bickford, Andrew. 2003. "The Militarization of Masculinity in the Former German Democratic Republic." In Paul R. Higate (ed.), *Military Masculinities*, 157–73. Westport: Praeger.

———. 2011. *Fallen Elites: The Military Other in Post-Unification Germany*. Stanford: Stanford University Press.

Boene, Bernard. 1990. "How Unique Should the Military Be? A Review of Representative Literature and Outline of Synthetic Formulation." *European Journal of Sociology* 31 (1): 3–59.

Burk, James. 1998. "The Logic of Crisis and Civil Military Relations Theory: A Comment on Desch, Feaver and Dauber." *Armed Forces and Society* 24 (3): 455–62.

Castro, Celso. 2016. "Interviewing the Brazilian Military: Reflections on a Research Experience." In Helena Carreiras, Celso Castro, and Sabina Frederic (eds.), *Researching the Military*, 87–93. London: Routledge.

Cushman, Thomas. 2004. "Anthropology and Genocide in the Balkans: An Analysis of Conceptual Practices of Power." *Anthropological Theory* 4 (1): 5–28.

Da Matta, R. 1984. "Carnival in Multiple Planes." In J. J. MacAloon (ed.), *Rite, Drama, Festival, Spectacle*, 208–40. Philadelphia: Institute for the Study of Human Issues.

Danielsen, Tone. 2015. "Making Warriors in the Global Era: An Anthropological Study of Institutional Apprenticeship; Selection, Training, Education and Everyday Life in the Norwegian Naval Special Operations Commando." Doctoral diss., Department of Social Anthropology, University of Oslo.

Der Derian, James. 2001. *The Virtuous War: Mapping the Military-Industrial-Media-Entertainment Network*. London: Routledge.

Duncanson, Claire. 2013. *Forces for Good? Military Masculinities and Peacebuilding in Afghanistan and Iraq*. Basingstoke: Palgrave Macmillan.

Eisenhart, Wayne. 1975. "You Can't Hack It Little Girl: A Discussion of the Covert Psychological Agenda of Modern Combat Training." *Journal of Social Issues* 31 (4): 13–23.

Enloe, Cynthia. 2000. *Maneuvers: The International Politics of Militarizing Women's Lives*. Berkeley: University of California Press.

Finley, Erin. 2011. *Fields of Combat: Understanding PTSD among Veterans of Irac and Afghanistan*. Ithaca: Cornell University Press.

Fitz-Henry, Erin E. 2011. "Distant Allies, Proximate Enemies: Rethinking the Scales of the Antibase Movement in Ecuador." *American Ethnologist* 38 (2): 323–37.

Frederic, Sabina. 2016. "An Ethnographic Research in the Military Field: Rethinking Academic Autonomy in the Study of the Exodus of Junior Military Personnel in Argentina."

In Helena Carreiras, Celso Castro, and Sabina Frederic (eds.), *Researching the Military*, 119–30. London: Routledge.

Frese, Pamela. 2008. "Guardians of the Golden Age: Custodians of Military Culture and the Fortified 'Home' in Time and Space." *Home Cultures* 5 (1): 11–26.

Frühstück, Sabine. 2007. *Uneasy Warriors: Gender, Memory and Popular Culture in the Japanese Army*. Berkeley: University of California Press.

Giddens, Anthony. 1985. *The Nation-State and Violence*. Cambridge: Polity.

Gill, Lesley 1997 "Creating Citizens, Making Man: The Military and Masculinity in Bolivia." *Cultural Anthropology* 12 (4): 527–50.

———. 2004. *The School of the Americas: Military Training and Political Violence in the Americas*. Durham, NC: Duke University Press.

Gonzalez, Roberto J. 2004a. "Anthropologists in the Public Sphere: Speaking Out on War, Peace, and American Power." In Roberto J. Gonzalez (ed.), *Anthropologists in the Public Sphere*, 1–20. Austin: University of Texas Press.

———. 2004b. "Epilogue. Unconventional Anthropology: Challenging the Myths of Continuous War." In Roberto J. Gonzalez (ed.), *Anthropologists in the Public Sphere*, 257–72. Austin: University of Texas Press.

Gonzalez, Roberto (ed.). 2010. *Culture: Essays on the Warfare State*. Walnut Creek, CA: Left Coast Press.

Graham, Stephen. 2009. "Cities as Battlespace: The New Military Urbanism." *City* 13 (4): 384–402.

Grassiani, Erella. 2013. *Soldiering under Occupation: Processes of Numbing among Israeli Soldiers in the Al-Aqsa Intifada*. Oxford: Berghahn.

Grätz, Tilo. 2007. "Vigilante Groups and the State in West Africa." In Keebet Von Benda-Beckman and Fernanda Pirie (eds.), *Order and Disorder*, 207–33. Oxford: Berghahn.

Greenhouse, Carol J. 1989. "Fighting for Peace." In Mary Lecron Foster and Robert A. Rubinstein (eds.), *Peace and War*, 49–60. New Brunswick, NJ: Transaction.

Gustavsen, Elin. 2016. "The Construction of Meaning among Norweigan Afghanistan Veterans." *International Sociology* 31 (1): 21–36.

Gusterson, Hugh. 1993. "Exploding Anthropology's Canon in the World of the Bomb: Ethnographic Writing on Militarism." *Journal of Contemporary Ethnography* 22 (1): 59–79.

———. 2003. "Anthropology and the Military: 1968, 2003 and Beyond?" *Anthropology Today* 19 (3): 25–26.

———. 2007. "Anthropology and Militarism." *Annual Review of Anthropology* 36: 155–75.

Haaland, Torunn Laugen. 2008. "Invisible Women and Friendly War-Fighters: Perceptions of Gender and Masculinities in the Norwegian Armed Forces." *Norma* 2: 167–81.

Halpern, Joel M., and David A. Kideckel. 2000. *Neighbors at War: Anthropological Perspectives on Yugoslav Ethnicity, Culture, and History*. Philadephia: Pennsylvania University Press.

Hautzinger, Sarah, and Jean Scandlyn. 2014. *Beyond Post-Traumatic Stress*. Walnut Creek, CA: Left Coast Press.

Hawkins, John P. 2001. *Army of Hope, Army of Alienation*. Westport, CT: Praeger.

Heiselberg, Maj Hedegaard. Forthcoming. "Families at War in Time and Space." *Critical Military Studies*, Special Issue, coedited with Mads Daugbjerg.

Higate, Paul R. 2003. *Military Masculinities: Identity and the State*. London: Praeger.

Hodder, Ian. 2012. *Entangled*. Oxford: Wiley-Blackwell.

Hoffman, Danny. 2011. *The War Machines*. Durham: Duke University Press.

Hoffman, F. 2007. *Conflict in the 21st Century*. Arlington: Potomac Institute for Policy Studies.

Holmes-Eber, Paula. 2014. *Culture in Conflict: Irregular Warfare, Culture Policy, and the Marine Corps*. Stanford: Stanford University Press.

Huntington, Samuel P. 1957: *The Soldier and the State*. Cambridge, MA: Harvard University Press.

Inoue, Masamichi. 2007. *Okinawa and the U.S. Military*. New York: Columbia University Press.

Janowitz, Morris. 1971. *The Professional Soldier*. New York: Free Press.

———. 1976. "Military Institutions and Citizenship in Western Societies." *Armed Forces and Society* 2 (2): 185–203.

Kaldor, Mary. 1999. *New and Old Wars*. Cambridge: Polity.

Kelly, John D., and Beatrice Jauregui (eds.). 2010. *Anthropology and Global Counterinsurgency*. Chicago: Chicago University Press.

Kertzer, D. I. 1988. *Ritual, Politics and Power*. New Haven: Yale University Press.

Kilshaw, Susie. 2007. "Toxic Emissions: The Role of Semen in Gulf War Syndrome Illness Narratives." *Anthropology and Medicine* 14 (3): 251–58.

———. 2009. *Impotent Warriors*. Oxford: Berghahn.

Kirke, Charles. 2000. *Red Coat, Green Machine: Continuity and Change in the British Army 1700–2000*. London: Continuum.

Krohn-Hansen, Christian. 1994. "The Anthropology of Violent Interaction." *Journal of Anthropological Research* 50: 367–81.

Kronsell, Annica, and Erika Svedberg. 2012. *Making Gender, Making War*. New York: Routledge.

Lomsky-Feder, Edna. 1998. *As If There Was No War: The Perception of War in the Life Stories of Israeli Men* (Hebrew). Jerusalem: Magnes.

Lomsky-Feder, Edna, and Eyal Ben-Ari. 2000. *Military and Militarism in Israeli Society*. Albany: State University of New York Press.

Lucas, George R., Jr. 2009. *Anthropologists in Arms*. Lanham: Rowman & Littlefield.

Luckham, Robin A. 1971. "A Comparative Typology of Civil–Military Relations." *Government and Opposition* 6 (1): 5–35.

Lutz, Catherine 2001. *Homefront: The Military City and the American Twentieth Century*. Boston: Beacon Press.

———. 2002. "Making War at Home in the United States: Militarization and the Current Crisis." *American Anthropologist* 104 (3): 723–35.

——— (ed.). 2009. *The Bases of Empire: The Global Struggle against U.S. Military Posts*. New York: Pluto Press.

Lutz, Catherine, and Donald Nonini. 1999. "The Economies of Violence and the Violence of Economies." In Henrietta Moore (ed.), *Anthropological Theory Today*, 73–113. London: Polity Press.

MacLeish, Kenneth T. 2012. Armor and Anesthesia: Exposure, Feeling, and the Soldier's Body. *Medical Anthropology Quarterly* 26 (1): 49–68.

MacLeish, Kenneth T. 2013. *Making War at Fort Hood*. Princeton: Princeton University Press.

Maguire, Mark, Catarina Frois, and Nils Zurawski. 2014. *The Anthropology of Security*. London: Pluto Press.

Mann, Michael. 1988. *States, War and Capitalism*. Oxford: Blackwell.

Marcus, George, and Erkan Saka. 2006. "Assemblage." *Theory, Culture & Society* 23 (2–3): 101–9.

Masco, Joseph. 2014. *The Theater of Operations*. Durham, NC: Duke University Press.

McCaffrey, Katherine T. 2002. *Military Power and Popular Protest*. New Brunswick, NJ: Rutgers University Press.

McFate, Montgomery. 2005. "Anthropology and Counterinsurgency: The Strange Story of Their Curious Relationship." *Military Review* 85 (2): 24–38.

McFate, Montgomery, and Janice H. Laurence (eds.). 2015. *Social Science Goes to War*. Oxford: Oxford University Press.

McSorley, Kevin (ed.). 2013. *War and the Body*. London: Routledge.

Messinger, Seth. 2009. "Incorporating the Prosthetic: Traumatic Limb-Loss, Rehabilitation and Reconfigured Military Bodies." *Disability and Rehabilitation* 31 (25): 2130–34.

———. 2013. "Vigilance and Attention among U.S. Service Members and Veterans after Combat." *Anthropology of Consciousness* 24 (2): 191–7.

Moskos, Charles C. 1976. "The Military." In Alex Inkeles, James Coleman, and Neil Smelser (eds.), *Annual Review of Sociology* 2: 25–77. Palo Alto, CA: Annual Reviews.

Mosse, George L. 1990. *Fallen Soldiers*. Oxford: Oxford University Press.

Mosse, Pamela, and Michael J. Prince. 2014. *Weary Warriors*. Oxford: Berghahn.

Münkler, Herfried. 2005. *The New Wars*. Cambridge: Polity.

Nordstrom, Carolyn. 1997. *A Different Kind of War Story*. Philadelphia: University of Pennsylvania Press.

———. 2004. *Shadows of War*. Berkeley: University of California Press.

Nordstrom, Carolyn, and Antonius C. G. M. Robben (eds.). 1996. *Fieldwork under Fire*. Berkeley: University of California Press.

Nørgaard, Katrine. 2004. "The Technology of Trust: The Military Ethos and the Will to Culture" (Danish). Ph.D. diss., Department of Anthropology, University of Copenhagen.

Ong, Aihwa, and Stephen J. Collier. 2004. *Global Assemblages*. London: Blackwell.

Price, David. 2002. "Lessons from the Second World War Anthropology: Peripheral, Persuasive and Ignored Contributions." *Anthropology Today* 18 (3): 14–20.

———. 2008. *Anthropological Intelligence*. Durham, NC: Duke University Press.

———. 2011a. Counterinsurgency, Vietnam, Thailand and the Political Use of Militarized Anthropology. In Laura McNamara and Robert Rubenstein (eds.), *Dangerous Liaisons: Anthropologists and the National Security State*, 51–76. Santa Fe: SAR Press.

———. 2011b. *Weaponizing Anthropology*. Petrolia, CA: AK Press.

Robben, Antonius. 1995. "The Politics of Truth and Emotion among Victims and Perpetrators of Violence." In Carolyn Nordstrom and Antonius C. G. M. Robben (eds.), *Fieldwork under Fire*, 81–103. Berkeley: University of California Press.

Rubinstein, Robert A. 1998. "Methodological Challenges in the Ethnographic Study of Multilateral Peacekeeping." *Political and Legal Anthropology Review* 21 (1): 138–49.

———. 2003. "Peacekeepers and Politics: Experience and Political Representation among U.S. Military Officers." In Pamela R. Frese and Margaret C. Harrell (eds.), *Anthropology and the United States Military*, 15–28. New York: Palgrave.

———. 2012. "Master Narratives, Retrospective Attribution, and Ritual Pollution in Anthropology's Engagements with the Military." In Robert A. Rubinstein, Kerry Fosher, and Clementine Fujimura (eds.), *Practicing Military Anthropology*, 199–33. Sterling VA: Kumarian Press.

Rubinstein, Robert A., Kerry Fosher, and Clementine Fujimura (eds.). 2012. *Practicing Military Anthropology*. Sterling, VA: Kumarian Press.

Schober, Elisabeth. 2016. *Base Encounters: The U.S. Armed Forces in South Korea*. London: Pluto Press.

Schäuble, Michala. 2014. *Narrating Victimhood*. Oxford: Berghahn.

Segal, David R., and H. Wallace Sinaiko (eds.). 1986. *Life in the Rank and File*. Washington, DC: Brassey's.

Shatan, Chaim F. 1977. "Bogus Manhood, Bogus Honor: Surrender and Transfiguration in the United States Marine Corps." *Psychoanalytic Review* 64 (4): 585–610.

Simons, Anna. 1997. *The Company They Keep: Life Inside the U.S. Army Special Forces*. New York: Free Press.

———. 1999. "War: Back to the Future." *Annual Review of Anthropology* 28: 73–108.

Sion, Liora. 2004. *Dutch Peacekeepers: Between Soldiering and Policing*. Doctoral thesis, Free University of Amsterdam.

Stachowitsch, Saskia. 2013. "Professional Soldier, Weak Victim, Patriotic Heroine: Gender Ideologies in Debates on Women's Military Integration in the U.S." *International Feminist Journal of Politics* 15 (2): 157–76.

Sylvester, Christine. 2014. "Bodies of War." *International Feminist Journal of Politics* 16 (1): 1–5

Sørensen, Birgitte Refslund. 2013. "Soldaterfamilier: sociale fordringer og forandringer" [Soldierfamilies: social demands and changes]. In Hanne Mogensen and Karen Fog Olwig (eds.), *Familie og slægtskab – antropologisker perspektiver* [Family and kin – anthropological perspectives], 97–114. Copenhagen: Samfundslitteratur.

———. 2015. "Veterans' Homecomings: Secrecy and Post-deployment Social Becoming." *Current Anthropology*, Supplement, 56 (12).

———. Forthcoming. "Public Commemorations of Danish Soldiers: Monuments, Memorials and Tombstones." *Critical Military Studies*, Special Issue, coedited with Mads Daugbjerg.

Sørensen, Birgitte Refslund, and Jeppe Trolle Linnet. Nd. *Courage and Coziness: Soldiers Made in Denmark*. PDF available at Academia.edu.

Sørensen, Birgitte Refslund, and Thomas Randrop Pedersen. 2012. "Homecoming Parades: A Ceremonial Celebration of the Warrior and the Warrior Nation" (Original in Danish: *"Hjemkomstparader: ceremoniel fejring af krigeren og den krigsførende nation"*). *Slagmark. Tidsskrift for idehistorie* 63: 31–48.

Thiranagama, Sharika. 2014. "Making Tigers from Tamils: Sri Lankan Tamils and Long Distance Nationalism in Toronto, Canada." *American Anthropologist* 116 (2): 265–78.

Thomas, Nicholas. 1991. *Entangled Objects*. Cambridge, MA: Harvard University Press.

Tierney, Kathleen, and C. A. Bevc. 2007. "Disaster as War: Militarism and the Social Construction of Disaster in New Orleans." In David Brunsma, David Overfelt, and J. Steven Picou (eds.), *The Sociology of Katrina*, 37–54. Plymouth: Rowman & Littlefield.

Tilly, Charles. 1995. "States and Nationalism in Europe 1492–1992." In John L. Comaroff and Paul Stern (eds.), *Perspectives on Nationalism and War*, 187–204. Luxembourg: Gordon and Breach.

Tomforde, Maren. 2009. "'My Pink Uniform Shows I Am One of Them': Socio-Cultural Dimensions of German Peacekeeping Missions," in Gerhard Kümmel, Guiseppe Caforio, and Christopher Dandeker (eds.), *Armed Forces, Soldiers and Civil–Military Relations*, 37–57. Wiesbaden: VS Verlag für Sozialwissenschaften.

———. 2010. "Introduction: The Distinctive Role of Culture in Peacekeeping." *International Peacekeeping* 17 (4): 450–6.

Tsing, Anna. 2005. *Friction: An Ethnography of Global Connections*. Princeton: Princeton University Press.

Vigh, Henrik. 2006. *Navigating Terrains of War: Youth and Soldiering in Guinea-Bissau*. Oxford: Berghahn.

Vine, David, and Laura Jeffrey. 2009. "'Give Us Back Diego Garcia': Unity and Division among Activists in the Indian Ocean." In Catherine Lutz (ed.), *The Bases of Empire*, 181–217. New York: Pluto Press.

Wax, Murray L. 2003. "Wartime Dilemmas of an Ethical Anthropology." *Anthropology Today* 19 (3): 23–24.

Weber, Claude. 2016. "Immersion Experience within Military Organizations." In Helena Carreiras, Celso Castro, and Sabina Frederic (eds.), *Researching the Military*, 131–40. London: Routledge.

Whitworth, Sandra. 2004. *Men, Militarism and UN Peacekeeping*. London: Lynne Rienner Publishers.

Winslow, Donna. 1997. *The Canadian Airborne Regiment in Somalia: A Socio-Cultural Inquiry*. Ottawa: Canadian Government Publishing.

Winter, Jay. 1995. *Sites of Memory, Sites of Mourning*. Cambridge: Cambridge University Press.

Woodward, Rachel. 2004. *Military Landscapes*. Oxford: Blackwell.

Woodward, Rachel, and K. Neil Jenkings. 2013. "Soldiers' Bodies and the Contemporary British Military Memoir." In Kevin McSorley (ed.), *War and the Body*. London: Routledge.

Wool, Zoë. 2012. "On Movement: The Matter of US Soldiers' Being after Combat." *Ethnos* 78 (3): 1–31.

———. 2015. *After War: The Weight of Life at Walter Reed*. Durham, NC: Duke University Press.

Wool, Zoë, and Seth D. Messinger. 2012. "Labors of Love: The Transformation of Care in the Non-Medical Attendant Program at Walter Reed Army Medical Center." *Medical Anthropology Quarterly* 26 (1): 26–48.

Chapter 1

The Invisible Uniform
Civil–Military Entanglements in the
Everyday Life of Danish Soldiers' Families

Birgitte Refslund Sørensen and Maj Hedegaard Heiselberg

This chapter aims to make a contribution to thinking about civil–military relations by exploring how the international deployment of Danish soldiers turns their families' everyday lives into a space in which civil–military relations are lived, reflected upon, negotiated, and given shape. To many scholars of civil–military relations, this may appear an odd place to initiate an exploration of civil–military relations, but in this chapter we argue that the everyday lives of soldiers' families offer a unique insight into how the contemporary civilian and military worlds are related, indeed entangled and embedded in each other. Families' experiences show how the international deployment of soldiers generates multiple practical, material, and emotional ripples in everyday social worlds that are physically remote from government offices, military headquarters, barracks, battlefields, and army camps. But rather than simply seeing soldiers' spouses and families as victims of deployment, or indeed of militarization, we contend that their everyday lives possess a critical potential that subtly contributes to defining contemporary civil–military relations.

Given recent transformations in the global security landscape, which call for new kinds of military operations, many Western nations have embarked on a reorganization of their armed forces, typically moving away from conscript armies toward smaller and more flexible professional armies (Joenniemi 2006; Mannitz 2012). The professionalization of armies and the reshaping of soldiering has made the complex figure of "the

Notes for this chapter begin on page 39.

modern soldier" a favorite object of interest in studies of civil–military relations and military studies more generally (Dempsey 2010; Feaver and Kohn 2001; King 2010; Mannitz 2012). The changes mentioned above, however, not only affect soldiers' recruitment, training, and operations, but also reverberate strongly in the civilian world, as political and military authorities alike become increasingly keen on obtaining civilian support for the troops and their missions (Gee 2014). Consequently, the home civilian world emerges as a critical terrain in which to engage for both political and military leaderships.

Efforts to increase support of the military among civilian populations are many, as documented by the burgeoning anthropological literature on "militarization" (Ben-Ari 2004; Enloe 2000; Frühstück 2007; Gonzalez 2010; Lutz 2001). In its most overt form, militarization works through propaganda and recruitment materials, public military shows and parades, or through the configuration of landscapes with war memorials commemorating and celebrating soldiers' sacrifices (Sørensen 2017). However, as Cynthia Enloe (2000: 2) remarks, "militarization is never simply about joining a military. It is a far more subtle process." Several studies, for instance, have demonstrated how the entertainment, fashion, and toy industries, as well as the worlds of the arts and museums, are often implicated in processes of militarization (Dean 2009; Der Derian 2009; Gonzalez 2010). Militarization not only shapes the public space and popular culture, it "creeps into ordinary daily routines; [and] threads its way amid memos, laundry, lovemaking, and the clinked of frosted beer glasses," as Enloe (2000: 3) phrases it. Ethnographic studies of militarization make a useful contribution to the field of civil–military relations by showing how they are never reducible to institutional arrangements alone, but are always also about the everyday lives of ordinary people. While we will probably all discover traces of militarization in our everyday lives if we scrutinize our kitchens, children's playrooms, wardrobes, and bookshelves, the families of soldiers, we argue, are particularly entangled in webs of militarization (Åhäll 2016; Heiselberg 2017; Hyde 2016; Sørensen 2013). As one spouse remarked to anthropologist Kenneth MacLeish (2013: 177), "Military spouses bridge the gap between civilians and the military." Although hinting at militarization as a possible consequence of civil–military entanglements, recent sociological studies of military families tend to focus instead on the conflicting demands of the military and the family respectively. Often the family and the military are portrayed as equally "greedy" institutions, both reliant on time and devotion, and resulting in so-called work-family or family-work conflicts (De Angelis and Segal 2015; Moelker et al. 2015).

The militarization and greedy institution perspectives help us see how the civilian world becomes implicated in security policies and military worlds, but unfortunately these perspectives pay scant attention to how ordinary civilians, some of whom are intimately connected to military personnel, are not only acted upon by militarization, but also act upon it. By approaching the encounters of soldiers' families with the military from the perspective of the everyday, we wish to draw attention to the various ways in which military spouses act upon militarization and greedy demands, and reject, negotiate, or adapt to the presence of the military in their private lives, thus co-producing particular manifestations of civil–military entanglements (see also Heiselberg 2017; Sørensen 2013).

Drawing on Hodder's (2012: 91) understanding of entanglement, we wish to demonstrate how the influence of the military on the daily lives, personal relationships, and private spaces of soldiers' families, far from being uncritically adopted, are always mediated, negotiated, and interpreted in specific social circumstances. In other words, whereas militarization is usually portrayed as a one-way process, entanglement captures the dialectical and transformative relationship of civil–military relations. Civilian reactions to war and militarism may be vociferous, as when people take to the streets protesting with banners (Inoue 2007; Schober 2016), but as we shall show in this chapter, like militarization itself, they may also be subtly embedded in the conduct of everyday life.

The concept of everyday life is commonly perceived in terms of routines, repetition, and reproduction, which give it an air of mundaneness and taken-for-grantedness (Ehn and Löfgren 2009; Gullestad 1991). However, as numerous researchers have shown, the conduct of everyday life is shaped by improvisation (Amit 2015) and creativity (Löfgren 2001), also being interspersed with signifying "extraordinary experiences" (Shokeid 1992). And, as feminist scholars have pointed out, it is inherently political and may even constitute an arena of conflicts and struggles, a potential site of "resistance and subversion" (Felski 2012: 290). Moreover, as Mike Featherstone (2012: 237) argues, critique anchored in everyday life points at its counterpositioned "heroic life," with its emphasis on the (masculine) exceptional, adventure, courage, and sacrifice. This observation reverberates with our accounts of Danish soldiers' families, where one member is cast as a "hero" and the others are simply derivative "kindred" (*pårørende*). However, as we shall show, families' responses to "heroic life" as a dominant contrast and parameter of their everyday lives are not consistent, but waver between positions of all-out support, being reluctant and doubtful, or rejecting and resisting it. In that sense, civil–military relations are always uniquely created within each family setting, constantly being negotiated, transformed, and entangled in new ways.

Civil–military relations and everyday life are both inherently gendered fields, as reflected in approaches to soldiers and their families.[1] In the academic and policy fields alike, soldiers' families are commonly referred to as "military families," "military spouses," or "military wives," all of which stress their belonging and subjection to the military. While this may in some cases indeed be an apt analytical rendering, we opt for "soldiers' families" and "soldiers' spouses" as descriptive categories that highlight our interlocutors' conjugal bond with soldiers, but do not assume in advance any particular relationship to the military. Our female interlocutors were very conscious that labels matter, and many actively engaged in a politics of categorization in order to maintain some control over their own lives. When the soldiers were deployed, their female family members were exposed to particular social and military imaginaries of their gendered roles and social identities, which were often at odds with the women's self-understandings and their notions of modern family life and parenthood. Thus, as Catherine Lutz (2001) has argued, militarization is always gendered, but everyday negotiations of civil–military relations reveal new grounds for exploring how gendered social identities are shaped and reconsidered.

Our account of how the families of Danish soldiers with a deployment history are affected by and respond to this experience draws on semi-structured interviews with fourteen soldiers, twenty-four spouses, one sister, and two mothers of soldiers who went on tours of duty to Iraq or Afghanistan between 2005 and 2015.[2] Everyday time spent with soldiers' families in their homes constitutes another important source of ethnographic data, as do observations and casual conversations with soldiers' family members at public events in honor and recognition of the veterans, and family events hosted by the military before, during, and after deployment. Having outlined our analytical approach to civil–military entanglements and the fieldwork on which this analysis builds, we will briefly introduce the political context before entering into the everyday lives of some Danish soldiers' families to follow how they reflectively engage with things military in their everyday lives.

Contemporary civil–military relations in Denmark are a product of the political switch from a long-established pacifist approach to foreign policy to the so-called "activist foreign policy" of the 1990s, when Danish troops became a new instrument in the foreign-policy toolbox (Kristensen 2013). Since then, the government has deployed Danish armed forces on UN and NATO missions to the Balkans, Kosovo, Iraq, Afghanistan, Libya, the Gulf of Aden, Mali, and Syria, some of which were destined to engage the troops in combat with insurgency groups.[3] The inevitable risk of casualties and severe injuries did not affect popular support, nor did it discourage young men and women from joining the armed forces and signing up for deployment (Pendersen 2017).

Civil–military relations and entanglements are not only shaped by security policies, they are also marked by the particular spatial organization of the military, which influences the everyday social environment of soldiers' families. The literature on civil–military relations, and especially on the militarization of soldiers' families, has long been dominated by the experience of the United States, where many families live in communities established at and around military bases (Enloe 2000; Lutz 2001; MacLeish 2013). In many other countries, including Denmark, the military does not provide housing for families at army bases, and it is important to examine to what extent their lives are influenced by the military, and how.

Taking our point of departure in Felski's (2012: 294) important reminder that everyday life is lived in many different spaces, we begin our analysis with a discussion of soldiers' families' first encounters with the Danish military as an institution. In the following section, we then direct our analytical gaze at the social environment of the soldiers' families, demonstrating how public opinion about warfare in general and deployment in particular affects their social standing and identity. We then zoom in on the private sphere, looking at how "things military" and "things civilian" are negotiated and manifest themselves in the routines and spatial organization of the home. In all three sections, we demonstrate how deployment necessitates soldiers' spouses reflecting on and negotiating the social meanings of family, parenthood, and their identity as women, but most importantly, the military's part in these. We conclude with some reflections on civil–military entanglements as an analytical approach to examining the presence of the military in the everyday lives of soldiers' families.

Lingo and Discipline: Encountering the Military

Just as many parents recall how their child's decision to join the armed forces and go to war had surprised or even shocked them, many wives tell how the first tour came about unexpectedly, although most had been well aware of the obligations of a military career when they got married.[4] The announcement of an upcoming tour of duty, we argue, constitutes a "disjuncture" (Amit 2015) or a "decision-event" (Humphrey 2008) for the family, which ruptures and challenges established ways, demands numerous adjustments, and opens up a space for change. The first deployment sends most soldiers' families on a journey into a largely unknown military world with a distinct culture, which, in the case of repeated deployments, may become increasingly familiar and normalized, while the challenges of how to manage everyday family life with one parent absent usually remain.

The participation of the Danish armed forces in international operations has required closer and more frequent contact with the soldiers'
families, whose support is deemed both important and necessary. This is
primarily facilitated through family gatherings and network groups and
the appointment of family liaison officers, who keep families informed
about the mission and offer them support. The regular family meetings
at garrisons constitute an important arena for the initial military socialization of soldiers' families. Here they are introduced to basic military
terminology and receive instructions regarding their new social roles as
soldiers' relatives.

Lingo

A clash between civil and military and a subtle sign of the growing militarization of families are revealed already in the formal letter of invitation
to a family event that one of our interlocutors receives. It is addressed to
pårørende (kindreds) and invites them to a "light lunch" and a "chat in network groups" at the garrison. Colloquialisms are scarce in the letter, which
is dominated by military lingo like "B Coy," "PNINF," "ISAF," "KC," and
"KTO/GHR," which all envelop and socialize the families into the military world of specialized functions, weaponry, missions, regiments, ranks,
etc. At the meeting, the list of baffling abbreviations and terms continues
to grow, as army commanders and family liaison officers add "MOB,"
"FOB," "Hesco," "PMV," "IED," "minimize," "leave," "A&R," and many
more. The speakers aspire to provide the families with basic insights into
the troops' living conditions, tasks, and schedules, but judging from the
audience's mutterings, much of the information is incomprehensible to
them.

Soldiers' families respond and adapt to the military world and new
lingo differently. Pernille, whose son is on his first tour to Afghanistan, en-
thusiastically embraces the changes: "I try to learn their [the soldiers'] language. I read everything I can get my hands on related to the mission in
Afghanistan; I learn the names, and I know who is who, what groups and
sections there are, where they are, and how they are placed in relation to
the Helmand River." Knowing the basic military lingo, she explains, helps
her to interpret the scarce information the military releases about the mission and to communicate with her son on his own terms. Pernille smilingly adds, "Now I have a share in the armed forces," as she elaborates
on how she feels part of the whole effort. One could argue that Pernille is
thus attempting to elevate her own life by integrating it into a narrative
of "heroic life" (Featherstone 2012). Some relatives are far more reluctant
about letting the military world and perspective enter their everyday lives

and insist on a "civilian" conceptualization of the situation. After a meeting at the garrison, one spouse angrily remarks that, "They keep talking to us about "our soldiers." To me and to us [the family] he's not a soldier, he's just Martin—my husband and the girls' father. I really hate it when they say that." Other women resist subjection to military culture by refusing to learn and adopt military terms or abbreviations, not paying attention when their husbands talk about their work in technical terms, and mocking military expressions and abbreviations.[5]

The military lingo plays a crucial role in the formation of relationships between the military and the soldiers' relatives. The military institution demonstrates its dominance by assuming that soldiers' families know or will gradually learn the military language. And it appreciates knowledge of the military lingo as a sign of commitment, warily viewing the lack thereof as a sign of insufficient support. So does the individual soldier sometimes. Although Sandra takes a keen interest in her husband's military career, she finds it difficult to remember what her husband refers to as simple abbreviations. "You have heard that word a hundred times. How can you still not know?" she imitates him, while shaking her head to indicate how difficult it can be to master the military terminology. Similarly, one mother reveals that she had been scolded and blamed by her son when he learned that she had been asking the meaning of what in his view were very basic terms in an Internet forum for soldiers' families.

Family members' knowledge of military lingo and the world it refers to is a sensitive matter. Simple conversations among relatives may on some occasions turn into subtle trials of the level of one's commitment, and contribute to the creation of a moral hierarchy within the *pårørende* category. Charlotte explains that, as a young woman whose husband has recently deployed for the first time, you are allowed to be ignorant and ask questions, and more experienced people will happily explain the many terms, but you are nonetheless expected to learn them yourself.

Discipline

The military has been described as a "total institution" that transforms the social identity of its "inmates" through separation and discipline (Goffman 1957; Scott 2011). Following Segal's (1986) analysis of the military as a greedy institution, we contend that its disciplinary practices also include the families in order to create good *pårørende* subjects. The fact that families live outside the garrison gates in Denmark obviously limits the disciplinary reach of the military institution, but family liaison officers, family gatherings, network groups, homecoming parades, commemoration days, etc. all create potent openings for disciplinary practices and negotiations.

At meetings of *pårørende*, soldiers' families receive instructions on how to communicate with the deployed soldiers: "Don't complain over a broken washing machine or a car that doesn't start," or "Don't bother him with the humdrum of everyday life, even if it is hard." Such directions are often justified pragmatically: "He can't do anything about it anyway" — but sometimes the expectation of families' compliance and endurance is also explained as crucial for the wellbeing of the soldiers and the success of the operation, which places a huge moral burden on the shoulders of the soldier's family. Lise, the fiancée of a soldier on his second tour of duty, explains that, although it is difficult to suppress her innermost feelings, "I try to sound happy when he calls. If I've been sad, I don't tell him until it's over." Some women refuse to be told how to communicate with their husbands during deployment and find ways to share the sorrows and joys of everyday life in agreement with their husbands, thereby challenging the military's authority over family life and intimate relations. Others seemingly comply with the instructions, but voice this as a sacrifice that has to be compensated for later, as when, in the presence of many other families, and with a disarming smile, the young wife of an army commander responds, when her husband asks on a direct video link to Afghanistan how she is, with a warning: "Fine, but you owe me big time when you return!"

The military's interference with family life becomes even more noticeable at a family meeting prior to the soldiers' upcoming leave: "Ask him what he would like to eat," "Don't make too many big plans for his leave period," "Make sure the day is structured, but let him sleep and spend time with his friends if that is what he wants." The audience listens attentively to pick up useful advice that can make the leave period, which is anticipated with some anxiety, a nice experience, but the practice of listing advice provokes some. After the meeting, Marianne states, "It is also important they [the soldiers] feel that there are certain demands on them. . . . Just because one is a soldier, it doesn't mean that one has no responsibilities as a human being." After a family event at which the family liaison officer persistently urged the families to be patient and show understanding toward the soldiers, Trine too feels annoyed and sarcastically remarks, "Yes, because the soldier gets to decide everything!" While women frequently shared with us their frustrations about the military's expectations of their compliance, many revealed a hesitation to voice their concerns openly to the military out of fear of the consequences. Marianne explains: "I have not been able to ask what was most important for me because I cannot figure out what consequences it might have for our soldier. And I think that many feel the same way. . . . Because we don't know how it will be handled, if it is noted down with a remark that there is a lack of support at home or something."

As this section has demonstrated, today the Danish military is making an effort to build stronger relations with the civilian home front as part of its operations. These efforts are generally welcomed, but the women's responses reveal a certain tension from being pulled into the military world, a tension that contains blends of necessity, fascination, pride, estrangement, uncertainty, ambivalence and sometimes aversion. Women who embrace the military typically stress their desire to stay connected to the soldier, but some are also persuaded to become part of the imposing military setup. When some wives are critical of the many well-intended efforts, this is mostly because they position the women's professional career, emotional lives, and practical trials as secondary to those of their husbands and their military career. This challenges their self-perceptions and meddles in their family's lives.

Victimhood and Familyhood: Contesting Social Categorization

Soldiers' families find that life with a deployed soldier forces them into a new and closer relationship with the military, and regardless of their sentiments about this, it is somehow expected. What surprises many, however, is that deployment also affects their relationships with their civilian friends, acquaintances, and even strangers, who suddenly regard them and relate to them differently. In the wake of Denmark's engagement in international military operations, the terms *kampsoldat* (combat soldier) and *krigsveteran* (war veteran) emerged as new social categories in both policy discourse and everyday speech, soon to be accompanied by the derivative category *pårørende*, which commonly denotes relatives or other persons with an intimate bond to a soldier. In colloquial Danish, *pårørende* inevitably connotes suffering, as it designates somebody close to a deceased, diseased, injured, or disabled person. These connotations therefore influence the common perception of soldiers' *pårørende*, and associate them with victimhood, with implications for how they are expected to behave (Hautzinger and Scandlyn 2014; Sørensen 2015).

Victimhood

On the way to a homecoming event, we strike up a conversation with a woman in her forties who is chatting to a young soldier in camouflage combat uniform standing next to her. She introduces herself as the soldier's mother, but immediately adds that she does not consider herself a *pårørende*, as she is not a victim! She explains that her professional and personal lives continue regardless of her son's deployment, and goes on to deplore the fact that too often events organized for or by relative network groups turn into "Kleenex gatherings with sobbing women," for which she has no need. On another occasion, Lise, who recently got engaged, expresses similar reservations about being categorized by others as *pårørende* and states that people's reactions have indeed been one of the most difficult aspects of her fiancé's deployment. "Oh no, he is not being deployed, is he? That's terrible," she says, mimicking the comments she has heard over and over again, and adds, "As if he isn't coming back! I am put in a box, a box for the weak, a box for victims, and I don't want that." Neither of the two women would deny that suffering and anxiety accompany deployment or that at times it is hard to endure. However, being considered a victim adds aspects of desolation, weakness, and helplessness that they do not fully recognize or accept, nor do they want to become objects of pity.

Natasja, married to a sergeant and the mother of two young children, similarly felt victimized when she turned to her sister for sympathy and comfort during her husband's tour of duty. While probably well intended, her sister's remark that she could not possibly fathom how Jacob [Natasja's husband] could leave his family hurt Natasja. The sister's words not only offended her husband, but also suggested that Jacob had sought deployment against Natasja's will and that she was subject to his decisions, with little if any say in the matter. "Then the day came, just like they [the armed forces] had warned us that it would, where I had to defend my husband's job," Natasja explained after the confrontation, indicating that her sister's ignorance had somehow been anticipated. Young Caroline recognizes the sense of being treated as a victim because her partner is a combat soldier, and she experiences this categorization as a restriction on her ability to express her feelings for her husband and what he is doing. She explains, "I was made into a victim . . . I did not feel like a victim. That is not how I felt . . . I was fucking proud of him."

The notion of victimhood being caused by a partner-soldier going to war generally evokes sympathy, but in some cases the women's intimate relationship with a soldier subjects them to other civilians' suspicion, condemnation, or even stigmatization. Caroline tells how she was constantly expected to comment knowingly on Denmark's decision to go to war and on shifting military tactics at the front, as well as on the suspected actions of her warrior husband. In the absence of the real soldiers, their relatives often become a kind of "proxy soldier" and thus are treated as complicit in war, individuals whom civilians can target with their questions and attitudes about war. Such questions may simply be expressions of people's curiosity about a world to which they have no direct access, but not always. One newly returned soldier told how his girlfriend had been challenged by an unknown person at a party who asked how she could possibly live with a person who could have taken or one day would take the life of another person? This disdainful question classified and stigmatized the girlfriend as a morally tainted person simply on the grounds of her being close to a soldier. Such confrontations consequently meant that some women refrained from talking about their husbands' jobs with friends and family, whereas others insisted on justifying their partners' actions and decisions.

Familyhood

Many of the social expectations that the relatives of deployed soldiers encounter reveal cultural ideas and norms of gendered family roles in contemporary Denmark, in particular those of mother or child-raiser and housewife (see also Segal 1986). Frustrations over unreasonable demands and fears of failing to live up to expectations characterize and strain relations with other civilians.

Birthe, a middle-aged mother, recalls what happened when she confided in the family's long-term neighbors and told them about her son's unexpected plans to do a tour of duty in Afghanistan. Hoping for some understanding and sympathy, Birthe was instead met with a condescending and hurtful, "That would never have happened in *our* family. We would *never* have allowed that." It was "as if there was something wrong in our upbringing of our son," she lamented. The neighbors' remarks not only marked war and a military career as "bad," with which Birthe as a former anti-war activist partly agreed, but also made her complicit and marked her out as an inadequate parent. Laila's experience in many ways echoes that of Birthe; she reports that many friends and acquaintances blame her for not having been able to dissuade her son from a soldier's career. Laila, however, considers herself a good parent who has succeeded in rearing an independent young man who is both reflective and responsible, and who she is adamant will not only be a good soldier, but a good person. Laila feels particularly hurt when on several occasions her academic colleagues insinuate that soldiers are "poor youths with few other options," because it tags her and her family as coming from a lower and marginalized social class.[6]

Similarly, soldiers' wives are subjected to gendered expectations regarding their roles as mothers and housewives during their husband's absence by the military, relatives, and friends. Like most Danish women, many soldiers' spouses work full time even while their children are young, and usually women expect their husbands to take an active part in domestic chores and childrearing (Lausten and Sjørup 2003; Deding, Lausten, and Andersen 2006). Acknowledging that deployment generates more work and new responsibilities for the spouse who remains at home, the military encourages spouses to mobilize their social networks and to ask friends and family to help out when the soldier is away. While apparently aiming to help and support the women, the advice confirms the military's expectations and interests in ensuring a stable home front. However, many women feel uncomfortable asking other people for help in this situation. Natasja explains that she usually turns down friends' offers to help out with her children because she does not want them "to see the piles of laundry or the dirty dishes" around the house. Alice likewise prefers to take care of things by herself because, as she explains, "You don't want anyone to know that you cannot handle it. That would be a failure, right?" The fear of being judged by others if they cannot "handle it" thus prevents many wives from seeking help, and ultimately, when they find themselves unable to cope with the pressures of everyday life, they blame themselves. Living up to others' (and their own) expectations also extends to their responsibilities as mothers. Trine admits being very ambivalent about having her mother look after her children during the weekends when she works: "When their father isn't at home, I think that they [her children] should have full access to me every day . . . and those weekends when they are staying at my mother's they will not." In their husbands' absence, Trine and many others feel even more responsible for being physically and mentally present for their children because, as Trine expressed it, "We didn't have children for someone else to take care of them." This, however, adds to the hardship of enduring deployment and affects their social interactions with others.

The relatives of contemporary Danish soldiers are not only left with the emotional and practical challenges of deployment. We see that the social categorization of soldiers' relatives as *pårørende* accentuates their intimate relations with the soldiers in particular and normative ways, as if almost embodying the civil–military binary. *Pårørende* may be considered pitiful victims, presumably knowledgeable proxy soldiers, subjects who are morally complicit in violence, or persons responsible for the choices and wellbeing of the entire family. The attitudes that accompany each of these positions are different, but none of them seems fully to recognize and respect the individual woman's self-understanding. These effects of the social categorization of soldiers' spouses thus seem to reveal a complex and maybe even unintended process of militarization in which other civilians, if to varying degrees, tend to push the soldiers' close relatives toward social isolation or a deeper entanglement with the military and other *pårørende,* where they feel better understood or at least less exposed (see also Heiselberg 2018a; Sørensen 2013).

Routines and Home: Military Inscriptions on Private Life

The everyday lives of soldiers' families are not only marked by the military in their social interactions with other civilians in the public domain. Even the private domestic domain becomes profoundly entangled with the military, changing everyday routines as well as the decoration and organization of the home (Enloe 2000).

Routines

For many, the soldier's deployment causes a reorganization of everyday life and its many routines and practical chores, which, we argue, not only reflects practical adjustments to the soldier's physical absence, but also demonstrates how women "make time" (Shove, Trentmann, and Wilk 2009: 4) as they synchronize their everyday lives with the rhythms of the military. Several women told us how they developed new daily routines, where, for instance, checking ISAF's (the International Security Assistance Forces) and DAF's (the Danish Armed Forces) webpages became synchronized with ordinary everyday routines and activities. Some devoted particular weekdays to writing and sending letters, preparing and dispatching parcels with goods for the soldier and his buddies. Lise explains that, "Until he was back on leave, I wrote to him every three days, partly for his sake, but also very much for my own so I could make him part of my everyday life, even though he was absent." What began as a reflective ritual (Ehn and Löfgren 2009: 101) to cope with a new situation gradually became integrated and normalized into Lise's everyday routines. Moreover, Lise's new routines and orientations affected when and how she spent time with her friends and eventually cost her several friendships because, as she said, "Some friends found it impossible to relate to war all the time."

Improved Internet connections in the army camps have increased the opportunities for regular communication, often making it possible to Skype, phone, email, text, and send MMS daily. Most spouses found this a positive development. As Trine explained, "I definitely think it was an advantage that you could see each other so that we could pick up on a few things along the way. He definitely became more part of our everyday lives, even though he wasn't here." However, for some the frequent contact and the need to synchronize the domestic and army worlds were experienced as an annoying interference with a new and often tightly scheduled everyday life. Trine continues, "There are some expectations that you talk every day. . . . It can be a bit stressful that you feel like you have to call or talk at least once a day, and also preferably send a picture. Sometimes I just didn't have the time." Staying connected with one's soldier during deployment was a constant reminder of his absence, but at the same time the very absence and the felt obligation to communicate regularly regulated the spouses' everyday lives, demonstrating how "questions of power, freedom and control" may be hidden in everyday routines (Ehn and Löfgren 2009: 99).

Coping with a soldier's absence entails creating new everyday routines and new roles and responsibilities for the remaining family members. Although the soldiers' mid-tour leave is much appreciated and anxiously anticipated, some wives also experienced it as an annoying rupture of these newly established routines. Reflecting upon her experiences with the leave period, Birgit, a mother of two and married to a soldier, says, "Well, I am a little ambivalent because I would never tell him not to come home, because it's time together, it's family time, and it's time with his children. . . . But that said, it's a disturbance in the everyday life that we have just made work, so to speak. Because you have just found your own rhythm, and now everything is on track, and we have everything under control, and everyone knows what to do and when. And whoops, then everything is changed." While families' everyday routines are disrupted by the soldiers' temporary returns home, soldiers, too, experience the leave period as something extraordinary, out of sync with both mundane everyday life and the "heroic" routines of war (Featherstone 2012; Heiselberg 2018b).

While many spouses go to great lengths to make the family function for the sakes of the soldier-husband, their children, or their own self-understandings as good mothers or wives (Heiselberg 2018a), many of them reflect critically on its consequences for family life, social relations, and their own personal lives. As Ehn and Löfgren (2009: 106) argue, "Certain routines are seen as crucial to people's ideas about what kind of person they really are." As one spouse phrased it, "Soldiers put their lives at risk, but we put ours on hold." For some, deployment proves to be too challenging a task for the family members at home, compelling the soldiers to reconsider their careers in the military, while for others it may be a chance to reevaluate everyday life as they know it. As Ehn and Löfgren (2009: 109) suggest, a rupture in everyday routines may "create a new platform, a feeling that there was a possibility of building up an alternative existence." Everyday life in the shadow of deployment, in other words, also offers opportunities to be grasped, or serendipities with openings for change (Amit 2015: 36). As we have shown, the military is present in very significant ways in the everyday lives of the soldiers' families, and, through processes of adjustment and reorganization, *pårørende* constantly negotiate this presence within the routines of their civilian lives.

Home

Although everyday life transgresses the public and private domains, a good deal of it is lived within the domestic sphere of the home, which endows it with particular practical and symbolic value (Felski 2012). Home refers to the place we inhabit, but also to activities, perceptions, and social relations there, and as such it may be critical for our understandings of who we are (Vacher 2010). In many cases, the husband's choice of a professional military career was one that impacted the spatial organization and decoration of the family home, which became a potent site for defining the boundaries between "things military" and "things civilian." When we meet, Caroline shows us around the three-room apartment where she lives with her partner, who is in Afghanistan. The heart of the apartment is the living room, sparsely decorated, clean and tidy. In one corner, a comfortable sofa is placed in front of a TV set, surrounded by their wedding photo, she in a white gown and he in his military gala uniform, and an electronic photo frame that runs a slide show with numerous pictures of her husband in different situations in Afghanistan, some of the couple together, and a few of the yellow "support our troops" ribbons. When Caroline opens the door to the adjacent room, an entirely new sensory-scape reveals itself: earth colors and camouflage patterns dominate the visual impression. The shelves are stacked with military gear, tokens of appreciation, war souvenirs, and video war games, and Caroline points to the computer and headset, and says, "When Mark is at home, he spends a lot of time in here!," suggesting that when he is away the room is not used, but awaits his return. Several family homes we visited have such densely militarized spaces, often in basements or other more secluded areas of the home, but as in Caroline's case, "things military" also creep into other parts of the domestic space that is used by all members, thus making them visible to visitors.

Sometimes the military impact on domestic space is more subtle. Thomas, a veteran diagnosed with PTSD, lives with his wife and two young children in a small house. After a long account of his traumatizing experiences in Afghanistan, Thomas gets up to make us coffee. As he opens one of the kitchens cabinets, a new narrative begins. Thomas shows how each cabinet and drawer in the kitchen is meticulously organized, often with a list on the inside mentioning all the items it contains. "I am in charge of the kitchen, but also most of the other rooms, as I do most of the cleaning," he smilingly informs me, and admits that this aspect of his military socialization has survived his time in the military, and indeed it is imperative for him in his current state to find some rest and ease in their common home.

Considerations and negotiations of the proper emplacement and distribution of civilian and military signs and objects in the home are an everyday concern that is not restricted to the home's materiality, but extends to the bodies of its inhabitants and their movements in and out of the house. One concrete example is soldiers' and their families' "rules" for when and where to wear military uniform, the symbol *sine qua non* of military affiliation and the marker of professional rank. While soldiers are obliged to wear their military uniforms while on duty and are allowed to do so when traveling between the barracks and home, most of the soldiers in our study refrained from doing so. While some soldiers explained that they did not want to provoke other people unnecessarily or risk unfriendly assaults, others considered their uniforms inappropriate in the private family domain. As Tina, the wife of an army officer, explained, "He does not wear it [the uniform] outside either. To and from work he usually brings clothes to change. If he is picking up [our daughter] Lucy or something he will change his clothes. It is very unusual to see him in his uniform." Many of our interlocutors agreed that the uniform does not belong in the private space.

Interestingly, we observed a relatively lenient attitude with regard to children's exposure to military symbols (see also Daugbjerg 2014). When Christian and Laila were getting married, for instance, Christian visited a custom store and bought an identical uniform for their four-year old son to wear at the wedding. Laila found it a fun feature, and the collection of wedding photos adorning the hallway wall showed a "military family," with her in a white wedding dress and her husband and son in military gala uniforms. Another powerful military symbol, the medal, which bears witness to the soldier's affiliation and special achievements, was similarly transformed into a symbol of identification between parents and children, and thus accepted. Trine was normally skeptical about military interference in her family life, but when the voluntary organization the Family Network (*Familienetværket*) launched the "children's medal" as a new initiative to recognize the hardships endured by children during a parent's deployment, she was excited. As she explained, "I think it is a nice way of recognizing them and what they have gone through, and also a way to make them feel like they are part of it in some way, because Martin [her husband] also gets one when he comes home." Acknowledging soldiers' children by offering them a medal resembling the one their parent receives after deployment is a clear example of the Danish military's efforts to strengthen civil–military relations by normalizing the physical presence of military symbols in a civilian setting. Unlike the soldiers' uniform, the medal as a military symbol was welcomed into the private sphere of some of the families in our study because it was considered an opportunity for their children to be recognized and to identify and connect with their father.

As our ethnography shows, in every soldier's family some kind of (un)witting negotiation takes place as to the extent to which, and the ways in which, "things military" can be accepted into everyday family life and its temporal and spatial organization.

Conclusion

When going on a tour of duty to remote war zones, Danish professional soldiers are typically absent from their families for up to six months, to which should be added several months devoted to predeployment training and postdeployment readjustment. The military acknowledges that deployment puts an extra demand on families, but it mainly considers this to be a practical and emotional challenge, one that the spouse is expected to handle by mobilizing her social network without unnecessarily involving the soldier. In this chapter, we have argued that deployment constitutes a far more profound "decision-event" (Humphrey 2008) or "disjuncture" (Amit 2015), one that mobilizes women to employ different kinds of "tactics" (De Certeau 1980) in order to maintain or produce what they each consider a good everyday family life and a positive self-understanding. What is particular about these women's efforts is that to a large extent they are configured as negotiations of the proper relationship between the "civilian" and "military" perspectives in different domains of life.

While we concur with the understanding in militarization studies of how the military subtly impacts the many facets of everyday life (Enloe 2000; Gonzalez 2010; Lutz 2001), we have attempted to go beyond this view by paying special attention to civil–military entanglements—that is, to how women are not only acted upon by the military, but also act on the military, which they sometimes approach as an institution and a site of power, and at other times more as a set of cultural values and potent symbols. Anchoring our exploration in the everyday concerns and perspectives of the mothers, sisters, girlfriends, and particularly wives of soldiers has not generated a unified (female, civilian) vociferous voice, but rather demonstrated how differently civil–military entanglements figure in these women's lives. The majority of the women in our study adopt what can be called a pragmatic approach. They focus on establishing stable everyday lives for their families, while more or less consciously accepting that military interests and symbols invade certain aspects of those lives, but not allowing them to become dominant. A few of our interlocutors went all out to embrace the military and synchronized their everyday routines with the soldiers' lives at the front, most often in an effort to ensure a sense of intimacy, but sometimes also in order to give their own lives more meaning and value by linking them to a greater purpose. Yet other women remained critical of the military and zealously resisted its presence in their everyday lives because it challenged their self-understandings as women, mothers, and wives in its demands for (temporary) submission to it. The diversity of ways in which women negotiate and accommodate the military in their civilian lives, we believe, demonstrates the potency and relevance of "civil–military entanglements" as a new way of capturing the social and personal consequences of contemporary wars that adds nuances and dynamics to the civil–military dichotomy.

Birgitte Refslund Sørensen is associate professor at the Department of Anthropology, University of Copenhagen. With her background in conflict studies and political anthropology, Sørensen has been both practitioner and researcher on issues of postconflict reconstruction for the United Nations Research Institute for Social Development and the Danish Refugee Council. She has also been a consultant on veterans' affairs in Denmark. Her latest publications include "Veterans' Homecomings" in *Current Anthropology*; "Public Commemorations of Danish Soldiers" in *Critical Military Studies*, and "Postconflict Reconstruction" in Palgrave MacMillan's interdisciplinary handbooks series on gender.

Maj Hedegaard Heiselberg holds a Ph.D. degree from the Department of Anthropology, University of Copenhagen and the Danish Veteran Centre. Her Ph.D. project investigates how military deployment affects everyday family life, and how ideas about intimacy and closeness are negotiated during times of physical separation. Heiselberg was also a member of the NATO HFM-258 research group "The Impact of Military Life on Children from Military Families."

Notes

1. The proportion of female soldiers deployed to Afghanistan by the Danish armed forces has ranged between 1 and 6 percent ("Udsendte," Forsvarsministeriet: Personalestyrelsen, accessed 31 August 2017, http://forpers.dk/hr/Pages/Udsendte.aspx). For a complete overview of women in the Danish military, see "Historik – kvinder I FSV; tal fra 2007-2017," Forsvarsministeriet: Personalestyrelsen, accessed 31 August 2017, http://forpers.dk/hr/Pages/Historik-kvinderiFSV.aspx. Female soldiers and their families are not included in this study.
2. Our research has been supported by the Danish Council for Independent Research and the Danish Veteran Center. Interviews were conducted in Danish and translated into English by the authors.
3. For an overview of Danish deployed soldiers since 1992, see "Udsendte," Forsvarsministeriet: Personalestyrelsen, http://forpers.dk/hr/Pages/Udsendte.aspx (accessed 31 August 2017).
4. The duration of basic training of Danish soldiers is four months. If they are interested in and qualify for international deployment, they are contracted and receive eight months' additional training. A soldier can be deployed once every three years, and a typical tour of duty lasts six months, including three weeks of leave mid-term.
5. This mode is expressively captured in the tragicomic theater play, *In Afghanistan They Shoot with Water Pistols*, about temporary war widows, when the four female characters engage in a frantic unintelligible conversation consisting exclusively of military abbreviations.
6. The assumption that soldiers come from a poor socioeconomic background is common, but a survey of Danish soldiers deployed 1992–2009 demonstrated that this is not the case (Lyk-Jensen et al. 2011).

References

Åhäll, L. 2016. "The Dance of Militarisation: A Feminist Security Studies Take on 'the Political.'" *Critical Studies on Security* 4 (2): 154–68.

Amit, V. 2015. "Disjuncture: The Creativity of, and Breaks in, Everyday Associations and Routines." In V. Amit (ed.), *Thinking through Sociality: An Anthropological Interrogation of Key Concepts*. Oxford: Berghahn, pp. 21–46.

Ben-Ari, E. 2004. "Review Essay: The Military and Militarization in the United States." *American Ethnologist* 31 (3): 340–48.

De Angelis, K., and M. W. Segal. 2015. "Transitions in the Military and the Family as Greedy Institutions: Original Concept and Current Applicability." In R. Moelker, M. Andres, G. Bowen, and P. Manigart (eds.), *Military Families and War in the 21st Century: Comparative Perspectives*, 22–42. New York: Routledge.

De Certeau, M. 1980. "On the Oppositional Practices of Everyday Life." *Social Text* 3: 3–43.

Daugbjerg, M. 2014. *Borders of Belonging: Experiencing History, War and Nation at a Danish Heritage Site*. Oxford: Berghahn.

Dean, D. 2009. "Museums as Conflict Zones: The Canadian War Museum and Bomber Command." *Museum and Society* 7 (1): 1–15.

Deding, M., M. Lausten, and A. Andersen. 2006. *Børnefamiliernes balance mellem familie- og arbejdsliv* (Danish). Copenhagen: SFI – The Danish National Centre for Social Research.

Dempsey, J. K. 2010. *Our Army: Soldiers, Politics and American Civil–Military Relations*. Princeton: Princeton University Press.

Der Derian, J. 2009 (2001). *The Virtuous War: Mapping the Military-Industrial-Media-Entertainment Network*. London: Routledge.

Ehn, B., and O. Löfgren. 2009. "Routines: Made and Unmade." In E. Shove, F. Tentmann, and R. Wilk (eds.), *Time, Consumption and Everyday Life: Practice, Materiality and Culture*, 99–114. Oxford: Berg.

Enloe, C. 2000. *Maneuvers: The International Politics of Militarizing Women's Lives*. Berkeley: University of California Press.

Featherstone, M. 2012. "The Heroic Life and Everyday Life." In B. Highmore (ed.), *Everyday Life: Critical Concepts in Media and Cultural Studies*, 225–45. London: Routledge.

Feaver, P., and R. Kohn. 2001. *Soldiers and Civilians: The Civil–Military Gap and American National Security*. Cambridge, MA: MIT Press.

Felski, R. 2012. "The Invention of Everyday Life." In B. Highmore (ed.), *Everyday Life: Critical Concepts in Media and Cultural Studies*, 287–306. London: Routledge.

Frühstück, S. 2007. *Military Manipulations of Popular Culture. Uneasy Warriors: Gender, Memory and Popular Culture in the Japanese Army*. Berkeley: University of California Press.

Gee, D. 2014. *Spectacle, Reality, Resistance: Confronting a Culture of Militarism*. London: Russell Press.

Goffman, I. 1957. "The Characteristics of Total Institutions." In *Symposium on Preventative and Social Psychiatry*. Washington, DC: The Walter Reed Army Medical Centre, and the National Research Council.

Gonzalez, R. J. 2010. *Militarizing Culture: Essays on the Warfare State*. Walnut Creek, CA: Left Coast Press.

Gullestad, M. 1991. "The Transformation of the Norwegian Notion of Everyday Life." *American Ethnologist* 18 (3): 480–99.

Hautzinger, S., and J. Scandlyn. 2014. *Beyond Post-Traumatic Stress: Homefront Struggles with the Wars on Terror*. Walnut Creek, CA: Left Coast Press.

Heiselberg, M. H. 2017. "Fighting for the Family: Overcoming Distances in Time and Space." *Critical Military Studies* 3 (1): 69–86.

———. 2018a. "The Battlegrounds of Everyday Life: Negotiating Motherhood and Career as a Danish Soldier's Partner." *Women, Gender and Research* 1: 84–97.

———. 2018b. "Operation 'Long Distance Parenting': The Moral Struggles of Being a Danish Soldier and Father." *Gender, Place & Culture* 25 (10): 1471–1479.

Hodder, I. 2012. *Entangled: An Archaeology of the Relationships between Humans and Things*. Oxford: Wiley-Blackwell.

Humphrey, C. 2008. "Reassembling Individual Subjects: Events and Decisions in Troubled Times." *Anthropological Theory* 8 (4): 357–80.

Hyde, A. 2016. "The Present Tense of Afghanistan: Accounting for Space, Time and Gender in Processes of Militarization." *Gender, Place and Culture* 23 (6): 857–68.

Inoue, M. S. 2007. *Okinawa and the U.S. Military: Identity Making in the Age of Globalization*. New York: Columbia Press.

Joenniemi, P. 2006. "Farewell to Conscription? The Case of Denmark." In P. Joenniemi (ed.), *The Changing Face of European Conscription*, 13–39. Aldershot: Ashgate.

King, A. 2010. "The Afghan War and 'Postmodern' Memory: Commemoration and the Dead of Helmand." *British Journal of Sociology* 61 (1): 1–25.

Kristensen, K. S. (ed.). 2013. *Danmark i krig: demokrati, politik og strategi i den militære aktivisme*. Copenhagen: Jurist- og Økonomforbundets Forlag.

Lausten, M., and K. Sjørup. 2003. *Hvad kvinder og mænd bruger tiden til – om tidsmæssig ligestilling i danske familier*. Copenhagen: The Danish National Centre for Social Research.

Löfgren, O. 2001. "The Anthropology of Everyday Life." *International Encyclopedia of the Social & Behavioral Sciences* 8 (2): 4969–72.

Lutz, C. 2001. *Homefront: A Military City and the American 20th Century*. Boston: Beacon Press.

Lyk-Jensen, S., C. Dohlmann Weatherall, J. Heidemann, M. Damgaard, and Ane Glad. 2011. *Soldater før og under udsendelse. En.* Copenhagen: SFI – The Danish National Centre for Social Research.

MacLeish, K. T. 2013. *Making War at Fort Hood: Life and Uncertainty in a Military Community.* Princeton: Princeton University Press.

Mannitz, S. 2012. *Democratic Civil–Military Relations: Soldiering in 21ˢᵗ Century Europe.* London: Routledge.

Moelker, R., M. Andres, G. Bowen, and P. Manigart (eds.). 2015. *Military Families and War in the 21ˢᵗ Century: Comparative Perspectives.* New York: Routledge.

Pedersen, T. R. 2017. "Soldierly Becomings: A Grunt Ethnography of Denmark's New 'Warrior Generation'." Ph.D diss., University of Copenhagen.

Schober, E. 2016. *Base Encounters: The US Armed Forces in South Korea.* London: Pluto Press.

Scott, S. 2011. *Total Institutions and Reinvented Identities.* New York: Palgrave MacMillan.

Segal, M. W. 1986. "The Military and the Family as Greedy Institutions." *Armed Forces and Society* 13 (1): 9–38.

Shove, E., F. Trentmann, and R. Wilk. 2009. "Introduction." In E. Shove, F. Trentmann, and R. Wilk (eds.), *Time, Consumption and Everyday Life: Practice, Materiality and Culture*, 1–13. Oxford: Berg.

Sørensen, B. R. 2013. "Soldaterfamilier: sociale fordringer og forandringer." In H. Mogensen and K. F. Olwig (eds.), *Familie og slægtskab: antropologiske perspektiver*, 97–114. Copenhagen: Samfundslitteratur.

———. 2015. "Veterans' Homecomings: Secrecy and Post-Deployment Social Becoming." *Current Anthropology*, Supplements, 56 (12): 231–40.

———. 2017. "Public Commemorations of Danish Soldiers: Monuments Memorials, and Tombstones." *Critical Military Studies* 3 (1): 27–49.

Vacher, M. 2010. "Looking at Houses. Searching for Homes: An Anthropological Analysis of the Relationship between Danish Homeowners and Their Houses." *Ethnologia Scandinavica* 40: 52–67.

Chapter 2

Capable Patriots
Narratives of Estonian Women
Living with Military Service Members

Tiia-Triin Truusa and Kairi Kasearu

Introduction

Scholarly literature on the military is abundant; however, most research concerning families of military service members has been carried out in the United States, and good quality research that takes into account the structural and contextual differences of other countries is scarce (Fossey 2012: 11). This is also the case in Estonia, where perhaps the main reason is that the military is a relatively young institution, as Estonia regained independence in 1991 and an entirely new Estonian Defence Forces structure was established at that time. Sociological studies involving and related to the military have focused on the formation and building of a military to suit the specific needs of Estonia. In designing our research, we therefore found very few studies involving Estonian military personnel and their families, and those we did find were bachelor's and master's level theses concentrating on the social guarantees provided by the state to military service members and their families. We, on the other hand, were interested in the wives and partners of military service members, and what it meant for them to be married to, or to live as a family with, a professional military service member.

The term "greedy institutions" is classically applied when the relations between the military and the family are discussed (Segal 1986). However, the greediness has changed over the decades due to the transitions that both of these social institutions have undergone (De Angelis and Segal 2015). Moreover, the military is not unique in its "greediness"; there are others, such as higher education institutions (Wright et al. 2004), which demand high levels of time and commitment from their members. However, the question of how the institutions of the military and the family are combined in everyday life is still relevant, as was also discussed in a 2015 work on military families and deployments in comparative perspectives (Moelker et al. 2015). The authors state that the transformation from conscription-based military organizations into occupational professional organizations has increased the need to take another look at the tensions between family and military. Heiselberg (2017) examines how the families of military service members become militarized, with military elements seeping into their daily lives, while trying to maintain close meaningful family ties and "good" or ideal family life over the course of deployment-induced separations. What society regards as good family life or considers to be normal is certainly time and culture-specific. Within the Danish military framework, the nuclear family persists as a normative ideal; this emphasis asserts pressure on the deployed father to perform fatherhood roles as intensively as possible (Heiselberg 2017: 72–81). At the same time, Gustavsen (2015), in an analysis of spouses of Norwegian professional military service members, indicates that the feelings of mastery and confidence that the spouses exhibit while their husbands are deployed dominate over the women's feelings of stress occasioned by being in charge of the whole household. The private and public spheres of people's lives are mutually interdependent (Pateman 1989: 3), meaning that entanglement of the civilian and military spheres is all but unavoidable, and that this is the case also when wives and partners of military service members create and negotiate their identities.

As we developed and conducted our interviews, we realized that the terms "military family" and "military spouse" are not expressions that are readily used in the Estonian context. One explanation for this might be that for the purposes of Estonia's laws and social security system, families of military service members are considered to belong to the civilian side of the society; moreover, it is not culturally common to identify oneself through one's spouse or partner. Most often, our interviewees would say that their husband or partner was in the military, but not that they were military spouses or that they were a military family. Therefore, we shall also endeavor to avoid such expressions, though it might at times make the text cumbersome to read.

Research Considerations

In our research, we concentrated on the stories that the wives and partners of military service members tell us about what it means to them to build a life and a family together with a professional military service member, and how these experiences influence their identity creation. The accounts of their experiences give us access to these women's narrative reality—a term first used by Gubrium and Holstein (2009: 15–16). In this context, we use the term "narrative reality" to denote the sets of narratives that are shaped and constantly re-created collectively in our interactions and allow people to make sense of the events and experiences in their daily lives and their surroundings, as well as their inner worlds. Baker (2006: 28–34) also describes them as collective and public narratives, the first of which are the stories that have become widely accepted in a given society, and the second being narratives that are reproduced in society by institutions such as the media and which can change fairly rapidly. The public and collective narratives are the so-called big narratives, and, in addition to these, we also study "small stories" where people are agentive actors by positioning themselves, and thereby also become positioned, in certain roles in the big stories (Bamberg 2011: 10). Thus, we are looking at identity creation in two ways—both how people create the world with respect to which they position themselves, and how people in the context of the interview "want to be understood" (Bamberg 2011: 10). Narratives mirror the identity of the narrator, the preferred identity in that moment of interaction (Gergen 2005). We are characterized simultaneously by a continuous personal identity and by discontinuous personal diversity (Davies and Harré 1990: 46). This personal diversity is how we form our sense of self in different social and personal dimensions though discursive acts available to us (Harré 2015: 2). The forming of the sense of self starts from the self/other and agency expressions.

In this chapter, we shall be looking at the ways the women we interviewed establish their identity in their domestic partnership or marriage to a professional military service member and how civil–military entanglement becomes expressed in the context of comprehensive national defense.

Understanding the Context of Narratives of the Wives and Partners of Professional Military Service Members in Estonia

Estonia adheres to the principles of total defense—that is, all means will be employed to anticipate and prevent any possible military action against it (Estonian Ministry of Defence 2011). The security is strengthened by the civil society, where civic initiative plays an important role in the enhancement of national security and advancement of the sense of security (Estonian Ministry of Defence 2017). The initial military defense of the nation is carried out by territorial and nonterritorial units. The territorial units are comprised of the Defence Forces and the Estonian Defence League (EDL), the latter being a militarily organized, armed, voluntary defense organization. These aspects of the Estonian defense concept are important to consider because in addition to professional military service members, a part of the national defense is carried out by people who volunteer as a part of their civic duty to perform defense duties without pay. These are people who choose to participate in military training and preparation for defense as part of their lifestyle. The Defence League is a well-known organization throughout the country, and its units are based on the administrative subdivisions in Estonia, meaning that the EDL can be seen as a "security blanket" covering the whole country. Thus, entanglement of the civilian and the military spheres has been encoded into the recent security documents and strategies in Estonia and is also evidenced by annual large-scale military exercises that include the military (active duty, conscripts, reservists, and allied troops), the EDL, the police, local municipalities, hospitals, and other parties, thus transforming civilian spaces temporarily into simulated battlegrounds.

Taking into account the formalized or perhaps even normative entanglement of the civilian population and the military, we draw on the collective and public narratives that the wives and partners of professional military service members used as frames for positioning themselves during the interviews.

The first set of narratives describes the collective and public narratives of independence and the meaning of soldier and veteran in the Estonian context. Since the beginning of the twentieth century, the first period of independence for Estonia, the representation of the soldier has undergone a series of transformations in rather rapid succession. This transformation has not only been due to the warrior–peacekeeper tension that has become prevalent in recent decades in other Western democracies as well.

The Fight for Freedom and Independence as the Apotheosis of Estonian History

The core of Estonian nationhood has been the "struggle for independence"; though debatable, some believe that this has been the case since the thirteenth century (Tamm 2007: 505–8). This "struggle for independence" was at the very center of the first national awakening that led to the emergence of the Estonian nation-state in 1918 after the War of Independence. Independence was fairly short-lived, as the 1939 Molotov-Ribbentrop Pact led to the eventual occupation of Estonia by the Soviet Union in 1940. In the beginning of the 1980s, when Estonia was still a part of the Soviet Union, a group of young Estonian historians, who later became Estonia's political elite, managed to portray the nation's struggles as a continuation of the ancient "struggle for independence" (Tamm 2007: 505–8; Tamm 2016: 162–65), thus glorifying Estonians as freedom fighters. The need to create a purposeful history led to using the War of Independence as Estonia's founding myth (Tammisto 2015: 85), in which all the injustices of history were redressed. The soldiers that had fought and won the long sought-after independence for Estonia were honored as heroes. For Estonians, having a War of Independence participant in their family is a point of pride.

The Occupying Soviet Soldier

The Soviet era tainted some aspects of the image of the newly formed Estonian Defence Forces. During the Soviet period, the military had been considered an occupation force and conscription in the Soviet armed forces was greatly feared (Nugin 2016: 302). Estonians had fought on both the German and the Soviet side in WWII, but only the Soviet WWII veterans enjoyed additional benefits from the state, and, in general, Soviet Army officers and their families received special treatment (Danilova 2010: 900–2). At the same time, Estonians viewed the Soviet army as an occupying force, and tensions in the society were high. The status of soldiers in society today is still faintly affected by lingering resentment of the Soviet armed forces as a symbol of occupation. This does not extend to service in the Soviet army, as it was not associated with an occupier; the position was mostly "us" (Estonians) against "them" (the Soviets). There is another aspect to this narrative: because those who managed to avoid the unappealing prospect of serving for the required two years in the Soviet military were considered either lucky or smart enough to come up with a plan, those who did not manage to avoid service must have been unlucky or not smart enough, or worse, a voluntary enlistee, which on the background of opposition to all things Soviet bore out the societal perception of the Soviet soldier as a "dim-witted brute."

Fading Soviet-Afghan War Oppressor–Victim Dichotomy

When the Soviet-Afghan War (1979–1989) started, the populations in the Soviet republics of Latvia, Lithuania, and Estonia took a very critical stance and actively protested against the war. Clear historical parallels could be drawn between the Soviet-Afghan friendship treaty and a similar treaty, the Molotov-Ribbentrop Pact, concerning the Baltic States. In both cases the treaties were used to legitimize the entrance of Soviet troops into the respective countries (Philips 1986: 101). Estonians saw the Soviet troops in

Afghanistan every bit as much as an occupying force as the Soviet forces were seen as such in Estonia. At the same time, compulsory conscription into the Soviet army continued in Estonia, and those who did not manage to avoid the draft were sent as conscripts to fight in Afghanistan. The war itself would be recast as a "pointless" conflict (Aleksievich, 1992: 185) already during the Soviet period and even in Russia. In Estonia, this created a collective narrative that was internally conflicting. The Estonian soldiers who had fought in the Soviet-Afghan War were at once considered oppressors (in Afghanistan and sometimes even in their own eyes or as seen by their fellow Estonians), and, while at home, considered victims of the Soviet regime.

The New Capable and Persevering Veteran

In the re-independence era—1991 to the present—the meaning of soldier has undergone a shift from the symbol of Soviet occupation back to a defender or fighter for Estonian independence. Since 2008, public polls have shown that the Estonian Defence Forces (EDF) has enjoyed high rates of trust in society, and up to 79 percent of the population say they have a positive attitude toward military personnel (Kivirähk 2017: 16–17). However, in 2003, when Estonia deployed forces to Iraq and, later, Afghanistan, the perception of the soldier as oppressor was quick to reemerge. This was partly because Estonia had not been involved in any combat missions prior to Iraq and Afghanistan, but also because of the Soviet-Afghan War. This attitude was countered by high-ranking Estonian officials' unwavering support for these missions. Prior to the adoption of the Veterans Policy in 2012, the support system for deployed soldiers was still in need of enhanced measures to match the support needed by the Estonian soldiers. Prior to the policy, media attention centered on wounded soldiers and their need for additional social guarantees, while the Veterans Policy succeeded in introducing measures to boost public recognition. This led to the emergence of the new image of a capable and persevering veteran (Truusa 2015). It is important to keep in mind that in Estonia, the official definition of veteran predominantly includes those who have served on missions abroad.

Closed Off and Separate

Unlike some Central and Eastern European countries, Estonia did not inherit armed forces from the previous Soviet-aligned socialist system, and after regaining its independence in 1991, Estonia set out to build and develop its military structures from the ground up. Estonian indepen-

dence was restored on the basis of legal continuity with the republic of
1918–1940 and, as such, reinstated many of the interwar era's principles
governing fields such as military organization (Maigre 2006: 12). However, changes in how Western democracies regarded civilian–military
relations had also changed, and in striving for NATO membership, the
country had to conduct civil–military reforms as outlined by NATO. The
public debate in the second part of the 1990s was largely concentrated on
enhancing civilian control over the military, the main purpose of which is
to keep the lethal power of the military under the guidance of democratically elected governments and to minimize the possibility of a coup. The
official approach to civil–military relations carried characteristics inherent
to the Huntingtonian model that, among other things, advocates a large
separation between the civilian and military spheres. This focus left little leeway in developing Estonia's own unique mode or balance between
the military and the civilian society, and even hindered public debate on
"softer" issues connected to the military, such as families of soldiers. Thus
the military and all things military are by and large conceptualized as not
a part of the civil society, which is in turn supplemented by the special and
separate status of Soviet officers.

The second set of collective and public narratives that emerged from
the interviews help us to understand the context of women's position and
identity in the Estonian society. Just as the collective and public narratives
of the soldier create tensions in the self-forming process that incorporates
soldiering, the next set of narratives does the same with being a woman.

The Dedicated Mother

Estonia has a family policy that in general is considered pro-natalistic,
with a long paid parental leave, initially designed as a measure to increase
the birth rate in Estonia. Gradually, however, more gender equality and
equity principles are being incorporated. The parental leave period is
long, up to three years, and half of this period is covered by the parental
benefit, which is 100 percent of earnings from a previous period of a pre-
defined length (Karu 2011: 15). It is up to the family whether the mother
or the father goes on parental leave; however, the first seventy days are
only entitled to mothers. Fathers can take ten working days' additional
paternity leave before or after the birth of a child. This generous policy
measure has fed into the preexisting position that taking care of children
and domestic chores is mainly the responsibility of mothers (Karu and
Kasearu 2011: 26). The share of fathers who go on parental leave is still
rather modest (Karu 2011: 22). In addition, as Estonia was reestablished
under nation-state ideology, women were extolled for the sex-specific role

of replenishing the population (Kaskla 2003: 298–99), also tying into the previously mentioned narrative of independence as the apotheosis of all of Estonian history.

The Hard-Working, Model Employee

Previous studies have shown that paid work and being able to work are important aspects for women's self-realization and feeling that they are included in society (Pajumets 2007: 56–57). Due to the parental leave policy, it is the norm for mothers to stay at home with their children for the duration of paid parental leave, and they often time the birth of their second child so that they can either continue to stay at home with no interruption in income, or go back to work for only a short period between children. After that, though, mothers are expected to return to the labor market full time, as Estonian employers are reluctant to provide part-time working options. Partly due to that, Estonia has almost the highest rates of employment among mothers with children age three to twelve (Keck and Saraceno 2013: 308). This is reinforced not only by the dual-earner family model as the income subsidies and family allowances after the period of paid parental leave do not cover the absence of parental salary, but also the return of ideological equality that has stemmed from the influence of the Scandinavian equality model and the EU normative stance on gender equality (Kaskla 2003: 309–10). This is augmented by the narrative of Estonians as a hard-working nation, so women might find themselves locked into the collective narrative of hard-working, model employees.

The Center of the Family

Despite some change, there is a persistent narrative of the sensible Estonian woman supporting her family and husband, of the woman stoically accepting her role (Kaskla 2003: 302–3). The woman plays the significant role of the stabilizer of the family, yet does not have the status as head of the family. This is to a degree supported by the still-prevailing gender identity where nearly half (48 percent) of men and women without children feel that women should be ready to reduce their workload as employees in favor of taking care of the family, and 43 percent of men and women with children support the same idea. Although the previous studies, mostly carried out in the United States, have shown that serving in the military is associated with more traditional family behavior—earlier marriage and more children (Lundquist and Smith 2005: 8–9)—in Estonia this association is rather weak (Kangro 2015: 118). It could also mean that spouses of service members are also in other aspects quite similar to the whole female population, and that as far as their identity and self-perception go, the role of being active on the labor market and the main contributor in private life is prevailing over the other aspects.

Finding Our Interviewees

We found our interviewees in two separate waves. The first ten interviews were conducted as part of a graduate-level qualitative methodology course where students were taught interviewing on sensitive subjects. The main themes discussed during interviews were the identity of a military spouse, the differences between military families and civilian families, and the positive and negative experiences of having a spouse on active duty. Students started with a snowball method, introducing and announcing the research project through a Facebook call, which drew a fairly large number of potential participants. We employed the principles of voluntary participation, confidentiality, and keeping the participants exhaustively informed about the interview topic (Kvale 1996: 110–14). Finally, ten of the twenty-five people who were initially interested were interviewed. Several indicated that they would have been comfortable with a standardized digital survey, as they felt the degree of anonymity would be higher. As a reason for nonparticipation, some cited doubt about whether they were in a position to agree to an interview, or whether it should be a decision made together with their spouse, or even whether permission should be sought from the EDF.

This might have been because, more often than not, before the implementation of the Veterans Policy in 2012, media interviews often concentrated on the hardships of veterans and on raising awareness of veterans' need for more support. The tone of these articles often victimized the veteran and his or her family and also pointed to the shortcomings of the support system in place. Some of the women who refused to participate in the interviews might have felt it inappropriate to participate in a study that might, for all they knew, pursue the same angle.

Those who were concerned more with privacy and anonymity were given the option of participating in written interviews by email. The first wave of data gathering did not achieve data saturation, and thus we proceeded with asking for a recommendation from a colleague at the Estonian National Defence College and continued by asking for further recommendations from the interviewees. The final dataset consists of fourteen interviews with spouses and cohabiting partners of active-duty members. They were all women who either worked or were on three-year parental leave, between the ages of twenty-two and forty-five, with different levels of education ranging from vocational school to a Ph.D. They were all in relationships with an active-duty member, and had been in that relationship for a period of one and a half to fifteen years. Some of the couples had children; some did not.

There were no divorcees or women separated from their partner. In some cases, the interviewees had moved along with their partner relocating because of their job, but in other cases, the service member had asked to be rotated close to home to allow daily or weekend commutes. The interviews were semistructured and conducted from spring 2014 to autumn 2015.

Narratives of Wives or Partners of Professional Military Service Members

In this section, we will discuss the personal identity-forming narratives of the wives and partners of the professional service members of the Estonian Defence Forces.

Usually, we asked the interviewee fairly early in the interview how she would describe her relationship to the military, and all the interviewees pointed out that it was their husband or partner who was in the military and that they themselves had no connection to the military. In this way, they positioned themselves firmly in the civilian sphere. That was the case even with women who either worked as civilians in the military or were members of a voluntary defense organization:

> I do not really have a connection to the defense forces, only that I work at the Estonian National Defence College.

> Sometimes, being a civilian myself, not connected to the military, creates misunderstandings.

This links up with the narrative of "Closed Off and Separate" as the conventional way of conceptualizing the relationship in society between civilians and the military, but it might also be the product of the way military service personnel are separated from society—they have a perceived position as people who have less agency in their lives—after all, the military can reassign or rotate them from one job to another, and they are barred by law from belonging to a political party:

> Well, he is an officer now, so he can be assigned to a different position. So, he has been assigned to different postings in our area; there aren't too many op-

tions left. I don't know where he is going to be posted. My job is here; he can't really *not* accept a posting unless he wants to leave the forces.

Regardless of our interviewees' self-inspired reasons for seeing themselves as separate from the military sphere, the normative framework established by the laws and social welfare system of Estonia also lead these women to seeing themselves as belonging on the civilian side. This brings up the question of intrafamily power relations, taking into account the collective narrative of the woman as "The Center of the Family" and the family not being considered in the purview of the military.

Secrecy in Life

In describing the life of military families, Wertsch (1991: 33–61) discusses three aspects of military culture that have a bearing on the life of a family where one of the members is in the military: masks of secrecy, normalcy, and denial. Sørensen (2015: S232) calls it "secrecy work," where past experiences, present conditions, and hopes for the future are masked in concealment and silence. In the narratives of the women we interviewed, the habit of keeping things secret was also evident. However, it was not really seen as something that was particularly disruptive to family life, but rather as a part of the husband's or partner's job and something that the women shared in. It was even referred to as something that united the spouses or partners, a pragmatic aspect of family life, and something where one will learn fast enough what is appropriate to say in what situation:

> No, not for me . . . the secrecy doesn't really bother me. I mean you learn very early on in the relationship that things talked about at home aren't talked about outside of home. I mean, he talks to me, so I know . . . it's something that we share.

One reason that this might not be seen as very disruptive is the Soviet legacy, as during the occupation it was normal for people to watch what was being said in public for fear of repercussions. It is also considered culturally appropriate to be private about one's family life:

> Estonians are not big on talking about personal stuff in public anyway, like if you are sick or have problems. And, as well you remember, back then you knew where to say what and to whom.

Although it has been historically necessary to have very clear public and private life boundaries, the pragmatic attitude toward "secrecy work" might start changing in the globalizing world with the ever-increasing culture of sharing through social media.

Pride and Patriotism

The interviewees invariably found that through their spouse's or partner's job, they have either become more patriotic or prouder of the independence of Estonia, something that in the cultural narrative is seen as the apotheosis of all Estonian history. They express this by celebrating Estonian Independence Day and Victory Day, and estimate that they generally know and pay more attention to defense and security issues in Estonia than they did previously:

> Living with a professional service member has certainly made me more aware of issues connected to defense. I follow these topics more now than I used to. I have in fact educated myself in this area.

It becomes evident in the course of the interviews that patriotism plays a prominent role in the formation of their identity as wives or partners of professional military service members. It is equally clear that they position themselves on the civilian side by bringing up comparisons of how the same kind of patriotism is also displayed among families that do not have any connection to the military:

> We have not missed any Independence Day celebrations, not one, but this is not something special, not because I am married to someone from the military. I know many families, not connected to the military, that do the same thing. Going out for the raising of the flag at sunrise, the parade, a nice dinner. Freedom is not self-evident.

We see these women invoking simultaneously a cultural and public narrative where they fit in, but also positioning themselves at one end of the patriotism continuum. This resonates well with Bamberg's (2011: 9) story prerequisite that stories should not deviate from the perceived norm too much, but should still be different enough to be told. We can also follow the strategic narrative (Nissen 2015: 65) of comprehensive national defense—for example, the national defense paradigm involves the preparation and readiness of society as a whole, not only the defense structures, equating knowledge with better preparedness. Being aware and knowing defense and security issues supports preparedness, but also encourages the realization that this independence is something to be celebrated and commemorated.

As narratives often include not only the story of the protagonist, other characters were introduced to highlight the pride the interviewees felt that came with their husband's or spouse's chosen career through others. For example, in one story, a young child in a grocery store pointed at the uniform of the interviewee's husband, thus expressing joy at seeing an officer. Other stories tell of bank loans or insurance cases being handled with exceptional speed and efficiency due to their husband or partner being in the military.

These stories are told from the perspective of the interviewees being recipients of these benefits by proxy—that is, they themselves as wives or spouses of military service members would not have invited such behavior on the part of others. These were not stories of entitlement but of heartfelt pride that the career choice of their husbands was being valued on the societal level. This ties in well with social recognition as Honneth (1996: 92–130) sees it—namely, that it takes place in the conversational space, and moves beyond words to deeds (Warming 2015: 251).

However, the importance of preserving the nation's independence is also of central value. It is self-evident for our interviewees that it is a point of loyalty on their part that they take pride in the knowledge that their spouses or partners will be the ones fighting to preserve independence in case of war. This could also be interpreted as stoicism in the face of adversity, which Wertsch (1991: 33–61) identifies as one of the key values defining military culture.

The knowledge that their husbands and partners will be the ones who will stay and fight for the independence of Estonia if such a need arises carries with it an intense sense of pride and, to an extent, the spirit of sacrifice for a greater goal:

> I know that he is going to be here, fighting for our freedom, if things should come to that. I am an Estonian patriot, what can I say? I am proud that he is going to stay when so many others are going to be crowding the boats to get out of here.

Able, Capable, and Persevering

Regardless of the social recognition experienced by the wives and partners of the military service members in some instances—where the positive image of the soldier as someone dependable and trustworthy is prevalent—there are also instances where the cultural narratives of the "dim-witted" and untrustworthy Soviet soldier still arise. Though fading among today's younger generations, it is evident among older generations:

> In the beginning I was ashamed for my friends. Actually appalled, all these jokes about not being able to think, only following orders. I had to apologize to him in front of my friends, then it finally eased. It is like they couldn't understand that it is someone's choice to become a professional soldier.

> He sort of didn't want to tell my parents that he is a professional service member. Maybe he was afraid what they'd think of him. [Questions like] why the army, you know, what kind of a choice is that?

Negative attitudes had been encountered by most of the interviewees not only among friends and family members upon first introducing their spouse or partner, but also among professionals and specialists, such as a midwife criticizing the father for not being there for the birth of his child:

> I went into labor, got to the hospital and said that my husband is deployed. And that I was giving birth alone. They treated me like I was a single parent, like my child didn't have a father. I tried to pay it no mind . . . but the attitude from the doctors was exactly the same. It was uncomfortable to be at the hospital.

The latter strongly speaks to the rapid change that has taken place concerning customs and values connected to giving birth and the part that men play now. Even in the 1980s, birth was in most cases strictly the domain of doctors and other medical staff. Fathers and family members were not allowed into the maternity ward.

However drastic the narrated incidents, almost all of the interviewees assumed that these situations arose from people not understanding the military way of life or what being on active duty demanded from those serving in the military. Interestingly, the service members' partners themselves noted that their friends and acquaintances generally sympathized with the active-duty military personnel, as they are perceived as leading hard lives—unlike teachers, they have to be constantly away from their families. This sympathy for active-duty personnel suggests a cultural narrative where the woman is the one who has to shoulder the work of running the household, yet the man is the one who gets the sympathy for being deprived of a cozy existence, of hearth and home:

> I'm a teacher, people know and respect me for what I do, but they sort of pity him, because he has to spend so much time away from home and the kids.

The unplannable nature of everyday life was also narrated: plans often have to be revised and cancelled. This results in distance from friends and acquaintances, and the family finds it is unable—or indifferent—to attend various get-togethers. As discussed above, home and child-rearing is part of the female domain, but following independence, one of the new traditions that has become difficult to navigate for single mothers is Father's Day, celebrated on the second Sunday in November. It has become customary on these days to have celebrations in kindergartens and schools where fathers are invited for a breakfast or to talk about their work and life. This new custom has proven somewhat uncomfortable, as often the husbands or partners of our interviewees could not attend the celebrations. In addition, there seemed to be a prevalent desire not to make an issue of any difficulties that military families might experience due to the demands that the military way of life places on them—a sign of stoicism and denial, according to Wertsch (1991: 33–61).

There was a strong belief among the interviewees that they can overcome all the challenges because they are capable and independent; at the same time, it was noted that, in reality, this demands a great deal of resources from them and their family. Single motherhood is still considered a stigma, and this resonates through the interviews. Public debate around single motherhood is ongoing. In 2017, heated debate arose over the status of single mothers in light of a foundation's policy of allowing only married women to be nominated for a prominent "Mother of the Year" award. In addition, there is a relatively high rate of child poverty (Toots, Reetz, and Jahn 2014: 3), which is connected to the fact that the income subsidies and family allowances do not cover the absence of a parental salary. This means that the wellbeing of families is based on a dual-earner family model, where in order to attain the average standard of living, both parents have to be employed on a full-time basis. Thus, women's employment plays an important role in the material wellbeing of families, but also in their identity. The interviews revealed that for women, especially for those with university degrees, their own career and employment were significant status symbols, which also helped them to strengthen their position in the civilian world.

"We Are No Different"

In 2007, Estonia's Peacekeeping Operations Centre's Social and Psychological Support Section began developing a system to tackle the issues connected to military deployments abroad. During that period, the term "deployment family" was coined, and a Deployment Family Program was set up to help families before, during and after deployment (Truusa 2010: 46). The Veterans Policy adopted in 2012 also devoted attention to the families of veterans, but during Veterans Day on April 23, the attention and emphasis continues to be mainly on veterans and to a much lesser degree on the people that surround the veterans. The Estonian definition of a veteran is fairly exclusive, as Dandeker et al. (2006: 162–64) define it, encompassing mostly military service members who have been deployed, but the wives and partners of military service members whose husbands have not been deployed lack a conceptual framework for positioning. Instead, other possible reference groups are sought, and it can also be said that, to a certain degree, relief is found in positioning oneself in the civilian framework, namely that of the wives and partners of workers who have migrated to other European countries for employment. This correlates with a study conducted in Estonia in 2013–14 showing that 22 percent of the parents of children attending second, fourth, and sixth grade have either one or both parents working abroad (Talves 2013: 48). The specifics of deployment notwithstanding, the women see themselves as less unique than it might be conventionally presumed.

At the same time, even during deployments, there is a tendency to use the internet support forum, which was created by the EDF's Family Support Program for deploying soldiers and their families, mostly for pragmatic reasons, such as exchanging information about the beginning of the mid-deployment vacation, the best way to send packages, etc. (Truusa and Siplane 2015). Otherwise, there is a tendency to rely on one's family and friends for support during the deployment cycle—even to the extent of trying to avoid other deployment families, as it is felt that interaction with other families who either have someone deployed or who have someone serving as a professional in the military might compound feelings of stress or irrational fear, whereas being surrounded by one's friends and family allows for a larger degree of normalcy, keeping the focus on the mundane and everyday issues:

> I knowingly did not want to interact with other women who had men deployed. I got more support from friends—they would sometimes just help with the kids. They'd say: just leave the kids here, go give yourself some space, go have cake and coffee at a café or have a chat with friends. They just took me as a friend whose husband is away. Didn't try to give me advice or tell me how to live my life.

Again, the parallel of migrant workers is palpable, as these workers often are builders who for the duration of the construction season live abroad:

> So tell me how we're so different, or where do you draw the line? There are people who work abroad for six months at a time, there are the builders, and there are doctors and truckers. Deployments are a part of his job. I am also away with my job.

One of the reasons why this parallel is fairly persistent is that Estonia joined the EU in 2004, and by 2007, when the term "deployment family" was coined, migration of seasonal workers to neighboring EU countries had become a desired state and fairly common—much more so than, for example, being deployed, as Estonian contingents that deployed were small in relation to the size of the force.

Deployment as a Family Decision

Unlike in some armies, in the EDF deploying is voluntary and, as such, is seen as something that the family decides together. Moreover, in the EDF, the same regulations are applied as in the civilian world, which means that according to the Military Service Act, parents who have children three years and younger can only be deployed with the parents' consent. In fact, all deployments are ultimately voluntary, meaning that they most probably are family decisions and need to be negotiated:

> It is absolutely a family decision. I mean, even if I know that it's part of his job, the "when" was still up to us. We agreed that he'd deploy only after the kids are old enough that they have actual memories of their dad. That's how it happened too.

Furthermore, once the decision that the family member is going to deploy is reached, it becomes difficult to criticize the system or the support offered to the families through the Deployment Family Program. Deployment is seen as a normal part of a soldier's career and also a principle of equality. Allowing for career advancement for either of the partners is seen as the norm, and only very small children are viewed as a possible argument against joining a deployment at that particular time.

Conclusion

With regard to their relationship to the military, the women we had the privilege to interview demonstrated acceptance, ambiguity, ambivalence, and entanglement in their narrations.

The research process revealed that our understanding as researchers of Estonian women with military service members for spouses or partners has been strongly influenced by data gathered in the United States. Perhaps the most significant was understanding how the fact that Estonia lacks some of the concepts so readily used in the academic literature—such as "military family" and "military spouse"—both limits and opens up the negotiations of identity in the narratives as wives and partners of professional military service members. Berger and Luckmann (1991: 53) point out that the words and meanings that we have readily available about the reality we experience for our present and future actions provide us with "a ready-made possibility for the on-going objectification" of our continuously developing experience. Language also typifies experiences, but if one lacks categories and concepts in the language to describe one's experience, one has to find categories that are available. An example of such a category is the wife of a Finnish builder. The partners of the Defence Forces members indicated they were aware of the differences between such professions and that of a soldier, yet comparisons between the case of a soldier and that of an Estonian builder working in Finland are quite common, and this is true in our dataset as well. These women apparently chose a comparison group that is perhaps better understood in society, or at least more common than a professional soldier serving on a mission. At the same time, overlooking the specifics of the soldier's profession may be related to denial or stoicism. This can also be seen in their positioning patterns vis-à-vis the civilian–military axis, stressing their adherence to some military values but at the same time emphasizing their own position as civilians. It is also important to take into account that after regaining independence, Estonia began single-mindedly pursuing membership in the EU and NATO. The discussions on the topic of civil–military relations that reached the public concentrated mostly on the establishing of civilian control over the armed forces of the country, in accordance with principles of Western democracy. There was little scope in the public discourse to accommodate topics such as the families of professional soldiers and their place in society.

The interviewees were ambivalent about the topic of civil–military entanglement and perceived limits to what they felt they could talk about. Although these women perceive themselves as belonging to the civilian rather than military world, they face questions of confidentiality and uncertainty. The situation is complicated by their loyalty to their partner/husband.

The emergent collective narrative of the wives or partners of professional military service members accepts the positive recognition and patriotism as also applying to them and their whole family, but when coping with difficulties, solidarity with the civilian society is stressed. In other words, the cultural narrative of the "Fight for Freedom" and "Independence as the Apotheosis of Estonian History" is accepted as the leading narrative and used to position oneself as a protagonist aligned with the military. At the same time, when coping with everyday matters, strong alignment with the civilian society is stressed: support during difficult periods is expected from and also given by the personal support networks. Thus, in conclusion, we submit that in Estonia, the military finds its way into the lives of the wives and partners of professional military service members in more ways than just the uniforms and rucksacks in the corner, or in the form of absence during military exercises and deployments. Although we are used to thinking about the military and the civilian society standing apart, it is evident that there is entanglement; and military values are respected and to a degree adhered to by the women we interviewed. Perhaps because of the historical context, these military values of stoicism and secrecy are similar to the values in Estonian society in general.

Acknowledgments

We would like to extend our gratitude to the University of Tartu Associate Professor in Social Policy Judit Strömpl and her students, who in autumn 2014 conducted the interviews in the framework of the course "Research Methods and Research Methodology." The students who served as interviewers were Eliise Salla, Elin Kütt, Felika Tuul, Greten Sööl, Marje Reimund, Johanna Toplaan, Margit Metsmägin, Maarika Masikas, and Helina Paat.

Tiia-Triin Truusa, M.S.W., is currently a sociology Ph.D. student at the Institute of Social Studies, Faculty of Social Sciences at University of Tartu in Estonia. She is also a junior research fellow in the "Human Resource-Related Sustainability of the Estonian Defence Forces" research project and a member of the NATO HFM-263 research group "The Transition of Military Veterans from Active Service to Civilian Life."

Kairi Kasearu, PhD, is currently an Associate Professor at the Institute of Social Studies, Faculty of Social Sciences at University of Tartu in Estonia. She is also the head of the "Human resource-related sustainability of the Estonian Defence Forces" research project and a member of the NATO HFM-258 research group "The Impact of Military Life on Children from Military Families." Her research areas include family sociology, social problems and welfare, national insurance and military sociology.

References

Baker, M. 2006. _Translation and Conflict: A Narrative Account._ London: Routledge.

Bamberg, M. 2011. "Who Am I? Narration and Its Contribution to Self and Identity." _Theory & Psychology_ 21 (1): 3–24. Retrieved 1 February 2011 from SAGE Journals.

Berger, P. L., and T. Luckmann. 1991. _The Social Construction of Reality: A Treatise in the Sociology of Knowledge._ London: Penguin.

Danilova, N. (2010). "The Development of an Exclusive Veterans' Policy: The Case of Russia." _Armed Forces and Society_ 36 (5): 890–916.

Dandeker, C., S. Wessely, A. Iversen, and J. Ross. 2006. "What's in a Name? Defining and Caring for 'Veterans': The United Kingdom in International Perspective." _Armed Forces & Society_ 32 (2): 161–77. Retrieved 12 August 2014 from SAGE Journals.

Davies, B., and R. Harré. 1990. "Positioning: The Discursive Production of Selves." _Journal for the Theory of Social Behaviour_ 20 (1): 43–63. Retrieved 4 June 2017 from Wiley Online Library.

De Angelis, K., and M. W. Segal. 2015. "Transitions in the Military and the Family as Greedy Institutions: Original Concept and Current Applicability." In R. Moelker, M. Andres, G. Bowen, and P. Manigart (eds.), *Military Families and War in the 21st Century: Comparative Perspectives*, 22–42. London: Routledge.

Estonian Ministry of Defence. 2011. "National Defence Strategy." Accessed 12 May 2018, http://www.kaitseministeerium.ee/en/objectives-activities/basic-national-defence-documents.

———. 2017. "National Security Concept." Accessed 12 May 2018, http://www.kaitsemini steerium.ee/en/objectives-activities/basic-national-defence-documents.

Fossey, M. 2012. "Unsung Heroes: Developing a Better Understanding of the Emotional Support Needs of Service Families." Centre for Mental Health, 10 May 2012. Retrieved 20 November 2018 from https://www.centreformentalhealth.org.uk/unsung-heroes.

Gergen, K. 2005. "Narrative, Moral Identity, And Historical Consciousness: A Social Constructionist Account." ResearchGate. Retrieved 15 August 2017 from https://www.re searchgate.net/publication/298103687_Narrative_moral_identity_and_historical_consc iousness_A_social_constructionist_account.

Gubrium, J. F., and J. A. Holstein. 2009. *Analyzing Narrative Reality*. Los Angeles: SAGE.

Gustavsen, E. 2015. "The Veteran Experience from a Spousal Perspective." Paper, Inter-University Seminar on Armed Forces and Society, Chicago, IL.

Harré, R. 2015. "Positioning Theory." In K. Tracy, C. Ilie, and T. Sandel (eds.), *The International Encyclopedia of Language and Social Interaction*. Retrieved 3 April 2016 from Wiley Online Library.

Heiselberg, M. H. 2017. "Fighting for the Family: Overcoming Distances in Time and Space." *Critical Military Studies* 3 (1): 69–86. https://doi.org/10.1080/23337486.2016.1231986.

Honneth, A. 1996. *The Struggle for Recognition: The Moral Grammar of Social Conflicts*. Cambridge, MA: MIT Press.

Kangro, M. 2015. "Kas seotus Kaitseväega mõjutab meeste pereloomelist käitumist ja väärtusi?" In A. Trumm (ed.), *Riigikaitse inimvara arendamine: võimalused ja väljakutsed*, 111–28. Tartu: Tartu Ülikool.

Karu, M. 2011. "Fathers and Parental Leave: Slow Steps towards Dual Earner/Dual Career Family Model in Estonia." Ph.D. diss., University of Tartu, Tartu, Estonia.

Karu, M., and K. Kasearu. 2011. "Slow Steps towards Dual Earner/Dual Career Family Model: Why Do Fathers Not Take Parental Leave." *Studies of Transition States and Societies* 3 (1): 24–38.

Kaskla, E. 2003. "The National Woman: Constructing Gender Roles in Estonia." *Journal of Baltic Studies* 34 (3): 298–312.

Keck, W., and C. Saraceno. 2013. "The Impact of Different Social-Policy Frameworks on Social Inequalities among Women in the European Union: The Labour-Market Participation of Mothers." *Social Politics: International Studies in Gender, State & Society* 20 (3): 297–328.

Kivirähk, J. 2017. "Avalik arvamus ja riigikaitse." Tellija, Estonia: Kaitseministeerium. Retrieved 14 September 2017, http://www.kmin.ee/sites/default/files/elfinder/article_files/avalik_arvamus_ja_riigikaitse_marts_2017.pdf.

Kvale, S. 1996. *InterViews: An Introduction to Qualitative Research Interviewing*. London: SAGE Publications.

Lundquist, J., and H. L. Smith. 2005. "Family Formation among Women in the U.S. Military: Evidence from the NSLY. *Journal of Marriage and Family* 67 (1): 1–13.

Maigre, M. 2006. "Post-Communist Transition in Civil–Military Relations: The Case of Estonia." M.A. thesis, King's College London, UK.

Moelker, R., M. Andres, G. Bowen, and P. Manigart. 2015. *Military Families and War in the 21st Century: Comparative Perspectives*. London: Routledge.

Nissen, T. E. 2015. *Sotsiaalmeedia Kasutamine Relvasüsteemina. Tänapäeva Konfliktide Omadused*. Tartu: Riigikaitse Raamatukogu. Postimees.

Nugin, R. 2016. "Re-Constructing a Transition Generation: The 1970s Cohort." In R. Nugin, A. Kannike, and M. Raudsepp (eds.), *Generations in Estonia: Contemporary Perspectives on Turbulent Times*, 282–317. *Approaches to Culture Theory* 5. Tartu: University of Tartu Press.

Pajumets, M. 2007. "Why Mummy Goes to Work?—Subjective Expectations and Different Meanings Given to Work." In B. Vaher and K. Seeder (eds.), *Töö ja Pere: paindlik töökorraldus ja lastevanemate tööhõive*, 35–78. Tallinn: AS Ajakirjade Kirjastus.

Pateman, C. 1989. *The Disorder of Women: Democracy, Feminism, and Political Theory*. Stanford: Stanford University Press.

Philips, P. 1986. "A Soviet Estonian Soldier in Afghanistan." *Central Asian Survey* 5 (1): 101–15.

Segal, M. W. 1986. "The Military And the Family As Greedy Institutions." *Armed Forces & Society* 13 (1): 9–38. https://doi.org/10.1177/0095327X8601300101.

Sørensen, B. R. 2015. "Veterans' Homecomings." *Current Anthropology* 56 (S12): S231–40.

Talves, K. 2013. "Tööränne Ja Selle Mõju Laste Heaolule Eestis." *Ajakiri Sotsiaaltöö* 3: 47–49.

Tamm, M. 2008. "History as Cultural Memory: Mnemohistory and the Construction of the Estonian Nation." *Journal of Baltic Studies* 39 (4): 499–516.

———. 2016 "The Republic of Historians: Historians as Nationbuilders in Estonia (Late 1980s–Early 1990s). *Rethinking History: The Journal of Theory and Practice* 20 (2): 154–71.

Tammisto, P. 2015. "Commemoration of Independence Day in the Republic of Estonia 1919–1940." *Ajalooline Ajakiri-the Estonian Historical Journal* 1/2 (151/152): 85–119.

Toots, A., A. Reetz, and D. Jahn. 2014. "SGI Sustainable Governance Indicators: 2014 Estonia Report." Gütersloh, Germany: Bertelsmann Stiftung. Retrieved 15 September 2017, http://www.sgi-network.org/docs/2014/country/SGI2014_Estonia.pdf.

Truusa, T.-T. 2010. "Media Analysis of Deployment-Related Stress: Ideas for Developing Estonian Military Social Work." M.S.W. thesis, University of Tartu, Estonia.

———. 2015. "Supporting the Troops: The Effects of Estonia's Veterans Policy." Paper, 13th Biennial Conference of ERGOMAS, 8–12 June 2015, Open University of Israel, Ra'anana, Israel.

Truusa, T.-T., and A. Siplane. 2015. "Using Internet Forums to Support Military Families during Deployment." Paper, Third Annual Military Social Work Conference: Strengthening Military Families through Effective Community Practices, 16–18 September 2015, Joe C. Thompson Center, University of Texas, Austin, Texas.

Warming, H. 2015. "The Life of Children in Care in Denmark: A Struggle over Recognition." *Childhood* 22 (2): 248–62.

Wertsch, M. E. 1991. *Military Brats: Legacies of Childhood inside the Fortress*. St. Louis, MO: Brightwell Publishing.

Wright, M. C., N. Assar, E. L. Kain, L. Kramer, C. B. Howery, K. McKinney, B. Glass, and M. Atkinson. 2004. "Greedy Institutions: The Importance of Institutional Context for Teaching in Higher Education." *Teaching Sociology* 32 (2): 144–59. https://doi.org/10.1177/0092055X0403200201.

Chapter 3

Military, Society, and Violence through Popular Culture
Japan's Self-Defense Forces

Eyal Ben-Ari

Introduction

Militaries around the world use a plethora of images aimed at large groups to variously recruit potential troops, assure publics of their necessity, or portray the varied civilian activities they take upon themselves. Thus one finds live-fire exercises held for the public in the United States (Lutz 2001), annual air force fly-bys produced by the Israeli military, or the massive dissemination of posters by the German or Taiwanese forces containing slogans centered on freedom, democracy, and confidence in their armed forces (Frühstück 2010). In addition, the armed forces, often in alliance with commercial establishments, sell a multitude of products with emblems and signs of military units, including, for instance, hats and sweaters, key chains and lighters, or plaques and ornaments. But how does one make sense of such popular imageries (appearing in spectacles, films, or commercial products) conveyed by martial forces? How does one interpret the use of such images by "the" institution most often identified with the nation-state? How can one understand the use by the armed forces of popular culture as that accumulation of cultural products such as music, art, literature, fashion, dance, film, cyber culture, television, and radio that are consumed the majority of a society's population? As I show, the appeal of popular culture lies in its mass accessibility and reach, and its potential in influencing different publics' attitudes toward certain topics.

Notes for this chapter begin on page 76.

To answer these questions, this study begins with an analysis of relations between militaries, societies, and violence as portrayed in mass-produced and disseminated popular cultural products that are publicly offered by an alliance of the armed forces and commercial establishments: specifically, it centers on the ways the armed forces of the industrial democracies manage their public imagery through popular goods, merchandise, artifacts, applications (apps), videos, or television programs.

The study then proceeds to the wider theoretical question that is the center of this volume: how do contemporary militaries manage their relation to organized and legitimate violence within international conflicts through popular culture? Hence, I ask what can be learned about the classic problem of social order and violence through analyzing how states and their armed forces have moved into the realm of popular culture to try to "deal with" — order, manipulate, control — public representations centered on the potential use of organized violence in conflicts.

To be sure, various forms of popular cultural products have long been used as part of inter-state conflicts as the cartoons and caricatures of the two world wars attest to (Greene 2014; Naftali 2014). But the veritable explosion and increased acceptance of popular culture among affluent publics have turned its products into readily available means that states and militaries can use to represent themselves and their various roles. Arguably, nowhere is this truer than in the case of Japan, which has become one of the world's leading producers and consumers of popular cultural products. Among the abundance of such products and productions are many that include major elements of violence, such as monsters, samurai, criminals, or indeed the Imperial army and navy (Allison 2000; Gill 1998; Kinsella 2000). Moreover, manga and anime have been used extensively in order to explore and portray various narratives of World War II (Penney 2009: Napier 2005). Hence these products, it can be argued, lead to the population's "pre-exposure" to depictions of violence. Such pre-exposure seems especially true of younger generations, who were born into and have grown up in the context of a variety of images readily available through the touch of a screen.

It is against this background that Japan's military — the Self-Defense Forces (SDF) — has recognized and actively utilized — often in concert with conservative politicians and senior civil servants — the sophistication, innovation, and productive power of the country's popular culture industries. The main thrust of this usage has centered on the country's problematic military past during World War II, and on the need to convince wide swaths of the population of the seriousness of the threats posed by North Korea, China, and possibly Russia. At base, then, the SDF find themselves, as I show, needing to deal with public perceptions of their specializing in organized violence.

From the point of view of the study of civil–military entanglements, the study of popular culture and the military seems especially intriguing. Publicly available, and often commercially produced, imagery tie together both domains (the civilian and the military) in a way that is appealing and entertaining—that is, in ways that catch the attention, and often mobilize the interest, of consumers in ways that are very different from other modes of connection. In other words, looking at a YouTube film or viewing an air force fly-over of jets is different from the ways in which people view a news broadcast or a televised debate between experts, or how families negotiate with representatives of the armed forces. But there is more here. Hodder (2012) suggests that the concept of "entanglements" entails something qualitatively different than mere connection of separate entities. Rather, for him the concept should prod scholars to look for the complex dialectic relations between entities, to their mutual effects (positive and negative), and to the unique kinds of joint entities created by such relations.

In this chapter, I use the notion of entanglements to trace out the ripples and reverberations between the military and civilian spheres through popular cultural products. Popular culture—and especially those products related to the new media—tightly link production, dissemination, and consumption. As I show, this association implies two points: first, that civilian–military ties are evident through the whole process: production is done via military and civilian alliances; dissemination is carried out through commercial enterprises but controlled by the SDF; and consumption is done within both military spaces by civilians (as in their direct participation in activities like viewing public performances) or in civilian places (as when viewing movies and clips at home). Second, given the relative freedom of consumers and the close relations between production and consumption in popular culture, some people may send images of the SDF onward, add their own ornamentations or comments to them, or integrate them into new products. In this way, a popular cultural product reverberates and resonates outward from its initial point of reception to other venues and relations.

In the next section, I provide a few examples that may provide a flavor of the diverse products produced by the SDF and commercial businesses.

Popular Cultural Products and Japan's Self Defense Forces

The websites of the ground, air, and maritime services of the SDF include multiple links to beautiful YouTube presentations of equipment and activities (and links to Facebook and Twitter for further dissemination of their products) (see also Stein 2012). The website of the Air SDF includes an array of commercially fabricated products that can be downloaded, including wallpapers, screen savers, icons, and instructions for building paper planes.[1] The Maritime SDF website includes games for children (including matching flash cards and puzzles) and recipes (including one for a tangy Shirase seafood curry for the Shirase icebreaker).[2] According to the *Asahi Shimbum* newspaper (5 July 2013), from 2008 to 2013, page views on SDF websites nearly doubled partly as a result of the SDF's active involvement in relief, response, and rebuilding efforts following the Great East Japan Earthquake, tsunami, and the Fukushima nuclear disaster of March 2011. In order to further spruce up these websites, the forces appointed pop idol Shimazaki Haruka of the popular J-pop group AKB48 in 2014 as brand ambassador and the lynchpin of a new charm offensive to sign up young recruits (Jain 2014). She appears in an official thirty-second video wearing a neat dress and speaking about the necessity of the SDF; the accompanying link includes a picture and personal information about her.

Even before this charm offensive, the 2000s saw many television dramas centered on the SDF that were produced with the acquiescence and sometimes direct help of the Japanese military. The reason for this situation is that, as Jain (2014) explains, Japanese now attach the same degree of romance and glamor to their armed forces as people do anywhere in the world. One example is the cooperation of the Air SDF service in the production of a TV drama called "Public Affairs Office in the Sky," set in the public relations section of the Air Staff Office.

Indeed, these efforts are the latest of a long series of uses that the SDF has made of popular cultural products dating back to the 1980s, when it began to copy the strategies of large government offices and business corporations in using popular cultural products to promote images of themselves (Kinsella 2000). At that time, the SDF contracted professionals from Dentsu (one of the largest advertising agencies in the world) to produce a cartoon comic series called *Prince Pickles*, with the lead character and his female counterpart Princess Parsley becoming mascots for the forces (Frühstück 2010). In addition to adorning some service members' business cards, the Prince and Princess can be bought as plastic dolls in different sizes and as fluorescent stickers. The Prince is also the hero of three cartoon volumes published during the early 1990s by the public relations division of the then Japan Defense Agency (it is now a full-fledged ministry).[3] As Frühstück (2010) explains, between fourteen and thirty-four pages thick, the cartoon booklets were part of a larger campaign aimed at aggressively establishing new images of the Self-Defense Forces in Japanese society.

A different kind of popular cultural product produced by the SDF entails a very large array of public performances designed to advance its image, demonstrate its varied capabilities, and provide a human side to the force. These include opening military camps to the public, parades and fly-bys, live-fire exercises, and musical festivals (Ben-Ari 2011; Früh-stück 2010). For instance, every January, Japan's 1st Airborne Brigade—the force's only airborne unit—holds an annual exercise in Chiba prefecture, near Tokyo, that is open to the public.[4] In 2015, as a reflection of the SDF's popularity, an estimated fifteen thousand spectators came out to the para-chute and helicopter performance, compared with twelve thousand in 2014 and eleven thousand in 2013. Likewise, as part of a joint exercise with the U.S. Army, the SDF provided a performance by "ninjas" for the participating troops, which was widely reported on by the media (Witt 2012). A final example is an activity that has been going on for at least three decades, in which the ground forces regularly hold simulated basic training for a few days. This training is open to a variety of participants and has even been followed by Japanese versions of reality TV.[5]

At first sight, the use of popular cultural products can be understood as the means by which the Japanese military (like any public bureaucracy or business concern; Purcell 2005) manages its public relations so as to project good images of itself. Indeed, these various products are initiated, produced, and managed by the public relations office of the SDF, which today comprises about a thousand soldiers and civilians. As Frühstück (2014), explains, during the 1990s,

> the defense ministry's and SDF branch websites looked dull and bureaucratic. Now, they offer video clips and games, individual service members' accounts of their motivations and experiences, and other dynamic materials in addition to data about capabilities and missions. The military public relations apparatus is now appealing to a youthful audience that is largely clueless about the cir-cumstances of the Constitution's Article 9 [limiting the country's use of armed force] and the U.S.–Japan alliance. Many in the young generation tend to see the first as outdated and the second as *fait accompli* and unproblematic.

But the Japanese military, like any similar armed force, is unlike civilian organizations since the military is the organization most strongly identi-fied with the legitimate (if at times contested) use of organized violence in external (and sometimes internal) conflicts (Boene 1990). Since the end of the Cold War, public attitudes toward the use of military force have been changing around the industrial democracies (Ben-Ari, Kellen, and Michael 2009). In these countries, cultural transformations have led to a heavy emphasis on keeping casualties to a minimum and to justifications for using military power being much more contested than in the past (Moskos et al. 2000: 5–6). The recent incursions into Afghanistan and Iraq by coalitions of countries ironically attest to this: the violence perpetuated by various such forces is legitimated (among other things) by a strong rhetorical stress on precision warfare, a very strong control of the dissemination of media reports about the effects of violence (on both sides), and the minimization of casualties.

In such societies, as the means of violence have been monopolized by states, and as societies have been pacified, people have developed strong feelings about using and witnessing violence (Blok 2000). Thus, among wide publics in these societies, violence has come to be seen as anomalous, irrational, senseless, and disruptive—as the reverse of social order, as the antithesis of "civilization," as something that has to be brought under control (Blok 2000: 23). To be sure, the use of armed force is still a major characteristic of contemporary states, but the point is that the terms for using organized violence have now become more contested. Sociologists and political scientists have explored some of the explicit political strategies—gathering support, lobbying for funds, or handling the media, for example—by which political decision makers and military establishments handle these contestations (Feaver 1999: 235; Shaw 2005). As the editors state in the introduction to this volume, given their very heavy stress on the institutional and political arrangements characterizing civil–military relations, these studies have done little to explore the cultural imagery and practices by which the militaries of the technologically advanced democracies handle their problematic relation to violence. In this sense, I go beyond previous analyses offered by sociologists and political scientists to explore the popular cultural practices contemporary forces like the SDF use. Moreover, as explained earlier, popular cultural sites are especially intriguing for exploring the civil–military entanglements through which the images of the armed forces are produced, disseminated, and consumed.

But in the case of the Japanese military, identification with an institution charged with state-mandated organized violence is especially problematic because of the country's historical and political position (Ben-Ari 2015a; 2015b). The legacy of World War II meant that the country's defeat was blamed on "the generals," and that the word "military" (guntai) became synonymous with subjugation, destruction, and disaster. This meaning was underpinned by the effects of the atomic bomb which—beyond the sheer misery of hundreds of thousands of people—resulted in the Japanese having been victimized, both by America's actions and by the aggression of Japan's wartime military regime. These circumstances lead to the promulgation of Article 9 of a new constitution, prohibiting Japan from possessing offensive military capability (hence the name Self-Defense Forces), the rise of a significant anti-militaristic ethos in Japanese society, and the burgeoning of a host of social movements devoted to the promotion of world peace. The immediate postwar anti-militarist turn has sometimes echoed external interests, namely the continued strong resistance of Japan's Asian neighbors to signs of what they see as its remilitarization.

Yet despite these rather unfavorable circumstances, Japan does have a substantial military establishment that perceives enemy invasion as its primary threat, considers the combat leader the dominant military professional, and enjoys an increasingly supportive public attitude toward it in the wider population. The SDF is a full-fledged military establishment complete with three services, the latest military technology, and all of the organizational accompaniments common to armed forces (territorial divisions, brigades, and training methods). This situation thus underscores my questions about how the production, dissemination, and consumption of official popular cultural products are elated to the Japanese military's very *raison d'être*, to its violent potential in armed conflict? Here I follow Frühstück (2007; 2014), who has done more than any other scholar to systematically and innovatively analyze how the Japanese military uses popular culture for its own purposes. Concretely, following Galia Press-Barnathan (2016), I ask about popular culture as a policy tool.

The Messages

Let me provide an analysis of the main messages the SDF transmits to various publics and of the popular products and productions through which they do so (for a wider analysis of more messages using means other than popular culture, see Ben-Ari 2015b). To begin, the main aim of using popular culture has increasingly been to create understandings of the SDF's necessity as an armed force. In other words, given the still widespread anti-military ethos among wide publics in Japan, the SDF emphasizes more and more that the country needs the military for its defense. While in the past the major threat to the country was the Soviet Union, today the main adversaries are seen to be China and North Korea, a variety of terror organizations, and piracy. Among the more conventional strategies the Japanese forces (along with other groups) use to create a sense of their necessity are parliamentary debates, establishing various study groups, lectures and speeches by the Prime Minister and other politicians, creating think tanks populated by security experts, formulating party policies, cultivating news reporters, allowing television companies access to camps and bases, and the dissemination of informational videos about the country and its potentially dangerous environs. The use of popular cultural products should be seen alongside—accompanying and often complementing—these varied strategies.

A good example of the complementary function of popular culture was the publication in 2005 of the annual defense white paper in cartoon form centered on a young girl and her loveable bear (Frühstück 2014). A few years later, pirate attacks off the coast of Somalia led to the dispatch of Maritime SDF ships to the area and eventually to the establishment of a Japanese naval base in Djibouti. Accompanying this dispatch as Früh-stück (2007b) explains, the SDF published a manga pamphlet titled "Understanding through Manga: The Somalia Pirate Problem" to clarify that as piracy had become an international issue, Japan was contributing to the international community. More recently, the Ground SDF released an illustrated video showing it in action as part of the new *National Defense Program Guidelines for FY 2014 and Beyond*. I concur with Frühstück's (2014) conclusion that the SDF has come to emphasize a much more combative stance than in the past, at the center of which are effective deterrence and response capabilities. In fact, she goes on to say,

> To my knowledge, never before has the SDF public relations apparatus officially dared to adopt the hawkish rhetoric of becoming "more battle oriented," speaking of "combat vehicles" that are needed for "optimizing the force structure from an operational point of view," or the eventuality of responding "to attacks on remote islands." The smooth aesthetic, musically dramatized and enhanced with defense rhetoric more similar to American military public relations efforts than anything I have seen before in Japan, is a clear departure from earlier, more amateurish attempts to familiarize a broad audience with the Self-Defense Forces' mission and style.

A similarly explicit message is found in the following instance. After a public parachute exercise by the country's airborne brigade, Defense Minister Gen Nakatani gave a speech to troops reported on by the media. He said, "For the past few years, Chinese warships have increased their activities in Japan's adjacent seas . . . and the security environment surrounding Japan has become more severe. . . . We should always be ready to handle any possible situation, including aid activities overseas, the defense of Japan—our core mission—and the protection of islands." Hence, the public performance of an "entertaining" exercise open to the general public was directly linked to the policy message of a much more militarily oriented SDF.

The new emphasis on much more explicit messages about national defense should, however, be seen as the result of previous efforts by the SDF to prepare the public to accept the military's necessity. It is in this light that the publication of the "Prince Pickles" cartoon back during the 1980s should be seen—as a strategy to carefully, incrementally "train" wide publics for this message. Thus it is not surprising that by July of 2013 a DVD featuring SDF tanks became an instant hit with the public when it sold more than fifteen thousand copies during the first week of release (*Asahi Shinbun*, 28 July 2013). It marked the first time that a DVD themed on a cultural or pedagogical subject had beaten all other entries from music, movie, and other categories to lead Oricon Inc.'s weekly sales chart. As the *Asahi* article explained, the main track on the DVD, titled "Yoku Wakaru! Rikujo Jieitai" (Plain to see! The Japan Ground Self-Defense Force) with the subtitle, "Riku no Oja! Nihon wo Mamoru Sensha no Rekishi" (King of the land! A history of tanks that defend Japan), is narrated by a male voice, but a bonus track is narrated by the voice of a high school girl in a popular anime.

At the same time, however, one cannot understand the power of all these messages without noting the rise in the status of the SDF in the wake of the 2011 triple disaster of the Tohoku earthquake, tsunami, and nuclear crisis. Even more than previous crises (involving floods, snow avalanches, or earthquakes) the SDF utilized opportunities to carry out reconstruction and humanitarian efforts that usually receive considerable media coverage (Yeo 2012–13). If performed successfully and covered substantially, as in the case of the 2011 disaster, these humanitarian activities influence, change, or confirm public attitudes and understanding of a nation's military role and social acceptance. And, indeed, public support for the SDF has never been as high as it is now (Ben-Ari 2015b).

Entertainment, Aestheticization, and the Emotional Appeal of Violence

The analysis, however, is not complete. In order to understand the appeal of the popular cultural products the SDF uses, it is important to examine *how* its messages are conveyed. There seem to be four interrelated approaches used: humanizing and familiarizing the force through individual pictures, the aestheticization of performances of organized violence, the softening of soldierly imagery through manga and anime (especially with female figures), and holding open days in camps to host the general public.

The first approach includes a plethora of aesthetically pleasing pictures of individuals and typical scenes that appear in newspapers, posters, YouTube (and other) videos, and websites. These photos and videos purport to offer "representative" samples of life in the SDF and include faces and full-body figures (invariably smiling if not engaged in combat work), equipment and weaponry, or activities and workplaces. Such pictures seem to be akin to postcards since they offer exemplary pictures of "ideal-typical" scenes of places and peoples we visit, meant to arouse an emotional response. For instance, Frühstück (2014) tells how the Ministry of Defense homepage encouraged visitors to "Believe your heart." More dynamically, official websites often contain banner advertisements at their page peripheries that shimmer or produce repetitive loops designed to draw the eye of users and ultimately get them to mouse click on a picture where an embedded hyperlink is located. These hyperlinks, in turn, are almost always accompanied by other pictures of exemplary scenes and figures. The overall effect of these depictions in photos is to humanize the SDF by personalizing troops and everyday scenes. The reverberation with "postcards"—or, today, cellular phone pictures—seems to convey sentiments of familiarity and similarity to other organizations. Indeed, in 2014, the SDF released a smart phone app called *Kimi ni Eeru AR* (Your AR cheerleading shout). The app allows users to take selfies and use them to make cute military avatars of themselves by selecting gender, branch, uniform, and style. Users can then get "augmented reality cards" (or AR cards) downloaded from the JSDF website to make their avatars perform various actions, such as dancing or marching.

The second approach centers on "rehearsal," such as live-fire exercises that are open to the general public but require going through application processes (Ben-Ari 2011; Ben-Ari and Frühstück 2003; Grisafi 2014). Furthermore, footage of the maneuvers can be easily downloaded from official and unofficial websites.[6] In these live and video-recorded shows, the violence of the military is presented as spectacular through kinetic visuals, dynamic action, and accompanying sounds of guns shooting and vehicles moving. In addition, the live audiences can smell the oil of the tanks as well as that of the explosives. Closely orchestrated by the SDF, the videos contain footage that is much better than could be found in real firefights (where it is often difficult to get good angles for photographing). In this process of aestheticization, the violent qualities are transformed into something to be contemplated or experienced in the rather "safe" conditions of the audience in the stands or viewers at home (Handelman 1997: 395). In this sense, the live-fire exercise can be likened to a theater performance or perhaps more correctly a spectacle, a grand and impressive event meant to entertain. Undeniably, there is nothing more kinetic than the physical violence used by the military and its epitome of firefight—the heart of war (Moeller 1989: 3). My point is that while violence has been "civilized" or "tamed" in our societies, it is still an object of fascination, enjoyment, and celebration. The complex of official representations of (real and staged) firefights along with adoring audiences may be a part of what Michael Mann (1987) calls "spectator sport" militarism. Here modern urban dwellers participate not as foot soldiers their grandfathers did, but as consumers of (mediated) images.

The third approach involves the softening of the SDF's image and especially of its violent potential (see also Kuntzman and Stein 2015). A major means for doing so is the active use of anime and manga. Thus SDF offices in several prefectures designed sets of female anime characters—for use in ads, posters, calendars, handouts, and even cardboard cutouts—with figures representing the three services—ground, maritime, and air forces (Grisafi 2014). One revealing example are the narratives proclaiming a new "joint" SDF action policy disseminated by the Defense Ministry that actually remained cleansed of information on the potential death and destruction that follow the new missions (Frühstück 2014). Instead, many of these narratives blended with a plethora of popular cultural products whose key characters are gendered female, coded childlike, and unapologetically sexualized. As Kendall (2012) explains, Kisarazu city's aviation festival presented a new AH-1S Cobra helicopter to be used in "(defensive) tank-busting operations" that involved a *"moe* style" and a redhaired character. According to him, the term *"moe"* is hard to define but is used to describe a feeling of passion and burning usually for something like a pretty young girl that men desire. As Kendall goes on to describe, during the festival the helicopter quickly stole the show with hundreds taking photos and sharing videos of it on the internet. Reporting on the same event, Ashcraft (2015) shows that the tradition of painting pinups on aircraft lives on in Japan with an important difference: they are not cheesecake pinups but anime girls. Hence, while the old saucy nose art has been deemed offensive in the West, it is not that much of a concern in Japan: at this event, there was a cosplaying female actress on hand, with an explanation that her bust-waist-hip measurements were a "national secret." [7]

If this is not enough, the *Yomiuri Shinbun* (*Yomiuri Shinbun*, 22 July 2013) reported that the town of Oarai, Ibaraki Prefecture, had adopted an unusual symbol to attract visitors: a Ground SDF tank. Oarai is the setting of the popular TV anime series *Girls und Panzer*, in which high school girls learn *senshado*, a fictitious popular martial art that uses tanks as its main weapon. Many tanks appear in the series, in which various facilities and streets of the town are precisely re-created. And as the *Asahi Shinbun* (28 July 2013) went on to report, the voice of Yukari Akiyama, a character in the serial *Girls und Panzer*, exclaims, "Don't you perhaps believe that Japan, an island country, does not need tanks? That's absolutely not the case!" The anime, in turn, is credited with causing a record number of applicants—over a hundred thousand—to come observe the Japan Ground Self-Defense Force's annual Fuji live-fire exercise in August of 2013. During the event, the town displayed equipment and personnel as part of its efforts to attract sightseers, whose numbers fell after the 2011 Great East Japan Earthquake, and found the SDF very willing to cooperate to promote its tanks' role in the nation's defense. The festival saw about thirty-two thousand visitors, five times the number of the previous year, according to the town government (*Yomiuri Shinbun*, 22 July 2013). For the duration of the festival, then, the town becomes a civilian–military hybrid, an enmeshment of soldiers and visitors.

The fourth, and closely related, form of popular cultural production entails the tens of open days that the SDF holds in camps and bases around the country. One example is a yearly event held at a camp in the Osaka area taking place every February (Ben-Ari 2011). It includes a parachute jump at the edge of the base, a large display of weapons and vehicles in its main square, an exhibition of the regiment's soldiers in Iraq and disaster relief, and a performance of military bands, cheerleaders (from a women's university in Kyoto), and martial arts (performed by soldiers). The atmosphere is casual, with much interaction taking place between visitors and soldiers in and around the weapons and vehicles, with visitors climbing onto the tanks, taking rides in jeeps, holding weapons (such as light machine guns), or trying on flak jackets or gas masks. This kind of opportunity allows for tactile experiences: people can touch the vehicles, climb up on them, feel the relationship between their bodies and the bulk of the trucks and tanks, pick up and handle weaponry, aim rifles and machine guns, and smell the peculiar military odors of gas fumes and oil. To follow Beeman (2005: 25), because the deepest emotional expressions between people are usually tactile (perhaps even olfactory and gustatory) rather than linguistic, by touching and handling war machines—guns, artillery pieces, tanks, binoculars—outsiders become privy to and feel the power evinced by the metal and the sleekness of the weapons. Indeed, the fascination with the missile projectiles is complemented by the touching of the armor of the vehicles as one would stroke metal muscles. Indeed, to stretch an image, for the duration of the day, civilians not only temporarily take on parts of soldierly roles but become entangled in a bodily experience that links the military and civilian spheres.

Like other open-door activities (Ben-Ari and Frühstück 2003; *Japan Times*, 31 August 31, 2006), so here a primary aim is to bring the SDF closer to "the people" and—among other messages—show them that soldiers are "real persons." The troops and the weapons become objects that are both accessible and open to dialogue with civilian outsiders. Indeed, according to my impression, almost all the photographs taken are of individuals or small groups with military equipment or on armed vehicles. Hence the "stylistic choices" governing these photographs involve composites of family, relatives, or friends placed in, on, or near the vehicles, or handling weapons. Moreover, as visitors later view and show these pictures outside the camp, the SDF is further entangled into and within civilian places and activities. More generally, to follow MacAloon (1984: 246), the event partakes of the character of a festival rather than a spectacle because in festivals, the roles of actors and spectators are less distinguishable. This point is, again, important for our analysis, since it underscores how the relative lack of boundaries between performers (the soldiers) and audience (the external visitors) is a mechanism enmeshing the two spheres. Finally, the many food stalls, several staffed by soldiers, turn the event into a sort of mass picnic. Hence, throughout the day, tactile experiences, shared food and drink, and the breakdown of the boundaries between civilians and soldiers work toward domesticating and personalizing the event.

Conclusion

As I have shown in this chapter, because Japan is a country where organized violence has been extremely problematic for the past decades, it is a good case for exploring just how states and their armed forces work toward making military force accepted by wide publics (see also Daugsberg this volume; Susca 2012). The main problem faced by the leaders of the SDF—sometimes, but not always, in alliance with civilian decision makers—is how to "normalize" its links to the use of organized violence. However, the SDF—again like all armed forces—not only deals with legitimizing and justifying its links to violence but also strives to convey a wider variety of roles it fulfills, such as aiding in times of natural disasters, working toward ecologically friendly activities, or helping local communities. The wider point of this essay is that popular culture has become a prime set of means by which militaries are normalized into everyday understandings. Looking at today's industrial democracies, I would posit that the bewildering array of popular cultural products centered on war and militaries that saturate such societies as Japan work to preprepare wide publics for the use of organized state violence.

The particular power of popular cultural products, as I have demonstrated, lies in their multimodality (Aarseth 1997): they not only provide information to educate but also entertain through visual and audio modes that appeal to a greater range of the senses. Such products, in other words, create a dialogue between written, auditory, and visual images (and sometimes olfactory and gustatory dimensions) in a particularly emotional and embodied way (Golan and Ben-Ari 2018). It is this emotional accompaniment to messages and narratives that is so important for legitimation. Indeed, if one wants to understand the mobilization potential of contemporary states, it would seem that popular culture is a prime site for doing so. A focus on images and aesthetics, performances and spectacles, or festivals and open days, therefore, should caution us against too cognitive a bias in our analysis. Apart from being designed to convey or express certain messages, such popular cultural products are predicated on emotional resonances and sentiments that "move" (motivate and resonate with) people. Indeed, perhaps because these products and productions are so routine, and even labeled as "trivial," to date there has been very little criticism (let alone resistance) to their use of by the SDF.

To conclude, let me underscore two points. First, it is only through a focus on the interrelationships between emotionality, the body, and aesthetic appeal that we can understand how these events attempt to normalize the SDF, as any similar armed force, within current-day Japan. In this respect, the wide consumption of anime and manga within contemporary Japan provides an important reminder of the unique popular cultural heritage of each country and how its military forces use it. Second, to echo the editorial introduction to this volume, rather than viewing the civil–military divide as a given dichotomy, by focusing on such arenas as popular culture, we can disaggregate it to identify both the key actors, discourses, technologies, and objects through which they are entangled and to explore the ways that they are mobilized and reconfigured in innovative ways to end up in particular, sometimes unexpected, ways.

Eyal Ben-Ari is director of the Center for Society, Security and Peace at Kinneret College on the Sea of Galilee. He has carried out research in Israel, Japan, Singapore, and Hong Kong. His main areas of research are the sociology of the armed forces, early childhood education, and popular culture in Asia. Among his recent books are (with Zev Lehrer, Uzi Ben-Shalom and Ariel Vainer) *Rethinking the Sociology of Warfare: A Sociological View of the Al-Aqsa Intifada* (2010), (with Nissim Otmazgin) *The State and Popular Culture in East Asia* (2012), (with Jessica Glicken Turnley and Kobi Michael) *Social Science and Special Operations Forces* (2017), and *Japanese Encounters* (2018).

Notes

1. See "Gallery," JASDF website, http://www.mod.go.jp/asdf/English_page/gallery/.
2. See http://www.mod.go.jp/msdf/formal/family/kids/index.html (in Japanese). In a related manner, K. K. DeAgostini Japan, a publisher of magazines, bundled their publications with miniature models (even issuing a series titled "Japan Self-Defense Forces Model Collection") (*Asahi Shinbun*, 5 July 2013), and the UCC Ueshima Coffee Co. began offering assembly-type miniature models of tanks and other military paraphernalia as giveaway items with one of its canned coffee products.

3. "Prince Pickles in Action," AltJapan.com, 2 March 2007, http://altjapan.typepad.com/my_weblog/2007/03/prince_pickles_.html.
4. "Photos: Japan's New Year Parachute Exercise Entertains 15,000 Spectators" 2015.
5. "Photos: Japan's New Year Parachute Exercise Entertains 15,000 Spectators, *Wall Street Journal*, 28 Jan 2015, https://www.wsj.com/articles/photos-japans-new-year-parachute-exercise-entertains-15-000-spectators-1422496485.
6. One example can be found in http://www.mod.go.jp/gsdf/english/firepower.html.
7. Other examples can be found here: Michelle Lynn Dinh, 2014, "Japan Self-Defense Forces Show Off Their Feminine Side with 2014 Calendar," SoraNews24.com, 26 February 2014, http://en.rocketnews24.com/2014/02/26/japan-self-defense-forces-show-off-their-feminine-side-with-2014-calendar/; and Mac Denny, "Japan Self Defense Force Recruitment Posters Kill with Cute, 3 April 2012, http://en.rocketnews24.com/2012/04/03/japan-self-defense-force-recruitment-posters-kill-with-cute/.

References

Aarseth E. J. 1997. *Cybertext: Perspectives on Ergodic Literature*. Baltimore, MD: JHU Press.

Allison, Ann 2000. *Permitted and Prohibited Desires: Mothers, Comics and Censorship in Japan*. Berkeley: University of California Press.

Ashcraft, Brian. 2015. "Japan's Take on Military Pin-Ups Seems . . . Different." *Kotaku*. Accessed 25 June 2015, http://kotaku.com/5951730/japans-take-on-military-pin-ups-seemdifferent.

Ben-Ari Eyal. 2011. "Public Events and Japanese Self-Defense Forces: Aesthetics, Ritual Density and the Normalization of Military Violence." In Maria Six-Hohenbalken and Nerina Weiss (eds.), *Violence Expressed: An Anthropological Approach*, 55–70. Farnham: Ashgate.

———. 2015a. "Changing Japanese Defense Policies." Bar Ilan University, The Begin-Sadat Center. *Mideast Security and Policy Studies* 112.

———. 2015b. "Normalization, Democracy and the Armed Forces: The Transformation of the Japanese Military." In Sigal Ben-Rafael Galanti, Nissim Otmazgin, and Alon Levkowitz (eds.), *Japan's Multilayered Democracy*, 105–22. Lanham: Lexington.

Ben-Ari, Eyal, and Sabine Frühstück. 2003. "The Celebration of Violence: A Live-Fire Demonstration Carried Out by Japan's Contemporary Military." *American Ethnologist* 30 (4): 539–55.

Ben-Ari, Eyal, David Kellen, and Kobi Michael. 2009. "Introductory Essay. Wars and Peace Support Operations in the Contemporary World: Conceptual Clarifications and Suggestions." In Kobi Michael, David Kellen, and Eyal Ben-Ari (eds.), *The Transformation of the World of Warfare and Peace Support Operations*, 1–20. West Port, CT: Praeger Security International.

Ben-Ari, Eyal, and Nissim Otmazgin. 2011. "Cultural Industries and the State in East and Southeast Asia." In Nissim Otmazgin and Eyal Ben-Ari (eds.), *Popular Culture and the State in East and Southeast Asia*, 3–26. London: Routledge.

Boene, Bernard. 1990. "How Unique Should the Military Be? A Review of Representative Literature and Outline of Synthetic Formulation." *European Journal of Sociology* 31 (1): 3–59.

Blok, Anton. 2000. "The Enigma of Senseless Violence." In Goran Aijmer and Jon Abbink (eds.), *Meanings of Violence: A Cross Cultural Perspective*, 23–38. Oxford: Berg.

Burk, James. 1998. "Introduction, 1998: Ten Years of New Times." In James Burk (ed.), *The Adaptive Military: Armed Forces in a Turbulent World*, 1–24. New Brunswick, NJ: Transaction Books.

Da Matta, Roberto. 1984. "Carnival in Multiple Planes." In John J. MacAloon (ed.), *Rite, Drama, Festival, Spectacle: Rehearsals Toward a Theory of Cultural Performance*, 208–40. Philadelphia: Institute for the Study of Human Issues.

Der Derian, James. 2001. *Virtuous War: Mapping the Military-Industrial-Media-Entertainment Network*. Boulder: Westview.

Feaver, Peter D. 1999. "Civil-Military Relations." *Annual Review of Political Science* 2: 211–41.

Frühstück, Sabine. 2007a. *Uneasy Warriors: Gender, Memory and Popular Culture in the Japanese Army*. Berkeley: University of California Press.

———. 2007b. "AMPO in Crisis? US Military's Manga Offers Upbeat Take on US-Japan Relations." *The Asia-Pacific Journal* 8 (45.3). Accessed 12 December 2016, http://apjjf.org/-Sabine-Fruhstuck/3442/article.html.

———. 2010. "'To Protect Japan's Peace We Need Guns and Rockets': The Military Uses of Popular Culture in Current-Day Japan." *The Asia-Pacific Journal* 7 (34.2). Accessed 12 December 2016, http://apjjf.org/-Sabine-Fruhstuck/3209/article.html.

———. 2014. "A 'Dynamic Joint Defense Force'? An Introduction to Japanese Strategic Thinking." *The Asia-Pacific Journal*. Accessed 12 December 2016, http://apjjf.org/-Sabine-Fruhstuck/4790/article.html.

Gill, Tom. 1998. "Transformations of Magic: Some Japanese Super-Heroes and Monsters." In D. P. Martinez (ed.), *Japanese Popular Culture: Gender, Shifting Boundaries and Global Cultures*, 33–55. Cambridge: Cambridge University Press.

Golan, Oren, and Eyal Ben-Ari. 2018. "Armed Forces, Cyberspace and Global Images: The Official Website of the Israeli Defense Forces 2007–2015." *Armed Forces and Society* 44 (2): 280–300.

Greene, Linda. 2014. "Call to Arms." *Index on Censorship* 43: 45–9.

Grisafi, John. 2014. Japan Self-Defense Force Uses Anime, Technology to Draw More Recruits. *Penn Asian Review*, 29 September 2014. Accessed 25 June 2015, http://pennasianreviewonline.blogspot.jp/2014/09/japan-self-defense-force-uses-anime.html.

Handelman, Don. 1998. *Models and Mirrors: Towards and Anthropology of Public Events*. Oxford: Berghahn Books.

Hodder, Ian. 2012. *Entangled*. Oxford: Wiley-Blackwell.

"Ibaraki Town's Tank Attracts Tourists." 2013. *Yomiuri Shinbun*, 22 July 2013. https://www.questia.com/read/1P3-3032975521/ibaraki-town-s-tank-attracts-tourists.

Jain, Amit. 2014. "Japanese Armed Forces Get Image Makeover." *PR Week*, 28 November 2014. Accessed 6 June 2015, http://www.prweek.com/article/1324203/japanese-armed-forces-image-makeover.

Kendall, Philip. 2012. "Japan's Armed Forces Show Their Playful Side: Moe-Style Attack Helicopter Wows Crowd." *Rocket News* 24. Accessed 26 February 2015, http://en.rocketnews24.com/2012/10/19/japans-armed-forces-show-their-playful-side-moe-style-attack-helicopter-wows-crowds/.

Kinsella, Sharon. 2000. *Adult Manga: Culture and Power in Contemporary Japanese Society*. London: Curzon.

Lutz, Catherine. 2001. *Homefront: The Military City and the American Twentieth Century*. Boston: Beacon Press.

Mann, Michael. 1987. "The Roots and Contradictions of Modern Militarism." *New Left Review* 162: 35–51.

MacAloon, John J. 1984. "Introduction: Cultural Performances, Cultural Theory." In John J. MacAloon (ed.), *Rite, Drama, Festival, Spectacle: Rehearsals toward a Theory of Cultural Performance*, 1–15. Philadelphia: Institute for the Study of Human Issues.

Moskos, Charles C., John Allen Williams, and David R. Segal. 2000. "Armed Forces after the Cold War." In Charles Moskos, John Allen Williams, and David R. Segal (eds.), *The Postmodern Military: Armed Forces after the Cold War*, 1–13. New York: Oxford University Press.

Naftali, Orna. 2014. "Marketing War and the Military to Children and Youth in China: Little Red Soldiers in the Digital Age." *China Information* 28 (1): 3–25.

Napier, Susan. 2005. "World War II as Trauma, Memory and Fantasy in Japanese Animation." *Asia-Pacific Journal: Japan Focus 3 (5).* Accessed 7 January 2017, http://apjjf.org/-Susan-J.-Napier/1972/article.html.

Otmazgin, Nissim Kadosh. 2013. *Regionalizing Culture: The Political Economy of Japanese Popular Culture in Asia.* Honolulu: Hawaii Press.

Penney, Matthew. 2009. "Nationalism and Anti-Americanism in Japan: Manga Wars, Aso, Tamogami, and Progressive Alternatives." *The Asia-Pacific Journal: Japan Focus* 7 (17.2). Accessed 7 January 2017, https://apjjf.org/-Matthew-Penney/3116/article.html.

Press-Barnathan, Galia. 2016. Thinking about the Role of Popular Culture in International Conflicts. *International Studies Review* 19 (2): 166–84.

Purcell, Darren. 2005. "The Military in the Noosphere: ICT Adoption and Website Development in the Slovenian Ministry of Defense." *Information, Communication and Society* 8 (2): 194–216.

Schroder, Ingo W., and Bettinna E. Schmidt. 2001. "Introduction: Violent Imaginaries and Violent Practices." In Bettina E. Schmidt and Ingo W. Schroder (eds.), *Anthropology of Violence and Conflict*, 1–24. London: Routledge.

Shaw, Martin. 2005. *The New Western Way of War.* London: Pluto.

Stein, Rebecca L. 2012. "StateTube: Anthropological Reflections on Social Media and the Israeli State." *Anthropological Quarterly* 85: 893–916.

Susca, Margot A. 2012. "Why We Still Fight: Adolescents, America's Army, and the Government–Gaming Nexus." *Global Media Journal* 12 (20): 1–16.

Witt, Jamie. 2012. "Ninjas Leave Soldiers Seeing Stars." Army.mil (the official website of the United States Military), 6 November 2012. Accessed 23 February 2015, http://www.army.mil/article/90755/Ninjas_Leave_Soldiers_Seeing_Stars/.

Yeo, Yezi. 2012–2013. "De-militarizing Military: Confirming Japan's Self-defense Forces' Identity as a Disaster Relief Agency in the 2011 Tohoku Triple Crisis." *Asia Journal of Global Studies* 5 (2): 71–80.

Chapter 4

From Obligatory to Optional
Thirty Years of Civil–Military
Entanglements in Norway

Elin Gustavsen and Torunn Laugen Haaland

Introduction

This chapter analyzes the changing nature of civil–military entanglements in Norway. The starting point for the analysis are the claims made in the introductory chapter of this book: that all countries discussed in this volume have embarked on a process that implies some degree of militarization, and that we are witnessing a "deeper" and "subtler" penetration of "things military" into peoples' ordinary lives. In order to critically examine these claims in a Norwegian context, we argue first that today's expressions of "things military" must be seen in a larger historical context if we are to assess whether entanglements have become deeper and subtler. Second, a balanced analysis of entanglements should consider not only how "things military" penetrate ordinary people's lives, but also how "things civilian" penetrate military life. Third, an assessment of whether changing entanglements should be characterized as a "militarization" obviously depends on how this term is defined, and we question the adequacy of the definition offered by Ben-Ari and Sørensen. We therefore begin our analysis with a discussion of the terms "militarization" and "militarism" before we set out to describe and analyze entanglements in Norway from the last decade of the Cold War until the late 2010s.

Notes for this chapter begin on page 96.

Militarism and Militarization

Ben-Ari and Sørensen (introduction, this volume) define "militarization" as follows: "a discursive process involving a shift in societal beliefs and values in ways necessary to legitimate the use of force, the organization of large standing armies and their leaders, and the higher taxes or tribute used to pay for them." We find this definition to be too vague to be useful for our purposes. Moreover, taken literally it hardly fits with the claim that Western societies are in a process of "militarization." In Norway, societal beliefs and values, measured in surveys of support for the armed forces, have been remarkably constant over the last thirty years. To illustrate the point, surveys show that in 1980, 1992, and 2010, 86 percent of the Norwegian population answered yes when asked whether Norway should have a military defense (Alstad 1993; Nielsen 2010). In the years in between, the percentage sometimes dropped to 80 or rose to 90, but the overall picture is that societal belief and values in Norway are in favor of the country's armed forces. Furthermore, at no time has Norway had a large standing army. During the Cold War, Norway had a large mobilization army (more of this later), and presently Norway has a small semistanding army (approximately 4,100 army personnel, including conscripts, in a population of 5.2 million). When it comes to taxes and tribute to pay for the armed forces, the defense budget has declined from 2.9 of GDP in 1988 to 1.6 percent in 2016 (SIPRI 2018). These trends have been the same in most Western countries. To summarize, values and societal beliefs necessary to legitimate the use of force through the maintenance of a military organization have remained constantly supportive over the last thirty years; the standing army has never been large and is now smaller than ever; and the financial burden of the armed forces has declined. To characterize this development as a militarization (or its opposite—demilitarization) makes little sense, and we must look for another definition.

The crux of the definition problem is whether the presence outside the military sector of all "things military" should be seen as an indication of militarization of a society. The following statement from the Norwegian Chief of Defense (in England), 15 April 1944 (quoted in Sørlie and Rønne 2006:51), illustrates our point: "War, in our time, is everybody's concern, and everybody must prepare for such an event. . . . Almost all societal questions have a military side which must be taken under consideration when solved in times of peace. Society's civilian institutions and arrangements must, in peace, systematically prepare for their tasks in war." This policy, which in post–World War II Norway was labeled "total defense," was actively pursued by a large political majority in Norway throughout the Cold War. As will be further outlined below, it involved the entire society. It appears to prescribe a deeply militarized society. However, Norway did not develop into a garrison state, but an open liberal democracy.

Therefore, in our analysis of entanglements we find it useful to distinguish between processes aimed to maintain a military force in preparation for war on the one hand, and processes aimed to maintain a military force as a goal in itself on the other. We propose a more narrow definition of militarization, following Alfred Vagts's distinction between *the military way* and *the militaristic way*. Vagts defines militarism as "unlimited in scope. It may permeate all society and become dominant over all industry and arts. . . . An army so built that it serves military men, not war, is militaristic, so is everything in an army which is not preparing for fighting" (Vagts 1959:13–15). Following that, the existence of "things military" does not automatically lead to a militarization of society. It is only when "things military" begin to serve the military *as an end in itself* that a society become militarized.

Overview of the Chapter

The chapter continues with an account of the many entanglements existing in Norwegian society during the Cold War, a period when the armed forces had an extensive presence in ordinary people's everyday lives. The discussion is based on secondary literature, and we also use the experience of Torunn, one of the authors, to bring life to the mundane and ordinary aspects of these relations, as shared by many small communities throughout the country with a military campsite in their vicinity.

Thereafter, we analyze some of the most visible new "things military" that have surfaced in Norway since the Cold War ended, and discuss whether they represent a militarization of Norwegian society, or are in fact the military's efforts to counter the opposite: a significant demilitarization process. The new "things military" included in our analysis are a national Veteran's Day (instigated in 1996), a Memorial Sunday for deceased soldiers (instigated in 2007), public homecoming medal ceremonies for deployed soldiers (starting in 2009), the reinstitution of the War Cross (in 2009) — Norway's highest decoration for bravery during service — published soldiers' memoirs from recent wars, and TV documentaries from "inside" the military (aired between 2010 and 2018).

The analysis is based on documents from the Ministry of Defence (MoD) archive, newspaper articles, and official government documents located through their online database, manuscripts of public speeches, and observation of Veteran's Day and homecoming ceremonies in Oslo. All memoirs and TV documentaries published and aired between 2010 and 2018 are included to the best of our knowledge.[1] We must stress that in our analysis of these entanglements, we aim to provide an overview of these new phenomena rather than an in-depth analysis of the content of each contribution. Although not our primary focus, our analysis will also include how important societal reforms have been integrated in the armed forces over the last thirty years, bringing "things civilian" into the military. Through that, we aim to contribute to the understanding of the "deeper cultural constructs" (Levy 2016: 79) that shape civil–military entanglements at different times in different societies.

At the end of the chapter we revisit Ben-Ari's and Sørensen's claim that we are witnessing "what seems to be an ever deeper and subtler penetration of "things military" into ordinary lives"(introduction). Our basic argument is that whereas Cold War civil–military entanglements in Norway were secretive, obligatory, and direct, the entanglements of the late 2010s are (more) open, optional, and symbolic.

The Cold War Era: Pervasive Military Presence in Everyday Life

Coming out of World War II, Norway had experienced military defeat in 1940, followed by five years of Nazi occupation, before being liberated by allied forces in 1944–45. During the years of occupation, acts of military resistance were formed by a clandestine home front as well as by regular armed forces of the government-in-exile in Great Britain. Civic resistance took place in parallel, and despite the collaboration of Quisling and his followers, Norway came out of the war with a unifying collective feeling of a national resistance against the Nazi regime (Fure 2014). Before World War II, Norway pursued a policy of nonalignment in peace, aimed toward neutrality in war, but the collective lesson from World War II was that the strategic importance of Norway's geographic location would draw the country into war in case of major conflict in the Euro-Atlantic area. The nonalignment policy was formally abandoned in 1949, and Norway became a founding member of the Atlantic Alliance. Furthermore, under the slogan "Never again April 9th!," a large scale strengthening of the armed forces and civilian society's ability to repel an invasion ensued. Universal male conscription ensured that close to half of the population spent time in the military. The other half had the experience of sons, brothers, and friends going away, many to an isolated military base in the northern part of Norway, to receive twelve to eighteen months of military training.

Besides the regular armed forces, the entire society was to a considerable extent prepared for war in line with Norway's policy of "total defense." Municipalities had "readiness councils" in which civilian and military authorities, and local private enterprises, met and made plans for war preparation. The civilian support to the military in case of mobilization included means of production, transport, provisions, medical support, engineering, repairs, and maintenance (Børresen, Gjeseth, and Tamnes 2004: 71). To put it simply, every bus, tractor, tanker, and fishing boat had its own war service card and could be requisitioned and used in the mobilization defense of the country (Hansen and Higraff 2015). In case of war, between 20 and 30 percent of the population would be actively involved in the defense effort in preassigned roles, which were rehearsed on a regular basis (Børresen, Gjeseth, and Tamnes 2004: 372). As a result, the armed forces were notably present throughout the elongated landscape of the country.

The experience of Torunn illustrates how civil–military entanglements were part of many people's everyday lives. Steinkjer, her hometown, is a rural town in mid-Norway with approximately ten thousand inhabitants. Beginning in the 1950s, an army camp was located almost in the middle of the town, hosting an infantry basic training school, and every third month a new load of recruits would arrive for a three-month stay. Growing up there, the recruits' presence was very notable in the town's only discotheque (this was the 1980s). Besides that, the civil–military entanglements were everywhere: some of her childhood friends ended up marrying military conscripts; another friend's father was an officer working in the camp; her next-door neighbor worked in the uniform repair shop; and her mother, who was employed in the county administration, went away every other year rehearsing secret communication procedures to be used in case of war. In addition, her brother and all of her male friends served one year of conscription. A few of them also went away for six months or a year on UN peacekeeping missions. It was a "militarized" society in the sense that everyone's lives were influenced by the armed forces in one way or another.

The military presence was pervasive, reaching deep into peoples' lives. It was, at the same time, completely noncelebratory, but interwoven into everyday life in ways taken for granted and not reflected over. The military was, for instance, largely invisible on national occasions, such as the Norwegian day of independence (May 17); a national holiday that is extensively celebrated each year with children's parades.[2] On the other hand, the military offered extensive support to civilian sectors. Børresen, Gjeseth, and Tamnes (2014: 240) note that "the average Norwegian encountered the armed forces as a benefactor—one that guarded the borders, assisted the police and [assisted] at sporting events, and engaged in peacekeeping. The brutal reality of war and the military's use of violence faded into the background." The plans for use of the military forces in war were highly classified. The armed forces were at the same time closed off from the public *and* engaging the entire population, directly or indirectly, at some point in their life.

In parallel, the establishment of a welfare state changed the Norwegian military in fundamental ways. Most important in this respect was the introduction of extensive legal reforms in the 1970s and 1980s: In 1969, officers' work hours became regulated, and in 1981, the Working Environment Act (relating to working environment, working hours, and employment protection, etc.) was fully implemented in the armed forces. Officers were paid overtime for irregular work hours. Other novelties in this law, which challenged the traditional military hierarchy and command structures, was the right to codetermination given to conscripts and low rank military personnel. In 1978, the introduction of an Equality Act prohibited gender discrimination, and in 1984, women were given access to all services and combat positions in the armed forces. As more women worked full time, the duty of officers to move to new bases was made more flexible in 1983 (Børresen, Gjeseth, and Tamnes 2004: 354). Furthermore, almost all military personnel were organized in trade unions, which again were fully integrated in large civilian umbrella unions. These unions played and continue to play a pivotal role in the organization of the Norwegian work force. As a result, the military profession became similar to other professions. In the words of Charles Moskos, the military went from being an institution to an occupation (Moskos 1977; Haaland 2008)

Overall, Cold War entanglements were all-inclusive and obligatory. "Things military" were everywhere. At the same time, many "things military" became more and more similar to "things civilian" over the years. On the one hand, the military was exposed and well known in the population through the shared male experience of conscription and the many meetings between military and civilian decision makers entailed in the "total defense" policy. On the other hand, the military's preparation for war was secretive and closed off from the public eye.

Post–Cold War Reforms (1990–ca. 2015): Downsizing and New Military Assignments

The end of the Cold War did not lead to any immediate changes in this overall scenario. Even though the Soviet Union collapsed and a cautious cooperation with Russia was gradually established, the fundamental asymmetry in military strength between Norway and its eastern neighbor remained a constant in Norwegian defense and security planning. Thus defense cuts were slower than in many European countries. Universal conscription was maintained. At the same time, Norway's military engagements abroad both increased and changed character.[3] A crucial turning point occurred when NATO took over command of the UN operation in Bosnia in 1995. Within a few years, Norway changed its contribution to NATO's Balkan operations (in Bosnia and Kosovo) from supporting logistic and medical units to combat-ready forces, including infantry, Special Forces units, and fighter jets. The combination of (1) more extensive participation in coalition operations abroad and (2) the need to make land, air, and sea forces more professional and deployable on short notice to distant places climatically and topographically strikingly different from Norway put pressure on the defense budget. In retrospect, the 1990s are often referred to as "the lost decade" in the Norwegian defense and security policy debate, since reforms were postposed and Norway's focus only slowly and reluctantly turned away from homeland defense to deployment of forces to operations abroad. Characteristically, military expenditure as percentage of GNP remained around 2 percent until 2005 when it dropped to around 1.5 percent and remained there (SIPRI 2018).

During the first decade in the new century, Norwegian defense reforms picked up speed, and a dramatic downsizing commenced. This development was paralleled with an ever more combative role in the international arena. Thus Norway took part in the coalition wars in Iraq, Libya, and most importantly Afghanistan. The policy shift initially sparked some controversy in Norway, but politicians and the public soon became accustomed to the idea of Norwegian soldiers being involved in combat missions. The public response, even when the Norwegian engagement in Afghanistan became more warlike with an increased number of casualties, has been described as "silent acceptance" (Harpviken 2011; Oma and Ekhaugen 2014). The policy shift also created a new generation of veterans and transformed the public image of the armed forces, as will be further discussed below.

Back home, much of the everywhere-present, predominantly civilian readiness structure was dissolved, and many military camps throughout Norway were closed down as the armed forces were gradually restructured into a smaller, semiprofessional force. Thirteen mobilization brigades were reduced to one semiprofessional brigade. Some 160 camps, eighty coastal forts, ninety depots, and thirty-seven homeland defense constructions were divested (Hansen and Higraff 2015). By the end of 2010, the army was centralized into three main locations, the largest one in Northern Norway[4] and the other two in the South.[5] Navy and air force bases were equally reduced and centralized into significantly fewer geographical locations (Bogen and Håkenstad 2015). Conscription was maintained, but in 2015 only about one third of the male population was drafted. Thus, in the thirty-year span from 1985 to 2015, a great number of civil–military meeting points simply disappeared. In Torunn's hometown, the army regiment was dissolved in 2002. A few years later, the camp was sold to a private enterprise and turned into a hotel and a kindergarten, along with other functions. All military activities ceased, and uniformed personnel became a rare sight.

To summarize, by 2015 many of the traditional arenas for everyday contact between the armed forces and Norwegian civil society had disappeared. The majority of the new generations did not have firsthand experience with military service. At the same time, a new generation of veterans, with distinct wartime experience from former Yugoslavia, Iraq, Libya, and Afghanistan operations, had come into existence. These operations, and the veterans who returned from them, became the nexus of new ties that emerged between the civilian and the military sphere. Many of these new ties were purposely forged by the authorities from above in an effort to maintain good relations and display their support of the armed forces. Others developed from below as a result of, and in response to, broader societal changes.

New Forms of Civil–Military Entanglements

As mentioned in the introduction, the WW2 experience of total war created a sense among Norwegian decision makers of a need for a small state to engage the entire population and the resources of the entire society in defense against external threats. The resistance heroes in Norwegian folklore were ordinary men hiding in the woods conducting clandestine sabotage operations. Militarism was associated with the occupying Nazi regime. Additionally, the emerging post–World War II political leaders from the Labour Party carried a heritage of a deep skepticism toward the military, with its traditionally close ties to the conservative political parties. For all of these reasons, to build and maintain close relations between the armed forces and the entire population remained a high priority throughout the Cold War and after. For instance, in 1974 the defense planning commission stated, "A living democracy cannot leave to others to defend the country from external attacks. In this way, the people and the armed forces are bound together in a people's defense" (Børresen, Gjeseth, and Tamnes 2004: 358). Almost thirty years later, a new defense reform commission stated, "[Conscription] is important as a social and cultural melting pot and by providing a broad anchoring of the Armed Forces in the population" (Børresen, Gjeseth, and Tamnes 2004: 359). However, the modernized and semiprofessionalized armed forces needed fewer conscripts. As a result, a number of new measures were invented to maintain the close ties between the population and the armed forces. These measures were as much an attempt to prevent militarism—in the meaning of a military with values and a culture at odds with civil society—as an attempt to militarize society.

As mentioned above, the new deployments and the new generation of veterans became the nexus for the authorities' attempts to create new arenas for civil–military entanglements. In 2009, the government issued a white paper conveying a political commitment to improve the recognition of the veteran population (Forsvarsdepartementet 2009). In the following, we take a closer look at four of the concrete measures taken to fulfill that commitment.

Veteran's Day

The first attempt to forge new civil–military entanglements through recognition of veterans came in the form of the introduction of a Norwegian Veteran's Day. The process of instituting a national Veteran's Day started already in 1995, when a member of Parliament from the right-wing Progress Party took a personal initiative to establish a designated day to commemorate "military veterans from national forces and UN forces" (Stortinget 1996). A formal proposal was made to the Parliament in the fall of 1995, and all political parties unanimously agreed that a national Veteran's Day should be instituted on May 8—already celebrated as Liberation Day. Nevertheless, over the next fifteen years, May 8 was mostly observed as it had been in the past, through wreath-laying ceremonies at selected graves and monuments, marking central events and people from the Second World War.

In 2011, the government decided to give May 8 a completely new expression, with a distinct political profile. The political consensus from 1996 to leave Veterans' Day to be organized by the veterans was abandoned in favor of the new ambition to arrange number of prominent commemoration ceremonies encompassing all veterans from World War II until today (Regjeringen 2010). The program for the 2011 Veteran's Day set the precedent for how the day should be observed hereafter. A delicate balancing act had to be maintained between its original meaning as the day of liberation, and the incorporated focus on veterans from later missions. In an effort to tend to both needs, the final program displayed an ambitious itinerary consisting of traditional wreath-laying ceremonies, a church service at Oslo's main cathedral, a medal ceremony attended by the king, the president of the Parliament, the prime minister, foreign and defense ministers, and the chief of defense. It also included an official reception for specially invited guests, and an open day at Akershus Fortress in the capital, where a small-scale military camp was set up, visitors could see different military equipment, sit in vehicles, talk to soldiers, and visit a frigate that had docked by the harbor—all while eating hot dogs and drinking coffee (Forsvarsdepartementet 2011). An estimated six thousand people attended the 2011 Veteran's Day, and the organizers declared it a success (Forsvarsstaben 2011a). The Veteran's Day observance has later been arranged in slightly more modest, but mostly similar, fashion. The attendance has also been considerably lower, averaging two to three thousand when May 8 falls on a weekday (Oslo's population is approximately 660 thousand).

In addition to the national arrangement in Oslo, the government also encouraged municipalities to conduct their own local arrangements. Smaller ceremonies have been arranged throughout the country, especially in areas close to military bases. It is, however, not a day celebrated by most Norwegians. Returning quickly to Torunn's hometown Steinkjer—in 2017, the May 8 ceremony was attended by about approximately sixty people (Børstad 2017) (Steinkjer's population is approximately twenty thousand).

The last numbers from Steinkjer are particularly striking, and show that the attempt to engage the entire population in ceremonial recognition of the new veterans has failed. The event is by and large attended only by those directly involved with the military. This is even more the case for the other attempts the government made to promote new civil–military entanglements.

Memorial Sunday

A second novelty, introduced in 2007, was a Memorial Sunday in remembrance of those who have died or been injured while serving in the armed forces. The stated objective of this day is "to put our service in perspective with regards to the gravity and responsibility, the risks and consequences service in the armed forces may involve" (Forsvarsstaben 2011b). This day is not targeted at the wider society, but focused on the military organization and those who serve in the armed forces. The main arrangement on this day is a church service held in the chapel at the Akershus Fortress in Oslo, but all military bases are required to arrange some kind of commemoration ceremony either on that Sunday or on the Friday before. Family members of service members who have abruptly and unexpectedly passed away while enrolled in the armed forces in the past two years are specially invited to attend the ceremony in Oslo. That not only includes soldiers killed in action, but also victims of, for instance, suicide or accidents that occurred unrelated to their military service. The church service is attended by prominent guests such as Norway's King Harald, the president of the Parliament, the minister of defense, and the chief of defense. In addition to the church service, a wreath-laying ceremony is conducted at Akershus Fortress in Oslo, accompanied by a small reception for the invited guests.

Compared to May 8, which is designed as a public event focusing on the recognition of all veterans, Memorial Sunday is a much quieter and internally focused ceremony, with an emphasis on mourning and remembrance. It is a new "thing military," attended to by the highest civilian representatives of the state, but most Norwegians are unlikely to be even remotely aware of its existence. As such it signifies the absence of militarization of Norwegian society rather than the opposite. Remembering the war dead, on equal grounds with the ones who have died of causes unrelated to the military, has become an internal matter for the military and the relatives of the deceased.

Reinstitution of the War Cross

A third measure in the society–veteran nexus was the reinstitution of the War Cross, Norway's highest military decoration awarded for extraordinary acts of valor. Unlike most other military decorations, the medal is awarded by the government (Forsvarsdepartementet 1941). Originally, the War Cross could only be awarded to participants in World War II, but in 2009 the Norwegian government decided to reinstitute the War Cross by changing the statutes so service members from other missions would also qualify as recipients (Regjeringen 2009). The government stated in its announcement that "the reinstitution of the War Cross is intended to give our veterans greater recognition. It is important for us in the Government to improve the status of our veterans, not least veterans from modern day international operations" (Regjeringen 2009). Since 2009, nine veterans have been awarded the War Cross: one who received it posthumously from the Second World War, and eight veterans from missions at the Balkans and Afghanistan. In comparison, 273 people received the medal for their efforts during World War II. The medal is awarded during the main ceremony on Veteran's Day in Oslo. Once again, it is a new "thing military," but beyond brief media attention on Veteran's Day, there is hardly any impact of these award ceremonies outside of the armed forces.

Homecoming Ceremonies

A fourth and final new measure in this line of events initiated to acknowledge veterans from international operations, and to forge new ties between the military and civilian society, is the arrangement of formal homecoming medal ceremonies for deployed soldiers. Up until the late 1990s, participation in international operations was largely seen as a private choice of the individual participant, and the procedures for how to receive soldiers upon return were quite modest. Briefly put, it consisted of a handshake and a pat on the back, a medical examination, and a train ticket to your hometown (Haaland 2008). Starting in 2009, a public ceremony was arranged in which the soldiers were presented their medal of participation by the Norwegian chief of defense at Akershus Fortress in Oslo (*Aftenposten* 2009). Since then, similar ceremonies have been regularly conducted at Akershus Fortress or at a military air base outside the capital for soldiers returning during the winter. In both cases, the homecoming is observed in a formal, ceremonial manner and attended by a high-ranking politician, often the minister of defense. Both the media and family members of the returning soldiers are invited to attend the ceremony. Media coverage, however, has been modest.

The events described above share a duality. On the one hand, they are new "things military," initiated and attended to by the very highest levels of government. In comparison, the only other annual event that gathers the highest political and official elite in a similar manner is the opening of Parliament each fall. They honor the military profession in manners that are unparalleled in Norwegian society. On the other hand, the events have limited reach beyond the armed forces, their families, and their closest civilian superiors. As measures to uphold the ties between the population and the armed forces, and to replace the disappearing everyday entanglements of the Cold War's people's defense, they have not succeeded. As such they signify the strictly confined space for military expressions in Norwegian society rather than its militarization.

The Norwegian Version of the Military-Industrial-Media-Entertainment Complex

The media and the entertainment industry are other potential arenas for new "things military," in Norway as in other countries. Several authors have pointed out the multiple connections between the military, media, and the movie industry and how they form a massive entanglement system (see, for instance, González 2010 and Lutz 2000). To put these studies into perspective, we quote journalist Sveinung Bentzrød, defense specialist in one of Norway's largest newspapers *(Aftenposten)*:

> Insight about the armed forces among journalists have been weakened the last 20–30 years since so few of us have served conscription, and because the

armed forces are less visible for most people. Today very few serve, and except
from the local communities that are close to the remaining and rapidly shrink-
ing bases, the armed forces are invisible. . . . It is very worrisome that there
is not more knowledge about the armed forces in Norwegian media groups.
. . . Now, only a few in the Parliament's defense and foreign policy committee
have knowledge about the armed forces . . . so yes, it's a democratic problem.
(Akerhaug 2018)

Soldier's memoirs and TV documentaries about various aspects of military
life are two new cultural products that provide some insight into and promote "things military" to a civilian audience, who are now predominantly
lacking first-hand experience. What kind of pictures do they present? The
first Norwegian Afghanistan memoir, published in 2011 and titled *Brothers in the Blood: At War for Norway*, was written by Emil Johansen (2011), an
officer who had deployed to Afghanistan three times. The author presents
himself as a "warrior," writing candidly about life as a professional soldier
in Afghanistan, where he experienced combat and lost a fellow soldier in
a road bomb incident. The book sold thirty-three thousand copies, a huge
number in the Norwegian publishing context, and received overall good
reviews as "an honest and important book" (Hovde 2011; Solvang 2013).
Other memoirs followed, with similar proverbial tiles, such as *War and
Love* (Elden 2012) and *For King and Country* (Mella 2013). Common for the
abovementioned books is that they present Norway's wartime experience
to a wider civilian audience, providing a direct insight into the embodied
experiences of war, including emotions like fear, joy, and excitement. They
describe the attraction of war (Johansen 2011; Mella 2013) while also pre-
senting the soldiers as ordinary young men, sons and fathers, who fight
bravely, but end up disillusioned by a war that cannot be won (Elden 2012;
Gangdal and Gjestvang 2012; Widerøe and Aass 2012; Muradi and Gangdal 2015). In accordance with Woodward and Jenkings (2012: 505), we
find that while these memoirs are "vectors of militarization, mechanisms
by which military ideas, rationales, explanations for action are translated
into civilian discourse, they are also vectors of ideas about the soldier and
about the lived experience of military participation at odds with the dominant heroic soldier figure circulating in popular discourse."

The TV industry constitutes another arena for new civil–military entanglements. In recent years, the armed forces have facilitated the production
of various "reality" programs that portray different aspects of military
life. Topics include conscript service (Max 2015, 2018), the training and
selection of an all-female Special Forces unit (NRK 2016), the training and
selection of paratroopers (Max/Insider 2014), struggling veterans (Max/
Insider 2017), and life within Norway's only professional army unit (Max/
Insider 2015). Most of these programs come across as similar to other pro-

grams in the same genre, which portray the everyday life of other work-places, such as airports, hospitals, and police stations. They do not present military life as something extraordinary or particularly honorable, but rather as a job like others. Physical hardship and training comes across as the most unique feature of the profession.

TV documentaries have also portrayed units preparing for, and participating in, international operations (NRK 2011, 2013; TV2 Sumo 2011; Viasat 4 2012). The 2011 documentary "Norway at War – Mission Afghanistan," filmed during a six-month field visit to the Norwegian camp, is the first time the on-the-ground experience of Norwegian soldiers has been extensively documented for Norwegian viewers. "Exit Afghanistan," which aired two years later in 2013, documented both the Norwegian military effort and life among the civilian population during the exit phase of the ISAF operation (NRK 2013). Undoubtedly, these programs promote military life. As stated by the armed forces' media center in connection with the airing of the first documentary in 2015, "[In cooperation with Novemberfilm] we have selected units which show the breath and opportunities in the Armed Forces in a good way. . . . The soldiers are our best ambassadors" (Forsvaret 2015). The message conveyed is first of all one of tough physical training, and ordinary men's and women's reactions to that. The deployment documentaries are primarily concerned with the ethical dilemmas the soldiers are facing, and portray deployments as quite unglamorous. They do not criticize the Norwegian military as such, but provide an insight into the deployment experience.

These programs are a novelty. However, their coming into being is more than anything a result of the armed forces entering new arenas and opening themselves to external insights in the same manner as other professional organizations. As such they are as much a sign of the military becoming more like civilian organizations as a sign of the militarization of society.

Deeper Entanglements or More Separate Spheres?

Based on the thirty years trajectory sketched out above, are we witnessing a "deeper" and "subtler" penetration of "things military" into peoples' ordinary lives in Norway? Our basic argument is that whereas Cold War civil–military entanglements in Norway were secretive, obligatory, and direct, the entanglements of the late 2010s are (more) open, optional, and symbolic.

During the Cold War most people encountered "things military" in some form or another at some point in their life. Entanglements were mundane and often not reflected over, and an inescapable part of people's lives. The downsizing of the armed forces led to significantly fewer meeting points between the civilian population and the military organization, resulting in a perceived need to create new ones. Maintenance of broad support for the armed forces and close ties between the military and civilian society was a seen as a measure toward two goals: protecting Norway from external threat *and* preventing the development of a military separated from civilian society with other values than civilian ones.

Over the last decade, political authorities have taken an active role in forging new ties between the armed forces and society by instituting various new practices intended to show society's gratitude and respect toward military service members. Two defining features of these practices are that they are symbolic entanglements constituted of ceremonial events, and that civilian society are mainly represented by high-ranking officials, such as government ministers, members of parliament, and the Norwegian king. These new practices are dependent on an active choice of participation from the civilian population—who so far have overall shown a limited interest.

The trajectory presented in this chapter also suggests a development toward a new type of transparency between the realms. Universal male conscription and the total defense organization of the Cold War provided insight into military life and military concerns to a large segment of the population. Since then, far fewer people have access to these types of insight. Instead, the military has become a more open institution. The new openness is not only a result of a need to find new ways to uphold society's awareness of and interest in military matters, but also part of a general trend in society toward more openness in government affairs (Relly and Sabharwal 2009).[6] Letting cameras into the military camps at home and abroad offers insights into military life for those with no relation to the armed forces whatsoever. As such, transparency has increased. At the same time, these entanglements require an active initiative from potential consumers, and many people do remain uninterested—or merely interested in a brief peek. A few times, the candidness offered by soldiers has provoked debates about certain aspects of military deployments. People in Norway seem wary of tendencies of a military institution embodying different values than civilian society. This attitude clearly manifested itself in 2010, when a group of Norwegian soldiers interviewed for a magazine article commented on how combat encounters triggered a sense of enjoyment, which led to a widespread debate about the soldier profession (Andersen 2010; see also Langeland 2012).[7]

To be part of the new "things military" discussed in this chapter is optional for civilians. A vast majority of the youths growing up in Norway will have no "real-life" experience of military life. Even conscription is for all practical reasons voluntary in Norway in 2018, as a simple declaration of lack of motivation will let you off the hook. Furthermore, the integration of civilian reforms have continued. The military education system has been adapted to the European Bologna process standards, and New Public Management procedures has been incorporated into the military organization on equal footing with the civilian bureaucracy (Bjerga 2014). In 2016, gender-neutral conscription was implemented, not because of a lack of manpower in the military, but to meet the standard of gender equality prevalent in Norwegian society.

Conclusion

Based on the analysis above, we find little support for Ben-Ari and Sørensen's thesis of a "deeper" and "subtler" penetration of "things military" into ordinary people's lives. Quite to the contrary, in Norway we find that entanglements have become more open and less direct. We also find it problematic to call the trajectory sketched out above a "militarization" of society. In our view, such a definition rests on the argument that any kind of military activity is a step toward a militarization, which makes it difficult to separate military activities conducted within the mandate of the institution—even if it leads to new forms of civil–military entanglements—from military activities that are an end in themselves. Moreover civil–military entanglements are not necessarily a form of militarization per se, but may also point in the opposite direction. For the term "militarization" to become analytically useful, it must involve a subjugation of broader societal interests to meet the needs of the military. While relations between the armed forces and society have taken on new forms and entered new arenas since the Cold War, it seems unwarranted to describe contemporary entanglements in Norway as a militarization of society; they could just as well be understood as a civilization of the military.

Elin Gustavsen is a sociologist and wrote her doctoral thesis on meaning making among Norwegian Afghanistan veterans and their partners. Her research interests focus on the experience of war in the intersection between individual-level meaning construction and cultural context.

Torunn Laugen Haaland is assistant professor at the Norwegian Institute for Defence Studies and the Norwegian Defence University College in Oslo. She has a Ph.D. in international relations from the University of Oslo, and specializes in the Norwegian armed forces' international deployments, experience-based learning in the military, and war commemoration.

Notes

1. While these cultural expressions are not initiated by the authorities, they are partly enabled through access and facilitation provided by the armed forces. These practices are not only the result of changes in the global security landscape and the restructuring of the armed forces, but are also intertwined with broader societal trends unrelated to the military and security sphere.

2. An illustrating example of this attitude occurred in 1999, when the minister of defense canceled a military parade that was intended to be part of the event celebrating the 700th anniversary of Akershus Fortress in Oslo. To include a public parade in the program proved too controversial, not only because of the ongoing war in Kosovo, but also since it would have been the first military parade in the capital since the end of the Second World War (Hagen 1999).

3. Norway's longstanding tradition for participation in peacekeeping operations, the UNI-FIL engagement in Southern Lebanon being the most extensive mission, also changed during the 1990s (Forsvaret 2012). Other deployments were UNMOGIP (United Nations Military Observer Group in India and Pakistan) in two periods, 1949–52 and 1953–94; UNEF I (United Nations Emergency Force) between 1956 and 1967; UNTSO (United Nations Truce Supervision Organisation [in the Middle East]) between 1956 and 1992; UNOGIL (United Nations Observation Group in Lebanon) in 1958; ONUC (Opération Des Nations Unies au Congo) in 1960–64; UNYOM (United Nations Yemen Observation Mission) in 1963 and 1964; MFO (Multinational Force and Observers in Sinai) since 1982; UNIIMOG (United Nations Iran-Iraq Military Observer Group) between 1988 and 1991;and UNAVEM I (United Nations Angola Verification Mission) between 1989 and 1991. This engagement continued during the 1990s with participation in UNPROFOR (United Nations Protection Force [in Bosnia-Herzegovina and Croatia]) between 1992 and 1995; UNOSOM (United Nations Operation in Somalia) between 1992 and 1994; and UN-mandated IFOR/SFOR (Implementation Force/Stabilization Force) in Bosnia between 1995 and 2004.

4. This location hosts the brigade headquarters consisting of two maneuver battalions, intelligence, medical, and artillery forces.

5. Maneuver, logistics, and engineers forces are located at Rena, two hours north of Oslo. The Royal Guard is located in Oslo.

6. A potent example of the development toward more openness is the threat assessment report that since 2012 has been published yearly by the Norwegian intelligence service (Forsvaret 2014), the most secretive part of the armed forces, something unheard of a few decades ago.

7. Their statements were also quickly and sharply rebuked by both the chief of defense and the defense minister, who expressed their skepticism toward signs of a distinct warrior culture among Norwegian soldiers.

References

Aftenposten. 2009. "Hjem til medaljer" [Home to medals]. *Aftenposten,* 12 June 2009.

Akerhaug, L. 2018. "Få forsvarsjournalister igjen i de store mediene" [Few defense journalists left in the large media]. *Journalisten,* 20 March 2018.

Alstad, B. (ed.). 1993. *Norske meninger 1946–93. Norge og verden* [Norwegian opinions 1946–93. Norway and the world]. Søreidgrend: Sigma forlag.

Andersen, M. 2010. "Forsvarsledelsen til kamp mot ukultur: En hån mot de som ga sitt liv" [Armed forces' leadership to fight bad culture: An insult to those who gave their life]. *VG*, 27 September 2010.

Bjerga, K. I. 2014. "Forsvarspolitikk og forvaltningspolitikk: Organisering, reformer og militæreksepsjonalisme i Forsvarets sentrale ledelse mellom 1940 og 2003" [Defense policy and governance policy: Organization, reform and military exceptionalism in the armed forces' central leadership between 1940 and 2003]. Doctoral thesis, Department of Archaeology, History, Cultural Studies and Religion, University of Bergen, Norway.

Bogen, O., and M. Håkenstad. 2015. *Balansegang: Forsvarets omstilling etter den kalde krigen* [An act of balance: Restructuring the armed forces after the cold war]. Oslo: Dreyer.

Børresen, J., G. Gjeseth, and R. Tamnes. 2004. *Allianseforsvar i endring: 1970–2000* [Alliance defense in transition: 1970–2000]. Bergen: Eide Forlag.

Børstad, J. 2017. "Ønsker enda et minnesmerke" [Wants another memorial]. *Trønderavisa*, 9 May 2017.

Elden, E. 2012. *Krig og kjærlighet* [War and love]. Oslo: Kagge.

Forsvarsdepartementet. 1941. *Statutter for krigskorset* [Statutes for the War Cross]. Retrieved 7 May 2018, https://lovdata.no/dokument/INS/forskrift/1941-05-23-1. London: Forsvarsdepartementet.

———. 2009. *Fra vernepliktig til veteran: Om ivaretakelse av personell før, under og etter deltakelse i utenlandsoperasjoner* [From conscript to veteran: On taking care of personnel before, during and after participation in international operations]. St.meld.nr.34 2008–2009. Oslo: Forsvarsdepartementet.

———. 2010. *Egen dag for å hedre veteraner* [A separate day to honor the veterans]. Retrieved 4 December 2018, https://www.regjeringen.no/no/aktuelt/egen-dag-for-a-hedre-vetera ner/id627135/.

———. 2011. "8. mai—Frigjøringsdagen og nasjonal veterandag" [May 8 Liberation Day and Veteran's Day]. Letter to the Chief of Defence dated 10 February 2011. Oslo: Ministry of Defence Archives.

Forsvaret. 2012. *Med Norge—for fred 1945–2012. Norsk deltagelse i internasjonale militære operasjoner* [With Norway—for peace 1945–2012. Norwegian participation in international military operations]. Oslo: Forsvarets veterantjeneste.

———. 2014. "Etterretningstjenesten—Fokus" [The Norwegian intelligence service—Fokus]. Norwegian Armed Forces website Forsvaret.no. Retrieved 7 May 2018, https://forsvaret .no/fakta/undersokelser-og-rapporter/fokus.

———. 2015. "Følg soldatlivet via skjerm" [Follow the soldier life via screen]. Norwegian Armed Forces website Forsvaret.no. Retrieved 7 May 2018, https://forsvaret.no/aktuelt/ tv-serie-om-forsvaret.

Forsvarsstaben. 2011a. "Forsvarets evaluering av markeringer på frigjøringsdagen og Nasjonal veterandag 8. mai 2011" [The armed forces' evaluation of arrangements at the Day of Liberation and National Veteran's Day 8 May 2011]. Forsvarsstaben. Letter to Ministry of Defence dated 16 June 2011. Oslo: Ministry of Defence Archives.

———. 2011b. "Sjef Forsvarsstabens ordre for planlegging og gjennomføring av markeringer i forbindelse med Forsvarets Minnedag 2011" [Chief of the Defence Staff's order for planning and executing arrangements concerning the Memorial Day 2011]. Letter to the Armed Forces dated 30 June 2011. Oslo: Ministry of Defence Archives.

Fure, O.-B. 2014. "Developmental Societal Processes: Changing Configurations of Memories; The Case of Norway in a Comparative Perspective." In A. Bauerkämper, O. B. Fure, and Ø. Hetland (eds.), *From a Patriotic Memory to a Universalistic Narrative? Shifts in Norwegian Memory Culture after 1945 in Comparative Perspective*, 43–62. Essen: Klartex.

Gangdal, J., and B. Gjestvang. 2012. *Trond Bolle: alles helt—min mann* [Trond Bolle: Everybody's hero—my husband]. Oslo: Kagge.

González, R. J. 2010. *Militarizing Culture: Essays on the Warfare State.* Walnut Creek: Left Coast Press, Inc.

Haaland, T. L. 2008. "Small Forces with a Global Outreach: Role Perceptions in the Norwegian Armed Forces after the Cold War." Doctoral thesis, Department of Political Science, Faculty of Social Sciences, University of Oslo, Norway.

Hagen, G. 1999. "Militærparade på Karl Johan" [Military parade down Karl Johan]. *Dagbladet*, 21 May 1999.

Hansen, S., and M. Higraff. 2015. "Forsvaret stanser eiendomssalg på grunn av Putins Russland. Forsvaret stanser eiendomssalg på grunn av Putins Russland" [The armed forces end property sale due to Putin's Russia]. NRK Dokumentar, 14 October 2015. Retrieved 7 May 2018, https://www.nrk.no/dokumentar/forsvaret-som-forsvant-1.12601445.

Harpviken, K. B. 2011. *A Peace Nation Takes Up Arms: The Norwegian Engagement in Afghanistan.* Prio Paper. Oslo: Peace Research Institute of Oslo.

Hovde, K. 2011. "Nær ved å dø" [Close to death]. *Adresseavisa*, 21 December 2011.

Johansen, E. 2011. *Brødre i blodet: i krig for Norge* [Brothers in the blood: At war for Norway]. Oslo: Kagge.

Langeland, F. 2012. "Soldater med lyst til å drepe – Krigermaskulinitet i mannebladet *Alfa* [Soldiers with a desire to kill – Warrior masculinity in the male magazine *Alfa*]." *Norsk medietidsskrift* 19 (4): 312–32.

Levy, A. 2016. "What Is Controlled by Civilian Control of the Military? Control of the Military vs. Control of Militarization." *Armed Forces & Society* 42 (1): 75–98.

Lutz, C. 2000. "Making War at Home in the United States: Militarization and the Current Crisis." *American Anthropologist* 104 (3): 723–35.

Mella, H. 2013. *For konge og fedreland : 150 dager i Afghanistan* [For king and motherland: 150 days in Afghanistan]. Oslo: Kagge.

Moskos, C. 1977. "From Institution to Occupation: Trends in Military Organization." *Armed Forces & Society* 4 (1): 41–50.

Muradi, F., and J. Gangdal. 2015. *Ingen bror får bli igjen : en kamptolks beretning om krigen i Afghanistan og Norges svik* [No brother can be left behind: A combat interpreter's report of the war in Afghanistan and Norway's betrayal]. Oslo: Gyldendal.

Nielsen Consumer Research. 2010. *Holdninger til Forsvaret April 2010.* Retrieved 7 May 2018, http://www.folkogforsvar.no/resources/meningsmalinger/Holdninger_til_forsvaret_Mars_2010_NORSKNone.pdf.

Oma, I. M., and L. Ekhaugen. 2014. "Norwegian Lead in Afghanistan: A Small State Approach to a Large Commitment." In R. Allers, C. Masala, and R. Tamnes (eds.), *Common or Divided Security? German and Norwegian Perspectives on Euro-Atlantic Security*, 237–57. Frankfurt am Main: Peter Lang.

Regjeringen. 2009. "Krigskorset gjeninnføres" [The War Cross is reinstituted]. Regjeringen. no, 26 June 2009. Retrieved 30 January 2017, https://www.regjeringen.no/no/aktuelt/krigskorset-gjeninnfores/id570219/.

———. 2010. "Egen dag for å hedre veteraner" [A separate day to honor the veterans]. Regjeringen.no, 2 December 2010. Retrieved 30 January 2017, https://www.regjeringen.no/no/aktuelt/egen-dag-for-a-hedre-veteraner/id627135/.

Relly, J. E., and M. Sabharwal. 2009. "Perceptions of Transparency of Government Policymaking: A Cross-National Study." *Government Information Quarterly* 26 (1): 148–57.

SIPRI. 2018. Military Expenditure Database. Retrieved 7 May 2018, https://www.sipri.org/sites/default/files/3_Data%20for%20all%20countries%20from%201988%E2%80%932017%20as%20a%20share%20of%20GDP.pdf.

Solvang, O. 2013. "Boktrend: Norges nye soldater" [Book trend: Norway's new soldiers]. *Vårt Land*, 24 May 2013.

Stortinget. 1996. "Dok 8, n. (1995–96). Forslag fra stortingsrepresentant Hans J. Røsjorde om å innstifte en "veterandag" for tidligere soldater fra nasjonale styrker og FN styrker"

[Proposal from MP Hans J. Røsjorde about instituting a "veterans day" for former soldiers from national forces and UN forces]. Oslo: Stortinget.

Sørlie, S. C., and Rønne, H. K. 2006. *Hele folket i forsvar. Totalforsvaret i Norge frem til 1970*. Oslo: Unipub.

Vagts, A. 1959. *A History of Militarism: Civilian and Military*. Revised edition. New York: The Free Press.

Widerøe, R. J., and H. P. Aass. 2012. *Krigshelten. Historien om marinejegeren og etterretningsagenten Trond Bolle* [War hero: The story of the naval special forces and intelligence officer Trond Bolle]. Oslo: Gyldendal.

Wooward, R., and K. N. Jenkings. 2012. "'This Place Isn't Worth the Left Boot of One of Our Boys': Geopolitics, Militarism and Memoirs of the Afghanistan War," *Political Geography* 31 (2012): 495–508.

TV Programs

Max. 2015. *Forsvaret* [The armed forces]. Documentary.

———. 2018. *I kongens klær* [In the king's clothes]. Documentary.

Max/Insider. 2014. Episode 3 and 4, Season 3. Documentary.

———. 2015. Episode 7, Season 4. Documentary.

———. 2017. Episode 5, Season 6. Documentary.

NRK. 2011. *Norge i krig – oppdrag Afghanistan*. [Norway at war – Mission Afghanistan]. Documentary.

———. 2013. *Exit Afghanistan*. Documentary.

———. 2016. *Jenter for Norge* [Girls for Norway]. Documentary.

TV2 Sumo. 2011. *Krigens pris* [The price of war]. Documentary.

Viasat 4. 2012. *Livredderne i Afghnistan* [Lifesavers in Afghanistan]. 2012. Documentary.

Chapter 5

Framing the Other
in Times of War and Terror
Explorations of the Military in Germany

Maren Tomforde

L ast week it happened again. One of my colleagues at the Bundeswehr (Armed forces) Command and Staff College in Hamburg, a lieutenant colonel, asked me to take a substantial detour in order to pick him up from work and to drive him to a military meeting at the other end of town, a place where I had just been. My soldierly colleague was not too lazy to take public transportation. He would have liked to have taken the metro. However, as he was wearing his uniform, he felt he could not do so. This feeling is ubiquitous among German soldiers, who generally avoid wearing the uniform in public, especially in cities. Reasons for this widely shared discomfort and avoidance are manifold. Among others, service-members explain that they are tired of being mistaken for train personnel, of being stared at—especially female soldiers—of being spat at, or of being called a murderer.

The Bundeswehr, founded in 1955, is democratically legitimized. Article 87a of the German constitution states that the federal government must assemble armed forces. In March 2005, a law passed that strengthens the Bundeswehr as a parliamentary army, which is only sent to out-of-area missions after a majority in parliament has agreed upon a clear mandate for this deployment. Given this commitment to Germany's constitution and "the primacy of politics" over the armed forces, it is somewhat astonishing that more than seventy years after the end of World War II and the

Wehrmacht, servicemembers still feel uncomfortable wearing the uniform in public, foremost in cities and on public transport. However, due to the atrocities committed by the Nazi regime during the Third Reich, a fear of militarization of civilian spheres and of soldiers trained in the use of force is still widespread. This fear also affects civil–military relations and leads to insecurities during encounters on both sides (Tomforde 2015a). In comparison to other countries (like the United States, United Kingdom, Australia, the Netherlands, Denmark, Sweden, and Norway) where soldiers are publicly recognized and thanked for their service, Germany, with its deep sense of responsibility for the atrocities of the Third Reich and "culture of shame" (Schirrmacher 2014), still seems to struggle with its armed forces in many different ways. However, in the context of the main aim of this book—to reconceptualize civil–military relations—German society should not be perceived as a monolithic block opposing the military. Parts of German society are very open toward the military, and the German public has, as in other NATO countries, also undergone profound changes since the end of the Cold War, in parallel to a growing professionalization of the military (see, e.g., Leonhard 2017). Anthony King (2013: 429) speaks in this regard of "professional societies," and criticizes former visions of civil societies as "under-developed" and "crude" (see, e.g., Huntington 1957; Janowitz 1960). Moreover, armed forces in Germany are very diverse despite uniformity in appearance (Tomforde and Roggmann 2008). The main aim of this chapter is to scrutinize civil–military entanglements in Germany by looking at the different ways servicemembers are framed by German society.

It is important to understand these diverse, partly contradictory frames go beyond dichotomizing the civilian and military spheres, and open up for dynamic, never-ending constituting processes between the military and civil society. Military and civilian subjects constitute each other due to many existing interfaces in space and time (see also Bickford 2011). These two groups are entangled in so many different ways that they should not be conceptualized and studied as two opposing, clear-cut entities but rather as diversified actors who relate to each other in varying settings and ways (King 2013: 429). One such way is the framing of the "other." It is the main assumption of this chapter that servicemembers, who are, of course, also part of German society, are yet mostly conceptualized or framed as "the other" by members of German society—"the other" not being a stable imagery but changing depending on different settings, spaces, and conditions. Frames are understood here as the social construction and perception of "the other." Frames have shifted considerably due to the International Security Assistance Force (ISAF) mission in Afghanistan, as the Bundeswehr participated in active warfare for the first time since the end of World War II (see Biehl and Schön 2015; Biehl 2011). According to anthropological research among the Bundeswehr in Germany from 2003 until today, three main frames seem to be prevalent—each gaining more or less relevance at certain points in time and highlighting the dialectic co-production of "things military" and "things civilian." The three main frames are (1) soldiers as murderers, (2) soldiers as individuals, and (3) soldiers as marginal men. These three frames, analyzed in the course of this chapter, underline how parts of German society perceive the military and relate to soldiers, violence, and war, as well as to itself. The prevalent frames provide insight into how parts of German society constitute a "civilian we" in opposition to a "military other" in order to sustain the imagery of a violence-averse and peaceful society, while other parts of German society, as is highlighted during the analysis of frame two, add to the constitution of the soldier as an integral part of German society. German civil–military entanglements vary depending on settings, places, times, actors, and framework conditions.

During the Cold War, Germany had a strong peace movement; as in Nordic countries such as Norway or Sweden, "strong patriotic expressions linked to the military" (Åse and Wendt 2018: 27) had been nonexistent ever since World War II. Soldiers were still viewed with suspicion by large parts of German society, sometimes culminating in the usage of Kurt Tucholsky's phrase "soldiers are murderers" (1931) in interactions with servicemembers. German military sociologist Nina Leonhard (2017: 8) describes the reaction to this phrase by the military: "This also had an effect on the self-perception of the Bundeswehr. It provoked at least in parts of the armed forces the inclination to withdraw from the public and to seal themselves off from the outside world." At first glance, one might indeed have the impression that civil society and the military are two opposing entities in Germany.

Of course, not all Germans agree with the label or frame "soldiers are murderers," and not all soldiers support the idea of the military profession as a profession *sui generis*. Yet, this phrase draws our attention to German civil–military relations burdened by prevalent suspicions and distrust after World War II.

However, during the ISAF mission in Afghanistan, media coverage and society's entanglement with its armed forces clearly shifted as soldiers had to prevail in combat, and were wounded and killed. Between 2008 and 2014, journalists, publicists, and artists drew a more nuanced picture of deployed servicemembers. Instead of rejecting the Bundeswehr as a whole, formerly so common in German discourse, soldiers were presented as individuals with emotions and fears. The "military other" became less of a stranger and could be related to despite possible anti-war sentiments. Via in-depth documentaries, embedded accounts of mission experiences, or portraits of individual soldiers, to name a few examples, publicists and artists allowed glimpses into soldiers' everyday realities and lifeworlds in theaters of conflict. During the height of the German ISAF mission, the frame "soldiers as individuals" thus gained importance. Large parts of society were interested in soldiers' fates, realistic reports from the Hindukush, and insights into soldiers' experiences and wellbeing. In other words, in Germany, the individuality of the soldier helps members of society to deal with violent conflict and war instead of taking attention away from war-related issues.

These almost anthropological works subsided, however, after ISAF officially ended in December 2014. Upon the soldiers' return home, a third important frame became and still becomes apparent: "soldiers as marginal men" (Park 1928; see also Mannitz 2013). Due to the servicemembers' peculiar mission experiences in times of war and terror, moral challenges seem to exist in reintegrating them back into society. For many Germans, especially those belonging to the fourth generation of people growing up without war in their own society at home, violent conflict is experienced only in a mediated way. German servicemembers who have been to mission areas—for example, in the Balkans, Afghanistan, or Mali—are the ones who have seen the effects of war and terror and who have experienced combat, with heavy kinetic action resulting in killings and severely wounded comrades and enemies alike (Zimmermann 2014; Tomforde 2015a; see also King 2013). For historic reasons, involvement in any kind of war or armed conflict is generally viewed with suspicion (Bulmahn and Wanner 2013). In Germany, soldiers are often marked as being special "so that their experiences may be excluded as particular ones" (Langer 2013: 86). Members of society do not have to accept them as "normal experiences" by entering into direct confrontation with the effects of war. In other words, experiences of violence are not integrated into society. Instead, they are marginalized, as are the soldiers who experienced them. Servicemembers are largely perceived as traumatized returnees instead of as individuals with challenging insights for all members of society. In other words, while soldiers were in theater, the German public were interested in their fate and largely sympathized with their servicemembers under fire. Yet, upon the soldiers' return home, a distance is kept to safeguard the stability of society as a whole. The three frames discussed in the course of the chapter highlight the different ways the military is conceptualized and how these approaches affect civil–military encounters.

The chapter is structured as follows: first, processes of framing are tackled and presented as the construction of a social phenomenon. Processes of "othering" and "selfing" are discussed to gain an understanding of reasons for "reverse mirroring." In a second step, the three prominent frames are analyzed in detail on the basis of anthropological research on the Bundeswehr (2003 until today) as well as on the basis of secondary sources. The conclusion summarizes the main findings of the chapter and discusses reasons for partly contradictory frames on soldiers existing in Germany. Civil–military entanglements are multifaceted and are ever changing due to inter/national events and the security contexts of our times.

Theoretical Context: Framing the Other

Frames are defined as interpretative patterns, which are used in the course of sense making and appraisal of different topics that are part of our life realities (Entman 1993: 52). "To frame is to select some aspects of a perceived reality and make them more salient in a communicating text, in such a way as to promote a particular problem definition, causal interpretation, moral evaluation and/or treatment recommendation" (Entman 1993: 52). According to this definition, frames fulfill two central functions: first, the selection of certain aspects of our life realities, and, second, the structuring of communication and interpretation when dealing with these realities (Merton 1957). Framing thus involves social construction of a social phenomenon. This framing process can be done by mass media, social groups, political leaders, or any other social actors (Dahinden 2006). In social theory, framing is understood as a way of interpretation and a combination of anecdotes and stereotypes. Individuals rely on these interpretations to better grasp, understand, and respond to certain life realities and to make sense of the world (Goffman 1974; see also Geertz [1983] 2000). This article will focus on collective frames of thought and thus on the mental representations, interpretations, and pictures of the military that shape, among other factors, complex civil–military entanglements in Germany. These collective frames develop by way of public discourse as well as interpersonal interaction and communication between "people civilian" and "people military."

Let us move on to the concept of the Other. The notion of "otherness" lies in the heart of the anthropological discipline, as it has long focused on "other" societies and cultures, not our own. Also, processes of "othering" by anthropologists and others alike as part of a neocolonial, postmodern discourse have instigated heated debates in the discipline and triggered an epistemic crisis (see, e.g., Geertz 1988; Clifford and Marcus 1986; Marcus and Fisher 1986; Baudrillard 1984). According to Michel Foucault (1982), othering is strongly connected to power and knowledge. When we "other" another group, we highlight their perceived weaknesses to augment our own strength and self-value. Processes of othering reveal hierarchies and serve to keep power or order according to mainstream society. Colonialism is a good example of the powers of othering.

The process of othering is always linked to "reverse mirroring" (see, e.g., Hahn 1994). It is a dialectic process. "Each time we attach a connotation to the Other, we are in essence creating an imaginary Self." (Holslag 2015: 98.) Through this process of mirroring, we draw fictitious lines between groups (Baumann and Gingrich 2006). In any nation-state, internal others are produced in many ways: for example, due to wars, diseases, migration, or culture change. It is the main assumption of this chapter that soldiers in Germany are more often than not actively framed as the Other, revealing stereotypes on the basis of existing group identities. Although the axes of difference that undergird these expressions of othering vary considerably and are deeply contextual, they contain a similar set of underlying dynamics (Baumann and Gingrich 2006). It is claimed that soldiers are "othered" to draw moral boundaries between society and servicemembers who are "experts in violence." This is one way to create a sense of order and the certainty that atrocities of the Third Reich will never happen again. Through this othering process, German society is gearing to establish a normalized "self" and to protect itself from any form of military violence (see also Grassiani 2015).

Civil–Military Entanglements in Germany

After the end of the Cold War and the start of a severe reduction of its forces in numbers, former defense minister Peter Struck (2003) feared that German society would completely turn away from its armed forces, seeing them as irrelevant. Journalist Constanze Stelzenmüller (2004) observed that Bundeswehr servicemembers turned into "binmen of Germany's security politics," while the German public seemed to become largely disinterested in its military. Thus, former president Horst Köhler (2005) tried to characterize civil–military relations as a so-called "friendly disinterest" of German society toward its armed forces (see also Martinsen 2013b). German military sociologist Heiko Biehl did not agree with this observation of "friendly disinterest." Instead, he draws our attention to a prevailing "myth of a lack of societal support" (2011: 78) of the military in Germany. Quantitative surveys highlight that servicemembers are highly valued by German society, especially officers. Citizens communicate their positive attitude toward the Bundeswehr and take advantage of open days to visit barracks or ships by the navy. Four-fifths of the German population maintains a positive attitude toward its armed forces. This research result has been more or less consistent since 2000 (Steinbrecher et al. 2016: 48–49). However, knowledge about facts and figures concerning the Bundeswehr is relatively low: only 17 percent of the population know the approximate number of soldiers who are currently deployed. Most Germans agree themselves that they only know basic facts about Bundeswehr missions, and results of quantitative surveys underline the lack of knowledge about its armed forces (Steinbrecher et al. 2016: 123). German historian Klaus Naumann (2013) also calls for a broader public debate about the role of Germany's armed forces and society's relation with the military as a professional army deployed to out-of-area theaters. German publicist Cora Stephan (2013: 149) claims that a public that largely defines war as a crime has, of course, very little understanding of the role of its armed forces in a democratic society. Due to the prevailing supremacy of the German "peace paradigm," we seem to find a consistent opposition between society and the Bundeswehr, between pacifism and the military (Kempf 2013: 189).

Indeed, as shown in previous surveys, the more robust a mission, the more critical the attitude toward such a mission—a reason why the ISAF mission received less and less public support by the German public (Bulmahn and Wanner 2013; see also Martinsen 2013a).[1] However, instead of supporting ISAF, large parts of German society developed a new and unprecedented interest in the lifeworlds of deployed soldiers, as the many newspaper articles, radio features, TV documentaries, movies, theater plays, art exhibitions, and even graphic novels underline (Tomforde 2015a). This heightened interest in the Bundeswehr and its soldiers reached its peak when servicemembers were involved in heavy combat in Afghanistan between 2008 and 2013, and ebbed away again with the end of the ISAF mission in 2014. Despite more media coverage in those years that was not solely negative, as in the years before or after, soldiers themselves claimed in interviews that they did not feel supported by the German public—not during the ISAF mission and especially not since. Due to different contexts and the international security situation, the way soldiers are perceived and framed by the German public can shift, which highlights that civil–military entanglements are multifaceted and ever changing.

Three stereotypical frames will be discussed here. It goes without saying that these frames do not represent all notions of soldiers existing among the German population. Instead, they draw our attention to three frames that seem to be prevalent in Germany, according to 150 servicemembers interviewed between 2008 and 2015, as well as public discourse. These three frames were developed on the basis of semistructured individual interviews, as well as group interviews with servicemembers of all ranks.

In a second step, media articles, theater plays, movies, TV documentaries, YouTube videos, and graphic novels were examined for frames existing on soldiers. As frames are representations and constructions of reality, they are not congruent with empirical data collected by questionnaires, for example. It is claimed here, however, that alongside opinions that can be collected via quantitative methods, frames also exist and only become visible when one takes a second look—for example through interviews with the Other and/or a thorough media analysis to tackle public discourse. As an anthropologist, I largely focused on interviews and participant observation with servicemembers in order to gain an understanding of how they feel they are being framed by the German public. In addition, I inspected works on the military in the media and in art and tried to grasp the underlying notions about soldiers and the Bundeswehr by systematic document analysis and evaluation, and analysis of external documents (Bowen 2009; see also Gustavsen 2017).

Frame 1: Soldiers as Murderers

Although opinion polls showed some fairly positive responses, civil–military relations always remain ambiguous in Germany due to our World War II legacy. This could be witnessed again in media reports in 2017 on scandals within the Bundeswehr, such as reports on the right-wing extremist officer Franco A. or the cases of sexual abuse in the barracks of Pfullendorf. Even if bad news sells better than good news, German media's focus on Bundeswehr scandals over other Bundeswehr-related news has been apparent. One journalist even admitted in a personal communication on this topic in May 2017 that positive reports on the armed forces are less popular among the readership than negative news and scandals.

In some parts of Germany, negative perceptions and mistrust have turned into action against the Bundeswehr. For example, young officers are no longer allowed to inform students in some schools about the Bundeswehr. Instead, it is only permitted to discuss general security politics topics. Some schools and other institutions fear a growing militarization of their students as well as direct on-site recruitment by the Bundeswehr. Numerous institutions have now labeled themselves as "military free." Two schools in the federal state of Baden-Württemberg was even awarded the Peace Price by the city of Aachen for their work toward this end (Himmelrath 2015).

Servicemembers discuss costs like this, as well as the critical assessment of their work at schools and universities. Instead of understanding that criticism and fear of militarization of the public sphere is not directed toward individual soldiers personally, they feel, once again, rejected by parts of their own society. According to personal interviews with forty officers, they all have had at least one negative personal experience when in uniform in public. Most soldiers whose home bases are in the rural areas in Germany do not encounter problems in their small towns or cities. On the contrary, they feel valued and appreciated when the population gathers to bid them farewell before an out-of-area mission or when they are welcomed back. However, once they travel throughout Germany and are on duty in bigger cities, experiences change. Servicemembers report of (slight) beatings, people spitting at them, or phrases like "soldiers are murderers." As this phrase by German journalist, satirist, and lyricist Kurt Tucholsky is ever recurring in the discourse on the military in Germany, it is used here as the first frame that stands for civil–military relations still burdened by our history and a still-existing and ever-recurring mistrust and hostile perception of the armed forces (Kempf 2013).

"Soldiers are murderers" is a quotation taken from a brief article by Kurt Tucholsky, "Der Bewachte Kriegsschauplatz" (The guarded theater of war), published under the pseudonym Ignaz Wrobel in the weekly cultural and political journal of the German pacifist Left, *Die Weltbuehne*, on 4 August 1931. In it, he said, "During four years there were many kilometers of land on which murder was obliged — while only half an hour away from there it was highly forbidden. Did I say murder? Of course. Soldiers are murderers" (Tucholsky 1931). Leaders of the Reichswehr (former German national defense during the Weimar Republic) lodged a complaint for insult against the editor of the publication, the journalist Carl von Ossietzky, who had just been charged with divulging military secrets. This famous episode of the declining Weimar Republic was resolved by Ossietzky's discharge. Being afraid that Nazis would persecute him, Tucholsky fled Germany and did not attend the trial in July 1932 for his declaration that "Soldaten sind Mörder." Luckily, the phrase was considered too vague, as it was not aimed at anyone in particular, nor even particularly at the Reichswehr. As such, it was not considered an insult against the German military (Hepp and Otto 1996).

Kurt Tucholsky's phrase became part of the prominent German pacifist tradition and was regularly used by the strong pacifist movement during the Cold War. After the fall of the Berlin wall, this phrase triggered numerous court cases, heated debates in Parliament, arson attacks on the offices of solicitors who represented the pacifists, cabaret features, and endless (judicial) reports (Hepp and Otto 1996). During the First Gulf War, for example, a pacifist used a sticker with this phrase on his car. For this, he was charged with insult of the Bundeswehr and for public hate speech by the district court of Krefeld. This conviction, like many others related to the

Tucholsky phrase, was deferred to the Federal Constitutional Court. It was decided that judgments by district courts were not permissible restrictions on the right to freedom of opinion and did not impair personal honor of individual soldiers. This phrase may be understood as aiming above all at the entire institution of the military. In 1996, the debate about the phrase seemed to ebb away. It was, however, started again in 2010 when journalist and politician Thies Gleiss of the party Die Linke (The left) claimed that German "murder soldiers" have killed many more people in Afghanistan than the former German Democratic Republic killed along the Berlin Wall (136 individuals died trying to escape to West Germany) (Gleiss 2010). Controversial public debates about missions like ISAF in Afghanistan have even been criticized as a sign of a "'pathological' pacifism within German society" (Leonhard 2017: 11). As former linguist and anthropologist Andrew Bickford (2011) observes, after reunification, soldiers of the Nationale Volksarmee (armed forces of the former GDR) became even more the "military other," second-class soldiers, and the negative point of reference. However, this critical view of the NVA as an "improper military," a "foreign" army, and persona non grata did not necessarily prompt a more positive public image of the Bundeswehr as the "proper military."

According to soldiers interviewed, they hear the phrase "soldiers are murderers" on a regular basis. They are directly called murderers by people in the streets who see them in uniform or sometimes even by their own relatives who are critical toward the Bundeswehr. Soldiers who had served in Afghanistan were more often than not asked "How many people have you killed in combat?" upon their return home (Tomforde 2015b). These personal experiences underline the assumption that the frame "soldiers as murderers" persists and affects civil–military relations in Germany to varying degrees depending on certain contexts related to space, time, and settings in Germany and in the more general security context.

Frame 2: Soldiers as Individuals

I personally started to work for the Bundeswehr in 2003. Still writing my Ph.D. thesis after my two-and-a-half-years-long fieldwork on cultural spatiality in Thailand, I gained a position as a researcher at the Social Research Institute of the Bundeswehr in Strausberg, near Berlin. To be honest, until then I did not know much about the German armed forces. At the most, I had stereotypical images of drunken conscripts in uniform on trains on their way home on Friday afternoons. Studying the military, not only in Germany but also in theater in the Balkans and in Afghanistan, allowed me a deeper insight into the Bundeswehr and its personnel. Conducting research on the contingents deployed to mission areas, I had the chance to meet and get to know soldiers as individuals—a chance I had never really had and had not sought before. Insights into soldiers' life-worlds and life realities were slowly provided not only to me but to the German public in general when the ISAF mission gradually turned more robust in 2008 and after. The more combat situations Bundeswehr soldiers were involved in, the more German media reported on these events. In addition, radio and TV stations as well as newspaper publishers produced detailed accounts on the kinetic encounters and on the soldiers involved in combat. The fairly peaceful missions in Bosnia-Herzegovina (SFOR 1996–2004) and Kosovo (1999 until today) drew the attention of the German public only in terms of their political legitimacy and the question of whether Germany really wanted to participate in such a military endeavor in the Balkans. Newspaper stories, TV documentaries, and themes of theater plays changed, however, once Bundeswehr soldiers were directly involved in kinetic action in Afghanistan beginning in 2008. Soldiers were now presented as individuals, with emotions, fears, combat stories, and experiences that most people in Germany had thought belonged to the past. German photographer Herlinde Koelbl, for example, traveled to Afghanistan to interview soldiers on their war experiences and to gain an insight into their daily life in theater (Koelbl 2011). The frank interviews on motivations, emotions, fears, impressions of the enemy, and other details, published in 2011 by the famous German weekly magazine *Die Zeit*, are moving, enlightening, and sometimes shocking in their honesty. Soldiers interviewed openly talk about their being prepared to kill in combat and about their self-image as fighters, but also about their feelings for their comrades and their fear of being killed or wounded. These interviews, among many others, opened up new perspectives on the multiple facets of war, the military, and its soldiers. These differentiated perspectives on the military and focus on the individual soldier were not easy to find before the ISAF mission turned more robust for Germany. Other examples are TV documentaries, such as *Dying for Afghanistan: Germany at War* (*Sterben für Afghanistan – Deutschland im Krieg*), by Stefan Aust and Claus Richter, broadcasted by the national TV station ZDF in March 2010.[2] The journalists traveled to Afghanistan to provide insight into mission reality and into challenges soldiers had to master. In 2013, ZDF also broadcasted the well-received documentary *Our War: Combat Mission in Afghanistan* (*Unser Krieg – Kampfeinsatz in Afghanistan*), by Michael Renz und Christian Deick.[3] This film also focuses on soldiers and their individual experiences. In addition, stories of soldiers who have died in combat and of their relatives are presented in detail. Another good example is the theater play "Soldiers: A Mission Report" (*Soldaten – Ein Einsatzbericht*) by the Free Theatre Göttingen, put on stage in 2011 (Krug 2011). For this play, director Julia Roesler analyzed in-depth interviews with soldiers who had been deployed to Afghanistan to answer questions such as "Why does someone join the armed forces knowing that he or she will be send to missions like that in Afghanistan? How does daily life look like in theater? How do soldiers cope with experiences of violence? How do they deal with recurring images of violence? How do they feel when they return home?" It becomes apparent that director Roesler is genuinely interested in the soldiers' experiences and in an encounter with military lifeworlds beyond stereotypical images. Photojournalist Anja Niedringhaus (killed in Afghanistan in 2014) also helped to draw a more detailed picture of soldiers as individuals. With an eye for detail and a tenderness for the people she was documenting, she took a photo of a German soldier in remote northeast Afghanistan, who sat quietly outdoors, with four candles burning in a small box at his side to celebrate his thirty-fourth birthday. This photo was well received, as it showed the human side of war and conflict in times of terror attacks and insecurity.

Berlin graphic artist Arne Jysch (2012) claims that wars of the twenty-first century also have an impact on our Western societies, even if these wars are not officially called wars (but instead "military operations other than war") and even if these wars happen thousands of kilometers away. In Jysch's opinion, the Afghanistan conflict in which fifty-four German soldiers also lost their lives has not prompted a new commemorative culture in Germany but instead reinforced an already existing culture of suppression (see also Sørensen 2017; Danilova 2014; King 2010). German society was not and is not yet ready to accept the fact that military violence and war-related deaths have yet again become part of our reality. In his graphic novel *Wave and Smile* (2012), Jysch portrays in aquarelle the daily routine of German soldiers in Afghanistan—marked by IED attacks, combat, Skype sessions with the family at home, and taking care of the company's turtle, named "Rambo" (Jysch 2012). The graphic novel is yet another good example of an art project that takes a close look at the lifeworlds of soldiers and that portrays them as individuals and humans who should not be despised solely because they are part of the military.

The frame "soldiers as individuals" gained relevance during the "kinetic years" of the ISAF mission and has almost vanished since 2014. Even though around a thousand German soldiers are still in Afghanistan as part of the Resolute Support Mission and 1,030 soldiers are currently deployed to Mali and Senegal as part of the MINUSMA mission (to name just the largest missions), public discourse on out-of-area missions by the Bundeswehr has almost completely ceased. Someone who is interested in mission reality in Mali and soldiers' fate in this West African country would find it hard to find any in-depth information beyond those given on the official Bundeswehr homepage. Public discourse has instead focused more on the past years, particularly on returning soldiers, who will be discussed in the following part.

Frame 3: Soldiers as Marginal Men

U.S. American urban sociologist Robert Ezra Park described in his groundbreaking article "Human Migration and the Marginal Man" (1928) how migrants find themselves living in two different cultural groups—the one they have just left, as well as the one they have just entered. In the mind of "the marginal man," these two different cultures coalesce toward something new at the margins of society. Park argued that migrants struggle with an identity crisis due to different norms, values, and social roles in both societies to which they relate. Morally, the migrant is torn between both worlds. The third frame discussed in this chapter is called "soldiers as marginal men" because society perceives returning soldiers as still somehow belonging to the "other world" (in Afghanistan, Mali, Somalia, etc.), while servicemembers themselves struggle to reintegrate back into a society that does not have a veterans' concept like other nations (Bohnert and Schreiber 2016; see also Gustavsen 2017; Dandeker et al. 2006).

Soldiers are socialized as citizens within German society—a society that basically rejects violence. At the same time, in a so-called secondary socialization process, military personnel are being accustomed to military culture. Part of this military culture is to come to terms with the fact that soldiers have to use violence in their capacity as representatives of the state, adhering to clearly defined rules. The use of violence is a key element of training and is practiced and rehearsed again and again in practical as well as in theoretical exercises. When confronted with combat experiences during operations, German service members have to come to terms with the sometimes conflicting socialization as German citizens on the one hand and as members of the armed forces on the other. Personal interviews with combat soldiers (Tomforde 2015b) have highlighted that legitimization of the use of force by German society is for the majority of soldiers of utmost importance. They are willing and able to fight; however, to morally justify their actions in missions abroad, they ask for the support of their home society and a clear legitimization of their robust mission (Münch 2015). Due to the general denegation of violence still found in Germany, this legitimization was largely missing. Instead, returning soldiers with combat experiences were rather singled out as traumatized troops than as people who needed to be reintegrated into society. It is important for returning soldiers to emphasize their normalcy: "We're no freaks, for heaven's sake" (German captain, deployed to Afghanistan in 2013, quoted in Tomforde 2015b). They point out that there are indeed traumatized returnees and also soldiers who at first have problems with reintegrating into a peaceful society and getting back into "everyday mode"—but they do not want to be generally degraded as "freaks" or marginalized because of this prevalent image.

One way the ISAF mission has been dealt with in the German public is that service members returning from Afghanistan have often been marked as being special or, more often than not, as traumatized "so that their experiences may be excluded as particular ones" (Langer 2013: 86). In other words, their experiences of violence were not confronted and openly integrated into society; instead, the affected soldiers were being ostracized by focusing on psychopathology. Subsequently, says social scientist Phil Langer (2013: 84), ISAF soldiers with experiences of violence are seen as outsiders who cannot be integrated, and they are "isolated from social discourse." According to him, the military personnel in question are being revictimized, and their experiences isolated as abnormal instead of being integrated and reinterpreted. For our so-called post-heroic society as a whole, "the abstinence from violence is the decisive moment of social cohesion in modern times" (Reemtsma 2008, quoted in Langer 2013). Problematizing the experiences of violence helps to maintain the violence-rejecting social canon of values. For the service members of the Bundeswehr, however, this perception as "marginal men" contributes to the feeling that they are left alone, on the one hand, and on the other hand, it reinforces the self-perception of belonging to a special profession with special experiences and specials merits—in the sense of a generation "Einsatz" (generation mission) clearly distinguishable from the rest of society (Seiffert 2013). This group of returning soldiers with combat experience in Afghanistan does not have any official veteran status. An official concept of "veteran," including a valid definition of the term, and clearly defined rights and duties of soldiers returning from mission areas, is still missing in Germany. This lack and the often emotional debate about an official recognition of veterans underline how difficult it still is for German politics in particular and German society in general to be confronted with effects of war.

The term "veteran" is still closely linked to World War I and World War II. Neither politics, the armed forces, nor the social sciences were successful in clearly defining the term "veteran" or institutionalizing the concept of veterans in Germany. In 2013, former minister of defense Thomas de Maizière presented a definition, which was never passed officially and is still waiting to be released in an updated version. German psychologist

Michael Daxner (2016) claims that no other country has more difficulties in accepting returning soldiers as part of being a changed international actor in global foreign and security politics. In Germany, no special research institutions and/or large-scale projects dealing with returning soldiers, let alone a Department for Veterans' Affairs in the government, exist. Former Parliamentary Commissioner for the Armed Forces Königshaus stressed in 2012, "In this regard, we live in the Stone Age" (cited in Daxner 2014). Returning soldiers are thus not framed as veterans but rather as people at the margins of society. Therefore, servicemembers call for a clear definition of the term and a legal-political concept that clarifies the rights and status of veterans just like in other countries that also had no combat experiences after World War II such as the Netherlands, Denmark, or Norway. In these countries, social recognition for the efforts made by armed forces on behalf of the state and society is expressed, for example, in a veteran's day or with publicly accessible monuments and memorials (see, e.g., Gustavsen 2017; Sørensen 2017; Martinsen 2013b). In the Netherlands, a Veterans Institute was created in 2000 that promotes mental and physical healthcare for veterans and their families, as well as scientific research on topics relevant to veterans' care and policy (see. e.g.. Weerts 2015). Additionally, in commemorating the dead, major differences can be identified between (to name a few examples) the United Kingdom, Denmark, and Germany. While in the United Kingdom and Denmark returning dead soldiers are honored in public ceremonies, and hero worship is even actively encouraged in Denmark, the opposite takes place in Germany. Funeral services are mostly conducted in military encampments closed to the public and any notion of "militaristic hero worship" is avoided (Martinsen 2013a: 3).

Due to the World War II legacy and the particular situation in Germany, returning soldiers find their own means to deal privately with their mission experiences and to commemorate wounded and dead comrades in their own ways (de Libero 2014; Zimmermann 2014). Apart from the Bundeswehr Memorial (Ehrenmal) at the Ministry of Defense in Berlin and the Forest of Remembrance (Wald der Erinnerung), inaugurated by the Bundeswehr in November 2014 near the Operations Command in Potsdam, official commemoration sites are nonexistent, and an official mourning of the dead is hardly existent (see also Sørensen 2017; Martinsen 2013b; King 2010; Ben-Ari 2005). Thus, returning soldiers meet in primarily unofficial places of remembrance, maintained by individual units or operational soldiers in Germany. By doing so, returning soldiers no longer merely form a community of experience; more and more they are also transforming into an important community of remembrance (see also Leonhard 2011). Michael Daxner (2016) goes even further by stating that thirty thousand returning German soldiers now form a "social group." The members of this group commemorate the fallen and the wounded together and in a variety of different ways, mostly unnoticed by members of society even though "the dead have brought the war home" (Martinsen 2013a: 4). German society at large still shies away from public commemoration of dead soldiers and avoids a closer examination of how soldiers have really returned home from theater and how they need to be reintegrated into society not as "marginal men" but as full members of society.

Conclusions

Studying civil–military entanglements in Germany, this chapter focused on ascertaining changing frames among the German population on its soldiers and examining how the frames shape interrelations. Three important frames were singled out as a way of interpretation of the military in Germany and as a way of constituting "things military" and at the same time "things civilian." Of course, these three mental representations of the Other change over time and are more prominent in one group or the other. Differences in perception could be found between rural and urban areas, between people who actually know soldiers and who do not, between times of a robust mission like ISAF or times of rather quiet theaters, or also between times affected by terrorist attacks and a feeling of insecurity or rather peaceful times. Also, further differences might be found between younger and older people. For example, in May 2017, I interviewed ten young privates who had voluntarily joined the armed forces as enlisted personnel for a period of nine to twenty-four months. When asked about their motivation to become a soldier, most stated that, among other things, they personally wanted to get to know the Bundeswehr. They wanted to question stereotypes and prejudices existing among peers, parents, and relatives, and learn how this organization worked and what it means to be a soldier. Personal encounters with servicemembers are rather seldom if one does not have any relatives or friends who are soldiers or if one does not live near a base or navy port. These young adults interviewed wanted to take the opportunity of a time-restricted enlistment to see for themselves and make their own experiences. Of course, not all Germans have this opportunity and due to the suspension of conscription, the reduction of the forces, and the shutdown of numerous bases throughout Germany, personal encounters between civilians and servicemembers are the exception rather than the rule. As a result, processes of othering develop, especially in times of robust missions, war, and terror. As a cultural expression, the process of othering is closely related to "selfing."

The first frame, "soldiers as murderers," seemed especially virulent during the strong pacifist movement throughout and shortly after the Cold War. However, as it came up again in Parliament in 2010 and iteratively in personal communications between soldiers and civilian members of society, it still seems to persist. As this frame is closely related to Germany's historical past, it reveals the fear of German citizens that atrocities committed by the Nazi regime and its forces might possibly happen again. It illustrates the deep-seated mistrust in the Other (the military) but also in one another. For example, the right-wing party AFD won 12.6 percent of the vote during federal elections in September 2017. Extreme right-wing political positions seem to be acceptable again, at least for a certain number of Germans. The omnipresent fear of militarization of civilian life in Germany and the subconscious mistrust of soldiers who carry arms lie behind the frame "soldiers as murderers" and reveal a historically based mistrust and fear concerning not only the military, but potentially all members of German society.

The second frame, "soldiers as individuals," gained strength especially during the ISAF mission in the years 2008 to 2014 when German soldiers were involved in combat, and had to fight and kill. Before these years, the mission in Afghanistan was already demanding for the servicemembers, costing three to five lives each year. Most people died in 2010: ten soldiers were killed in combat that year. In total, fifty-four German soldiers died in Afghanistan between 2002 and 2014. Looking at these figures, one could suspect that a frame "soldiers as individuals" could have occurred before the mission turned more robust in 2008. Before that date, soldiers had already died in Afghanistan, had had to cope with hardships, and had at times been severely attacked by IED (Improvised Explosive Devices). Interestingly enough, interest in individual fates, experiences, and stories, however, only rose when German soldiers actually had to engage in combat. Violence presumes physical strength, which is perceived as "sexy," and it thus triggered a heightened interest in soldiers' realities in theater. One might also argue that members of society started to feel empathy for its soldiers, whom they had formerly perceived only as members of a military that can potentially be harmful, as it had been in the past.

Members of the German public started to become genuinely interested in the mission reality of the soldiers once they had to persist in combat. People started to frame soldiers as individuals as they felt for them and wanted to understand the hardships they had to put up with. Most of all, German society tried to understand why the Bundeswehr had to fight in a distant country like Afghanistan to defend Germany. In Afghanistan, German soldiers had to fight and kill for the first time since the end of World War II—a caesura for German society and soldiers alike. By taking a close look at ISAF combat soldiers, society tried to show its sympathy for its servicemembers but also tried to make sense of a confusing stabilization and anti-terror mission (Tomforde 2015a).

The third frame, "soldiers as marginal men," started to be constituted once returning soldiers became apparent as a social phenomenon. Once might suspect that the second frame "soldiers as individuals" maintained its relevance for German society, which continued to show its sympathy for returning soldiers. However, people tend to strive for a self-definition "that provides continuity and guides one's life. Difficult conditions threaten the self-concept" (Staub 1989: 15) As concepts of the Other always mirror concepts of the self, the frame "soldiers as marginal men" and the lack of a concept of veteran reveal how much German society shies away from dealing with the consequences of a robust mission in Afghanistan. Returning soldiers who have been in combat—have seen violence, terror, and war—jeopardize peaceful life in Germany. Society often marks returning soldiers as marginal so that their combat experiences need not be integrated into life reality in Germany. If civil society focuses on PTSD when portraying Bundeswehr soldiers' mission experiences, military personnel are isolated as abnormal instead of being integrated as normal and their experiences reinterpreted for their own sake. Langer (2013: 83) posits that, "from a psychoanalytical point of view, it is logical to speak of a 'crooked cure' by individualizing in psychological terms the subject of experiences which are actually related to the entire society." Coming home to their peace-minded societies means that soldiers not only have to come to terms with their mission and combat experiences but also have to find a way to reintegrate into a society for which experiences of war, conflict, and violence in theater are kept as distant ones. Civil–military entanglements are burdened by this distancing effect. Time will tell whether or not this effect will persist or whether it will be countered by new situations, settings, and frames.

Maren Tomforde received her Ph.D. in sociocultural anthropology from the University of Hamburg in 2005. For her thesis, she carried out research in Thailand (1999–2002) on "cultural spatiality." In 2003–2007 she worked as senior researcher at the Social Research Institute of the Bundeswehr and conducted anthropological research on peacekeeping missions. Since March 2007, she is a senior lecturer at the Staff and Command College of the German Armed Forces in Hamburg. She carries out research on civil–military relations, culture change, and peace and conflict studies. Since 2015, Maren Tomforde has been an Honorary Fellow at the Department of Anthropology at Macquarie University, Sydney, Australia.

Notes

1. This decline in support for ISAF when the death toll rose did not happen in, for example, Denmark (see Jakobsen and Ringsmose 2015).
2. For information on the film, see https://www.fernsehserien.de/frontal21/folgen/6-ster ben-fuer-afghanistan-deutschland-im-krieg-670887, accessed 13 November 2018.
3. Maximus, "54 tote Deutsche: ZDF zeigt Bundeswehr Doku Krieg Afghanistan," Kriegs berichterstattung.com, 22 October 2013, accessed 13 November 2018, https://www.kriegs berichterstattung.com/id/2890/ZDF-zeigt-Bundeswehr-Unser-Krieg-Afghanistan/.

References

Åse, C., and Maria Wendt. 2018. "Gendering the New Hero Narratives: Military Death in Denmark and Sweden." *Cooperation and Conflict* 53 (1): 23–41.

Baudrillard, J. 1995. *Simulacra and Simulation*. Translated by Sheila Faria Glaser. Ann Arbor: University of Michigan Press.

Baumann, G., and A. Gingrich. 2006. *Grammars of Identity/Alterity: A Structural Approach*. New York: Berghahn Books.

Ben-Ari, E. 2005. "Epilogue: A 'Good' Military Death." *Armed Forces & Society* 31 (4): 651–654.

Bickford, A. 2011. *Fallen Elites: The Military Other in Post-Unification Germany*. Stanford: Stanford University Press.

Biehl, H. 2011. "Belastungen, Angebote und Ansprüche: die Bundeswehr als Armee im Aufbruch und die Neuverhandlung der zivil-militärischen Beziehungen." In S. Bayer and M. Gillner (eds.), *Soldaten im Einsatz: Sozialwissenschaftliche und ethische Reflexionen*, 65–94. Berlin: Duncker & Humblot.

Biehl, H., and H. Schön (eds.). 2015. *Sicherheitspolitik und Streitkräfte im Urteil der Bürger Theorien, Methoden, Befunde*. Wiesbaden: VS Verlag.

Bohnert, M., and B. Schreiber (eds.). 2016. *Die unsichtbaren Veteranen – Kriegsheimkehrer in der deutschen Gesellschaft*. Berlin: Carola Hartmann Miles Verlag.

Bowen, G. 2009. "Document Analysis as a Qualitative Research Method." *Qualitative Research Journal* 9 (2): 27–40.

Bulmahn, T., and M. Wanner. 2013. *Ergebnisse der Bevölkerungsumfrage 2013 zum Image der Bundeswehr sowie zur Wahrnehmung und Bewertung des Claims "Wir. Dienen. Deutschland."* Potsdam: Zentrum für Militärgeschichte und Sozialwissenschaften.

Clifford, J., and George E. Marcus (eds.). 1986. *Writing Culture: The Poetics and Politics of Ethnography*. Oakland: University of California Press.

Dahinden, U. 2006. *Framing: Eine integrative Theorie der Massenkommunikation*. Online Publisher: beck-shop.de.

Danilova, N. 2014. "The Politics of Mourning: The Virtual Memorialisation of British Fatalities in Iraq and Afghanistan." *Memory Studies* 8 (3): 267–81.

Dandeker, C., S. Wessely, A. Iversen, and J. Ross. 2006. *What's in a Name? Defining and Caring for Veterans*. London: King's College.

Daxner, M. 2016. "Einsatzrückkehrer und Veteranen." *Aus Politik und Zeitgeschichte*, 9 May 2016. Accessed 15 May 2018, http://www.bpb.de/politik/grundfragen/deutsche-vertei digungspolitik/220648/veteranen.

——— (ed.). 2014. *Deutschland in Afghanistan*. Oldenburg: BIS-Verlag.

De Libero, L. 2014. *Tod im Einsatz: Deutsche Soldaten in Afghanistan*. Potsdam: Zentrum für Militärgeschichte und Sozialwissenschaften.

Entman, R. 1993. "Framing: Toward Clarification of a Fractured Paradigm." *Journal of Communication* 43 (4): 51–58.

Geertz, C. (1983) 2000. *Local Knowledge: Further Essays in Interpretative Anthropology*. New York: Basic Books.

———. 1988. *Works and Lives: The Anthropologist as Author*. Stanford: Stanford University Press.

Gleiss, T. 2010. "Rat zur Bescheidenheit." *Junge Welt*, 20 May 2010.

Goffman, E. 1974. *Frame Analysis: An Essay on the Organization of Experience*. Cambridge: Harvard University Press.

Grassiani, E. 2015. "Moral Othering at the Checkpoint: The Case of Israeli Soldiers and Palestinian Civilians." *Critique of Anthropology* 35 (4): 373–88.

Gustavsen, E. 2017. *Construction Meaning after War: A Study of the Lived Experiences of Norwegian Afghanistan Veterans and Military Spouses*. Oslo: University of Oslo.

Hahn, A. 1994. "Die soziale Konstruktion des Fremden." In Walter Sprondel (ed.), *Die Objektivität der Ordnungen und ihre kommunikative Konstruktion*, 140–63. Frankfurt: Suhrkamp.

Hepp, M., and Viktor Otto (eds.). 1996. *Soldaten sind Mörder. Dokumentation einer Debatte*. Berlin: Ch. Links.

Himmelrath, A. 2015. "Bundeswehr an Schulen." SPIEGEL Online, 13 April 2015. Accessed 10 May 2018, http://www.spiegel.de/lebenundlernen/schule/bundeswehr-an-schulen-30-millionen-euro-fuer-nachwuchswerbung-a-1027935.html.

Holslag, A. 2015. "The Process of Othering from the 'Social Imaginaire' to Physical Acts: An Anthropological Approach." *Genocide Studies and Prevention: An International Journal* 9 (1): 96–113.

Huntington, S. 1957. *The Soldier and the State*. Cambridge, MA: Belknap Press.

Jakobsen, P. V., and J. Ringsmose. 2015. "In Denmark, Afghanistan is Worth Dying for: How Public Support for the War Was Maintained in the Face of Mounting Casualties and Elusive Success." *Cooperation and Conflict* 50 (2): 211–27.

Janowitz, M. 1960. *The Professional Soldier*. New York: Free Press.

Jysch, A. 2012. *Wave and Smile*. Hamburg: Carlsen Verlag.

Kempf, L. 2013. "Der Soldat als Feindbild im Inneren?." In M. Böcker, L. Krempf, and F. Springer, *Soldatentum: Auf der Suche nach Identität und Berufung der Bundeswehr heute*, 185–200. München: Olzog.

King, A. 2010. "The Afghan War and 'Postmodern' Memory: Commemoration and the Dead of Helmand." *The British Journal of Sociology* 61 (1): 1–25.

———. 2013. *The Combat Soldier: Infantry Tactics and Cohesion in the Twentieth and Twenty-First Centuries*. Oxford: Oxford University Press.

Koelbl, H. 2011. "Bist du in der Lage, auf einen Menschen zu schießen? Das konnte ich klar mit ja beantworten. Zehn junge Männer erzählen, wie es ist, in den Krieg zu ziehen. Oberleutnant Jens K. ist einer von ihnen." *Zeitmagazin* 49.

Köhler, H. 2005. *Einsatz für Freiheit und Sicherheit. Rede von Bundespräsident Horst Köhler bei der Kommandeurtagung der Bundeswehr am 10. Oktober 2005 in Bonn*. Berlin: Bundespräsidialamt.

Krug, H. 2011. "Soldaten: ein Einsatzbericht." *Deutschlandfunk*, 25 June 2011.

Langer, P. 2013. "'Wenn's nicht näher als 30 Meter neben mir knallt, dann nehmen wir es nicht mehr persönlich.' Zum gesellschaftlichen Umgang mit potenziell traumatischen Erfahrungen vom Krieg am Beispiel des Afghanistan-einsatzes der Bundeswehr." *Freie Assoziation: Zeitschrift für das Unbewusste in Organisation und Kultur* 16 (2): 69–86.

Leonhard, N. 2011. "Das Ehrenmal der Bundeswehr – ein Gedenkort voller Ambivalenzen." In S. Bayer and M. Gillner (eds.), *Soldaten im Einsatz: Sozialwissenschaftliche und ethische Reflexionen*, 134–46. Berlin: Duncker & Humblot.

———. 2017. "Towards a New German Military Identity? Change and Continuity of Military Representations of Self and Other(s) in Germany." *Critical Military Studies* (online), 10 October 2017. DOI: 10.1080/23337486.2017.1385586.

Mannitz, S. 2013. "Democratic Soldiers as Marginal Men. The Impact of Security-Cultural Transformations on the Military in Europe." In G. Kümmel and B. Giegerich (eds.), *The Armed Forces. Towards a Post-Interventionist Era?*, 173–90. Wiesbaden: Springer VS.

Marcus, G. E., and M. M. J. Fischer. 1986. *Anthropology as Cultural Critique: An Experimental Moment in the Human Sciences*. Chicago: University of Chicago Press.

Martinsen, K. D. 2013a. *Soldier Repatriation: Popular and Political Responses*. Surrey: Ashgate.

———. 2013b. "Totgeschwiegen? Deutschland und die Gefallenen des Afghanistan-Einsatzes." *Aus Politik und Zeitgeschichte*, 21 October 2013. Accessed 21 April 2018, http://www.bpb.de/apuz/170806/deutschland-und-die-gefallenen-des-afghanistan-einsatzes.

Merton, R. 1957. *Social Theory and Social Structure*. New York: Free Press.

Münch, P. 2015. *Die Bundeswehr in Afghanistan. Militärische Handlungslogik in internationalen Interventionen*. Freiburg i.Br.: Rombach.

Naumann, K. 2013. "Geleitwort: Soldatentum?! Zur Notwendigkeit einer Debatte." In M. Böcker, L. Krempf, and F. Springer, *Soldatentum: Auf der Suche nach Identität und Berufung der Bundeswehr heute*, 9–13. München: Olzog.

Park, R. E. 1928. "Human Migration and the Marginal Man." *American Journal of Sociology* 33 (6): 881–93.

Schirrmacher, T. 2014. *Culture of Shame / Culture of Guilt*. Holzgerlingen: Verlag für Kultur und Wissenschaft.

Seiffert, A. 2013. "Generation Einsatz." *Aus Politik und Zeitgeschichte*, 21 October 2010. Accessed 9 April 2018, http://www.bpb.de/apuz/170804/generation-einsatz.

Sørensen, B. 2017. Public Commemorations of Danish Soldiers: Monuments, Memorials, and Tombstones. *Critical Military Studies* 3 (1): 27–49.

Staub, E. 1989. *The Roots of Evil: The Origins of Genocide and Other Group Violence*. Cambridge: Cambridge University Press.

Stelzenmüller, C. 2004. "Kleiner und kräftiger. Die Bundeswehr vor dem radikalsten Umbau ihrer Geschichte." *Die Zeit* 3 (8 January 2004): 12.

Steinbrecher, M., H. Biehl, C. Höfig, and M. Wanner. 2016. *Sicherheits- und verteidigungspolitisches Meinungsklima in der Bundesrepublik Deutschland: Ergebnisse und Analysen der Bevölkerungsbefragung 2016*. Forschungsbericht 114. Potsdam: ZMS Bw.

Stepahn, C. 2013. "Bundeswehr und Öffentlichkeit: Militärische Tradition als gesellschaftliche Frage." In M. Böcker, L. Krempf, and F. Springer, *Soldatentum: Auf der Suche nach Identität und Berufung der Bundeswehr heute*, 141–56. München: Olzog.

Struck, P. 2003. "Jedes Land entscheidet souverän." *Der Spiegel* 49 (1 December 2003): 24.

Tomforde, M. 2015a. "Einsatzkultur und die Deutung von Gewalt beim Militär." In S. Salsborn and H. Zapf (eds.), *Krieg und Frieden: Kulturelle Deutungsmuster*, 109–36. Frankfurt a. Main: Peter Lang.

———. 2015b. "Good Shot: Gewalterfahrungen von Bundeswehrsoldaten im Auslandseinsatz." In J. Franke and N. Leonhard (eds.), *Einhegung und Legitimation militärischer Gewalt in Deutschland: Stand und Perspektiven*, 213–50. Berlin: Duncker & Humblot.

Tomforde, M., and K. Roggmann. 2018. *Uniformierte Vielfalt: Diversität in der Bundeswehr*. Hamburg: Funke Mediengruppe.

Tucholsky, K. 1931. "Der bewachte Kriegsschauplatz." *Die Weltbühne*, 4 August 1931.

Weerts, J. 2015. "Beyond the Line: Military and Veteran Health Research." *Medicine Conflict and Survival* 31 (2):1–2.

Zimmermann, M. 2014. "'Kämpfen können und es auch müssen': Wie verändern Gewalterfahrungen die Bundeswehr und ihre Soldaten?" Unpublished dissertation, General Staff Officer Course 2013, Staff and Command College of the German Armed Forces, Hamburg.

Chapter 6

Domesticating Civil–Military Entanglements
Multiplicity and Transnationality of Retired British Gurkhas' Citizenship Negotiation

Taeko Uesugi

Introduction

This chapter investigates civil–military entanglement observed in citizenship negotiation by immigrant veterans. To this end, I explore the case of Gurkha veterans who have retired from the British Army to the United Kingdom.

Military history books often cite the fact that the Greco-Roman citizenship concept, with its emphasis on citizens' military duty, was revived through the American and French revolutions in the late eighteenth century. Indeed, since these revolutions, citizen soldiers have become the norm in contemporary militaries, and the employment of mercenaries has been an object of reproach.

Nevertheless, the history of modern military forces has not been unilineal. In order to optimize manning and deployment on a global scale, some military forces (e.g., the French Foreign Legion) have hired foreign or native soldiers according to the given "state elite's ethnic security map" (Enloe 1980: 23–4) or outsourced their duties to private military companies, which are often multinational corporations.[1] On the one hand, this shows a denationalized aspect of national military forces. On the other hand, some such forces have conferred legal citizenship upon their noncitizen soldiers in a bid to recruit noncitizen youths and assure their allegiance

---

and military effectiveness. Thus, new citizen soldiers are born, military forces are renationalized, and the linkage of military service and citizenship is recovered. The modern military force, supposedly the most national type of institution in existence, is, paradoxically, an arena in which denationalization and nationalization frequently occur.

This process of renationalizing military forces does not operate automatically. Immigrant soldiers are qualified for citizenship in grades related to the requirements of military strategy and manning policy, and therefore not all immigrant soldiers are entitled to receive full citizenship rights immediately. Additionally, in modern states, with their complex political systems, multiple stakeholders, path dependencies in decision making, and varied discourse on the military, the decision-making process regarding the military tends to be extremely complicated. Because the access to important assets is mediated through national belonging (Loveman 2005 cited in Brubaker 2016: 41), conferment of citizenship on immigrant soldiers inevitably changes the pattern of resource distribution in the state, as well as within the military forces. Therefore, the conferment of citizenship necessitates negotiation with various stakeholders at different levels of sociopolitical and legal organization. After all, the linkage between military service and citizenship is not activated in the inexorable unfolding of a pre-established harmony, but is rather situational and needs substantiating by particular stakeholders' initiatives and efforts, as exemplified by the minority soldiers' citizenship negotiation (Berry 1977; Krebs 2006).

In the study of soldiers' citizenship negotiation, immigrant veterans are especially noteworthy because, like all veterans, they are dually positioned as both military and civilian persons and can engage in sociopolitical activities more freely than active soldiers. At the same time, as immigrants they have to accomplish social integration. As occasion demands, they exploit almost all resources to make the situation favorable to their advocacy; thus, they may nurture civil public opinion, negotiate or cooperate with multiple civil stakeholders, create their new civil identity as well as reinforce their military identity, and so on. In this way, they overstep the boundary between "civil" and "military" and manipulate a binary opposition between those two spheres. Further, in the process of citizenship negotiation, their advocacy may go between the national and subnational levels and across national borders, and produces a kind of civil–military entanglement. I would like to examine such civil–military entanglement as engendered in immigrant veterans' citizenship negotiation at multiple levels and across national borders.

Regarding the multiplicity of citizenship negotiation and transnationalism of immigrants, the previous scholarship has examined this concept in migration studies (e.g., Basch et al. 1994; Ong 1996; Glick Schiller and Fouron 1998).[2] However, for immigrant veterans, neither multiplicity nor transnationality of citizenship negotiation has received much attention, as long as active soldiers' military effectiveness or allegiance to military forces has not been influenced by such.

In this chapter, to illustrate the civil–military entanglement observed in immigrant soldiers' citizenship negotiation on multiple levels and in a transnational setting, I focus on Nepalese soldiers (Gurkhas) retired from the British Army. This group is of particular significance as a subject for the examination of civil–military entanglement, because their home country, Nepal, is thought to have been a part of the "informal British Empire" (Gallagher and Robinson 1953).[3] Accordingly, their position was weak compared with other immigrant soldiers from the Commonwealth countries, the former formal British Empire. The relative weakness of the Gurkhas' position has obliged them to dedicate great effort to citizenship negotiation.

In the next section, I provide an outline of Gurkha employment until the 2000s in order to clarify the historical background to Gurkhas' citizenship negotiation. I then describe how the terms and conditions of their employment were changed and brought within the fold of the wider British Army. In the following section, in order to clarify citizenship negotiation at the national level, I deal with the argument that occurred within the British public sphere over the granting of settlement rights to Gurkha veterans who had retired before the Handover of Hong Kong to China in 1997. I then describe the activities of a veterans' voluntary association, the British Gurkha Welfare Society (BGWS), to explore aspects of their citizenship negotiation at subnational levels and in a transnational setting.

My description and analysis are based on data that I collected intermittently from 1997 to 2015, in addition to a literature survey. With the permission of the Brigade of Gurkhas, I engaged in participant observation of events and interviews with soldiers in the United Kingdom (1997–1998, 2005, and 2007) and Brunei (2001–2003 and 2005). I also conducted research on retired Gurkhas in the United Kingdom (2008, 2010, 2011, 2013, and 2018), Nepal (1999, 2008, 2009, 2013, 2015, and 2016), Australia (2012), and Japan (2003 and 2013).

Historical Background

Fighting for the United Kingdom's Cause

Gurkha employment officially originated in 1815, when the Honourable East India Company recruited Gurkha prisoners of war with the intention of reducing Nepal's military power during the Anglo–Nepalese War (1814–16). After the start of employment, Gurkhas were deployed to the North East Frontier and Burma (1824–1912), the First Sikh War (1845–1846), and the North West Frontier (1852–1947).[4]

Due to the Gurkhas' distinguished service in the Indian Mutiny (1857–1859) as well as other battles, the United Kingdom recognized their military value for the rule and defense of the overseas territories where the United Kingdom's interests resided, and thus it reinforced the Gurkha troops, particularly in the second half of the nineteenth century. After the dissolution of the Honourable East India Company (1858), Gurkhas became soldiers of the force of the Bengal Presidency, which was incorporated into the new (British) Indian Army in 1895.[5] In addition to the North West Frontier, Gurkhas were deployed to Bhutan (1864–1866), the Malay States (1875–1876), the Second Afghan War (1878–1880), Sikkim (1888), China (1900), Tibet (1903–1904), North West Persia (1918–1921), the Third Afghan War (1919), Kurdistan (1919), Iraq (1919–1920), Malabar (1921–1922), Palestine (1945), Java and Sumatra (1945–1946), and Indo-China (1945–1946).

In order to obtain "pure Gurkhas" with superb military skills, military policy makers in colonial India specified the ethnic groups, lineages, and families to be prioritized for recruitment (Vansittart [1890] 1993: 76, 85). It was ethnic peoples of the Tibet-Burman language groups, who tended to be subjugated by high-caste Hindus, that the United Kingdom recruited heavily.[6]

On the other hand, as the result of their defeat in the Anglo–Nepalese War, Nepal ceded part of its territory to British India and accepted the Resident. Nepal could do "nothing" (Banskota 1994), including the importation of arms and ammunition or the building of a diplomatic relationship with other countries, without the permission of the Resident—that is, Nepal was only a quasi-independent state.[7] In the early stages of the British employment of Gurkhas, the Nepalese government obstructed their recruitment on Nepalese soil. However, after recognizing the United Kingdom's hegemony, in the second half of the nineteenth century, Nepal's prime ministers gradually became cooperative with the United Kingdom in order to secure Nepal's independence and the prime ministers' power in domestic politics (Banskota 1994; Izuyama 1999). Gurkhas were the "currency" (Des Chene 1991: 3–4) that Nepal paid to the United Kingdom to ensure its independence and to obtain support for the existing regime.

The two world wars comprised the apex of Gurkha employment. During World War I, when new recruits were added, Gurkha soldiers totaled no less than two hundred thousand (Banskota 1994: 126). They were deployed to France and Belgium, Gallipoli, Egypt and Palestine, and Mesopotamia. Evaluating Nepal's cooperation during World War I and recognizing the necessity to favor Nepal for the recruitment of Gurkhas, the United Kingdom admitted Nepal's independence by concluding the Treaty between the United Kingdom and Nepal, Together with Note Respecting the Importation of Arms and Ammunition into Nepal. This treaty made World War II the first large-scale war for Gurkhas as foreign soldiers from an independent country officered by the British. In World War II, the Gurkha regiments were reinforced, increasing from twenty battalions in peacetime to forty-five battalions during World War II. From 1939 to 1945, they were deployed to North Africa, Italy, Greece, the Middle East (Persia, Iraq, and Syria), Malaya and Singapore, and Burma. Approximately 112 thousand Gurkha soldiers were deployed to the theaters (Gurkha Brigade Association n.d.). Without proclaiming war against the Axis powers, Nepal made a great war effort as a "friend" of the United Kingdom.[8] Besides allowing the recruiting officers to penetrate deeply into the hills, some units of the Nepalese Army were placed at the disposal of the British Crown. The then prime minister also gave arms to the government of India and donated a significant amount of money to the victims of German air strikes in the United Kingdom and to the British war funds (Banskota 1994: 133). During the two world wars, casualties in Gurkha regiments reached nearly forty-three thousand (Gurkha Brigade Association n.d.).

Following the partition and independence of India and Pakistan (1947), Gurkha regiments were divided between the Indian and British armies, with Gurkhas becoming regular soldiers in both. The 1947 Tripartite Agreement (TPA) between Nepal, India, and the United Kingdom formally settled the terms and conditions under which Gurkha soldiers would serve. With the headquarters of the Brigade of Gurkhas in Malaya (1947–1970) and Hong Kong (1970–1997), Gurkhas' theaters extended to Malaya (1948–1960), Brunei (1962), Borneo (1962–1966), the Malay Peninsula (1964–1966), the Falkland Islands (1982), the Gulf (1990–1991), the Balkans (1994–2002), East Timor (1999), Sierra Leone (1999–2003), Iraq (2000–2011), and Afghanistan (2002–).

Being Nepali in the British Military

The Gurkhas, being neither the colonizer nor the colonized, comprised a convenient force for the practice of "divide and rule" in colonial India. That is they could be deployed to any region or any ethnic people in order to effectively suppress a riot without provoking direct hatred against the British. Hence, their collective national identity as Nepalis was preserved (Ragsdale 1989: 49).[9] The confirmation of Nepal's independence in 1923 also had significance as part of this "divide and rule" policy within the (British) Indian Army.

Even after the independence of India, the British Army, the new employer of Gurkhas, continued its policy of maintaining Gurkhas' Nepalese identity, as well as the substantial and symbolic ties between Gurkhas and

Nepal (Uesugi 2007). Under the TPA, the Gurkhas could be discharged if Nepal went to war. Their service began with attestation parades held in Nepal at enlistment, and they were also discharged in Nepal; however, they did not receive permission to work in the United Kingdom, much less British citizenship. Additionally, from 1964 to the present, the various versions of the Nepal Citizenship Act have never stipulated that Nepalese citizenship should be renounced on the grounds of foreign military service. Spouse-accompanied service was limited to soldiers with a designated duration of service and rank, so that most Gurkhas left their families behind in Nepal during their service. This inevitably meant transnational exchanges of money, letters, presents, and messages between Gurkhas and their families. Furthermore, the Brigade of Gurkhas adopted a cultural policy based on Nepal's national culture, formed after the 1960s under the leadership of King Mahendra. For instance, Gurkha soldiers of various ethnic/caste backgrounds use the Nepalese language as their lingua franca. A Hindu religious policy was also promoted: in Gurkha camps, Hindu festivals, including Dasain, were observed by Hindu religious teachers according to Bikram Sambat (the solar-lunar calendar).[10] This policy made Gurkha soldiers, who came from various family or religious traditions (and not all of whom were orthodox Hindus), subjects of the world's only Hindu monarchy, and it provided Gurkha units with a basis for cohesion that went beyond ethnic/caste lines.

Recognizing this policy, Gurkha officers also endeavored to strengthen their Nepali identity from within. In 1997, during the Dasain festival of a Gurkha unit, a cultural show was opened with the national anthem of Nepal, while greeting cards (Dasain cards) printed with the national flags of the United Kingdom and Nepal were distributed. During my field research, the Gurkha majors told me that the purpose of Dasain festival was to ensure that Nepalese culture is not forgotten.[11] Before the Handover of Hong Kong, the Gurkha officers even discouraged their men from marrying foreigners in order to maintain the cohesion of the Gurkha community based on national and cultural homogeneity.

The policy of sustaining the Gurkhas' ties with Nepal was also economically favorable for the British Army. The Gurkhas were paid lower salaries and pensions, justified by their family lives being based in Nepal, where the cost of living is far cheaper than in the United Kingdom.

*The Relationship between British Society
and the Gurkhas until the mid-2000s*

During the Indian Rebellion, the Gurkhas were portrayed in the British mass media as a true "martial race" who had saved British women from

Indian insurgents (Streets 2004); moreover, their valor, loyalty, honesty, and sense of humor were repeatedly praised as being similar to the British soldiers rather than to other Indian classes in the Indian Army (Caplan 1995).

However, before the Handover of Hong Kong, Gurkhas were stationed exclusively on foreign soil; they were foreign soldiers, beloved by the British public but nevertheless utterly far-removed in the geographical sense from mainland British society. Their acquisition of British citizenship was therefore never discussed, unlike the case of nonwhite subjects in the former British Empire (Rush and Reed 2014).

Nepal and the Gurkhas

Gurkha employment made Nepal's independence secure and brought cash income to the families in rural Nepal. Furthermore, the British Army's policy of preserving national identities introduced "Pan-Nepali values" into ethnic communities that speak Tibeto-Burman languages (Gurung 1997: 504), from which over 80 percent of Gurkhas came. However, as Onta (1996: 11) points out, Gurkhas have been given no place in the pantheon of brave Nepali heroes. In Nepal's public sphere, the relationship between Gurkhas and Nepalese society is not recognized as an ordinary type of civil–military connection between defenders and the defended. Also, the role that Gurkha employment played in Nepal's independence and the nation-building beyond caste/ethnic lines seems to have been underestimated to some extent. This may be partly because many Gurkhas were from the Tibet-Burman language groups, which did not compose the ruling class or influence the press much.

Including Gurkhas in the Wider British Army and British Society

In the 1990s and 2000s, Gurkha employment underwent drastic changes. The integration of Gurkhas into the wider British Army and British society had begun. Following the Handover of Hong Kong, the headquarters of the Brigade of Gurkhas moved to the United Kingdom for the first time. Along with the handover, the end of the Cold War and the so-called revolution in military affairs resulted in the downsizing of the Gurkhas, who tended to be regarded as superior infantry soldiers.

At the same time, Gurkha veterans started to assert the improvement of terms and conditions, which was enabled by Nepal's democratization after the 1990s, and the terms and conditions of their service were gradually integrated into that of the wider British Army. As a result, Gurkhas' wages were increased to resemble those of their British counterparts, and the ranking system of the Queen's Gurkha Officers became equivalent to the ranks of their British peers.[12] Gurkhas can now select the same terms and conditions as their British counterparts and serve in other British regiments.[13] Some Gurkha soldiers serve in British regiments together with Commonwealth soldiers, such as Fijians, who began to be recruited in 1997. Considering the religious diversity that pertains among Gurkha soldiers, in 2005 the Brigade began to employ Buddhist as well as Hindu chaplains for pastoral care in a civilian capacity.

Furthermore, in 2004, Tony Blair's government announced that in 2007 all Gurkhas who had served for more than four years and had retired after the Handover of Hong Kong would be granted the right to settlement in the United Kingdom. As legitimate dwelling is one of the requirements for citizenship application, it can be said that the door for British citizenship has been opened for Gurkhas. Some children of Gurkhas now enter service in the British military as "Hindu" or "Buddhist" British soldiers. In this work environment, Gurkha officers have abolished the informal rule discouraging international marriages, stating that such is meaningless since some Gurkhas have served together with Commonwealth soldiers. As a result of these policy changes, Gurkhas and their families have settled in military towns in southern England, such as Aldershot and Farnborough.

Due to these policy changes, the Gurkhas' national identity, or "Nepaliness," seems to have been diluted. However, even now, their "Nepaliness" and the transnational ties between Gurkhas and Nepal are still recognized as precious assets for the Brigade. As a British officer noted to Ware (2014: 128), "What makes Gurkhas Gurkhas . . . is that they maintain their cultural identity. We find it important to make them as good as they are, their strengths inherent from Nepal." In the context of the War on Terror, the Gurkhas' employment seems to be useful in allowing the United Kingdom to maintain a foothold in South Asia, and the British Army refers to its activities in Nepal as "Firm Base activity" (British Army 2015).[14]

Argument Regarding the Settlement Rights of Pre-1997 Gurkhas: Citizenship Negotiation at the National Level

Although many Gurkhas were granted settlement rights, those Gurkhas who had retired before the Handover of Hong Kong (pre-1997 Gurkhas) were excluded from the granting. Dissatisfied with this decision, the pre-1997 Gurkhas and their British supporters organized the Gurkha Justice Campaign. During the campaign, the pre-1997 Gurkhas exerted their political subjectivity in a visible way in mainland British society for the first time; they appeared before the mass media with visible symbols that signified their military careers (e.g., the Gurkha hat, khaki coat or blazer, and war medals) and demonstrated their collective identity as veterans, not merely as ordinary Asian immigrants, while other Gurkhas assisted them by donating money and gathered at important occasions in the same attire.

The Course of Events

In order to examine the Gurkhas' citizenship negotiation at the national level, I will here outline the course of events and the argument that ensued.

In 2007, Tulbahadur Pun, a Gurkha winner of the Victoria Cross military decoration, initiated legal action to seek settlement in the United Kingdom. The actor Joanna Lumley, famous for her roles in *On Her Majesty's Secret Service* (a James Bond film made in 1969) and the TV drama *Absolutely Fabulous*, also came out in support of the Gurkhas. Her father had been an officer of a Gurkha regiment and had been saved by the above-mentioned Pun in a battle with the Japanese Army during World War II ("Gurkha War Hero" 2007). In addition, five other Gurkhas and one widow, representing two thousand comrades, filed a test case in London's High Court, demanding recognition of their right to settle (Bailey 2008).

The court ruled that the policy of the Home Office was not legal and should be reexamined to allow entry clearance officers to make a different decision. A High Court judge stated that it was irrational for pre-1997 Gurkhas to be denied settlement while other foreign soldiers serving in the army could settle (Irvine 2009). By "other foreign soldiers," the judge was referring to soldiers from Commonwealth countries. On the day of the ruling, hundreds of people rushed to the High Court, attesting to the British public's considerable interest in the issue.

Subsequently, a nationwide argument broke out in the mass media. It exploited various current interests of the British public to stand for or against the Gurkha Justice Campaign irrespective of their civil/military character. As a result, the issue attracted a great deal of public attention. The incessant articles by online newspapers aroused public sentiment via the Internet, and, at the climax of the controversy, five articles were published in the online version of *The Guardian* on 21 May, with another article (Allen and Hickley 2008) receiving 135 comments from readers. As time went by, public opinion in support of the Gurkhas snowballed, eventually overwhelming support for the Cabinet. For instance, the Royal British Legion was paying for the campaigners' rent and giving them food vouchers ("Gurkhas' Charity Launched" 2009). On 29 April 2009, the Liberal Democrats proposed a motion in the House of Commons in favor of the settlement rights of pre-1997 Gurkhas. The motion was passed with 267 votes (including twenty-eight MPs from the ruling Labour Party) in favor and 246 against, as well as more than seventy abstentions from the Labour Party. Although the passage of this motion was not legally binding, it dealt a serious blow to the Labour government. Finally, on 21 May, Home Secretary Jacqui Smith announced that all ex-Gurkhas who had served for four or more years would be allowed to settle in the United Kingdom.

Following this incident, the British prime minister's approval ratings dropped. Labour lost the next general election, and the winning parties, the Conservative Party and Liberal Democrats, formed a coalition government in 2010. Furthermore, the victory for the pre-1997 Gurkhas won their solicitors' office the 2009 Human Rights Campaign of the Year award, as is proudly proclaimed on the office's website (Howe+Co Solicitors 2015).

Argument

The Cabinet had rejected the granting of settlement rights to pre-1997 Gurkhas on the grounds that (1) Gurkhas did not have sufficiently strong ties with the United Kingdom before the handover because the previous headquarters of the Brigade of Gurkhas were located overseas, and (2) doing so would increase the expenditure needed for pensions and other expenses (Bailey 2008).[15] Thus, the government set criteria for selection of Gurkhas according to geographical proximity of the civil–military relationship between Gurkhas and the British public. Defending the government, some discussants denied pre-1997 Gurkhas' settlement right from the perspective of sharing the common cause of the British Empire. For example, Simon Jenkins (2009), a freelance journalist, wrote, "They are not British or Commonwealth citizens. They are soldiers of fortune, with less claim to settle in Britain than Commonwealth soldiers who likewise decide to take the Queen's shilling and a career in the British forces. . . . The wages are beyond any imaginable in their own country. That they serve under British officers and for British interests does not give them special moral standing." In their opinion, the military service of pre-1997 Gurkhas was not deserving of citizenship because Gurkhas were not from the formal British empire and did not share its cause.

As opposed to the government, the supporters of the Gurkhas focused on Gurkhas' loyalty and contribution to the defense of the United Kingdom. Joanna Lumley's family history reminded the British public of the Gurkha soldiers' contribution to the United Kingdom and awakened a sense of justice and political correctness among the British public. The supporters asserted that the United Kingdom had a "moral debt of honour" (Naughton 2008) toward the Gurkhas, that it was a national shame to leave Gurkhas in poverty in Nepal, and that allowing the pre-1997

Gurkhas to settle would restore the United Kingdom's justice, morality, and decency. Padam Bahadur, the president of the Gurkha Army Ex-Servicemen's Organisation (GAESO), a Gurkha veterans' self-organization, also asserted that they became the British in their mind, by saying that he wears the Union Jack pin every day "to represent the British flag in [his] heart" (Fletcher 2008).

In addition, those who sided with the pre-1997 Gurkhas also cast light on almost every possible relevant issue, including "nonmilitary" issues to affirm the Gurkhas' claims and deny the government's assertions, which succeeded in drawing the attention of the wider public. Justifying expenditure related to Gurkhas, the supporters asserted that the government had engaged in several instances of improper expenditure (e.g., MPs' misuse of government funds for personal expenses).

Pre-1997 Gurkhas' civil supporters even utilized the argument for their own collective, corporate, or personal interests. *The Daily Telegraph* and other tabloids appropriated the pre-1997 Gurkha issue as a means to criticize the politics of the Labour government in general. The tabloids, which were alert to the rapid increase in immigrants, contended that pre-1997 Gurkhas should be given priority over other undesirable immigrants, such as refugees with criminal records, refugees with a low level of education, and immigrants from former enemy countries, to stay in the United Kingdom. Raising the issue of employing illegal immigrants as security guards, one reader also added that loyal Gurkhas should be hired instead ("Public Opinion in Favour of the Gurkha" 2009). Furthermore, the media and politicians criticized the prime minister for his lack of leadership and for being "out of touch" (Pierce and Kirkup 2009). Conservatives did not miss out on the opportunity to attack the Labour government, despite the party's traditional caution with respect to accepting immigrants. Expecting the general elections within one year and being nervous about the trend of public opinion, even members of parliament from Labour Party began to criticize Prime Minister Gordon Brown. Ultimately, there were many civil stakeholders of diverse personal, collective, or corporate interests that entangled the process linking pre-1997 Gurkhas' military service and citizenship.

Citizenship Negotiation by the BGWS at Multiple Levels and across National Borders

Respect and Embarrassment

It was also the case that in local communities, most local residents respected and welcomed the Gurkhas (Castle 2011). During the argument in favor of or against the pre-1997 Gurkhas, a statue of a Gurkha was built in the town of Maidstone, the home base of the Queen's Gurkha Engineers, using residents' donations. At the unveiling ceremony, the local councillor noted, "The statue will remain in Maidstone as a constant reminder of the debt of gratitude that we owe to this unique band of fighting men and of our admiration of them" (Salter 2008).

However, local residents felt embarrassment, as well as respect, for the former heroes. In the past, military hometowns in southern England had not had huge populations of nonwhite immigrants, unlike megacities such as London.[16] Therefore, some local residents were ambivalent about the growth of the Nepalese community. Two years after the dramatic victory by the pre-1997 Gurkhas, Gerald Howarth, the MP representing Aldershot and Farnborough, wrote in a letter to the prime minister that 10 percent of the Borough of Rushmoor's population was then Nepalese, and that the services of the local authority, the National Health Service, the Citizens Advice Bureau, and schools were in danger of being overwhelmed by the dependents of Gurkhas and elderly former soldiers due to their low levels of English literacy ("Hampshire MP Gerald Howarth's Letter" 2011). A tabloid also reported on the poverty levels of retired Gurkhas and their reliance on social welfare (Jones 2014).[17] Now they are required to fulfill a citizen's "civil" duty "to reduce their burden on society" (Ong 1996:739).

Furthermore, various types of personal friction have arisen since the immigration. At schools, incidents of bullying and quarrels between Gurkha children and others have occurred, while some locals have complained about the outdoor barbecues of retired Gurkhas. Other immigrants (e.g., those from Eastern European countries), who do not necessarily share the British national memory of the Gurkhas' contribution, have cast insults at old veterans walking on the streets of the towns in which they have settled.

In sum, the Gurkhas' glorious military career has somewhat receded into the background for some local residents, and they tend to regard Gurkha veterans as ordinary types of nonwhite immigrants. The veterans have experienced the ontological turn from the "military" being to the "civil" being.

Trying to adapt to this ontological turn from the military to civil, Gurkha veterans and their families have deployed citizenship negotiation in their everyday lives, on both an individual and a collective basis. Yet, it is the skill and knowledge acquired while they were on active service that they use.

As individuals, applying their military skills, many Gurkha veterans now work in the security industry, while their wives also work to bolster the family finances.[18] The BBC has reported that many such veterans play

a vital role in maintaining social order as employees of security companies (McClatchey 2011), although, of course, some Gurkhas are engaged
in other kinds of business (e.g., Nepalese restaurants). The change in the
security environment accompanying the War on Terror has offered Gurkha veterans new roles, thus enabling them to be engaged in another type
of civil–military relationship in the business world.

The BGWS

On a collective basis, Gurkha veterans have formed self-organizations to
deal with various issues. It seems appropriate at this juncture to discuss the
efforts of the British Gurkha Welfare Society (BGWS) to deal with the civil–
military entanglement that they experience in the process of collective citizenship negotiation in national, subnational, and transnational contexts.

Established in 2003, the BGWS comprises the largest self-organization
of former Gurkhas, with more than three thousand members. The BGWS
is among the two Gurkha veterans' organizations whose views were
sought by the command secretary of the Adjutant General's Command
when revising the terms and conditions for Gurkhas in the mid-2000s
(Land Forces Secretariat 2006: 2-1).[19] The society is financed by membership fees, donations, and investment profits. It is headquartered in Farnborough, has branch offices in Forkestone, Maidstone, and London, and
has an office in Nepal. Its officials are chosen by election, and important
matters are decided by majority vote in conferences of regional representatives. Its headquarters is accommodated in a barrack-like building with
the chairman's office, a lounge, and a radio station inside and a barbecue
area outside.

The Activities of the BGWS in the Locality

Responding to the above-cited frictions, the BGWS is engaged in voluntary activities to build better community relations, and cooperates with
local government bodies such as the Rushmoor Borough Council, the Citizens Advice Bureau, and the Hampshire Police.

Although the BGWS is a civil organization, it seems to have received
hints regarding these activities from the practice of the Brigade of Gurkhas. For example, the BGWS offers local residents the chance to watch
performances of Nepalese dances, and dispatches its members to local
schools to teach Nepalese languages. Considering that, in the Brigade of
Gurkhas, the British officers are expected to respect and learn Nepalese
culture, the BGWS seems to expect locals to have the same understanding
of their culture as do British officers. Besides that, as a voluntary activ-

ity, its chairman sits on the governing board of the Oxfam Education and Lindley Educational Trust, nongovernmental educational organizations. The local government greatly appreciates these interactional activities, and the chairman of the BGWS was awarded the Operational Command Unit (OCU) Commander's Commendation by the chief superintendent of the OCU commander in the North and East Hampshire Constabulary on 26 January 2009. Thus, the BGWS has established itself as a civil-society organization of active citizens.

Service to the Members

The BGWS provides various services to its members and their families so that they can adapt to the change of positionality from soldiers to nonwhite immigrants, and transform themselves from heroic fighters to model citizens. Again, it applies the practice of the Brigade of Gurkhas to this situation. The BGWS's officials provide a variety of services as if it were a unit in the Brigade of Gurkhas. They provide paternal protection, guidance for becoming model citizens, and social space to members, and mediate between them and the British, as Gurkha officers do in the units. For example, the BGWS provides information on social benefits and benefits for veterans. The chairman, an immigration advisor authorized by the Office of the Immigration Services Commissioner (OISC), negotiates with immigration officials for Gurkha veterans' family reunions.[20] The chairman also provides educational advice to members who are having difficulties with childrearing to observe their children's behavior during after-school hours at the Chairman's Surgery. The BGWS throws a party to celebrate Dasain and creates social gatherings for members and their families, as do the units in the Brigade of Gurkhas. The BGWS arranges collective assistance to widowed members, just as the Family Unit officer in the Brigade of Gurkhas does. Finally, the BGWS airs Nepali programs through Radio BGWS, as the British Forces Broadcasting Service does in the major Gurkha stations.

Activities at the National Level

Gurkha veterans' citizenship negotiation at the national level is ongoing. As did the Gurkha Justice Campaign cited in the previous section, the BGWS uses the history of Gurkha military careers as a ground for negotiation.

In the past, the BGWS conducted campaigns for equal pensions at the national level and beyond. Regarding service after 2007, Gurkhas can choose the terms and conditions of the Gurkha Pension Scheme or the Armed Forces Pension Scheme (AFPS). The BGWS is also campaigning for the availability of choice for those who served before 2007 and has filed suits in the High Court, Court of Appeal, and the European Court of Human Rights, which in 2016 decided that the United Kingdom's legislation on Gurkha soldiers' pensions was not discriminatory (European Court of Human Justice 2016: 19–20; "Gurkhas Lose" 2008). The knowledge that the chairman acquired as a clerk of his unit on active service helped the BGWS prosecute the British government.

Currently, the BGWS attends the annual Remembrance Sunday in London on the second Sunday in November, an event to commemorate casualties in World War I and subsequent wars. On this day, the BGWS asks the attendees to wear items signifying Gurkha veterans' military careers and artificial remembrance poppies.

Negotiating for Legislation of Dual Citizenship under Nepalese Law

The BGWS is also involved in activities to maintain legal, political, and economic ties with Nepalese society.[21] The activities include the campaign for the retention of Nepalese citizenship.

The current version of the Nepalese Citizenship Act does not permit dual citizenship and requires those who obtain a foreign nationality or citizenship to renounce their Nepalese citizenship. Until 2007, foreign nationals could not own real estate or involve themselves with businesses in certain key fields, such as cottage industries. Therefore, upon attaining British citizenship, Gurkhas sold their property in Nepal and were required to obtain visas every time they visited children or parents left behind in Nepal. However, some Gurkha veteran entrepreneurs wish to invest capital in Nepal, while others are interested in the political movement of the ethnic peoples of the Tibet-Burman language groups in Nepal. Therefore, the veterans have been campaigning to retain Nepalese citizenship. Asking for the support of politicians, in 2009 the BGWS dispatched its own contingent to Nepal. Handing over a booklet entitled *The Current Gurkha Plight* (BGWS n.d.) to the president, prime minister, and politicians of major political parties, it claimed that because the Gurkhas had faced a great deal of trouble even after migrating to the United Kingdom, the Nepalese government should support them and allow them to retain their Nepalese citizenship. A Gurkha veteran said,

> The government of Nepal has an obligation to let our citizenship continue because they sent us. . . . Thus, the government of Nepal has to take care of the Gurkhas. If a factory sends its people to another factory, it takes care of them. . . . I will say to them [Nepalese officials and party politicians] again that the government of Nepal should say to us, "Don't give up your citizenship." But we say on the contrary. In wrong ways [*sic*]. (Fieldnote, 11 March 2013)

Thus, comparing Gurkha employment by the British armed forces to the "civil" employment of factory workers, Gurkha veterans have even constructed a demilitarized cause to persuade the Nepalese government to allow them to retain their Nepalese citizenship. This can be said to be one kind of civil–military entanglement created by Gurkhas themselves.

The veterans' campaign for dual citizenship means that Gurkhas try to link their military service to legal citizenships of two countries: the country that "sent" them for military service to a foreign nation, and the foreign state for which they performed that service. Beyond the imaginations of the state elites of the two countries, the Gurkhas' experience of defending the United Kingdom while maintaining ties with Nepalese society has led them to negotiating their citizenship under the two different citizenship regimes of the United Kingdom and Nepal. They thus resemble what Schiller (2005: 27) calls "transborder citizens," who live their lives across the borders of two or more nation-states and claim and act on a relationship with more than one government.

However, as cited above, in Nepal there is not much recognition of the Gurkhas' diplomatic role in defending Nepalese independence. Therefore, it would be difficult for the BGWS to successfully conduct the campaign for themselves alone. In its campaign for the retention of their Nepalese citizenship, the BGWS joins the Non-Resident Nepali Association (NRNA), a civil organization. The BGWS encourages its members to enroll in the NRNA.

The NRNA, established in 2003, consists of Nepalese expatriates scattered across seventy-eight countries as of December 2018 (except India); it aims to support Nepal's development and to promote Nepali immigrants' welfare.[22] The NRNA members believe that the capital, experience, skills, and knowledge they have gained on foreign soil could be used to develop Nepal. For the smooth transfer of these resources, they insist that the retention of Nepalese citizenship be necessary, even after naturalizing in other countries. The NRNA has dispatched teams to Nepal to lobby party politicians, ministers, and bureaucrats regarding various matters, including dual citizenship legislation in the new constitution or Citizenship Act. The above-cited Gurkha veteran led the campaign to retain Nepalese citizenship as the vice president of the NRNA and the head of the working group.

As a result of the campaign, the NRNA succeeded in legalizing the status called Non-resident Nepali, and their broad economic rights were stipulated in the Non-resident Nepali Act, which was passed in 2007. Moreover, Nepal's newly promulgated 2015 Constitution has institutionalized non-resident Nepali citizenship with economic, but not political, rights.

The Nepalese government is thought to have legalized non-resident Nepali citizenship in appreciation of the NRNA's help with earthquake relief activity and the expectation of emigrants' further contribution to Nepal's economic development—civil factors, not Gurkha-related factors.[23] Three weeks after the new constitution was declared, the Non-resident Nepali Global Conference was held by the Nepalese government, the NRNA, and the Federation of Nepalese Chambers of Commerce and Industry, but it did not address any issues in relation to Gurkhas' rights, as asserted by veterans. Nevertheless, their efforts were surely one of the engines that drove the NRNA's campaign. As of September 2017, the veterans' campaign was still working for dual full citizenship.

Conclusion

This chapter has examined civil–military entanglement using the case of citizenship negotiation by Gurkha veterans.

The modern ideology of linking military service with citizenship is the most promising factor for the politics of belonging of Gurkha veterans who had accomplished the military duties of citizens by defending the country before they in fact became citizens. However, their weak position as nonwhite immigrants from the informal British Empire has obliged them to conduct a context-determined citizenship negotiation at multiple levels and in a transnational setting.

In some contexts, they have used "military" things and reasoning to make their claim maximally persuasive, while in others they have used invisible but practical resources, skills, and knowledge acquired in their military careers. Otherwise, where it is more beneficial to demilitarize their claim, they have not used "things military" but developed "civil" discourse and cooperated with "civil" people or organizations. In so doing, they have redefined the civil and the military, blurred the boundary between the civil and the military, and gone back and forth across the boundary. The linkage of citizenship and military service is activated through the most relevant stakeholders' efforts to domesticate such civil–military entanglement.

Acknowledgments

Research permission from the Brigade of Gurkhas and the cooperation of the BGWS, the NRNA, the GAESO, and the Runnymede Trust made it possible for me to collect data and subsequently to write this chapter. I would like to thank everyone who aided and cooperated in this research. Any views or opinions expressed in this chapter are those of the author;

unless specifically attributed to an institution or organization, they do not in any way represent the views, opinions, or policies of them. The field and literary research and the writing of this essay were supported by the Japan Society for the Promotion of Science (JSPS) (JSPS KAKENHI, Grant Numbers JP19401047, JP20320134, JP23520998, JP24320175, and JP15K03054).

Taeko Uesugi teaches cultural anthropology at Senshu University, Tokyo. From March 2007 to January 2008, she was a visiting scholar at the School of Oriental and African Studies, University of London. Her publications include *Dividing up the Ancestral Tablets: Changing Ancestor Worship in the Nagano Region, Japan* (Daiichi Shobo, 2001, in Japanese) and "Re-examining Transnationalism from Below and Transnationalism from Above: British Gurkhas' Life Strategies and the Brigade of Gurkhas' Employment Policies," in *Nepalis Inside and Outside Nepal* (edited by Hiroshi Ishii, David N. Gellner, and Katsuo Nawa, Manohar, 2007).

Notes

1. An "ethnic security map" comprises the concentric circles that illustrate state elites' cognition of ethnic groups' potential for political mobilization, political reliability, and accessibility to the state apparatus (Enloe 1980: 23–24).
2. Ong (1996) reports that Chinese immigrants are controlled by states and other organizations at multiple levels in the United States. Here, the term "transnationalism" describes the process or phenomenon whereby multiple ties or interactions are constructed and maintained across national boundaries by people or institutions. It has been examined in migration studies since the 1990s.
3. Gallagher and Robinson (1953), who were a major influence for later scholars, did not give an exact definition. In my interpretation, Gallagher and Robinson (1953) use the term "informal British Empire" for territories that were not directly administered by the United Kingdom like colonies, dominions, and protectorates, but were forced to accept the principle of free trade due to the United Kingdom's hegemonic influence.
4. I referred for the theaters and years of Gurkhas' main deployments to the epitaph on the Gurkha Memorial statue located in London. "North East Frontier" and "North West Frontier" mean those of colonial India.
5. In order to clarify the difference of the current Indian Army, I add "British" in parentheses.
6. High-caste Hindus, some of whom represent less than 15 percent of Gurkhas, do not necessarily view Gurkha employment in a positive light.
7. Originally, a "Resident" was an official who supervised a native state as the proxy of the Viceroy in colonial India.
8. The prime minister is said to have remarked, "Does a friend desert a friend in a time of need? If you win, we win with you. If you lose, we lose with you" (Bullock 2009: 96; Gurkha Brigade Association n.d.).

9. The origin of the British Army's "militarized multiculturalism" (Ware 2014) can be found in this "divide and rule" policy in the (British) Indian Army.
10. Dasain is the most important Hindu festival celebrated in the Brigade of Gurkhas (Uesugi 2007; 2015).
11. "Gurkha major" is a post for a Gurkha officer who assists a battalion's commanding officer.
12. Gurkhas' take-home pay was increased by adding an overseas allowance to an amount equal to that of their British counterparts. However, the Gurkhas did not receive overseas allowances while staying in Nepal during furloughs.
13. All these changes coincided with the application of the Race Relations Act of 1976 to prevent discrimination on racial grounds (Land Forces Secretariat 2006) and the effectuation of the Employment Equality Regulations in 2003 with the integration of the European Employment Framework Directive into the British legal regime (Ware 2014: 135).
14. According to a source that has direct contact with an Indian officer, the British Army attempted to forge ties with the Indian Army through the Gurkhas. See British Army (2013: 22) for the definition of "Firm Base."
15. As cited above, the government had paid lower salaries and pensions to Gurkhas since they were based in Nepal; so settling more ex-Gurkhas in the United Kingdom was thought to possibly increase the overall amount of pensions paid.
16. Personal communication with Ms. Jessica Mai Sims of the Runnymede Trust.
17. I also encountered an old Gurkha veteran who did not qualify for a generous pension and lived in poverty in Farnborough.
18. Until 2006, all serving Gurkhas were male. McClatchey (2011) reported that the employment rate was particularly high among Gurkha veterans and their wives.
19. Another organization was the GAESO.
20. The migration of Gurkhas has engendered transnational families, divided by national borders. As Nepalese nationals over eighteen years old cannot stay as Gurkhas' dependents, they are obliged to remain in Nepal. The chairman of the BGWS wrote letters to the prime minister and MPs regarding the treatment of Gurkha veterans, family reunions, or acquisition of settlement rights by the United Kingdom Border Agency or the British Embassy in Kathmandu, using the letterhead of the BGWS with the mark of the OISC (BGWS n.d.).
21. For example, it conducts charity projects, such as building a Gurkha hospital for poor people in Nepal.
22. At the border between India and Nepal, no passport check is conducted, and people move freely back and forth; thus, the NRNA does not consider it necessary to have a branch in India.
23. On 25 April and 12 May 2015, large earthquakes hit Nepal.

References

Allen, V., and M. Hickley. 2008. "Joanna Lumley Celebrates Victory for Gurkhas as They Win Legal Battle to Stay in Britain." *MailOnline*, 1 October 2008. Accessed 27 January 2010, https://www.dailymail.co.uk/news/article-1065117/Joanna-Lumley-celebrates-victory-Gurkhas-win-legal-battle-stay-Britain.html.

Bailey, C. 2008. "Joanna Lumley to Present Gurkha Petition to Government." *Telegraph*, 20 November 2008. Accessed 22 November 2009, https://www.telegraph.co.uk/news/celebritynews/3486948/6.15AM-Joanna-Lumley-to-present-Gurkha-petition-to-government.html.

Banskota, P. P. 1994. *The Gurkha Connection: A History of the Gurkha Recruitment in the British Indian Army*. Jaipur: Nirala Publications.

Basch, L., N. G. Schiller, and C. S. Blanc. 1994. *Nations Unbound: Transnational Projects, Postcolonial Predicaments and Deterritorialized Nation-States*. New York: Gordon & Breach.

Berry, M. F. 1977. *Military Necessity and Civil Rights Policy: Black Citizenship and the Constitution, 1861–1868*. New York: Kennikat Press.

BGWS (British Gurkha Welfare Society). n.d. *The Current Gurkha Plight*. Booklet obtained 26 April 2013.

British Army. 2015. "British Gurkhas: Nepal." Army website. Accessed 2 December 2018, https://www.army.mod.uk/who-we-are/corps-regiments-and-units/brigade-of-gurkhas/british-gurkhas-nepal/.

Brubaker, R. 2016. "Migration, Membership, and the Nation-State." In R. Brubaker, *Globalizing World and the Politics of Belonging: Migrants, Citizenship and Nation-State*, translated into Japanese by Shigeki Sato et al., 37–64. Tokyo: Akashi Shoten.

Bullock, C. 2009. *Britain's Gurkhas*. London: Third Millennium Publishing.

Caplan, L. 1995. *Warrior Gentleman: "Gurkhas" in the Western Imagination*. Providence: Berghahn.

Castle, P. 2011. "Howarth Hits Back at Lib Dem's Criticism." *getHAMPSHIRE*, 11 March 2011. Accessed 27 March 2011, http://www.gethampshire.co.U.K./news/local-news/howarth-hits-back-lib-dems-5349339.

Des Chene, M. K. 1991. "Relics of Empire: A Cultural History of Gurkhas, 1815–1987." Ph.D. diss., Stanford University, Stanford, CA, USA.

Enloe, C. H. 1980. *Ethnic Soldiers: State Security in Divided Societies*. Athens: University of Georgia Press.

European Court of Human Justice. 2016. *Information Note on the Court's Case-Law* 199 (August–September 2016). Accessed 21 July 2017, http://www.echr.coe.int/Documents/CLIN_2016_09_199_ENG.pdf.

Fletcher, H. 2008. "Gurkha Veterans Fight for Equal Rights." *TimesOnline*, 20 March 2008. Accessed 31 March 2018, http://www.freerepublic.com/focus/f-news/1988589/posts.

Gallagher, J., and R. Robinson. 1953. "The Imperialism of Free Trade." *The Economic History Review* n.s. 6 (1): 1–15. Accessed 8 February 2018, https://www.jstor.org/stable/2591017?seq=3#page_scan_tab_contents.

Glick Schiller, N., and G. Fouron. 1998. "Transnational Lives and National Identities: The Identity Politics of Haitian Immigrants." In M. P. Smith and L. E. Guarnizo (eds.), *Transnationalism from Below*, 130–61. New Brunswick: Transaction Publishers.

Gurkha Brigade Association. n.d. "The Second World War." Gurkha Brigade Association website. Accessed 25 February 2018, http://www.gurkhabde.com/the-second-world-war/.

"Gurkhas' Charity Launched in Town." 2009. *BBC News*, 22 January 2009. Accessed 11 February 2009, http://news.bbc.co.U.K./2/hi/U.K._news/england/berkshire/77845126.stm.

"Gurkhas Lose U.K. Army Pension Fight." 2008. eKantipur.com, 22 July 2008. Accessed 4 July 2008, http://www.kantipuronline.com/kolnews.php?&nid=152333.

"Gurkha War Hero Allowed to Stay in U.K. after Home Office U-turn." 2007. *MailOnline*, 1 June 2007. Accessed 23 January 2010, https://www.dailymail.co.uk/news/article-457426/Gurkha-war-hero-allowed-stay-UK-Home-Office-U-turn.html.

Gurung, H. 1997. "State and Society in Nepal." In D. N. Gellner, J. Pfaff-Czarnecka, and J. Whelpton (eds.), *Nationalism and Ethnicity in a Hindu Kingdom: The Politics of Culture in Contemporary Nepal*, 495–532. Amsterdam: Harwood Academic Publishers.

"Hampshire MP Gerald Howarth's Letter Re: Nepalese Immigration to the PM in Full." 2011. *Gurkha.com*, 14 February 2011. Accessed 15 February 2011, http://www.gurkhas.com/ShowArticle.aspx?ID=1518.

Howe+Co Solicitors. 2015. "About Us." Accessed 27 October 2015, http://www.howe.co.uk/our-company.html.

Irvine, C. 2009. "Gurkhas Drafted to Repair Britain's Railways." *Telegraph*, 23 January 2009. Accessed 22 November 2009, https://www.telegraph.co.uk/news/newstopics/onthefro ntline/4318665/Gurkhas-drafted-to-repair-Britains-railways.html.

Izuyama, M. 1999. "British Imperial Strategy and the Gurkha Negotiations." *Journal of the Japanese Association for South Asian Studies* 11: 51–70.

Jenkins, S. 2009. "Sir Humphrey Would Never Let His Minister Be Ambushed by Gurkhas." *Guardian.com*, 21 May 2009. Accessed 26 February 2010, https://www.theguardian.com/commentisfree/2009/may/21/gurkhas-government-lumley-gordon-brown.

Jones, D. 2014. "Joanna Lumley's Legacy of Misery: She Fought to Allow Retired Gurkhas into Britain with Her Heart in the Right Place. Five Years On, Even They Say It's Back-fired Terribly." *Daily Mail*, 14 November 2014. Accessed 18 November 2014, https://www.dailymail.co.uk/news/article-2835216/Joanna-Lumley-s-legacy-misery-fought-al low-retired-Gurkhas-Britain-heart-right-place-Five-years-say-s-backfired-terribly.html.

Krebs, R. R. 2006. *Fighting for Rights: Military Service and the Politics of Citizenship*. Ithaca: Cornell University Press.

Land Forces Secretariat. 2006. *A Review of Gurkha Terms and Conditions of Service*. D/LF SEC(GURKHAS) 1407.

Loveman, M. 2005. "The Modern State and the Primitive Accumulation of Symbolic Power." *American Journal of Sociology* 110: 1651–83.

McClatchey, C. 2011. "How Gurkhas Came to Be Britain's New Security Army." *BBC News*, 14 November 2011. Accessed 25 October 2015, https://www.bbc.com/news/magazine-15634938.

Naughton, P. 2008. "Gurkhas Celebrate Court Win for Right to Settle in Britain." *Times On-line*, 30 September 2008. Accessed 10 October 2008, https://www.thetimes.co.uk/article/gurkhas-celebrate-court-win-for-right-to-settle-in-britain-s5kkhv0jjxs.

Ong, A. 1996. "Cultural Citizenship as Subject-Making." *Current Anthropology* 37(5): 737–62.

Onta, P. R. 1996. "The Politics of Bravery: A History of Nepali Nationalism." Ph.D. diss. Phil-adelphia: University of Pennsylvania.

Pierce, A., and J. Kirkup. 2009. "Duchess of Cornwall Backs Campaign against Government's Treatment of Gurkhas." *Telegraph*, 5 May 2009. Accessed 22 November 2009, https://www.telegraph.co.uk/news/uknews/theroyalfamily/5279989/Duchess-of-Cornwall-backs-campaign-against-Governments-treatment-of-Gurkhas.html.

"Public Opinion in Favour of the Gurkhas Shows That Political Leaders Don't 'Get It'." 2009. *The Telegraph*, 1 May. Accessed 10 January 2009, https://www.telegraph.co.uk/comme nt/letters/5252014/Public-opinion-in-favour-of-the-Gurkhas-shows-that-political-lead ers-dont-get-it.html.

Ragsdale, T. A. 1989. *Once a Hermit Kingdom: Ethnicity, Education, and National Integration in Nepal*. New Delhi: Manohar.

Rush, A. S., and C. V. Reed. 2014. "Imperial Citizenship in a British World." In E. F. Isin and P. Nyers (eds.), 498–507. *Routledge Handbook of Global Citizenship Studies*. London: Routledge.

Salter, J. 2008. "Gurkhas Honoured by Statue in Garrison Town." *Telegraph*, 2 October 2008. Accessed 22 November 2009, https://www.telegraph.co.uk/news/3118560/Gurkhas-honoured-by-statue-in-garrison-town.html.

Schiller, N. G. 2005 "Transborder Citizenship: An Outcome of Legal Pluralism within Trans-national Social Fields." In F. B. Beckmann and K. B. Beckmann (eds.), *Mobile People, Mobile Law: Expanding Legal Relations in a Contracting World*. London: Ashgate. Accessed 6 September 2017 from eScholarhip, University of California.

Streets, H. 2004. *Martial Races: The Military, Race and Masculinity in British Imperial Culture, 1857–1914*. Manchester: Manchester University Press.

Uesugi, T. 2007. "Re-examining Transnationalism from Below and Transnationalism from Above: British Gurkhas' Life Strategies and the Brigade of Gurkhas' Employment Policies." In H. Ishii, D. N. Gellner, and K. Nawa (eds.), *Nepalis Inside and Outside Nepal*, 383–410. New Delhi: Manohar.

———. 2015. "How Have Gurkha Veterans Become British Citizens? Immigrant Veterans' Multiple Self-Inclusions and Reconstruction of Citizenship" [in Japanese]. In M. Tanaka (ed.), *Cultural Anthropology of the Military*, 459–485. Tokyo: Fukyo-sha.

Vansittart, E. [1890] 1993. *The Gurkhas*. New Delhi: Anmol Publications.

Ware, V. 2014. *Military Migrants Fighting for YOUR Country*. Basingstoke: Palgrave Macmillan

Chapter 7

Civil–Military Relations from International Conflict Zones to the United States

Notes on Mutual Discontents and Disruptive Logics

Robert A. Rubinstein and Corri Zoli

Introduction

Civil–military relations in the United States are much more militarized today than they were thirty years ago. In this chapter we take stock of one way this came about. We describe how efforts to improve humanitarian action and warfighting by taking a "cultural turn" created a web of relationships that at first entangled and later entrapped institutions and actors. The processes involved began in the 1990s and accelerated as the "cultural turn" became more central to post-9/11 security developments in the United States. Thus we consider the mutual dependences and dependencies attendant to these processes and consider the emergence of the militarization of local policing an exemplar of the broader societal arrangements they entailed.

Since 9/11, the patterns of civil–military interactions that have characterized institutional relations between the military and civil society in the United States have changed, prompting concerns that once separate, bounded spheres of social and political life have become increasingly convergent and fraught (Adams and Murray 2014; Hart 2013; Feaver 2009). To understand how security developments over the last three decades have contributed to these shifting boundaries in traditionally separated realms

---

Notes for this chapter begin on page 160.

of military and civilian spheres in the United States, we examine linked international and domestic developments: the militarization of humanitarian action in the post-9/11 wars of Afghanistan and Iraq, and the militarization of policing efforts at home, including disruptive responses to them. We also situate each of these developments in the context of the "cultural turn"— the institutional moments in which culture and cross-cultural understanding is made the focus of security policy responses and interventions.

In focusing on these security shifts, we are interested in the ways in which the thickening entanglements that flow from military and civilian organizational efforts to collaborate spread from military strategic initiatives abroad to local law enforcement trends at home—with unexpected effects. To flesh out these developments, we focus on several examples. In the international context, we examine, first, coordinated cross-cultural military and civilian humanitarian efforts to improve crisis response to complex emergencies in conflict and postconflict settings, and, second, the role of cross-cultural understanding as a military strategic framework adapted by the United States Department of Defense (DoD) to address setbacks in the wars in Afghanistan and Iraq. These instances reveal well-intentioned efforts by both military and civilian organizations in conflict settings to use culture as a strategic tool to advance respective mission priorities. We then turn to homeland security developments in the United States in which the military "cultural turn" abroad come to shape domestic policing policy at home in ways that often reveal the extension of military logics to emergency responses. As may be expected, none of these developments are without their discontents and disruptions.

In conducting our investigation, we have narrowed our engagement with the current voluminous social science literature on U.S. civil–military relations to the process of interactions occurring between federal institutions and matériel. We adapt Hodder's (2016) conceptualization of entanglement—the dialectic of dependence and dependency between humans and things—as one of our main interpretive threads for making sense of the changes in how U.S. military and law enforcement agencies work together with civilian organizations. In the course of such collaborative work, both civilian organizations and military actors make local operational adjustments in their efforts to work more effectively together, thus, creating entanglements.

We also show, however, that as military and law enforcement agencies pragmatically try to improve their efficacy by collaborating with civilian organizations, these engagements may bind the two organizations together into a dynamic system, whose very organizational structures may then come to "trap" or constrain future actions. Entrapment, as Hodder (2016: 67) explains, describes the ways in which "particular investments and networks of resources" can trap agents into constrained relationships that far exceed the original purpose of the collaboration. Hodder's description of the movement from entanglement to entrapment also resonates with Bateson's (1979: 67) observation that "for all objects and experiences, there is a quantity that has optimum value," but "above that quantity, the variable becomes toxic." In effect, such entanglement and entrapment dynamics—born out of well-intentioned efforts to create cultural interoperability—have far-reaching implications for military and policing policies and practices. By examining cross-cultural collaboration in these areas of U.S. security policy and practice, one can see important dynamics whereby organizational collaboration both enables and constrains actions. Such civil–military entanglements may also result in making permeable previously discrete boundaries between categories, resulting in new forms of matériel and organizational activity reflected in policing.

One broader theoretical implication of this work, consistent with that of Ingold (2010), Bateson (1979), and Laughlin (2017), is that distinctions among categories do not form absolute boundaries, especially when moving between levels of analysis, but are permeable, their contents changeable through interaction. This does not mean that the categories are of no importance. To the contrary, categories inform social action (Zerubavel 1991), yet categories may be blended, thus, reframing the meaning of action. Importantly, blending creates entanglements leading to new ways of organizing and understanding social life. In other words, in addition to actions and practice, cognitive blending is one of the mechanisms though which entanglement arises. Yet, when blending occurs, social actors may find the value of the blend to be less than that of its component parts (Coulson 2001) or uncomfortable, even perceived as a category error (Ryle 1949), which describes the point at which entanglement becomes entrapment. Whether the entanglements that result from category blending are a boon or a bane depends on whether they facilitate or dominate action, in a pragmatic sense (cf. James 1907, Rubinstein et al. 1984, Rubinstein 1991, Wimsatt 2007). Local operational adjustments made by humanitarian, law enforcement, and military organizations in their efforts to work across boundaries by taking a cultural turn creates such potentially effective or disruptive entanglements and entrapments with effects on these activities, their perception, and those involved in them.

The "Cultural Turn" in Warfighting and Humanitarian Intervention

After initial successes in the wars in Afghanistan and Iraq, the U.S. military faced setbacks as local and proxy resistance movements led to insurgencies in both places. As these setbacks became increasingly serious, these military strategic failings were often attributed to a lack of cross-cultural understanding. In a pragmatic move, the Department of Defense embraced cultural explanations for on-the-ground military strategic matters in what ultimately became a reified notion of culture as a strategic tool for advancing military and stabilization missions (Gray 1999; Dept. of the Army 2011; Norris 2012; U.S. Army Combined Arms Center 2012; Rosen 2011). Likewise, broad-based postconflict reconstruction projects involved intensive culture-based efforts and cross-cultural understanding initiatives, which played an equally significant and often troubled role in these missions.

The emergence of culture as a category of concern for contemporary civil–military relations arises out of multidisciplinary attempts to make sense of the role of culture in new forms of warfare, often associated with both the attacks of 9/11 and their aftermath, including direct U.S. interventions and counterinsurgent forms of warfare.

Once U.S. governmental leadership identified a gap in cultural understanding, significant efforts were undertaken to bring a variety of military units and civilian organizations into close contact (Rubinstein, Keller, and Scherger 2008), leading to the pragmatic choice that they work together for practical advantage. Some military and civilian organizations adjusted their on-the-ground ways of engaging in the world drawing on static, reified conceptions of culture, and used these for a variety of purposes, from setting up civilian affairs and civilian engagement teams to incorporating local municipal authorities directly in conflict resolution efforts and reconstruction planning. Thus, these adjustments aimed to make joint action more successful, creating interdependencies among government and civilian agencies and between U.S. government and local partners.

Attempts at improving their joint action were instantiated as arrangements for better understanding each other's organizational cultures. The changes were mainly at the operational and tactical level, but those also affected strategic perspectives (Rubinstein 2008), again creating entanglements among them. But military–civilian interactions in the field ultimately affected conceptions of risk and response at broader levels, entrapping these actors in mutual dependencies. Thus the post-9/11 embrace of a reified notion of culture brought with it unintended consequences, both for the military in theater, for peacebuilding initiatives (Rubinstein 2005), for conflict and postconflict reconstruction efforts, and for U.S. civil society in the aftermath of these wars—a much less appreciated development.

While civil–military entanglements create tensions that are at times deeply challenging, the story of civil–military entrapment is neither simple nor one-sided. There is a fairly robust accounting of how the cultural turn, relying on similar reified notions of cultural understanding and collaboration, created mutual dependencies between U.S./coalition military forces in both Iraq and Afghanistan and humanitarian organizations. Results in these cases were both complex and divergent (Rubinstein 2014). On the military side, for instance, the insistence that leaders needed to know the culture (reified and stereotyped) led to a push for closer understanding, coordination, even integration, with humanitarian NGOs working in their area of operations, and to militaries engaging in humanitarian-like activities (which went by various names, such as "Quick Impact Projects"). This pattern of practices prompted shared efforts to educate or retrain military personnel so that they better understood and respected the core values held by humanitarian organizations.

As part of these collaborative efforts, humanitarian actors have also invested in trying to figure out how to collaborate more effectively with military counterparts (The Sphere Project 2010) and to gain organizational understanding of the military, often seeking to link to a reified notion of military culture, by learning how militaries approach problem solving, with emphasis on security infrastructure, training, and logistics. Such learning efforts have paralleled the use of military resources and assets, especially for humanitarian organizations' basic security in conflict zones, to ensure personnel security and to achieve humanitarian goals, especially in complex operational theaters.

Entanglements in Military–Humanitarian Interactions: Phases in Military–Civilian Cooperation and Counterinsurgency (COIN) Doctrine

Adjustments made by humanitarian workers and militaries to allow better cooperation in the field have quite naturally been affected by the organizational cultures of each group. At first, these adjustments—framed as cultural understanding—contributed to better outcomes for humanitarians and for militaries. As these efforts became more institutionalized, they took on a life of their own, shaping and constraining the practices and relations among the people involved.

Shortly after the fall of the Soviet Union, a number of conflicts erupted either following or leading to complex emergencies—humanitarian crises in settings where political authority has broken down. In those situations, humanitarian workers and military interveners operated simultaneously in environments that were extremely violent and where security was hard to guarantee. In those settings—like Somalia and the former Yugoslavia—humanitarian actors often found themselves relying on military counterparts to protect some of their efforts. This led to some cooperation in the field, which we will call phase one cooperation—limited, pragmatic, and situational—but not always successful or welcomed by humanitarian organizations. Phase one cooperation also did not necessarily provide "best practices" or implicit guidelines for future collaborative efforts, but it did increase the dependence of humanitarian organizations on military resources and matériel.

Nevertheless, in the decade of the 1990s, considerable attention was devoted to trying to make the coordination between military and humanitarian actors go more smoothly in what we describe as a phase two collaborative effort. A considerable literature developed around this topic (e.g., Aall, Miltenberger, and Weiss 2000) as the U.S. Department of Defense and humanitarian organizations individually and collectively engaged the challenges of coordination, often framed, in a static and stereotyped way, as a problem of cross-cultural communication (Rife 1998; Davis and Paparone 2012). These often program-based initiatives focused on educating respective communities about the organizational and value differences that made collaboration in the field difficult. For example, training programs for humanitarians introduced them to military commitments, unity of command, and the hierarchical rank system. Training programs for military actors focused on explaining humanitarian commitments and the organizational structures and dynamics of civilian organizations. These phase two efforts intensified the web of relationships between humanitarian and military actors, making their entanglement both broader and denser.

Phase three collaborative efforts were implicit in some of the early humanitarian critiques of phase two collaboration. From the beginning, some humanitarians argued that coordination with militaries would be fundamentally disruptive, not only of the humanitarian mission, but of the organizational dynamics and roles that enable and ground that mission (e.g., de Waal 1995). Until the 2000s, their argument rested on the observation that the simple fact of humanitarians being seen cooperating with military units would confuse local populations (e.g., Sida 2005), and since humanitarians' effectiveness depended on this perception of their neutrality, a blurring of organizational identity would occur that some feared would put both humanitarians and the humanitarian enterprise at risk. Insofar as the levels of interaction characterizing military–humanitarian interaction in the 1990s were low and largely relationships of situational convenience, such as the provision by military units of security for humanitarian convoys, these concerns associated with phase three collaboration in the blurring of organizational mission and identity remained more fear than demonstrated reality. This changed in the 2000s, and entanglement became entrapment.

In the context of the response to 11 September 2001, and U.S./coalition interventions in Afghanistan, and later Iraq, humanitarian organizations and military units found themselves increasing their engagements in theater significantly, and in that process turning to the lessons learned in the 1990s to coordinate more effectively. Given the complexity of the missions undertaken in Iraq and Afghanistan, which included both broad-scale military kinetic missions, as well as sociocultural, political, and reconstruction initiatives, such collaboration promised to be especially challenging.

There were essentially three lines along which such collaborations held potential risks that could result in blurred organizational missions and identities, which could undermine both organizations' goals in theater, yet propelled further activities. First and foremost, there was a concerted, intentional effort among many humanitarian organizations and military partners to push for deeper, integrated collaborations among military and civilian experts in recognition of the challenging circumstances they faced—countering irregular, transnational actors who attacked "soft targets" among local communities, while rebuilding such nations so as to prevent them from providing safe havens for such conflict actors.[1] Military analysts often referred to this multipronged challenge as national building "under fire" (Gompert et al. 2009; Lawson Stearns et al. 2010). As the wars in both Afghanistan and Iraq progressed, these dynamics only increased, as insurgencies dug in, organized, and even banded together, often with the assistance of foreign fighters and other actors. This transformed the U.S./coalition effort into a counterinsurgency-style conflict in which the U.S. military increasingly adopted a form of "population-centric" warfare in both theaters.

Even before COIN doctrine placed "winning the population" at the center of the military campaign, Provincial Reconstruction Teams (PRTs) were designed to embed with local communities, and hearty reconstruction and development programs were unleashed at the local-municipal levels, amounting to trillions of dollars invested, as detailed in the Special Inspector General for Afghanistan Reconstruction (SIGAR) 2013 and 2016 reports. In the context of trying to fight a multifront war—at once political, military-kinetic, cultural, and even regional—the U.S. military leaned hard on humanitarian actors as force multipliers, working with them strategically. Although many humanitarian organizations, especially Médecins Sans Frontières / Doctors Without Borders, resisted allying with the military for many reasons, several influential humanitarian organizations embraced this relationship, even if they did so cautiously or with reservations (de Waal 2013: 296). The move from entanglement to entrapment is probably most clearly seen in the changing kinds of skills, experiences, and expertise that humanitarian organizations built into their job descriptions (Autesserre 2014). Recognizing that former military members had organizational and logistical skills and security experiences that could be valuable to them, those organizations sought to employ former military members for their technical expertise.

A second area of potential risk involved military units increasingly acting as providers of humanitarian aid—either offering direct-aid programs or supporting humanitarian groups for large-scale projects—thus adding another layer to blurred lines of humanitarian and military missions and identities, as well as confusion in traditional roles and responsibilities. Working from the belief that humanitarian and development assistance could help forces "win hearts and minds" and achieve international development goals, the humanitarian–military divide was often totally collapsed—exemplified in such mechanisms as fielding Provincial Reconstruction Teams (PRTs).

Third, the logic of improving coordination between military and humanitarian actors brought with it the promise that doing so would be good for both organizations and for the local communities served. From the humanitarian perspective, improved humanitarian–military relations might benefit those hard-to-reach communities most in need, whether due to insecure settings or lack of infrastructure, if coordination could make the delivery of assistance more feasible, streamlined, and effective.

The results of applying this phase three integrative logic have, however, not in the main lead to such hopeful results. Rather, the fruits of these entanglements and entrapments are that the organizational cultures of some humanitarian agencies have begun to change in response to privileging the logics and logistics of prioritizing security, brought to them by the influence of military–humanitarian partnerships, or by the expertise of former military personnel integrated into these humanitarian organizations who apply such military expertise to problems faced in the field. That is to say, they have organized themselves in the service of the affordances that these partnerships made possible. So, for example, concern with the technical aspects of security and logistics leads to a restricted scope in humanitarian agencies' actions. That is, where they will go and how they will go there to render assistance was often subtly reshaped by military-mission sensibilities newly incorporated into their own structure. At the same time, activities like "quick impact" projects and PRTs have had the effect of militarizing humanitarian projects and identities, even putting at risk humanitarians who act in complex emergencies.

Perhaps inevitably, the two and a half decades of applying the logic of cooperation, coordination, and integration did not play out as predicted, for the arc of these efforts shows once again that the dynamics of social life are not just the results of rational actions and predetermined decisions. Indeed, as Hodder (2016), Ingold (2010), and Bateson (1979) suggest, such a web of relationships creates unanticipated emergent products from the complex interdependent system. In the case of humanitarian action, the nature of the dependencies resulting from military entanglement has been distorted by many factors, notably the power differentials between military actors and humanitarians. The complex conflict and emergency settings in which such partnerships were supposed to work also often turned into "practical messes" (see Hodder 2016: 66). Generally speaking, humanitarianism has become a more militarized activity than it was just two decades ago—a development owing in part to the changing nature of post–Cold War conflict settings. As a result of the spreading entanglements wrought by the logic of coordination brought to military–humanitarian interaction, this has been disruptive to the basic functioning of the humanitarian community and associated with the rise of attacks on humanitarian workers (deWaal 2013; Rubinstein and Zoli, in press).

The ill effects of such disruption has also had negative or, at the least, mixed results for military organizations—notably, in recent years, the elemental cultural and humanitarian priorities of COIN doctrine have been downgraded in army planning and projection documents and in national security policy priorities.

The operational and tactical changes that flow from efforts to coordinate also have had ramifications in larger contexts. Principally, the effects have been to shift the logics applied in response to crises from considering whether and what kind of action should be undertaken to a default for intervention, though this is changing. Instead of focusing on the local effects of changes in relationships among military and civilian actors, there is now a presumption that militarized humanitarian intervention is legitimate if it meets certain abstract criteria, such as "just war" criteria (Seybolt 2008) rather than on the pragmatic evaluation of the lived experiences of communities or the shifts in organizational culture to better support military–civilian coordination. Similarly, although Fassin and Pandolfi (2008) are critical of the presumption for military intervention, their objections are built around what they see as the "extralegal" use of intervention, preferring intervention that has been legitimated by the authorization of appropriate international legal institutions, such as the United Nations Security Council. Their argument marks a shift away from the ethnographic particular to broader global and legal governance concerns bound up with the legitimacy of interventions. In this focus, they also conflate responses to disasters and conflicts, seeing them as equally embedded in the politics of the "global logic of intervention" (Fassin and Pandolfi 2008: 10; Keen 2008).

In contrast, observations of particular interventions reveal that responses to disaster and to conflicts are very different ethnographically (Duffield

1994), and responses to both kinetic and humanitarian interventions on the ground have highly localized and unexpected effects. What this shift of focus signifies for us is that the blending of categories of military and civilian humanitarian action prompted a shift in the broader cultural predisposition to militarize responses, a development that is not always effective or manageable for either military or humanitarian organizations (see, e.g., Rubinstein and Zoli, in press).

Entrapment: From National Security Reticence about Standing Armies to Militarizing the Local

For most of its history, the United States has been organized institutionally as anything but a national security state, as that term implies the predominance of national security priorities above all other socioeconomic affairs (Mares 2007: 387–88; Stuart 2008; Katzenstein 1996). Early on in the republic's history, the Continental Army, Navy, and Marines, constituted by the Thirteen Colonies' Second Continental Congress in 1775, were designed to combat British rule (Kohn 1975: 41) and then were permanently demobilized in the aftermath of the Treaty of Paris in 1783, whose first article providing for U.S. independence from Britain is still in force. The newly adopted constitution granted to Congress the power to "raise and support armies"—precisely because the assumption was that "standing armies," notoriously "dangerous to liberty" in early Anglo-American political thought, would not automatically exist.[2] Such early existential suspicion of a permanent national military not only pervades foundational debates, but frames formal, law-based civil–military relations and specific limited mobilizations of militia and, later, federal forces throughout the nineteenth and early twentieth centuries. As Adler and Keller (2014: 172) note, "A resistance to standing armies was at the heart of the revolutionary ideology of America."

It was only with the Second World War, as Jablonsky (2002–2003) describes, that the modern organizational arrangement of the military was expanded, in large part through the National Security Act of 1947, alongside the very broad conception of national security with "social, political, economic, and military implications" (Jablonsky 2003: 5). One lasting puzzle at the intersection of American political history and modern national security policy remains in this transformation in civil–military relations, given such early American antipathy to a meddling military in civilian affairs—a worry exemplified in enumerated grievances against King George III who had "quarter[ed] large bodies of armed troops among us" and "affected to render the Military independent of and superior to the Civil Power" (Declaration of Independence; Banks and Dycus 2016).

Following 9/11, perceptions of the external threats facing the homeland and conceptions of U.S. national security shifted drastically, propelled in part by the cultural turn described earlier. The risk and threat of terrorism emerged as a national narrative, which was soon translated into national strategy documents with terms such as "Global War on Terror." The effects of this framing were almost immediately felt in the ways that state and local first responders related to federal government mandates (Fosher 2008) in light of the expansion of lawful foreign intelligence surveillance authorities associated with the U.S.A. Patriot Act of 2001 and the Homeland Security Act of 2002, which significantly reorganized the security and intelligence communities.

While these shifting security laws and policies coincided with the ongoing war in Afghanistan in 2001 and the subsequent invasion of Iraq in 2003, these conflicts in turn created a range of opportunities with implications for humanitarian collaborative efforts, with a pronounced role for economic opportunities for a wide range of contractors and consultants who supplied expertise and services to support and enhance military efforts on the ground. The militarization of humanitarian efforts, described above, was one result of these developments. In addition, a considerable amount of military matériel was required for the conduct of these wars — some of which found its way back into the U.S. homeland through the evolving relationship between the national security apparatus in local law enforcement and policing initiatives.

The militarization of policing in the United States has long been a concern for civil libertarians and others. In the last decades of the 2000s, militarization of policing was driven in part by the cooperation between the military and police departments allowed by the 1981 Military Cooperation with Law Enforcement Act, a response in part to the desire for more effective drug enforcement (Hall and Coyne 2013). The continued militarization of policing was further encouraged by federal programs that allowed additional cooperation between law enforcement agencies and the military. Those programs include especially the 1033 Program under the auspices of the Department of Defense, which allowed the transfer of military matériel to local police departments, and, after the bureaucratic reorganizations that followed 9/11, the Department of Homeland Security's Grant Program, meant to allow local law enforcement agencies to better prepare to prevent and respond to terrorism threats (ACLU 2014).

From 2006 to 2015, the value of transferred military equipment to local police departments accounted for $2.2 billion dollars. This included "helicopters and airplanes, armored trucks and cars, tens of thousands of

M16/M14 rifles, thousands of bayonets, mine detectors, and other types of weaponry" (Open the Books 2016). Much of this redistributed military matériel was made surplus by the winding down of the large-scale conventional campaigns in Iraq and Afghanistan. This transfer of military equipment has importantly been paralleled by the militarization of the tactics used by local police, both initiatives understood as necessary given post-9/11 national security threat assessments that included homegrown terrorism.

The confluence of these changes—reframing national security law and policy priorities, law enforcement tactical innovations reliant on military–law enforcement collaborations, and the acquisition of military equipment and techniques from combat zones—helped to reinforce the sense of a militarized response to the heightened risks associated with the global threat of terrorism and large scale catastrophic events (as in the case of Hurricane Katrina in 2005). Scholars and analysts are still trying to understand these relationships and their meaning, including for federal agencies charged with providing for public safety, particularly in relation to terrorism. While there are a range of complex policy, empirical, and institutional developments here, there is little doubt that the role of militarized response in relation to risk perception is part of the emerging picture, reflecting what Giddens (1999: 26) calls manufactured risk—that is, "risk created by the impact of our own developing knowledge upon the world . . . [in] situations which we have very little historical experience confronting." To a considerable extent, these shifts can be traced to the ways in which the cultural turn entrapped American society into the organizational networks associated with military matériel and the need to dispose of resulting surpluses.

Worrisome to many is when this reshaping of local conceptions of risk—bound up with broader national and even global security developments—are glossed as unbounded fears, or more broadly fear of difference, particularly in cultural or identity-oriented terms. A number of studies have demonstrated that militarized police tactics in conjunction with acquiring military equipment can contribute to threat-oriented forms of ethnic, racial, and economic discrimination in policing, evident in work associated with the Minority Threat Hypothesis (see Blalock 1967; Ferrandino 2015; and Rudell and Thomas 2010). Such perceptions of risk, seeing threats to safety as residing in specific minority communities (defined culturally, religiously, by neighborhoods and geographic locations, etc.), which then must be aggressively managed, can create severe, often counterproductive tensions during times of crisis in the delicate balance between civil liberties and public order. Some studies have begun to examine the degree to which such factors contribute to police killings throughout the United States (e.g., Dansky 2016). In this case, the militarization of local law enforcement can contribute to disrupting the history and logic of community–police relations and accordingly create discontent and underserved communities within the polity.

An example of this matériel militarization is seen in Syracuse, New York, a city of just fewer than 145 thousand people. Like many cities in the northeast of the United States that once had robust manufacturing-based economies, Syracuse is now a "rustbelt" city in distress. It is one of the ten cities with the most abandoned homes (Herbert 2014), and more than half of its public schools have been documented as "failing" (New York Department of Education 2015); it has among the highest levels of lead poisoning in the United States, one of the highest per capita murder rates in New York State (Lane et al. 2017), and the "highest level of poverty concentration among blacks and Hispanics of the one hundred largest metropolitan areas" (Jargowsky 2015:8) in the United States. All of these challenges are best addressed through public policy and community-engagement initiatives that build the cultural, social, and economic capital of the community. Yet, according to the U.S. Defense Logistics Agency, the city police department received a little over three-quarters of a million dollars in military equipment, including a mine-resistant vehicle. These are in addition to the military matériel and training received by other agencies in Onondaga County, the county of which Syracuse is the capitol.

Entrapment: Disruptive to Military Logics

Yet part of the story of changing security and culture logics, particularly in the post-9/11 security environment, involves important and underappreciated instances of disruption, including unexpected and critically reflective actors intervening in these security developments. The term disruption, as we use it following Christensen (2006), refers to any social innovation that transforms traditional value networks and thus practices.

U.S. Military Veterans as Critics of Militarized Policing

"The first thing that went wrong was when the police showed up with K-9 units," King told a journalist on the scene. "The dogs played on racist imagery . . . it played the situation up and [the police department] wasn't cognizant of the imagery." In the days following the 2014 Ferguson, Missouri, protests of the fatal shooting of eighteen-year-old Michael Brown, Scriven King, a ten-year veteran of the U.S. Air Force's law enforcement component and a SWAT officer, made these comments to *Washington Post* journalist Thomas Gibbons-Neff (2014), himself a post-9/11 veteran. Another veteran onsite, Jason Fritz, a former Army officer and an international policing operations analyst, pointed out, "You see the police are standing online with bulletproof vests and rifles pointed at peoples [*sic*] chests." Fritz noted, "That's not controlling the crowd, that's intimidating them."

In the midst of a legitimacy crisis in local policing in Ferguson—a symptom of broader civil–military tensions associated in part with over-militarized police departments, as discussed above—veterans offered both some of the most critical commentary on the civil–military dynamics playing out in crowd control and took it upon themselves to offer incisive advice to police and to report this story to the public. King specifically mentioned the issue of militarism, noting that "instead of deescalating the situation on the second day, the police responded with armored vehicles and SWAT officers clad in bulletproof vests and military-grade rifles." King explained the violent protests in response as a product of the lack of leadership evident in such decision-making processes, which included the mismanagement of public perception on the part of the Ferguson Police Department.

More curiously, in both veterans' commentary to journalist Gibbons-Neff (2014), one could also detect elements of both operational training and cultural awareness attributable to their military experiences in theater and to their cross-cultural training there. Both veteran commentators made the express link between the protest violence and their experiences during combat in Afghanistan—underscoring what should have been obvious tactical differences, in keeping with traditional American civil–military boundaries. "We went through some pretty bad areas of Afghanistan, but we didn't wear that much gear," explained Kyle Dykstra, an Army veteran and former security officer for the State Department. In fact, Dykstra pointed out to the journalist that "the bulletproof armor the officers were wearing around their shoulders [was] known as 'Deltoid' armor," a familiar accoutrement of urban warfare and insurgency. Jason Fritz, clearly unsettled by the law enforcement response, explained, "I can't think of a [protest] situation where the use of M4 [rifles] are merited"—in fact, "I don't see it as a viable tactic in any [homeland] scenario."

In addition to noting instances of civil–military boundary-breaking in the protest response, the veterans interviewed mentioned less obvious concerns—beyond using tactics and weapons made for warfare, not community policing. Both interviewees mentioned more subtle problems of communication and de-escalation. King explained, "They've kept people in an information black hole," thus questioning any law enforcement decision-making that did "not share details about operations more widely," and which "only exacerbated the situation." Giving the officers the benefit of the doubt, he also pointed out that "there has not been a dialogue about the tactical situation the officers faced," explaining "there might have been a reason that caused the officers to respond with such heavy equipment." Nevertheless, he continued, even if there were "threats to the officers . . . that information has not been shared to the public."

As violence escalated over the week, the veteran commentators explained that Ferguson police unwittingly fueled tensions by allowing individual officers to engage with protesters: "Officers were calling the protesters 'animals,'" King said. Again, he made the comparison with his own military background and law of war expertise: "I can't imagine a military unit would do that in any scenario." Instead, King noted, "If it were a military unit in a similar situation there would be a public affairs officer or civil affairs engagement team that would help bridge the gap between the riot control elements and the general population." In fact, he continued, "I would hate to call the Ferguson response a military one," he emphasized, "because it isn't, it's an aberration," implying that an actual military engagement would have been more effective and respectful of civilians. Distinguishing an appropriate military–civil affairs engagement paradigm with militarized police, King, like many other veterans, did not see events in Ferguson as a problem of military and local law enforcement convergence—but as aberrant policing with military tactical gear added to the bad mix.

Ferguson was not the only instance in which U.S. military veterans were critical of police approaches to protests and used their civil affairs and culture-based military training to identify inappropriate instances of boundary breaking in civil–military relations. Many thoughtful observers also addressed the broader implications of these issues. As journalist Kriston Capps (2014) explained in the case of the Ferguson protests, veterans used online and social media venues to discuss the need for police departments to receive "military-level de-escalation training to go with all that war gear." Many drew on their military training for awareness of core domestic law-based civil–military boundaries implied in law enforcement approaches to public welfare. For many service members, what was an obvious bright-line distinction between civilian policing and military stabilization efforts was beginning to break down in U.S. community contexts under pressure.

We raise this example to emphasize that entrapment, the ways in which organizational structures and logics can trap agents into constrained relationships, run both ways—in this case, military expertise combined with cross-cultural training was more protective of civilian populations than engaged police.

Escaping Entrapment

A critically aware approach to new civil–military challenges is also occurring in defense and military policy debates—reflective discussions
often undertaken in explicitly cultural terms. In assessing U.S. efforts to
stand-up the Afghan National Army, Sergeant First Class Keith Norris in
a military review for the Combat Studies Institute at Fort Leavenworth
notes, for instance, that "capacity building [had] become culture building"
in the U.S.–Afghan context. Norris explains, "For the foreseeable future,
the Afghan National Army is, for all intents and purposes, deployed to its
own country," a transgression of civilian dominance of the military, itself
designed for external not internal operations (except under exceptional
emergencies). Norris's concern is that U.S. security force assistance initiatives are unwittingly applying U.S. civil–military relations paradigms for
an entirely different polity and, furthermore, failing to deliver on those
misplaced goals.

Outgoing Joint Chiefs of Staff Chairman Martin Dempsey also recently
reminded colleagues of the importance of the deliberately "rocky road of
civil military relations," arguing for a positive embrace of this tension-
filled relationship as one of "intentional" friction, stemming in part from
the necessary "gulf between two cultures" and the need to bridge them (in
Wilkie 2014). Dempsey went on to identify the source of differences in organizational mission and problem-solving approaches. When confronted
by a national security problem, Dempsey (in Wilkie 2014) explains,

> military men and women tend to ask, "What's the objective?" And once you
> know what you are trying to achieve, we go through this rather exquisite pro-
> cess of building a campaign plan to achieve it with intermediate objectives and
> milestones. . . . Whereas civilian leaders are generally more interested in what
> [policy] options they have when confronted by a problem. Such fundamentally
> different ways of approaching a problem can . . . cause both sides to talk past
> each other . . . as we literally come at this from two different cultures. (Special
> Inspector General for Afghanistan Reconstruction 2013)

But Dempsey's distinct sense is that this "rocky" relationship cannot
and should not be fixed—even though civilian policymakers and military
leaders need to understand the others' cultures and priorities better to
achieve what must remain essentially a civilian policy mission.

This well-known issue in the politics literature—of civilian control of the
military—hinges on what Huntington also called the "different cultures"
thesis, a premise on which much civil–military relations theory was built,
including notions of overlapping bureaucratic convergence (Desch 1999).
Part of the difficulty remains, however, that the reified, static ideas about
culture manifest in the cultural turn continue in political definitions of

culture as national culture. From this lens, culture remains large, abstract, focused largely on government bureaucracies and political elites, thus lacking in exactly those areas of precise formulation and on-the-ground knowledge common in anthropology, cultural studies, and culture-oriented fields sensitive to detail, human agency, the multiplicity of groups in societies, and the diversity of behaviors and viewpoints.

From this point of difference, however, Dempsey (in Wilkie 2014) again offers a curious, possibly disruptive solution: "to find ways to bridge that gap between these two different cultures," including by educating young officers, "because it can be a source of enormous frustration when we speak past each other about whether we start with options or start with objectives." In effect, this recommendation relying on the static, reified notions of culture is designed to acculturate next-generation decision makers, those whom today's military leaders can shape for the future, to be made culturally bilingual, to speak both languages of military objective-oriented and policy option-oriented cultures. That way, while military commanders have their own missions and mandates for which they are held publically and legally accountable, they can also understand the approaches of their policy masters, explain to them how and why they are approaching a mission in a given way, and appropriately incorporate policy concerns and input.

There are, of course, many ways in which anthropological approaches might contribute to moving civil–military relations from militarized entrapment back to productive entanglement, from dependency to mutual dependence—for instance, by focusing on interoperability in peacekeeping, strategic scaffolding, and/or civic obligations of social scientists and anthropologists. But this chapter has tried to take a more integrated tack, beyond using anthropological concepts to simply reframe military–civilian relationships. Drawing on both anthropological and security studies perspectives, we have argued for detecting and identifying—especially for complex, conflict environments—some key ways in which the cultural turn has created entrapment for both civilian and military organizations.

Robert A. Rubinstein is distinguished professor of anthropology and professor of international relations at the Maxwell School of Syracuse University. He is the author or editor of nine books and more than a hundred journal articles and book chapters. He received the Victor Sidel and Barry Levy Award for Peace from the American Public Health Association in 2016, and the Robert B. Textor and Family Prize for Anticipatory Anthropology from the American Anthropological Association in 2010.

Corri Zoli is director of research at the Institute for National Security and Counterterrorism at Syracuse University and research assistant professor in the Department of Political Science in the Maxwell School of Syracuse University. She is widely published in the areas of military affairs and veterans' postservice transition, and is a specialist in international humanitarian law and security policy. Her work has been supported with awards from the U.S. State Department, Department of Homeland Security, Social Science Research Council, and United States Institute of Peace.

Notes

1. Perhaps the best example is the *U.S. Army/Marine Corps Counterinsurgency Field Manual*, Army 3-24/Marine Corps 3-33.5, collaboratively written by military commanders and academic policymakers, among others, and distributed by an academic press (University of Chicago Press, 2007).
2. See, for example, *Federalist Papers* No. 8 and 29 (Hamilton 2008) versus *Anti-Federalist Papers*, Brutus No. 10 (Ketcham 2003).

References

Adams, Gordon, and Shoon Murray (eds.) 2014. *Mission Creep: The Militarization of US Foreign Policy*. Washington, DC: Georgetown University Press.

Aall, Pamela, Daniel Miltenberger, and Thomas G. Weiss. 2000. *Guide to IGOs, NGOs, and the Military in Peace and Relief Operations*. Washington, DC: United States Institute of Peace Press.

Adler, William D., and Jonathan Keller. 2014. "A Federal Army, Not a Federalist One: Regime Building in the Jeffersonian Era." *Journal of Policy History* 26 (2): 167–87.

American Civil Liberties Union (ACLU). 2014. *War Comes Home: The Excessive Militarization of American Policing*. New York, NY: ACLU Foundation.

Autesserre, Séverine. 2014. *Peaceland: Conflict Resolution and the Everyday Politics of International Intervention*. Cambridge: Cambridge University Press.

Banks, William C. 2016. *Soldiers on the Home Front: The Domestic Role of the American Military*. Cambridge, MA: Harvard University Press.

Bateson, Gregory. 1979. *Mind and Nature: A Necessary Unity*. New York: E. P. Dutton.

Blalock, Herbert. 1967. *Toward a Theory of Minority-Group Relations*. New York: John Wiley.

Capps, Kriston. 2014. "War Veterans Criticize the Tactics of Military-Armed Police in Ferguson." *CityLab*, 14 August 2014, http://www.citylab.com/crime/2014/08/war-veterans-criticize-the-tactics-of-military-armed-police-in-ferguson/376071/.

Christensen, Clayton M., Heiner Baumann, Rudy Ruggles, and Thomas M. Sadtler. 2006. "Disruptive Innovation for Social Change." *Harvard Business Review* 84 (12): 94.

Coulson Seana. 2001. *Semantic Leaps: Frame-Shifting and Conceptual Boundaries in Meaning Construction*. Cambridge, UK: Cambridge University Press.

Dansky, Kara. 2016. "Local Democratic Oversight of Police Militarization." *Harvard Law and Policy Review* 10: 59–75.

Davis, William J. Jr., and Christopher R. Paparone. 2012. "Departments of State and Defense Relations: Are Perceptions Important?" *Interagency Journal* 3 (1): 31–39.

Dept. of the Army. 2011. "Culture Cards: Afghanistan and Islamic Culture" (GTA 21-03-0222, September 2011). Fort Benning, GA: Department of the Army, Maneuver Center of Excellence. Available at https://fas.org/irp/doddir/army/culture.pdf.

Desch, Michael, C. 1999. *Civilian Control of the Military*. Baltimore: Johns Hopkins University Press.

de Waal, Alex. 1995. "Humanitarianism Unbound: The Context of the Call for Military Intervention in Africa." *Trócaire Development Review* 10: 29–45.

———. 2013. "An Emancipatory Imperium?: Power and Principle in the Humanitarian International." In Didier Fassin and Mariella Pandolfi, eds, *Contemporary States of Emergency: The Politics of Military and Humanitarian Interventions*, 295–316. New York: Zone Books.

Duffield, Mark. 1994. "Complex Emergencies and the Crisis of Developmentalism." *IDS Bulletin* 25 (4): 1–14.

Ferrandino, Joseph. 2015. "Minority Threat Hypothesis and NYPD Stop and Frisk Policy." *Criminal Justice Review* 40 (2): 209–29.

Fassin, Didier, and Mariella Pandolfi. 2008. "Introduction: Military and Humanitarian Government in the Age of Intervention." In Didier Fassin and Mariella Pandolfi, eds, *Contemporary States of Emergency: The Politics of Military and Humanitarian Interventions*, 9–25. New York: Zone Books.

Feaver, Peter. 2009. *Armed Servants: Agency, Oversight, and Civil–Military Relations*. Cambridge, MA: Harvard University Press.

Fosher, Kerry. 2008. *Under Construction: Making Homeland Security at the Local Level*. Chicago, IL: University of Chicago Press.

Gibbons-Neff, Thomas. 2014. "Military Veterans See Deeply Flawed Police Response in Ferguson." *Washington Post*, 14 August 2014, https://www.washingtonpost.com/news/checkpoint/wp/2014/08/14/military-veterans-see-deeply-flawed-police-response-in-ferguson/.

Giddens, Anthony. 1999. *Runaway World: How Globalization is Reshaping our Lives*. London: Profile Books.

Gompert, David C., Terrence K. Kelly, Brooke Stearns Lawson, Michelle Parker, and Kimberly Colloton. 2009. *Reconstruction under Fire: Unifying Civil and Military Counterinsurgency*. Santa Monica, CA: RAND.

Gray, Colin S. 1999. "Strategic Culture as Context: The First Generation of Theory Strikes Back." *Review of International Studies* 25 (1): 49–69.

Hall, Abigail, and Christopher Coye. 2013. "The Militarization of U.S. Domestic Policing." *The Independent Review* 17 (4): 485–504.

Hamilton, A., J. Madison, J. Jay, and L. Goldman. 2008. *The Federalist Papers*. Oxford: Oxford University Press.

Hart, C. 2013. *21st Century Civil-Military Relations: Disharmony and Dysfunction*. Carlisle Barracks, PA: Army War College.

Herbert G. 2014. "Syracuse Named One of Top 10 U.S. Cities with 'the Most Abandoned Home.'" *The Post-Standard*, 15 July 2014, Sect. A1.

Hodder, Ian. 2016. *Studies in Human-Thing Entanglement*. Published online at academia.edu, researchgate, and ian-hodder.com under the Creative Commons Attribution (CC BY 4.0) license.

IASC. 1994. *Working Paper on the Definition of Complex Emergencies*. New York: Inter-Agency Standing Committee Secretariat, United Nations.

Ingold, Tim. 2010. *Bringing Things to Life: Creative Entanglements in a World of Materials*. Manchester, UK: Realities/ESRC National Centre for Research Methods.

Jablonsky, David. 2002–2003. The State of the National Security State. *Parameters* 32 (4): 4–20.

James, William. 1907. *Pragmatism*. London: Longmans Green.

Jargowsky, Paul A. 2015. *The Architecture of Segregation: Civil Unrest, the Concentration of Poverty, and Public Policy.* New York: Century Foundation.

Katzenstein, Peter J. 1996. *The Culture of National Security: Norms and Identity in World Politics.* New York: Columbia University Press.

Keen, David J. 2008. *Complex Emergencies.* Cambridge: Polity Press.

Ketcham, Ralph. 2003. *The Anti-federalist Papers and the Constitutional Convention Debates.* New York: Penguin.

Kohn, Richard. 1975. *Eagle and Sword: The Beginnings of the Military Establishment in America.* New York: The Free Press.

Lane, Sandra D., Robert Rubinstein, Dessa Bergen-Cico, Timothy Jennings-Bey, Linda Stone Fish, David A. Larsen, Mindy Thompson Fullilove, Tracey Reichert Schimpff, Kishi Aminashaun Durcre, Jonnell Robinson. 2017. "Neighborhood Trauma Due to Violence: A Multilevel Analysis." *Journal of Health Care for the Poor and Underserved* 28: 446–62.

Laughlin, Charles D. 2017. "Conceptual Systems Theory: A Neglected Perspective for the Anthropology of Consciousness." *Anthropology of Consciousness* 28 (1): 31–68.

Lawson, Brooke Stearns, Terrence K. Kelly, Michelle Parker, Kimberly Colloton, and Jessica Watkins. 2010. *Reconstruction under Fire: Case Studies and Further Analysis of Civil Requirements.* Santa Monica, CA: RAND Corporation.

Mares, David R. 2007. "The National Security State." In Thomas Halloway (ed.), *A Companion to Latin American History*, 386–405. Chichester, UK: Wiley-Blackwell Publishing.

New York State Department of Education. 2012. "Syracuse City School District, 2012." Accessed 26 July 2015, https://reportcards.nysed.gov/.

Norris, Keith W. 2012. "The Afghan National Army: Has Capacity Building Become Culture Building?" *Military Review* 36 (November–December 2012). Fort Leavenworth, KS: Combat Studies Institute. *http://usacac.army.mil/CAC2/MilitaryReview/Archives/English/MilitaryReview_20121231_art007.pdf*

Open the Books. 2016. *The Militarization of Local Police Departments.* Burr Ridge, IL: Openthebooks.com.

Rife, Rickey L. 1998. *Defense is from Mars, State is from Venus: Improving Communications and Promoting National Security.* Carlisle, PA: United States Army War College.

Rosen, Lawrence. 2011. "Anthropological Assumptions and the Afghan War." *Anthropological Quarterly* 84 (2): 535–58.

Rubinstein, Robert A. 1991. "Reflection and Reflexivity in Anthropology." In Robert A. Rubinstein (ed.), *Fieldwork: The Correspondence of Robert Redfield and Sol Tax*, 1–35. Boulder, CO: Westview Press.

———. 2005. "Intervention and Culture: An Anthropological Approach to Peace Operations." *Security Dialogue* 36 (4): 527–44.

———. 2008. *Peacekeeping under Fire: Culture and Intervention.* London: Routledge.

———. 2014. "Humanitarian–Military Collaboration: Social and Cultural Aspects of Interoperability." In *Cultural Awareness in the Military: Developments and Implications for Future Humanitarian Cooperation*, 57–72. Basingstoke, UK: Palgrave Macmillan.

Rubinstein, R. A., D. M. Keller, and M. E. Scherger. 2008. "Culture and Interoperability in Integrated Missions." *International Peacekeeping* 15 (4): 540–55.

Rubinstein, R. A., C. D. Laughlin, and J. McManus. 1984. *Science as Cognitive Process: Toward an Empirical Philosophy of Science.* Philadelphia, PA: University of Pennsylvania Press.

Rubinstein, R. A., and C. Zoli. In press. "Culture and Humanitarian Actions: Short-Term Gains and Long-Term Losses." In H. C. Breede (ed.), *Culture and the Soldier: How Identity, Values, and Norms Intersect with Contemporary Military Engagements.* Vancouver, BC: University of British Columbia Press.

Ruddell, Rick, and Matthew O. Thomas. 2010. "Minority Threat and Police Strength: An Examination of the Golden State." *Police Practice and Research* 11 (3): 256–73.

Ryle, Gilbert. 1949. *The Concept of Mind.* New York: Barnes and Noble.

Seybolt, Taylor B. 2008. *Humanitarian Military Intervention: The Conditions for Success and Failure*. Stockholm: SIPRI/Oxford University Press.

Sida, Lewis. 2005. *Challenges to Humanitarian Space: A Review of Humanitarian Issues Related to the UN Integrated Mission in Liberia and to the Relationship between Humanitarian and Military Actors in Liberia*. Liberia: Monitoring and Steering Group. http://reliefweb.int/sites/reliefweb.int/files/resources/BC75B030FE472FF5C125700D004DBAA1-msg-lbr-30apr.pdf.

Special Inspector General for Afghanistan Reconstruction. 2013. *Quarterly Report to The United States Congress*, 30 October 2013. Arlington, VA: Special Inspector General for Afghanistan Reconstruction.

———. 2016. *Quarterly Report to The United States Congress*, 30 October 2016. Arlington, VA: Special Inspector General for Afghanistan Reconstruction.

The Sphere Project. 2011. *Sphere Handbook 2011: Humanitarian Charter and Minimum Standards in Humanitarian Response*. Rugby, UK: Practical Action Publishing.

Stuart, Douglas T. 2009. *Creating the National Security State: A History of the Law that Transformed America*. Princeton: Princeton University Press.

U.S. Army Combined Arms Center. 2012. *Understanding Afghan Culture: Observations, Insights and Lessons*. Special issue of the Center for Army Lessons Learned (CALL) *Newsletter* 12–18 (12 September 2012). Available at http://www.globalsecurity.org/military/library/report/call/call_12-18.pdf.

Wimsatt, William C. 2007. *Re-Engineering Philosophy for Limited Beings: Piecewise Approximations to Reality*. Cambridge, MA: Harvard University Press.

Wolf, Eric. 1990 "Facing Power: Old Insights, New Questions." *American Anthropologist* 92: 586–96.

Zerubavel, Eviatar. 1991. *The Fine Line: Making Distinctions in Everyday Life*. Chicago: University of Chicago Press.

Chapter 8

The Entangled Soldier
On the Messiness of War/Law/Morality

Thomas Randrup Pedersen

Forward Operating Base Ouellette, Helmand. Over a decade after the United States–led invasion of Afghanistan in October 2001, the mission of the International Security Assistance Force (ISAF) is drawing to a close. The NATO-led coalition is in the process of "redeploying," and military installations are being dismantled or handed over to Afghan forces. Forward Operating Base (FOB) Ouellette and the adjacent Observation Post (OP) Dara are no exceptions. During the closure of the two British-operated "hill forts" in the north of Helmand's Upper Gereshk Valley, the Danish Tank Platoon Loki and its intelligence, surveillance, target acquisition, and reconnaissance (ISTAR) assets are providing force protection to their British coalition partners. On day four of the operation there is an incident. Two of Loki's three battle tanks are positioned on the foreland of FOB Ouellette, scanning the surroundings for suspicious activity. In search of fortune as metal scavengers, or "scrappers" as they are known among the ISAF forces, over a hundred Helmandi men and boys have—as on the previous three days—gathered at what are now the ruins of the demolished OP Dara. However, on this day a group of five to seven children between eight and sixteen years of age make their way around the back of Battle Tank 5 and disappear behind cover. Reappearing shortly afterwards, they start to kick sand into the air. "What are they up to? What kind of game are they playing?"[1] the Platoon Commander, First Lieutenant Frederiksen,[2] asks himself in the turret of Battle Tank 5. The children move across the tank track behind a screen of dust before disappearing into the desert, and

---

Notes for this chapter begin on page 182.

Frederiksen and his crew soon forget all about them, at least until it is time to relieve the guard, and Battle Tank 3 drives along the tank track between the FOB and the battle position.

Boom! There is an ear-splitting explosion. Battle Tank 3 comes to a halt, engulfed in a thick cloud of dust. It has hit an improvised explosive device (IED) at the very spot where the children had moved across the track just a few hours earlier. Apparently, they had not just been playing, but shielding someone strong enough to deploy a Russian anti-tank mine. Apparently, there are so-called "insurgents" who have no scruples about making children carry out acts of war. At least that is the conclusion Frederiksen, outraged and frustrated, draws when I interview him back at Camp Bastion a few days later. Apparently, the use of "child soldiers" not only goes against the laws of war, but also against the first lieutenant's personal morality. Apparently, "insurgents" had turned law and morality into weapons against the Danish forces. The platoon commander and his men did not see what was coming because they were not anticipating children playing a direct part in hostile activities other than the occasional stone-throwing. Significantly, it was not only Battle Tank 3 that was damaged in the Ouellette incident. So too were the civil–military relations between Helmand's children and Loki's tankers, making yet another small cut in the coalition's battle for Afghan "hearts and minds." As Frederiksen emphasized, "We no longer have any trust in the kids whatsoever. When we drove home [from Ouellette], all those children who stood [at the roadside in Gereshk] and waved at us, we simply ignored them."

This chapter anthropologically explores civil–military relations intimately involved in entanglements of war, law, and morality within the context of Denmark's military engagement in the U.S.-led war in Afghanistan. Empirically, I probe into civil–military relations implicated in two entangled yet conflicting processes, namely what I shall call the "civilianization of the Western way of war" and the "warriorization of the Danish way of soldiering," respectively. Here, the former must not be conflated with the increasing numbers of civilian employees in the armed forces (Moskos 2000), nor with the growing numbers of private security contractors hired to undertake tasks traditionally carried out by the military (Mandel 2002). Rather, the "civilianization of war" refers to the increasing efforts within Western militaries to show consideration to civilians—that is to say, to make war in a hypermediatized reality ever more legitimate in the eye of those civilian electorates in whose name, and/or among whom, the wars are fought. With that end in view, today's Western way of war involves legitimizing means, such as "hearts and minds" campaigns (Egnell 2010), "precision warfare" (Ben-Ari et al. 2010), and, as I will emphasize in this chapter, "juridification of war" (Jones 2016). These means all aim

at minimizing (civilian) casualties and "collateral damage," and, by implication, at stemming growing moral sensibilities about killing and injuring
(fellow) human beings at war (see Ben-Ari and Frühstück 2003).

As for the "warriorization of the Danish way of soldiering," it refers not
simply to the Danish Helmand campaign's movement, however temporarily, toward the war-fighter end of the continuum of hyphenate-soldiers,
ranging from the capacity-building soldier-trainer to the trust-building
soldier-diplomat, to the law-enforcing soldier-constabulary, to the warfighting soldier-warrior. Rather, it refers above all to professional Danish
soldiering in present-day expeditionary forces as a voluntary project primarily driven neither by patriotism nor by humanitarianism, but instead
by a search for personal experience and development embodied in a quest
for warriorhood, for self-becoming in the hypermasculinized image of the
hard-hitting, hawkish warrior, be that the revived Viking warrior, or the
revitalized Special Operations Force operator (Pedersen 2017a). Additionally, a rising "warrior culture," drawing upon Nordic mythology, is cul-
tivated through names, symbols, memorials, and commemorative events
not only among individual soldiers, but also at the level of military units,
covering everything from sections to battalions across the Danish army's
combat arms (Pedersen 2017b).

In the present inquiry, I ethnographically describe how Danish grunts,
low-ranking soldiers in the combat arms, seek to strike a balance between
resisting the violence-discouraging civilianization of war and advancing
the violence-encouraging warriorization of soldiering—that is, how they
seek to renegotiate the entanglements of war, law, and morality by way
of judging self and other in relation to the virtue of courage and thereby
regaining a sense of agency—a sense of dignity, a sense of the warrior's
honor. Illuminating the roles that law and morality play in forging the
conduct of war, the study aims to improve our understanding not only
of how war gets done on the ground (see Jones 2016), but also of how
soldiers struggle to become hawkish warriors and, by implication, moral
beings, through their reflections on their doings at war. In this regard, I
argue that those Danish troops with whom I have done fieldwork struggle
to embody a hard-line warrior ethos through their contestation of ISAF's
strict rules of engagement (ROE), as well as of their civilian compatriots'
moral sensibilities about Danish war kills. By extension, I argue that the
grunts in question resort to military violence, in deed and word, as an ethical response to moral breakdowns in their pursuit of warriorhood.

Analytically, this chapter looks into civil–military relations from the
perspective of entanglement. Archaeologist Ian Hodder has defined entanglement of humans and things as a "dialectic relationship between
dependence, often productive and enabling, and dependency, often con-

straining and limiting" (Hodder 2012: 88). Adapting this definition to the entanglement of war, law, and morality, or in broader terms, of humans and "things civil" and "things military" (see Lutz 2001), I endeavor to come to grips with how the use of military violence relies on and is restrained by the civilianization of war and the warriorization of soldiering. Taking inspiration from Hodder's line of thinking differently about things (Hodder 2012), I conceive war, law, and morality as complex things, however evanescent they may be: things we make and that make us as humans; things we give duration, presence, and significance; things that bring us and other things together; things that unleash potentials in us; things that we invest in; things that get in our way and "object" us; things we try to fiddle and fix to solve our problems; things that we get further entangled and entrapped in (Hodder 2012). That said, in this study I do not merely probe how Danish ISAF troops, through their complex civil–military interactions, get caught up in the messy things of war, law, and morality. Rather, I first and foremost scrutinize how the grunts seek to resist their entrapments through renegotiations of the entanglements with "things civil" and "things military" (see Harman 2014).

The inquiry is based on ethnographic fieldwork with two of the very last Danish combat units deployed with ISAF: the Loki Tank Platoon from the Jutland Dragoon Regiment's 1st Armored Battalion, and the Fenrir Force Protection Section from the Guard Hussar Regiment's 3rd Recce Battalion.[3] The fieldwork has been a matter of coming and going in the course of a year, following Loki and Fenrir periodically before, during, and after their six-month tour of duty. In theater, Loki and Fenrir were deployed to southern Afghanistan's Helmand province at the "war's end." Both units were stationed at the gigantic Bastion-Leatherneck-Shorabak base complex in the Desert of Death. More precisely, both units were based at Camp Viking, the Danish operating base inside the British Camp Bastion. Loki was equipped with three battle tanks (Leopard 2A5) and one infantry mobility vehicle (Mine Resistant Ambush Protected [MRAP] Cougar 6x6). Each vehicle was operated by four crew, all male, and all deployment-experienced except for the platoon commander. Equipped with four Cougars, Fenrir, too, was staffed with sixteen personnel, all but one male, and all first-time deployees apart from the section's second-in-command.

The chapter is organized into six sections. First, I contextualize Loki and Fenrir's tour of duty in relation to the reinvention of Denmark as a warring nation. Second, I contextualize the war/law/morality entanglement and unfold the study's analytical key concepts. Third, I pay analytical attention to how Loki and Fenrir contest the legitimacy of ISAF's defensive ROE in relation to stone-throwing youths and, by extension, that of the very authority of the guardian of ISAF's ROE par excellence, the military legal advisor. Fourth, I direct my analytical gaze at how Loki and Fenrir make claims to the legitimacy of their "savage restraint." Fifth, I analyze how Loki's tankers contest the legitimacy of ISAF's offensive ROE and the taboo on killing with regard to "insurgents" and "collateral damage." Finally, in the conclusion, I recap the chapter's key insights and situate the study's contribution to our understanding of entangled agency, soldierly and otherwise.

A Warring Nation Once Again

In this section, I offer a very short introduction to the Danish warring nation that Loki and Fenrir were spearheading in Helmand. Denmark joined the U.S.-led coalition wars in Afghanistan and Iraq in 2002 and 2003, respectively, and today there is still a relatively strong Danish military presence in both countries. With these military adventures in South Asia and the Middle East, Denmark's activist, yet largely peaceful, foreign policy in the post–Cold War era has to a great extent been downgraded in favor of a militant counterpart in the post-9/11 years. As such, the wars in Afghanistan and Iraq have brought an end to an epoch in Danish history, an epoch of pacifism/defeatism stretching back to the Second Schleswig War of 1864, a war in which the Danish army was severely defeated, and the subsequent peace agreement resulted in Denmark being reduced from a medium-sized power into a midget state. Today, Denmark is still a small state. Yet, as it was the case for centuries prior to 1864, Denmark has once again become a warring nation, however temporarily it may be (Daugbjerg and Sørensen 2017; Pedersen 2017b). On foreign battlefields, the Danish army has become involved in regular combat on a regular basis for the first time since 1864. This was particularly so in the case of the Danish Helmand campaign (2006–2014). At the home front, a plethora of public and private initiatives offering support to and recognition of Danish veterans and their families have emerged since the late 2000s. Indeed, although film director Janus Metz's box-office hit, the war documentary *Armadillo*, in 2010 caused a public outcry over its portrayal of Danish ISAF troops not only as victims of war, but also as perpetrators of violence (Fredensborg 2010; Jensen 2010), Danish soldiers and veterans are today publicly celebrated and commemorated as heroes (Christensen 2015; Daugbjerg 2019; Pedersen 2017b; Sørensen 2017; Sørensen and Pedersen 2012). So much for the scholarly descriptions of contemporary Western warfare as "post-heroic" (Luttwak 1995; Scheipers 2014; cf. Frisk 2018), and for the long-established Danish who-do-you-think-you-are mentality, known as the Law of Jante.

War/Law/Morality

The aim of this section is twofold: to conceptualize war, law, and morality, and to contextualize their entanglements in relation to Loki and Fenrir's tour of duty in Helmand.

War. What kind of war did Loki and Fenrir take part in? To be sure, they participated in the global U.S.-led "war on terror" that was waged locally in Afghanistan as a counterinsurgency war, involving a "soft approach" to the use of military violence in the attempt at winning the battle for "hearts and minds" (see Egnell 2010) "at the front" as well as "at home" and "on the international stage." However, taking into consideration that the very nature of war has arguably changed more or less radically in the post–Cold War era (Strachan and Scheipers 2011), we can say that Loki and Fenrir were serving in what has been described as everything from a "new war" (Kaldor 2012) to a "war amongst the people" (Smith 2005) to a "risk-transfer war" (Shaw 2005) to a "precision war" (Ben-Ari et al. 2010). In other words, Loki and Fenrir were deployed to an unconventional counter-guerrilla war fought between a coalition of states and networks of nonstate actors (see Kaldor 2012)—a war fought among Afghan and Pakistani civilians; a war in which "the Taliban" and other "insurgents" in varying degrees formed part of the civilian population (see Smith 2005); a war in which casualty aversion was deemed imperative to win the battle for popular support; a war in which force protection was essential to minimize the risk of casualties within the ranks of the coalition (see Straw 2005); a war in which the juridification of the coalition's conduct of war was crucial, if not so much to the coveted minimization of civilian casualties, then at least to the actual or, at any rate, apparent legality and precision of the coalition's warfare (see Ben-Ari et al. 2010).

Law. What role does law play for Loki and Fenrir in theater? Here, geographer Craig A. Jones (2016: 2) reminds us that war is "shot-through with law." *Jus ad bellum* (acceptable justifications for resorting to war) and *jus in bello* (limits to the acceptable conduct of war) are both regulated by the law of war, namely by international law under the United Nations' Charter and by international humanitarian law respectively. *Jus in bello* is also governed by mission-specific ROE defining when, where, how, and against whom military violence may be lawfully used. In the post–Cold War era and particularly in the 9/11 years, the ever more hypermediatized wars imply that Western military interventions are, in the words of geographer Michael D. Smith (2014: 152), "always already public relations campaigns." Accordingly, the relationship between war and law has become increasingly intertwined, since "the good war" today has become the legal war (Jones 2015)—that is, a war *of* law (when waged by states of law), a war *through* law (when governed by law), and a war *for* law (when fought in the name of the rule of law) (Smith 2014). In this chapter, I explore the growing entanglements of war and law in terms of "lawfare" and "savage restraint." Charles Dunlap (2001: 5), former deputy judge advocate general of the U.S. Air Force, has described lawfare as "the use of law as a weapon of war." However, whereas Dunlap regards lawfare primarily as a weapon of the weak, of "the insurgent," Jones (2016) argues that lawfare has counterinsurgent potential too. Jones invokes the Comaroffs' (2008: 30) definition of lawfare in the postcolony as "the resort to legal instruments, to the violence inherent in the law, to commit acts of political coercion, even erasure." Following this line of thinking, the present study probes not only how ROE permits soldiers in Loki and Fenrir to use lawful military violence, but also how these troops turn their ROE into a weapon of what sociologist James Ron (2000), in his account of the Israeli Defence Forces (IDF) during the First Intifada, refers to as "savage restraint." In a nutshell, the question is how security forces deviate from their ROE without bypassing them altogether, thereby keeping up the appearance of legality and restraint while resorting to clandestine operating codes.

Morality. What does morality have to do with Loki and Fenrir's war? Drawing upon Cheryl Mattingly's (2014) anthropology of morality/ethics, this inquiry approaches soldiering as a self-transformative project of moral becoming—in essence, as a struggle for becoming a moral self based on virtuous action tied to a vision of "the good life" within the ranks of Loki and Fenrir and the wider Danish combat arms. In this context, a warrior ethos tends to be a highly valued ideal, a moral ideal encompassing what I call the "hawkish warrior," understood as one who fights fire with fire and seeks to conquer the moral high ground through actions embodying military virtues, such as loyalty, forcefulness, and, as I highlight in this chapter, courage. However, whereas Mattingly (2014) conceives humans as moral actors because we are evaluative in moral terms, I contend that we are not always consciously reflecting on the moral character of action, let alone always being self-aware of acting morally in terms of undertaking virtuous actions. Recalling Jarrett Zigon's (2007, 2014) anthropology of morality/ethics, we can say that our reflecting self, which is engaged in ethical deliberation and aspiration, only becomes manifest in moments of "moral breakdown." As Zigon (2007, 2014) conceives it, morality is an unreflective mode of being-in-the-world with others, while ethics is a tactic performed in moments of moral breakdown—that is, in moments that "shake one out of the everydayness of being moral" and thus make one "need to consciously consider or reason about what one must do" (Zigon 2007: 133). Ethics, Zigon (2007, 2014) argues, is primarily about responding to moments of moral breakdown in order to regain a sense of dwelling comfortably in the world with others. As such, ethics is not so much about evaluating as about caring for relations (Zigon 2014). Integrating Mattingly's neo-Aristotelian approach with Zigon's Heideggerian counterpart, this study illuminates soldiering as a project of moral self-becoming by paying analytical attention to moral breakdowns in which soldiers in Loki and Fenrir perform ethical tactics cultivating the hawkish warrior and, by implication, come to judge themselves and the world according to military virtues, such as courage.

The Eye and the Flesh

In Afghanistan, as of mid-2016, more than thirty-one thousand civilians have been killed and over forty thousand wounded since the U.S.-led invasion in October 2001 (Crawford 2016). The lion's share of the casualties has been attributed to the "Taliban" and other "insurgents," while the percentage ascribed to ISAF and other pro-government forces has to date risen and fallen between an all-time high of 41 in 2007 and a low of 12 in 2012 (Crawford 2016). Presumably, this fluctuation partly reflects two developments: the shift in emphasis of ISAF's campaign from combat to capacity-building, and the coalition's growing concern to minimize "collateral damage" (see Beljan 2013). In the wake of several high-profile incidents with civilian casualties, each ISAF commander-in-chief (COMISAF) has since 2009 issued tactical directives providing guidance and intent for ISAF's "use of force," and the coalition's ROE have increasingly been tightened over the years (Beljan 2013). In this section, I examine how soldiers in Loki and Fenrir contest not only the legitimacy of their defensive ROE, but also the authority of their military legal advisor.

Tactical Operations Centre (TOC), Camp Viking. Military Legal Advisor Holm takes the floor in front of Loki's dragoons. Holm is deployed with Defence Command Denmark and is an integral part of the hussar-formed staff in the Danish ISAF force. She is in her late twenties, a graduate of a civilian law school with subsequent military training. She is attached to the Danish Defence's Legal Advisory Service, which was established in 1997 to provide military commanders with legal advice, particularly in the field of international humanitarian law. However, Holm also performs other duties. In 2009, COMISAF made judgmental training mandatory for all troops in the multinational ISAF force. Thus, in effect, every fortnight Holm trains all Danish units in lawfare—that is, in judging when one can make use of military violence with legal impunity, and when one would be breaking the law and committing a punishable offence. As usual, Holm encourages dialogue about one or more experience-based scenarios: how to observe ROE and tactical directives in a given situation? Holm is very enthusiastic in her teaching. In contrast, most of the grunts are almost lying on their chairs and seem to be taking part in the class only reluctantly. "What's going on?" I wonder to myself in the last row; "Why such little interest?"

HQ, DANCON/ISAF, Camp Viking. Holm has agreed to do an interview. We are sitting in the shade at a table in the outdoor smoking area at the back of the staff tent. Touching on her at times thankless job as judgmental trainer, Holm states,

> The old boys . . . they've heard it all hundred times before . . . the younger ones who are on their first tour . . . there you just have a lot of questions asked . . . the young ones experience it as very frustrating to have stones thrown at them . . . it's not like I'm trying to put them into a straitjacket: they must duck, they must drive on . . . they're the ones out on the ground. They're the ones who have the feeling of what's going on. They just have to consider it because the important point is to use the least possible force. Especially when we deal with civilians.

Operational Zone Loki, Camp Viking. Tank Commander Sergeant First Class Hansen lights a cigarette, inhaling, then exhaling. We are sitting at Loki's long work table, doing an interview. Hansen is in his late twenties, yet I suspect he is one of Holm's "old boys." Although a fully qualified bricklayer, he has worn the Queen's uniform for almost a decade. This is his fourth tour of duty. He has strong but not exceptional opinions within the ranks of Loki:

> Judgmental training is a waste of time. . . . our military legal advisor doesn't understand a word of what's going on in real life. She calls it "boyish pranks" when kids run about throwing mines and stones . . . when our lads come back in with cracks in the side windows and with scratches on their facial protectors, because they're showered with stones, as they drive through a town, then her solution is to pull your head in . . . it's as plain as it can be that she has not tried to be in it. . . . When you're forced to stand still, and they ["the locals"] steal left, right, and center, then you cannot just pull your head in. It's not a solution. You cannot just put up with that . . . she's living in cloud-cuckoo land.

Echo Pod, Camp Midgaard. Gunner Private Lyngby is one of Holm's "young ones" and one of Hansen's "lads" insofar as that category also applies to non-Loki personnel.[4] Lyngby is a university graduate in his mid-twenties and a first-time deployee. He mans the heavy machine-gun in the open turret of one of Fenrir's four Cougars. I am interviewing him at the back of Fenrir's accommodation pod in the Danish quarters adjacent to Camp Viking. He says,

> Last time we were out . . . about one hundred meters from the gate into the camp [Main Operating Base (MOB) Lashkar Gah], a boy came up asking for water. I waved him away, as I always do. But then, when I looked back, I saw that he was standing with the largest stone ever—which he then threw up at me [in the Cougar turret]. I just managed to dodge it. I just lost my temper and took a [mini-]flare up and shot it directly down at him, and he then ran away . . . those ROE, up yours! We've told that to her [Holm]. Swell! First, [to observe the ROE's escalation of force procedures][5] you have to instruct, then you have to shout and then . . . come on now! Shut your face! You don't even dare to come along outside the wire to see how it is. Of course, you cannot manage to do all that in the situation. You only have a few seconds.

Leaving Holm's account aside for a moment, we can say that Hansen and Lyngby face moral breakdowns not so much because of the stone-throwing children but because of the ways in which Holm advises Loki and Fenrir to respond. Hansen and Lyngby do not simply deem Holm's solutions inappropriate in operational terms; rather, they go against the moral dispositions of the two grunts. To pull one's head in is not simply an anti-retaliatory act of turning the other cheek, but also a defensive act that reverberates with the Aristotelian vice of cowardice. In that sense, Holm's advice, so to speak, gets in Hansen and Lyngby's way of becoming a self in the image of the hawkish warrior. What is more, observing ISAF's escalation of force procedures entails a "soft approach" that apparently does not have the intended effect. Adapting a phrase from Susie Kilshaw's (2008) work on the Gulf War Syndrome, we can say that the juridification of ISAF's way of war threatens to reduce Hansen and Lyngby and their like to "impotent warriors"—existentially speaking, that is.

Yet, Hansen and Lyngby are not backward in performing ethics by which they resume their quest for warriorhood. Shooting a mini-flare directly at the stone-throwing boy, Lyngby embodies a hard-line warrior ethos and reestablishes the moral order that Michael D. Jackson (2005), with an intersubjective logic of reciprocity in mind, argues should ideally obtain between senior and junior persons, and between rulers and ruled. What is more, both Hansen and Lyngby reclaim soldiering as an ethical project of self-becoming, and, although she was actually on the road in Kabul and in Lashkar Gah, Hansen and Lyngby judge Holm by positioning her and themselves on opposite sides of the wire of Camp Bastion. The wire draws a fundamental boundary between frontline and rear-base personnel, between danger and safety, between courage and cowardice, between potential and entrapment. Importantly, it also marks a basic distinction between two competing ways of knowing war: with the eye and with the flesh. Whereas the authority of the eyewitness rests upon criteria of objectivity, that of the flesh-witness assumes that war experience is impossible to understand for those who were not there themselves (Harari 2009). Accordingly, we can say that, on the basis of their frontline experiences, Hansen and Lyngby make claims to the authority of the flesh-witness, while in the same breath they position Holm as an eyewitness who does not know the realities of war outside the wire. Not on her own body, that is. As such, the two troopers contest Holm's authority on *jus in bello* and the very legitimacy of ISAF's ROE and tactical directives. However, as Hodder (2012: 214) reminds us, "entanglements look different from different social positions and in relation to different interests." Thus, in countering the flesh-witnessing grunts, Holm lays claim to the moral high ground by taking account of the minimization of civilian casualties and, by extension, the strategic considerations of the battle for "hearts and minds." In short, she advocates the lawfare of the precision war rather than the force protection of the risk-transfer war.

The Warrior's Heart and Mind

Foxtrot Range, Bastion-Leatherneck-Shorabak. We are on one of the unfenced ranges in the desert just outside the wire. Fenrir is doing target practice with its Colt Canada assault rifles. The "lads" are waiting their turns. Time is dragging. But then Driver Private Ishøj, visibly excited about something finally happening, cries "scrappers!" The scrappers frequently turn up at the ranges, collecting the brass bullet casings in order to resell them at the market. Four motorcycles, each carrying two riders, are approaching. Scrappers are known to be light-fingered, and Sergeant Andersen will not have them anywhere near the section's Cougars. "Fetch the stick, but leave the rifles behind," the energetic sergeant orders Scout Private Hirtshals, and adds, directed at me, "They know that we're not going to shoot them. We bring the stick just in case. They respect the stick." Andersen is Fenrir's second-in-command. He is in his early twenties, yet the only one in the unit with previous deployment experience—a tour of duty in Lebanon. Andersen shoulders the stick and tells Ishøj, Hirtshals, and me to come along to receive "the locals." The wooden stick measures about one-and-a-half meters and has an iron hook at one end. The stick is a low-tech counter-IED instrument, not a bludgeon. All the same, here and now it serves as a simple yet intimidating strike weapon materializing the field of tension between the civilianization of war and the warriorization of soldiering, between the institutional demand for a "soft approach" and the individual potential for stepping into character as a hawkish warrior. This "creative" use of the counter-IED stick amounts to one of the subtle operating codes of savage restraint that I scrutinize in this section.

Command Post Loki, Camp Viking. Platoon Commander First Lieutenant Frederiksen opens a can of energy drink. I am interviewing him at his desk. Although he is in his late twenties, and although he has served in the Danish Armed Forces for nearly a decade, this is his first tour of duty. Recounting how the Ouellette incident has strained Loki's relationship with Helmandi children waving at the platoon as it passes by, Frederiksen makes it clear that his crew has not only stopped waving back:

> We know that they throw stones at us, or give us the finger, the second we turn around . . . I don't really think they realize what they're doing . . . it's boyish pranks, but we have zero tolerance of all that. Those mini-flares, right? Instead of shooting them into the air, as we used to do, they shoot as close by them [the children] as it's at all possible without striking them . . . because we want to send a signal that you shall damn well not do any shit.

Pod Echo, Camp Midgaard. In the interview with Gunner Private Lyngby, mentioned in the section above, Lyngby reflects further on the stone-throwing incident near MOB Lashkar Gah:

> We all agree [in the section] that you just got to do what you got to do. What's the point of aiming [mini-flares] into the air? He [the stone-throwing boy] just needs to get a good spanking. It doesn't do him any harm [to get hit by a mini-flare] . . . sometimes we also take our weapons up and aim a bit at them. We do frequently have good experiences with taking out the signal-light pistol . . . it would just have been so much easier for us to keep them ["the locals"] at bay if we could just do what we want to do. They do not have much respect for us.

YMCA, Camp Viking. Frederiksen has loaded up on coffee and cake. This time I am interviewing him in the TV room at the recreation center run by the Soldiers' Mission of the Young Men's Christian Association (YMCA) in Denmark. Frederiksen recounts an incident at FOB Ouellette the day before the IED hit:

> In general, we're very cautious . . . but when they [the higher authorities] start to question whether warning shots have to be fired. Listen . . . we have crew standing [exposed] in a battle tank, right? They're having stones thrown at them [with slings] left, right, and center. There's a crowd that doesn't respond to shouts, instructions, or shots fired with a signal-light pistol . . . what the hell does that say about the authority that we're supposed to have down here? . . . when they react to neither one thing nor the other, then there's only a warning shot left. And that proved to have the desired effect. I could also just simply have shot them, right [ironic tone of voice]? That too would have had the desired effect . . . two warning shots like these would have been lost in trivialities compared to what has happened on previous tours of duty down here . . . yet it has to be probed into.

On the basis of these three accounts, we can say at present that Lyngby and Frederiksen go through moral breakdowns triggered by children on whom the defensive use of military violence on the lower steps of the escalation of force ladder apparently has no effect. Consequently, Loki and Fenrir resort to clandestine operating codes, though they do not embody a *policy* of savage restraint, as Ron (2000) argues in the Israeli case. Rather, Loki's and Fenrir's clandestine operating codes embody a hard-line warrior ethos, entailing savage restraint either in terms of applying defensive measures not included in the ROE's repertoire, or in terms of bending the ROE to one's own advantage. In any event, Loki and Fenrir resort to these more or less subtle operating practices arguably not so much to maintain their own force protection in line with the risk-transfer war as to return to their moral ordinary. As such, we can consider the hidden operating practices, however intimidating they may be, as an ethical response empowering Lyngby and Frederiksen to make claims to authority and respect, thus carrying out moral acts of caring for the reciprocal relationship that should ideally exist between men and boys, rulers and ruled (see Jackson 2005). To put it differently, the dependency on ISAF's ROE constrain the use of lawful military violence and "objects" the quest for warriorhood. Yet, the very same ROE, upon which the clandestine operating codes depend, enable soldiers in Loki and Fenrir to cultivate their warrior ethos through investments in the "savage" detail of their otherwise "civilized" use of military violence. The hawkish warrior is in the details.

Speaking of details, let us return to Frederiksen's account of the warning shots he fired with his assault rifle. The children are seemingly not the only ones giving rise to a moral breakdown—so too are the higher Danish military authorities that subsequently questioned Frederiksen's decision to fire the two warning shots. Did Frederiksen breach ISAF's ROE? Did he carry out an act of excessive violence? After all, when Frederiksen and his crew took over the watch from Battle Tank 2, Frederiksen had jumped directly on to the second highest step on the escalation of force ladder: the warning shot. The next step would have meant shooting to kill. In the end, the case was closed without any action being taken against Frederiksen. First, the tankers that Frederiksen and his crew were relieving had taken all the lower steps on the ladder prior to the warning shot. Second, it is not as if one must climb the ladder from the very bottom. Rather, one should jump on to that step of the ladder that one judges necessary to exercise one's right to self-defense in relation to the given threat. That said, the severity of a threat is often likely to leave room for differing interpretations. In any case, we can say that Frederiksen responds to his moral breakdown with an ethical performance by which he once again dwells comfortably in the world: he fires the two warning shots to protect his men and to reestablish ISAF's potency. What is more, Frederiksen emphasizes that he did not go to the extreme of shooting to kill. As such, we can say that, however savagely, Frederiksen acted with restraint, even with courage, understood once again not as a heroic act, but as a mode of virtuous action between the vices of cowardice and recklessness. In short, by firing the warning shots, Frederiksen invested in the warrior's "heart and mind" and took a step toward unfolding his potential as a hawkish warrior fighting fire with fire.

One's Own Worst Enemy

In October 2011, a Danish ISAF company commander called in close air support against "targets" that subsequently turned out to be civilians. It was not the first time that Danish forces had caused civilian casualties in Helmand. It was, however, the first time that the Danish Military Prosecution Service charged a responsible commander with gross dereliction of duty (Westh and Aagaard 2015), thus provoking widespread outrage in the Danish army. The dragoon company commander was charged with breaching ISAF's ROE by failing to obtain a "positive identification" of "the enemy." If the commander were to be convicted, he would face up to three years' imprisonment (Westh and Aagaard 2015). Yet, in December 2012 the case was dropped because central evidence, including ISAF's ROE, was deemed too secret to be used in a civil court (Military Prosecution Service 2013). In this section, I focus on encounters in which the civilianization of war, including the trial of the dragoon company commander, is manifest in the act of killing or not killing. I explore how tankers in Loki contest the legitimacy of ISAF's offensive ROE and, by extension, first, the very character of the officers giving, or not giving, the order to shoot, and, second, the very taboo on killing at the crux of the moral sensibilities about Danish war kills.

Operational Zone Loki, Camp Viking. Tank Gunner Lance Corporal Nielsen is drinking Mountain Dew. He joined the army at eighteen and is now in his late twenties. This is his third tour of duty, the second to the Afghan "sandbox." I am interviewing Nielsen at Loki's long table. Reflecting on a recent operation in which Loki and its ISTAR assets were providing combat support to U.S. Marine Corps infantry, Nielsen states,

> There were actually some of these Taliban who began to shoot at our Finder Bird[6] . . . there were some frustrations because we were not allowed to engage. . . . he [the "insurgent"] was opening fire with a PKM[7] . . . and then there was another one who had, with certainty, some kind of long-barrel weapon. And then there were two others . . . they were all Taliban. That's almost a copper-

bottomed guarantee. They were all standing together and hiding behind the same wall . . . it would have been really nice to take out all four men. Then we might have had a group less to fight another day. . . . in the end, the Americans said that it was actually up to us to decide [whether to shoot or not], but I think that no one really dared to give the order—especially because . . . there's this precarious case with an officer from [the Jutland Dragoon Regiment in] Holstebro . . . he was dragged through a major trial back home. . . . they couldn't be hundred percent positive about whether they [the "targets"] were Taliban . . . it has then had the effect that those officers, who are down here now, they're so god-damned afraid of doing anything because they only think of their careers . . . you play a game of chess at the cost of pawns. I'd rather not shoot anyone— children least of all. Yet it can't be avoided that someone goes now and then, a few to the left, a few to the right, and a few to the center.

Nielsen, we can say, has a moral breakdown due to Loki's lack of engagement with "the enemy," which was carrying out a hostile act qualifying him as a lawful "target." The conditions for conducting an act of lawfare were in place. Yet, resonating with Holm's account above, Nielsen seems to suggest that Loki refrained from opening fire because the officers at the top of the kill chain are more concerned with precision war than with risk-transfer war. However, such concerns are, in Nielsen's view, and contrary to Holm's, not rooted in the strategic interests of the battle for "hearts and minds." Rather, they have to do with the notion of "the omelet of war" (Lutz and Millar 2012: 492), a notion to which Nielsen subscribes with his chess metaphor, and through which he accepts that just as one cannot make an omelet without breaking eggs, one, regrettably, cannot wage war without taking civilian lives. As the trial against the dragoon company commander indicates, this notion has come under pressure with the growing juridification of war. In Nielsen's opinion, his officers fear the legal consequences of "collateral damage" more than they fear the damage done to their own forces, being more preoccupied with taking care of themselves than with caring for their troops. Thus, the officers can be said to offend the military virtue of loyalty that arguably lies at the heart of the warrior ethos to which soldiers in Loki and Fenrir aspire.

Disloyal selfishness is one thing; lack of decisive action on the battlefield, another. Nielsen associates such inaction with the absence of courage and an abundance of cowardice. As such, he expresses a breakdown in the moral order that should ideally exist not only between officers and their troops, but also between the realities of war and dreams of warriorhood. However, by positioning the officers at the top of the kill chain as selfish, disloyal cowards (to push things to the extremes), Nielsen can be said to perform ethics as a tactic empowering him to morally dwell comfortably in the world once again (see Zigon 2007). This is a tactic whereby Nielsen not only attributes Loki's impotence to its commanding officers, but also indirectly ascribes unselfishness, loyalty, and courage to rank-and-file soldiers like himself. Thus, while the realities of the civilianized war may in practice make a mockery of the hard-line warrior ethos, Nielsen retrospectively performs a narrative maneuver enabling him to re-warriorize his soldierly becoming.

Operational Zone Loki, Camp Viking. Tank Commander Warrant Officer Second Class Overgaard takes yet another gulp of lukewarm coffee during our interview. Overgaard is in his late thirties, having joined the army fresh out of high school. Today he is one of Loki's most experienced and respected crewmembers. This is his sixth tour of duty, his second to Afghanistan. Things have changed since he was here several years ago, both "at the front" and "at home":

> Then there comes one or another kid around from the university, who has never tried to be shot at, and asks if it can be true that you've shot someone. Yes, that's actually the truth . . . back home in Denmark people are just not allowed to die. There, we're so civilized and so decadent that we cannot kill people. But that's exactly what we do out here. Not that it's totally legitimate any longer. Yet it's still acceptable. And when you're up against people who do not care if they have to point out one of their many sons and say: "now you must go and blow yourself up," then you cannot fight with the restrictions we have . . . it's like we have become too civilized.

Another moral breakdown, this time caused by a university kid, by someone who could resemble the author, someone who, in Overgaard's view, resembles Danish civilians in general, someone who hits the moral panic button when people are killed at the hands of Danish soldiers in Helmand. In other words, someone who carries the taboo on killing on the friendly Danish home front over to the hostile Afghan battlespace. Someone whose moral sensibilities about Danish war kills embody the growing civilianization of war. Someone who embodies the "civilizing process" of the Western way of war, understood, with sociologist Norbert Elias (2000), as a process of growing self-restraint rooted in Europe's historical process of gradually suppressing, out of shame and revulsion, our brute nature. That is, someone who embodies the vice of cowardice and thereby the very antithesis of the "barbaric" suicide-bomber who epitomizes the vice of recklessness. It is another ethical response, this time in the shape of Overgaard's renunciation of ISAF's ROE as a form of entrapment, namely as self-defeating constraints in the face of an unbounded enemy. As an unrelenting form of morality (see Csordas 2013), or as values as such (see Willerslev 2013), ISAF's ROE have, as it were, rebounded and created their opposite, their shadow immorality. As an idea of "the good war," the legal war, taken to its extreme, ISAF's ROE, and the taboo on killing they reflect, have, when we follow Overgaard's line of thought, flipped over and become "evil" — a trap.

Conclusion

In this chapter, I have aimed at throwing new light on contemporary civil–military relations through an anthropological investigation of war/law/morality entanglements within the context of Denmark's military engagement in Afghanistan. Drawing upon Ian Hodder's notion of entanglement as a dialectic of dependence and dependency between humans and things, I have ethnographically explored the use of military violence as relying on and restrained by two entangled yet conflicting processes, which I have referred to as the growing "civilianization of the Western way of war" and the emerging "warriorization of the Danish way of soldiering." The former refers to growing efforts among Western militaries to attempt legitimizing hypermediatized wars in the eyes of civilian electorates. The warriorization of soldiering, on the other hand, concerns two trends within the Danish army that have been rising particularly in the wake of the Danish Helmand campaign that saw Danish soldiers deployed in a combat role without precedence since 1864: first, professional combat soldiers in Danish expeditionary forces tend to be motivated above all by a search for personal experience and development embodied in a quest for warriorhood; and second, a "warrior culture," based on Nordic mythology, has been revived in the army's combat arms, both among individuals and units.

As for entanglement, its appeal is, as Hodder (2012) points out, its messiness. Seen from an entanglement perspective, the civil–military relations deeply involved in war, law, and morality are messy, not neatly divided between "things civil" and "things military." Based on ethnographic fieldwork with Danish ISAF troops deployed to Helmand at the "war's end," this chapter has explored how soldiers in the Loki Tank Platoon and in the Fenrir Force Protection Section got caught up in the messy things of war, law, and morality. I have showed how the Danish grunts struggled with such messiness; how they struggled between entangling webs of demands and potentials; how the Afghanistan War was, if not unleashing, then at least nudging the grunts' potentials of becoming hawkish warriors; how the constraining demands of ISAF's ROE got in the grunts' way of fulfilling their warrior dreams; how the civilianized war entrapped them into care for civilian concerns; and how they tried to invest in the warriorization of soldiering, fiddling and fixing the juridification of the battlespace, as well as the moral taboo on killing.

More specifically, I have argued that soldiers in Loki and Fenrir were struggling to become hawkish warriors through their contestation of ISAF's strict ROE and their civilian countrymen's moral sensibilities about Danish war kills. I have further argued that the grunts were carrying out acts of violence, in deed and word, as an ethical response to moral breakdowns in their quests for warriorhood. As such, I have endeavored to show not only how war gets done on the ground, but also how Danish grunts were struggling to escape existentially impotentizing entrapments of the civilianized war and re-potentizing themselves in terms of seeking to warriorize their way of soldiering. Accordingly, I have portrayed Danish soldiers as agents of change by virtue of their capacity for renegotiating the entanglements of war, law, and morality, however entrapping they may be. To be sure, this is not to say that things do not have effects, but to say that some things have more impact than others, including the complex things of humans (see Harman 2014). In saying this, the present chapter can be read between the lines as an attempt to contribute to the reconstitution of the individual subject as the basis of agency (see Mattingly 2014; Pedersen 2017b). In that sense, this study can be seen as an implicit attempt not only to modify Hodder's (2012: 215) conception of entangled agency as "the ever-present force of things," let alone Latour's closely related actor-network theory (ANT) notion of actants as everything in the world that "have some sort of effect on other actants," as the philosopher Graham Harman (2014: 37) puts it. Rather, the present inquiry can more generally be heard as a voice speaking against a long-standing idea across the human and social sciences—namely the idea of the individual subject's death (see Humphrey 2008). We are as humans not free-floating, autonomous individuals, yet no matter how entangled and entrapped we may be, we do still have a certain autonomous character in the space of possibility between what we are given and what we choose, between the world we are thrown into and the world we make over to ourselves (Jackson 1989). This, I contend, holds for the soldiers in Loki and Fenrir, as it does for the rest of us.

Acknowledgments

This work emanates from the collaborative research project *Soldier and Society*, University of Copenhagen. It is generously supported by the Independent Research Fund Denmark – Humanities (FKK) (grant no. 0602-02345B) and the Danish Agency for Science, Technology and Innovation (grant no. 4070-00115A). Thanks are due to Defence Command Denmark and to the soldiers and officers with whom I have conducted fieldwork. For insightful comments on earlier versions of this chapter, I owe special thanks to Birgitte Refslund Sørensen, Eyal Ben-Ari, Nir Gazit, Sara la Cour, Ida Sofie Matzen, Camilla Ida Ravnbøl, and Line Richter.

Thomas Randrup Pedersen is assistant professor at the Institute for the Study of Military History, Culture and War, Royal Danish Defence College. He holds a Ph.D. degree in anthropology from the University of Copenhagen. His Ph.D. dissertation, *Soldierly Becomings: A Grunt Ethnography of Denmark's New "Warrior Generation,"* explores contemporary Danish soldering as a project of existential, moral, and social self-becoming. Thomas has, among others, published *Homecoming Parades for Danish Soldiers: A Ceremonial Celebration of the Warrior and the Warring Nation* (in Danish, with Birgitte Refslund Sørensen, 2012) and *Get Real: Chasing Danish Warrior Dreams in the Afghan "Sandbox"* (2017).

Notes

1. Interview extracts and emic terms in Danish have been translated by the author.
2. The author has changed names and other biographical details to shield the identity of the interlocutors.
3. In Nordic mythology "Loki" is the name of the god of mischief, and "Fenrir" is the name of a monstrous wolf.
4. In keeping with a cavalry tradition for hussars and dragoons, privates are named after their hometowns. In this chapter, this applies to "Lyngby," "Ishøj," and "Hirtshals."
5. Escalation of force procedures form part of the ROE and refer to a "ladder" of sequential actions that begins with nonlethal measures and may gradually escalate to lethal actions.
6. Unmanned Aircraft System (UAS) providing ISTAR data.
7. Kalashnikov's modernized machine-gun.

References

Beljan, R. 2013. "Afghanistan: Lessons Learned from an ISAF Perspective." *Small War Journal*, 30 May.

Ben-Ari, E., and S. Frühstück. 2003. "The Celebration of Violence: A Live-Fire Demonstration Carried Out by Japan's Contemporary Military." *American Ethnologist* 30 (4): 540–55.

Ben-Ari, E., Z. Lerer, U. Ben-Shalom, and A. Vainer. 2010. *Rethinking Contemporary Warfare: A Sociological View of the Al-Aqsa Intifada*. Albany: State University of New York Press.

Christensen, T. D. 2015. "The Figure of the Soldier: Discourses of Indisputability and Heroism in a New Danish Commemorative Practice." *Journal of War & Culture Studies* 8 (4): 347–63. doi:10.1179/1752628015Y.0000000026.

Comaroff, J., and J. L. Comaroff (eds.). 2006. *Law and Disorder in the Postcolony*. Chicago: University of Chicago Press.

Crawford, N.C. 2016. "Update on the Human Costs of War for Afghanistan and Pakistan, 2001 to mid-2016." Watson Institute for International & Public Affairs, Brown University. Accessed 15 May 2018, http://watson.brown.edu/costsofwar/papers/human.

Csordas, T. J. 2013. "Morality as a Cultural System?" *Current Anthropology* 54 (5): 523–46. doi:10.1086/672210.

Daugbjerg, M. 2019. "Heroes Once Again: Varieties of Danish 'Activism' in Conflated Commemorations of the War in Afghanistan and the Prusso-Danish War of 1864." *Ethnos: Journal of Anthropology* 84 (1): 160–78. doi:10.1080/00141844.2017.1396232.

Daugbjerg, M., and B. R. Sørensen. 2017. "Becoming a Warring Nation: The Danish 'Military Moment' and Its Repercussions." *Critical Military Studies* 3 (1): 1–6. doi:10.1080/233374 86.2016.1231994.

Dunlap, C. J., Jr. 2001. "Law and Military Interventions: Preserving Humanitarian Values in 21st Century Conflicts." Humanitarian Challenges in Military Intervention Conference, Washington, DC, 29 November 2001. Carr Center for Human Rights Policy, Kennedy School of Government, Harvard University. Accessed 15 May 2018, http://people.duke .edu/~pfeaver/dunlap.pdf.

Egnell, R. 2010. "'Winning Hearts and Minds'? A Critical Analysis of Counter-insurgency Operations in Afghanistan." *Civil Wars* 12 (3): 282–303. doi:10.1080/13698249.2010.509 562.

Elias, N. 2000. *The Civilizing Process: Sociogenetic and Psychogenetic Investigations*. Revised edition. Oxford: Blackwell.

Fredensborg, R. 2010. "Mellem helte og bødler." *Filmmagasinet Ekko* 48. Accessed 15 May 2018, http://www.ekkofilm.dk/artikler/mellem-helte-og-bodler/.

Frisk, K. 2018. "Post-Heroic Warfare Revisited: Meaning and Legitimation of Military Losses." *Sociology* 52 (5): 898–914. doi:10.1177/0038038516680313.

Harari, Y. N. 2009. "Scholars, Eyewitnesses and Flesh-Witnesses of War: A Tense Relationship." *Partial Answers: Journal of Literature and the History of Ideas* 7 (2): 213–28. doi:10.1353/ pan.0.0147.

Harman, G. 2014. "Entanglement and Relation: A Response to Bruno Latour and Ian Hodder." *New Literary History* 45 (1): 37–49. doi:10.1353/nlh.2014.0007.

Hodder, I. 2012. *Entangled: An Archaeology of the Relationships Between Humans and Things*. Malden, MA: Wiley-Blackwell.

Humphrey, C. 2008. Reassembling Individual Subjects: Events and Decisions in Troubled Times. *Anthropological Theory* 8 (4): 357–80. doi:10.1177/1463499608096644.

Jackson, M. 1989. *Paths toward a Clearing: Radical Empiricism and Ethnographic Inquiry*. Bloomington: John Wiley & Sons.

———. 2005. *Existential Anthropology: Events, Exigencies and Effects*. New York: Berghahn.

Jensen, C. 2010. "Velkommen til Armadillo." *Filmmagasinet Ekko* 49. Accessed 15 May 2018, http://www.ekkofilm.dk/artikler/velkommen-til-armadillo/

Jones, C. A. 2015. "Frames of Law: Targeting Advice and Operational Law in the Israeli Military." *Environment and Planning D: Society and Space* 33 (4): 676–96. doi:10.1177/ 0263775815598103.

———. 2016. "Lawfare and the Juridification of Late Modern War." *Progress in Human Geography* 40 (2): 221–39. doi:10.1177/0309132515572270.

Kaldor, M. 2012. *New and Old Wars: Organized Violence in a Global Era*. 3rd ed. Cambridge: Polity Press.

Kilshaw, S. 2008. *Impotent Warriors: Perspectives on Gulf War Syndrome, Vulnerability and Masculinity*. New York: Berghahn.

Luttwak, E. N. 1995. "Toward Post-Heroic Warfare." *Foreign Affairs*, 1 May.

Lutz, C. A. 2001. *Homefront: A Military City and the American Twentieth-Century*. Boston: Beacon Press.

Lutz, C., and K. Millar. 2012. "War." In D. Fassin (ed.), *A Companion to Moral Anthropology*, 482–99. Malden, MA: Wiley-Blackwell.

Mandel, R. 2002. *Armies without States: The Privatization of Security*. London: Lynne Rienner Publishers.

Mattingly, C. 2014. *Moral Laboratories: Family Peril and the Struggle for a Good Life*. Oakland: University of California Press.

Military Prosecution Service. 2013. *Årsberetning 2012*. Copenhagen: Military Prosecution Service.

Moskos, C. 2000. "Towards a Postmodern Military?" In S.A. Cohen (ed.), *Democratic Societies and Their Armed Forces: Israel in Comparative Context*, 3–26. London: Frank Cass.

Pedersen, T. R. 2017a. "Get Real: Chasing Danish Warrior Dreams in the Afghan 'Sandbox.'" *Critical Military Studies* 3 (1): 7–26. doi:10.1080/23337486.2016.1231996.

———. 2017b. *Soldierly Becomings: A Grunt Ethnography of Denmark's New "Warrior Generation."* Ph.D. diss., Department of Anthropology, University of Copenhagen.

Ron, J. 2000. "Savage Restraint: Israel, Palestine and the Dialectics of Legal Repression." *Social Problems* 47 (4): 445–72.

Scheipers, S. (ed.). 2014. *Heroism and the Changing Character of War: Toward Post-Heroic Warfare?* Basingstoke: Palgrave Macmillan.

Shaw, M. 2005. *The New Western Way of War: Risk-Transfer War and Its Crisis in Iraq*. Cambridge: Polity Press.

Smith, M. D. 2014. "States That Come and Go: Mapping the Geolegalities of the Afghanistan Intervention." In I. Braverman, N. Blomley, D. Delaney, and A. Kedar (eds.), *The Expanding Spaces of Law: A Timely Legal Geography*, 142–66. Stanford, CA: Stanford University Press.

Smith, R. 2005. *The Utility of Force: The Art of War in the Modern World*. London: Penguin Books.

Strachan, H., and S. Scheipers (eds.). 2011. *The Changing Character of War*. Oxford: Oxford University Press.

Sørensen, B. R. 2017. "Public Commemorations of Danish Soldiers: Monuments, Memorials and Tombstones." *Critical Military Studies* 3 (1): 27–49. doi:10.1080/23337486.2016.1184 417.

Sørensen, B. R., and T. R. Pedersen. 2012. "Hjemkomstparader for danske soldater: en ceremoniel fejring af krigeren og den krigsførende nation." *Slagmark* 63: 31–46.

Westh, R. R., and C. Aagaard. 2015. "En fejlvurdering med dødelig udgang." *Information*, 13 June.

Willerslev, R. 2013. "God on Trial: Human Sacrifice, Trickery and Faith." *HAU: Journal of Ethnographic Theory* 3 (1): 140–54.

Zigon, J. 2007. "Moral Breakdown and the Ethical Demand: A Theoretical Framework for an Anthropology of Moralities." *Anthropological Theory* 7 (2): 131–50. doi:10.1177/1463 499607077295.

———. 2014. "Attunement and Fidelity: Two Ontological Conditions for Morally Being-in-the-World." *Ethos* 42 (1): 16–30. doi:10.1111/etho.12036.

Chapter 9

Mobility through Self-Defined Expertise

Israeli Security from the Occupation to Kenya

Erella Grassiani

Introduction

On Saturday, 18 July 2016, the Westgate shopping mall, which featured in international headlines after the bloody attack by members of Al Shabaab in 2013, was reopened. A newspaper covering the opening reports: "IRG, the Israeli security company hired in 2014, insists that with its overhaul, Westgate is the safest mall in Nairobi today. Managing Director Haim Cohen's team of ex-Israeli commandos has trained the mall's security personnel assiduously. 'Our life is security. The difference is not on the number of guys–we know how to recognize anything suspicious,' Cohen said. '[Before] everyone didn't take it seriously'" (Zirulnick 2015).

This utterance by Cohen is an insightful example of how the many Israeli security professionals abroad frame their work: as the Israeli expert who is all-knowing within this field due to past experience, while the local Kenyans ("everyone" in Cohen's utterance) don't seem to take security very seriously. In this chapter, I will analyze the mobility of Israeli security professionals, who export specific knowledge, skills, and technologies from Israel (and the Occupied Palestinian Territories) to Nairobi, through their self-framing as security experts. I will argue that these professionals self-identify as experts while using different logics or "discourses" that are characterized by nationalist, racist, and colonial features. Israeli secu-

---

rity actors use ideas of a specific "Israeli-ness" and "African-ness" to create a space in which a need for "Israeli security expertise" and the special, "superior" characteristics of this knowledge and technologies reinforce each other.

Importantly, I will contextualize this "security mobility" by paying special attention to the intimate relationship between the global and mobile security industry and the fact that Israel is a highly militarized society and a state that has been conducting a military occupation for over fifty years. This causes a civil–military entangling of different scales; the first is the existence of a close-knit security network (Sheffer and Barak 2013) within Israel, where military and (private) security actors are almost interchangeable as they move in and out of public and commercial positions. On an international scale, as I will show in this chapter, the military knowledge, experience, and militarist logic Israeli security professionals export becomes entangled with the private security industry as part of the global military industrial complex. These civil–military entanglements, furthermore, work in two directions; the military background of security professionals helps them in their commercial efforts, while the global security industry, as part of the military-industrial complex, strengthens the reputation of Israeli military products and, simultaneously, its military engagements.

This work feeds into the work on other kinds of "security circulations" or "mobilities" of security workers, such as veterans in Sierra Leone who join foreign private security companies (Christensen 2017), and South African veterans joining private security companies after apartheid was abolished (Singer 2003). In these cases, military expertise is used in order to gain employment after becoming redundant as a result of political and or professional changes. While these studies usually focus on lower-level agents, I will look at the ways Israeli veterans who have become businessmen use a self-definition as experts and Israeli security branding (Grassiani 2017) in their private careers.

Israel is often perceived as a security hub; the country has succeeded in many ways in framing itself as *the* place to be when one needs security solutions. This Israeli security brand (Grassiani 2017), which is largely based on military experiences and on stories of Israel's battles in the past and present, is used by Israeli security professionals worldwide. During big security fairs, knowledge, expertise, and technologies belonging to Israel's security industry is celebrated with clients from all over the world, including Asian, African, and European countries and the United States.[1] Instead of looking at whether Israeli security is indeed so superior to that of other countries, I will look into the ways in which security actors define and frame themselves as experts when they sell their knowledge and products abroad as part of a global security market. Israel makes for an interesting and telling case here, as its brand seems to pay off: Israel is successfully selling its products worldwide, using its military experience as capital, and is internationally seen as a major player in the security industry.[2] Besides its successful branding, Israel invests heavily in military technologies that are later sold to foreign parties, and it has a big pool of retired military specialists who are eager to take their knowledge into the private sphere. As mentioned before, these civil–military entanglements, which go from the national to the global, make Israel quite unique and a good case to show the ways security expertise can be framed and how it mobilizes security technologies and knowledge.

I will examine the self-proclaimed expertise of these security professionals and the way they frame their knowledge and skills as authoritative, efficient, and "authentic" vis-à-vis an incompetent "Other." Through this focus I hope to shed light on the ways technologies and ideologies become mobile, and how specific, militarized ways of thinking and acting become entangled with the global security industry and civilian surroundings far away from where they were developed.

I will begin this chapter by briefly explaining my use of the concept of "security," together with my methods, and continue to discuss the social and political context of the phenomenon I am discussing. I will elaborate here on processes of militarization, the Occupation, and the resulting production of a pool of security professionals. I will then go on to look at the ways these professionals become mobile through the construction of a militarized, colonial expert discourse that is infused with logics of "Israeli-ness" and "African-ness," in order to understand more deeply how elements of militarization become entangled within the global security industry.

Using "Security" as an Emic and Etic Term

"Security," as has also been argued by Neocleous and Rigakos (2011), often hides the many asymmetrical power relations that stand behind it, the human rights violations that are done in its name, and its selective character. "Security" is not neutral and not something necessarily good (for all). "Security," furthermore, Neocleous and Rigakos (2011: 20) write, "alienates us from solutions that are naturally social and forces us to speak the language of state rationality, corporate interest and individual egoism." I largely agree with their statement and hence believe it to be important to explain how I intend to use the term here.

In the Israeli context, security has become an almost sacrosanct concept or a security fetish (Neocleous 2007), which dictates that you can never have enough of it. In her work, Juliana Ochs (2011: 2) shows the ways Israelis, who often call the political situation of conflict "the security situation" (or *hamatsav habitchoni*), have internalized ideas of security. Wars are fought in its name and peace is seen as only possible if there first is security (Ochs 2011: 2). Importantly, this security is limited to the Jewish Israeli majority of society.

Here I will use this term through the ways it is used by the people I have studied: the security actors. This emic use of the concept should of course be separated from an etic one, and I will use it while not forgetting that the concept should be seen through a critical lens, as Goldstein (2010) has argued for. I will thus not take the concept of security for granted, but investigate what it means for people who use it and, in this case, sell it and analyze its use by critically examining the contexts in which it is constructed.

Methods

This chapter is based on fieldwork in Israel and Kenya, consisting of participant observation and interviews and on the analysis of media reports (Kenyan, Israeli, and international). In both places, I have spoken to Israeli security specialists, consultants, and employees. Meeting with security professionals is not always easy as they have a tendency to be very closed and secretive. By using a snowball method, however, I managed to interview quite a few consultants and managers. When I started looking for Israelis working in security in Nairobi, it seemed at first they would be hard to find; however, very soon, with the help of my fellow researchers present in Nairobi, I found some names and stories about Israeli connections, such as the rumor, which proved to be true, of an Israeli security manager at one of Nairobi's many shopping malls. These men (they were all men, almost all between forty-five and sixty years of age), furthermore, all tended to know each other.

The fact that I am Israeli helped tremendously. The moment potential research participants learned this fact, their tone changed and their willingness to help me increased. Language also became important: the interviews I conducted with Israelis were in Hebrew, their mother tongue, which made communication and understanding each other much easier.

Israeli Militarization, Securitization, and the Occupation

While much work on the Israeli military (e.g., Ben-Ari 1998; Levy 1998) and the "security network" (Sheffer and Barak 2013) have insightfully analyzed the internal processes within the military and within Israel's society, these studies have rarely been outspokenly critical of Israel's occupation, leaving a distinct political point of view outside of their analysis. Here I have chosen to incorporate such a political view and to analyze Israeli society as context for the security industry with distinct colonial dimensions (Zureik, Lyon, and Abu-Laban 2010; Zureik 1979; Gregory 2004). This frame of analysis will emphasize the significant power differences that exist between Israelis and Palestinians and the way the colonial activities of Israel give way to an array of security technologies and self-proclaimed expertise to be sold elsewhere. Analyzing Israel as such means to critically look at its ongoing military occupation of the Palestinian territories. Rigakos (2011) defines a settler colonialist state as being wrapped up in a settlers' enterprise, which means it occupies and dispossesses land of a people who were already living on this land, tries to forcibly pacify this local people, and beats down any possible resistance. Israel, when looking at its activities in the Occupied Territories, definitely fits this definition. Israel has been maintaining a military occupation in Palestinian territory since 1967. While it can be argued that the colonial enterprise of Israel started with the establishment of the Israeli state in 1948 and even before, for our purposes I will focus on the occupation and settlement activities outside of the green line, as it is in these Occupied Territories and in the "fight against terror" that most technologies, skillsets, and knowledge have been acquired and developed (see also Graham 2011; Klein 2007).

Since its creation, Israel has fought many wars and has been seen by the international world and in particular by itself as the victim of the aggressive Arab world surrounding it. Always on the defense, Israel constructed an image of itself as a David fighting a Goliath, and used this image to legitimize its growing defense and security industry. This siege mentality that has taken hold of the state and society has only grown in recent decades. Since the first Intifada in the late 1980s and the suicide attacks following the defeat of the Oslo Accords in the early 1990s, Israeli society has grown increasingly obsessed with its security and with warding off any threat, real or imagined (Ochs 2011).

Israel's internal civil–military relations are crucial here. As stated before, the military itself and processes of militarization play an enormous role in society. Not only are all Jewish Israelis conscripted into the military, but society itself is drenched with "things military," with ideas about the military as the most moral and righteous in the world and about the "good soldier" who, after service, becomes a "good citizen." Children in schools are taught about the military and learn about soldiers protecting them at the "borders" (which are often not recognized physical borders in the Occupied Territories). Much has been written about this militarization

(Kimmerling 1993; Lomsky-Feder and Ben-Ari 1999) and the way military service creates hierarchies and inequalities in society (Levy 1998). Men with an extensive military (combat) background have much more chance of climbing up the career ladder (while using their military skills) than those who have not (including women). This can be seen in commercial companies where former officers and generals continue a military-like style in managing; politicians also come from the ranks and take their military network with them. And last but definitely not least, it is very visible in the (private) security and defense industry, which Israeli generals enter after their (early) retirement. Sheffer and Barak (2013) coined the idea of the security network where military and civil spheres overlap and cannot be separated anymore. This is a crucial point: the entanglement and intense relationship between military and civil elements of society, and the blurring between the public and the private spheres. It lies at the heart of the way the security professionals I describe here self-identify as experts. They are part of this entanglement and take it to a different scale when they export knowledge and technologies developed in military settings into the global civil and commercial realm. I will elaborate on this below.

The Occupation and the Security Industry

The occupation of the Palestinian Territories, which was the result of the Six Day War in 1967, is often not called as such in mainstream Israeli media and society. People speak about "the territories" or "Judea and Samaria," referring to the Biblical term for the region. The main message in the mainstream public debate is that Palestinians are a threat to Israel's security and that they should be controlled and separated from the Israelis. Human rights violations that have been the result of this occupation, violence and humiliation at checkpoints and during raids for example (Grassiani 2013), are not problematized within this discourse, if they are raised at all. When one looks at how this occupation materializes, one can't miss the walls, fences, cameras, military vehicles, helicopters, planes, military uniforms, weaponry, helmets, turnstiles, and communication equipment that are built, developed, and worn by the Israeli soldiers of the IDF (Israeli Defence Forces). But there is more: often we do not see all the weaponry that is used by the military, such as the Nano technologies and cyber tools that Israel develops and uses in its quest to control the Palestinian occupied population under the pretext of "security" and the defense of Israel. This has also been called a "system of pacification" (Neocleous and Rigakos 2011; see also Halper 2015).

Israel is known as a hub of high-tech development, sometimes even called "Silicon Wadi"; this image is directly connected to the Israeli military and intelligence service (Forbes 2015). It is common knowledge, for example, that high tech companies that are looking for skilled workers eagerly recruit people who have served in the prestigious intelligence unit 8200 (Swed and Butler 2015). Military knowledge that has been developed within the context of a military occupation and has produced systems of surveillance, cyber technologies, and weapons are used in civilian context, often outside of Israel. This clearly shows how both realms, military and the civilian/commercial, become entangled with each other; not only through knowledge and technologies that move between them but also, as we shall see below, through actors who come from one realm (the military) and continue to the next (private security) while still intensely using their military networks (Sheffer and Barak 2013). Not only does the military background of these professionals help their role on an international level within the commercial world; the success of Israeli security products on the global security market also helps to legitimize Israel's military activities and occupation. The entanglements thus work in both directions.

Importantly, the Israeli security professionals who take their knowledge and skills abroad are also products of this militarized society. They are former combatants, often having served as professionals in the IDF or in the ISA (Israeli Security Agency), after which they seamlessly enter the private security market (Grassiani 2017). Using their "military capital" (Swed and Butler 2015), former military personnel become successful in the private sector while still working with military actors as well, making the distinctions between both realms, as said before, very blurry and entangled. As I will show here, this entanglement takes on an international flavor when Israeli military skills are used on the global security market.

Security Mobility: From Israel to Kenya

The global mobility of this industry sheds a new light on the way anthropologists have traditionally written about mobility. Mobilities and circulations have caught the interest of anthropologists and other scholars in the last decades; see, for example, the call for a new mobility paradigm by Sheller and Urry (2006). Anthropologists in particular have been working mostly on human migration within this field. Glick Shiller and Salazar (2013), for example, have done extensive work about what they have called regimes of mobility to emphasize how mobility for some means immobility for others and the unequal power relations that are at play.

Interestingly, within these so-called mobility studies, discourses on security are seen as counter-discourses to moving, since security efforts are seen as things that cause immobility or disruption (Salazar 2014). Or as

Sheller and Urry (2006: 207) write, "There are places and technologies that enhance the mobility of some peoples and places *and* heighten the immobility of others, especially as they try to cross borders." I want to move beyond this focus on the mobility of people while security technologies are seen as countering movement, and focus instead on the very mobility of security expertise and technologies. This mobility, I argue here, is framed through different logics used by members of the Israeli security industry. I hope to contribute to the mobilities debate by tracing the movement of security logic and technology, also when not related directly to migration and border security. Here I argue that a discourse of expertise makes the mobility of security technologies, actors, and knowledge possible by making it logical, legitimate, and attractive for the client, the "lay" Other who is in apparent need of it. The discourse that Israeli security actors in Nairobi use, then, is drenched with notions about an expert self who comes to offer his help to the unknowing Other.

Chisholm (2015: 116) alerts us to the "culture of whiteness that pervades the industry" and asks how (post)colonial histories shape the security industry of today. Here I take up this challenge to include the colonial practices of Israel when analyzing the security industry. As Graham (2010) has shown, Israeli military knowledge and technologies are not only transported into other conflicts and wars, they also can be traced back to more civilian and urban spaces as security measures. Israel, when seen as a Western state, not only exports its colonial technologies extensively to other Western countries (such as the United States and Europe), but exports them to the South as well; to "developing" countries that are thought to be in need of Israel's expertise and tools to combat their problems with crime and terror. Within this mobility, racial discourses that differentiate between the "developed, white Israeli expert" and the "undeveloped, amateur, black Kenyan" become apparent, as I will show further on.

The Case of Kenya

Nairobi is a hub for Israeli security activities. Israel and Kenya have had diplomatic ties since 1963, when then prime minister of Israel Golda Meir met with Kenyatta, Kenya's prime minister, and they agreed to formalize their ties and to enter in a developmental program Israel launched to help developing countries (while still in development itself). This timing was not random; as African countries were establishing their independence, Israel was quick to create new relationships with these strategically located states. Already then, security ties were consolidated, with Israel training presidential security details and supporting the formation of the General Security Unit, a notorious paramilitary group (Otenyo 2004). After relationships cooled in reaction to the 1973 Yom Kippur war, they were picked up again soon and were formalized in 1988. Security and defense cooperation became especially strong after the attacks on Israeli targets in Mombasa in 2002. An Israeli-owned hotel was attacked, and there was an attempt to shoot an Israeli low-cost airplane out of the sky. Israel worked intensively with Kenya in the aftermath of these attacks as the Israeli intelligence service Mossad was sent to find the perpetrators ("Mossad Hunts Terror Leaders" 2002).

In the more contemporary context of the "fight against terror," Israel has become a "natural" partner for Kenya in fighting against fundamentalist Islam. Recently (November 2017), Prime Minister Netanyahu undertook a trip to the African continent, including Kenya, bringing many businesspeople with him, among them representatives of big players in the Israeli security industry. While such trips (former Foreign Minister Liebermann already visited the continent twice, in 2009 and in 2014) are planned under the heading of diplomatic ties and agricultural and development work, security and military ties are at the heart of it (Melman 2009; Sadeh 2016). In 2011, Israel and Kenya signed a treaty to help each other in times of need against terror attacks, which has been enforced by several visits by officials to and fro.[3] During a meeting in July 2016, Kenyan president Kenyatta was quoted as saying that "As they have done for years, the Prime Minister and the Israeli people continue to extend invaluable support to Kenya; helping us build capacity and bolster internal and regional security" (in Namunane 2016). Furthermore, PM Netanyahu has pledged to help Kenya with the building of the wall between that country and Somalia (Namunane 2016). Comparisons with the wall in the Occupied Territories are easily made here.

This intense security cooperation was again in the media headlines after the attack on the Westgate shopping mall in Nairobi, mentioned before, as rumors went around about "Israeli forces" that helped the Kenyans to end the siege.[4] And even though my investigation has not given me any evidence for this involvement, the mythical status of Israel helping out as experts on anti-terrorism persists and is very telling.

Over the years Kenya has become a major trading partner for Israel, and in November 2018 it signed a Memorandum of Understanding with Israel geared toward improving this partnership considerably (Kondo 2018). Much of this trade is agricultural. While Israel advertises the agricultural or economic empowerment projects under MASHAV, Israel's Agency for Development Cooperation, within this development discourse of "helping" and "educating" the needy in Kenya, there is also room for security. Israel frames itself as an expert, more knowledgeable partner who comes to help its friend in need, and offers training, expertise, and equipment

(DPPS 2015). Below I will indicate how we can analyze such discourse of expertise anthropologically in order to understand its effects on the mobility of these security goods.

Expertise: Israeli Security Actors in Kenya

Thinking about Experts

Dominic Boyer (2008: 39) defines the expert as "an actor who has developed skills in, semiotic-epistemic competence for, and attentional concern with, some sphere or practical activity." He starts out from the idea of "the expert" to investigate how the anthropologist should go about investigating him/her. Here, however, I am interested in looking at the way expertise comes into being through the use of distinct discourses. I am less interested in knowing whether someone is or is not a "real" expert, as much as I want to understand the ways expertise is performed and framed. Expertise is thus not only about "knowing," but also about "doing" or even "acting," and about "becom[ing] intimate with . . . culturally valuable things that are relatively inaccessible or illegible to laypeople" (Carr 2010). Thus the ways in which expertise is embodied and performed, but also the language that is used to self-identify as an expert, are equally important to consider here. In her review of anthropological work on expertise, Carr (2010) notes that besides behavior of an individual, expertise also belongs to the domain of the institution, which gives the expert his or her legitimacy. In this light, she continues to describe apprenticeship and the acquiring of a specific "expert register," which can be used to manifest one's expertise. As mentioned before, she emphasizes the importance of the way expertise is acted out. Authenticity and its enactment are important here, as experts need such claims vis-à-vis "lay" people in order to establish their position. She finally shows the way expertise and the coding systems that it is made out of come to be naturalized in a way that "erase[s] the debate that inevitably went into producing them [categorical distinctions]" (Carr 2010: 26).

A security actor, then, needs to perform, act, and speak as an expert in order to be accepted as one by those who are not "in the know." Joachim and Schneiker (2014) assert that for clients in the security business, expertise or the image of expertise is of utmost importance. Berndtsson (2012), for example, explored the way a Swedish private security firm constructed its identities vis-à-vis different audiences, at times emphasizing its military competencies and at times its business image or its Swedish-ness. I will now continue to explore the ways Israeli security professionals frame themselves and perform as experts who not only bring specific knowledge, but also define what products and services Kenya is in need of (Leander 2005).

Israelis in Kenya

The expertise of these security professionals is framed largely in complementary ideas about the self and the Other and consists of ideas about "Israeli-ness" and a certain "African-ness." Making their expertise "logical" and natural, I argue, makes the mobility of their services possible. By analyzing this two-tier discourse, I thus want to see how Israeli security actors, their knowledge, and technologies are framed as "authoritative" and become mobile in order to be sold abroad to a lay Other, and how this Other is portrayed as a proper "receiver."

I will begin by mapping out the "Kenyan segment" of the Israeli security community. Importantly, all actors I spoke to had a history of military service, after which they either continued into the intelligence services (such as the Israeli Security Agency, ISA) or worked for private security companies. Interestingly, most told me a common story; after their military service they in fact wanted to get away from things "security," but they "fell into" this work through circumstances. Of course, as we have already noted before, these circumstances are not random. Men finishing (combat) military duty, especially in the rank of officer or even higher, have a big chance of being recruited into the ISA or to find a job in the security sector straight after their service, using their military capital (Grassiani 2017). We could analyze their military service as an apprenticeship, in which these men have learned not only skills, but also specific codes and jargon that distinguish them from others who are lacking this background (Carr 2010: 20).

However, even though this aspect of their biographies is comparable, a distinction can be made. These security actors can be largely divided into two kinds; employees of Israeli companies who work in Kenya and then leave again, and Israelis who live and work in Kenya and who own or work for a local security company (often Israeli-owned). The first group is made up of Israeli "integrator" firms that sell complete security systems. These companies are registered in Israel and compete in tenders of the Kenyan government, for example, or of electricity/energy companies. Once they receive the job, they come in with Israeli personnel who stay in Kenya for months, sometimes years, to finalize the project. They offer a "turnkey" solution, meaning that they bring in all different aspects of technologies and services to the client, who then only needs to "turn the key" and ignite the "engine."

An example of such a company is company X.[5] A big contract that was given to this company was for a project at the Jomo Kenyatta International

Airport in Nairobi (JKIA). An employee of company X whom I had contacted already in Israel invited me to come to their office at the airport. I
took a taxi and undertook the forty-minute to two-hour-long journey (depending on Nairobi traffic) and found the company in a new office, which
was still messy from construction and setting up new systems. Several
employees were working behind the computer (some Israeli, some not)
and behind them a majestic view could be seen, not only of the tarmac, but
also of Nairobi National Park, where, as the employees told me, you could
see the giraffes walking by while sitting behind your desk. The job that
this Israeli company came to do at JKIA was setting up all security systems
in a new wing at the airport. While we toured the wing, I saw the many
cameras that were connected to the huge screens in the control room next
to the offices and the access control systems that were installed. The systems they were in the process of setting up were meant to provide a "turnkey" solution for full security coverage. The Israeli company won a tender
that was offered by the Kenyan Airport Authority with a contract worth
over US$6 million. Besides setting up an elaborate technological advanced
security system, they also assisted with the hiring of local personnel, who
were to man the control room. An Israeli trainer who was flown in from
Israel performed the training of these personnel.

The second group of Israeli security actors is more diverse. Within
this group one can find individual consultants who work with local and
international clients, but also consultants who are employed as security
managers at specific sites, such as shopping malls. They work with local security companies, train members of the Kenyan police forces, and
provide security consultancy for projects such as the renewed Westgate
shopping mall and the Mombasa port. Often they stay in contact through
an informal network of security professionals and Israelis living abroad.
These consultants typically had lived in Nairobi for years, some even decades. They know the local context well and have had relationships with
the local security industry as well.

An example of such a consultant was A, a relatively young Israeli man
who, after working for several years in a variety of functions for the Israeli
Security Agency (ISA), came to Nairobi. By chance he was asked to manage
the security of one of Nairobi's shopping malls, and hence his consulting
career began. He admitted he was asked because he was Israeli and thus
was marked as a "security expert." It took some time to gain his trust, as he
was quite suspicious, but once we were sitting in his office he opened up.
He had been in Nairobi for several years and believed the work of Israelis
in Nairobi's security business was crucial, as the Kenyans often could not
be trusted to do the job well and to be honest (and thus not corrupt).

The knowledge and the technologies such consultants and companies brings to Kenya can be traced back directly to the "security network" (Sheffer and Barak 2013). They find their origins in the strategies of control and notions on security that are constructed in Israel and the Occupied Territories, and that are used by Israeli security and defense agencies, of which the security actors were part of. Such ideas—about who the enemy is, how the enemy should be "taken out," for example—are also deeply embedded in society. Furthermore, fences, surveillance methods, and models of facility security are copied directly from the systems of control in place in the Occupied Territories (Berda 2011; 2013). Many of the Israeli security professionals I spoke to pride themselves, for example, in the use of Israeli security models that were based on proactive security instead of "just waiting till something happens," emphasizing the difference between these approaches and the inferior "African" ones (or the absence of the latter). Their approach has been developed in Israel in response to the threats of suicide bombers and similar "surprise" attacks Israel has known for decades. These threats, as will also become clear below, are not seen within a context of the occupation, and thus the methods to counter them are also sanitized from any reference to Israel's systems of control; no mention is made of Palestinians and their hardships.

My questions for the interviewees mainly focused on the reasons they were in Kenya and how they explained their success. In the answers to these questions, two logics surfaced: one that emphasized the Israeli characteristics of the business, and another that explained the attraction of their (perceived) expertise by emphasizing "African" needs. I do not in any way perceive these logics as being objective or constant. Instead, I see them as part of the way Israeli security experts perceive their own work abroad and as part of the discourse with which they enact this expertise and mobility. Obviously, the broader context is one of making money, of "capitalizing on expertise," as one of my interviewees insightfully said. But I am interested here in looking beyond those market forces to understand how its producers frame their expertise and identify as experts. Their appeal and imagined and performed expertise in light of a supposed security "vacuum" is, I argue, what makes them mobile.

The expert framing in this case, I pose, is characterized by colonialist and racist ideas, within which the Israeli specialist has something to teach the "incompetent and unaware African." This will become clearer by looking in more detail at the arguments these experts voice. As mentioned before, the discourse of Israeli security professionals is sanitized almost in its entirety from any reference to the military occupation that stands at the basis of their specialty.

Israeli-ness: A Zionist, Colonial Logic

Israeli security experts working in Kenya frame their expertise first by emphasizing a specific "Israeli-ness," which, I argue, consists of two main ideas. The first one is related to the Israeli experience in defense and security and Israel's vast experience with fighting terror, thus using historical notions of experience and victimhood related to Israel's past. The second idea with which security professionals explain Israeli presence and their own expertise in Kenya has to do with a specific Israeli style of working, of being able to improvise, get things done, think "outside of the box." Both ideas are thus part of the way expertise is "performed" and framed to the outside world.

When I asked the employees (both in Israel and in Nairobi) about what makes their systems and work typically Israeli, they answered almost unanimously that it was related to "where we come from," or "our reality." Being an Israeli myself, most interviewees looked at me in a way that said something like "seriously . . . you know why." This idea of Israelis being superior in the "security business" because of their vast experience with terror and with many enemies around is taken for granted completely, and it was hard for me to even ask people to verbalize it. When they did, they emphasized a certain reality that "we Israelis" live in, and have lived in for decades. Usually they uttered "unfortunately" afterwards to emphasize it was out of their hands: Israel was attacked and Israelis could not but defend themselves. Again, the political context of the occupation is absent in these explanations. One consultant in Nairobi told me, "It is about . . . being 'smart'—Jews who came to Israel were smart, educated, . . . went through a lot of wars and won most of them. This gave them experience to become experts in security." In his perception, taking it all the way back to the fight for independence strengthens his argument; as another consultant said, "Israel has been fighting terror for years. If you live in Israel this is what you have to do." Another added, "We (Israelis) have had bitter experience; that is why we know so much." The Israeli as a security and anti-terror expert (against his will) surfaces here. Following this idea and Israel's successful branding of its expertise, security models that have been developed in Israel in the "fight against terror" are incorporated in the security of local shopping malls in Nairobi, for example. One veteran consultant told me the most important aspect of the "Israeli security model" is "to be a hunter, not a fisher." By this he meant that Israelis do not wait around for something to happen, but act proactively to guard against any attack. Such ideas then find their ways to shopping malls, embassies, and airports.

Related to this historical reasoning is an idea that emphasizes the current reality, the reality of kids growing up while needing to learn about security: "you experience security as kids, you learn about it from your parents, about looking out for suspicious people . . . there is the security thought," said one consultant. He continued: "Afterwards you go into the military; there you become disciplined, you become patriotic. You are experienced even if you are very young, you are born into it." Here we see a notion of passiveness that also emphasizes the inevitability of Israel's situation and its negative relations with its neighbors, experiences with terror and attacks.

This notion, however, is compensated by a more active and related idea that emphasizes a specific Israeli working style and attitude. Closely related to what Tamar Katriel (1986) has called "talking straight, dugri speech," this style consists of a direct, to-the-point approach, hard work, and an ability to improvise and think outside of the box. In relation to this, Senor and Singer (2009) have written about the "chutzpah" of Israeli entrepreneurs in the "Start-Up" world, which could be defined as a specific confidence, "gall, brazen nerve, effrontery."[6] The idea is that Israelis are not afraid to say it as it is and, in taking this risk, often get much further (in business) than others. While one might expect elaborate security models to be the thing emphasized by Israelis, this particular daring working style was much more dominant in the way they framed their expertise.

One consultant told me the following in a comparison to the way U.S. consultants would work in Kenya: "Israelis say what they want, in the U.S. they are nice . . . try to connect. Israelis show confidence, are assertive, take it or leave it, [they] come from the point of view: 'we know everything.' Marketing is not needed." The person described here is thus confident in his skills and knows that by only mentioning where he comes from, he can sell those skills with ease. "Israeli security experience" becomes an actual brand that sells itself (Grassiani 2017).

Another consultant in Nairobi phrased it as follows: "Israel has experience, we live it, we work hard, [we are] creative, loyal to the working place." Yet another one told me that there is more "caring" (*ekhpatiut*) and he really felt "part of the company" (adding that he felt this way even though it was not his). It is all about a specific "way of thinking, speed, action, thinking ahead." Often this style of working is then compared to the way the Other, in this case the Kenyan, is working. One security professional told me, "What a local does in a week I can do in an hour. [To] think ahead, they [Kenyans] can't do two things at once. [These are] different standards. The question is how to bring people to this standard."

I will get into this comparison in the next paragraphs, but for now I want to underscore the "educational" argument that is brought to the fore here: this consultant is wondering how one could bring the high (Israeli) standards to the Kenyans in a way that will actually stick. In the same line another security professional said to me, "It is all about mentality; this takes time. In Israel we live this reality; here, people don't 'have' it (*ein lahem etze*)." In relation to this, he told me about an experiment he did in Kenya to find out what the levels of security were: they tested some sites, and everywhere they managed to get in with a bag and leave it without anyone taking notice. This way of framing expertise in relation to the in-abilities of the Other is typical for the way experts distinguish themselves from lay persons (Carr 2010).

African-ness: A Racist, Colonialist Logic

The second part of the expert framing security professionals use empha-sizes the expertise vis-à-vis the "Africans" who are in need of Israeli secu-rity. Often "Africa" or "Africans" is used when describing these features, without making particular distinctions between the different countries that the vast continent consists of. Amanda Chisholm (2016) asks us to examine the global security industry through a critical "postcolonial lens" to identify colonial and racial patterns in the way security professionals from the West (or North) sell their knowledge to the "South" and thus to emphasize the context within which such relationships come into being. The heritage of being part of a colonizing entity is clearly visible in the discourse of Israeli security professionals in Kenya, as ideas of an inferior (black) Other are central to it. In their explanations of the characteristics of Africa or Kenya that create space for them, as security experts, to work in the security industry, we can see the following two ideas: "African incom-petence" and a high regard for Israeli security. Often these explanations are inherently racist, and people speak of black Africans as corrupt and incompetent, as "to claim to be an expert is also a claim to masculine white privilege" (Chisholm 2016: 119) in this context.

Concerning the first idea then, one consultant explained to me, after I asked him about the need for security in Kenya, that "Kenya is fairly peaceful, people are lazy, quiet, are not used to what we are used to. They are not connected to it, they don't have it (*hem lo mehubarim le klum, ein lahem etze*)." Another emphasized how Kenyans do not care about real security, only about money (see the quotation this chapter opened with as well). He said that making money was more important to them, empha-sizing the Israeli work ethic: "[The] head of security can't be Kenyan; [he] will take money from you—cheat you out of money." He added, "We fight for our land. I don't have any other country; here [in Kenya] they are not patriotic; it is business, for money—that is African culture." Another interviewee, answering my question about local Kenyan security, enforced the same idea: "[It's] nothing; they want to ride the wave of business in security but they don't know anything." He continued to say that Kenyan security officials would come to him for advice and then they would repeat to others what they had heard from him; this happened even on television shows.

What we can see here is an outspoken distrust of local security skills. Israeli expertise is established against a very dark and pessimistic idea about Kenyan security. The Israeli consultants I spoke to almost unanimously agreed that Kenyans knew close to nothing about security, that they mostly did not care, and that their main concern was to make money off the security business. Only one consultant was somewhat more optimistic, and he said he saw real improvement in the attitude and skills of Kenyans compared with some years ago.

Management skills were also part of a theme that came back as lacking in the local skillset. The dominant idea was that Kenyans (or Africans in general) could not "look ahead" or "see the big picture." They didn't have a "big head" (*rosh gadol*), a distinct military conceptualization of "looking beyond," at the whole context used by Israeli commanders and officers (Ben-Ari 1998; Grassiani 2013). Israeli expertise, in contrast, is highlighted as consisting of all those characteristics, as we saw earlier.

Related to the idea of the bad and sloppy security and management skills of Kenyans, or Africans in general, is a second logic I encountered consistently: the respect Israeli security companies and actors receive from the locals. As one interviewee said, "We know what we are doing; Israelis are respected." "As a consultant, being Israeli works," said another informant; "you are taken more serious in this context." A manager of a big Israeli company that does a lot of work in Kenya talked about the image of authority (*samchut*) that Israel has. Another told me that people are in need of "knowledge, they ask for it, see you as different, also in tenders, when you say you are from Israel they look at you different." Again and again, people emphasized that being Israeli gave them extra standing in business; one security professional even told me they were "seen as gods."

Thus the ways that Israeli security expertise is framed through emphases on "Israeli-ness" and "African-ness" can be seen as two sides of the same coin. This racist discourse shows the white privileged security expert who comes to "Africa" in order to share his knowledge with the lay, black Other. With these different logics distilled from the discourse of these professionals, I have tried to understand how the experts self-identify and what ideas about the Other are part of this expert framing.

Conclusion

In this chapter, I analyzed the mobility of Israeli security professionals, together with their technologies and knowledge, through their self-framing as experts. This mobility is part of a civil–military entanglement that works on a local level in Israel, through the security network, and internationally through the involvement of security agents and their military capital in the global security market. By looking at the case of Kenya, a place that is historically connected to Israel and where the Israeli security community is relatively extensive, I have attempted to show in what ways they frame their expertise through a discourse that is largely characterized by two corresponding logics. This discourse creates a space in which a need for "Israeli security expertise" and its superior characteristics reinforce each other.

The first logic consists of notions of a specific "Israeli-ness" that include a distinct Israeli working style and the "Israeli reality" as backdrop to Israel's knowledge and experience in security. The Israeli security professional is here defined as an expert who comes to the African continent to bring his knowledge to the lay Other. This lay Other comprises the second logic used. This logic is infused with colonialist and racist notions about a certain "African-ness" that includes the "incompetent African" who looks at Israeli superiority in security with awe. This discourse emphasizes Israel's position as (historical) victim in need of self-defense, posits that years of this defense grew an experienced security workforce, and is sanitized of any reference to Palestinian suffering or the occupation in general. In order to make these claims, I chose to analyze Israel as a whole, but also the language used by the security professionals, within its militarized social context and that of the military occupation. By doing so, it is possible to recognize the relationships and entanglements between the global security industry and the specific militarized and colonial background the security professionals come from.

Erella Grassiani is an anthropologist and works as assistant professor at the University of Amsterdam. She is the author of *Soldiering under Occupation: Processes of Numbing among Israeli Soldiers in the Al-Aqsa Intifada* (Berghahn Books, 2013). Her current research is part of a wider project on privatization and globalization of security, with a specific focus on Israel and security mobilities (SECURCIT). It traces the flows of (Israeli) security worldwide and looks at the way cultural ideas, technologies, and consultants move around globally.

Notes

1. At the HLS/Cyber conference of November 2016, there were people from approximately eighty countries (Azulai 2016).
2. It is estimated that Israel is selling security and military products (including knowledge) to 190 countries (Halper 2015). In 2017, Israel was estimated to close export deals for defense products with the value of 9 billion USD. From https://www.haaretz.com/israel-news/israel-s-defense-export-sales-exceed-record-9-billion-1.6052046, accessed 29 November 2018.
3. See https://www.standardmedia.co.ke/article/2000179470/israel-pm-netanyahu-pledges-to-support-kenya-in-war-against-terrorists, accessed 13 October 2015.
4. See https://www.nation.co.ke/news/Israeli-forces-join-Kenya-battle-to-end-deadly-mall-siege/1056-2002830-t6rln8z/index.html, accessed 29 November 2018.
5. I have used pseudonyms for the companies and names of employees in order to keep their anonymity (my concern is foremost with my interviewees; anonymizing the companies protects them).
6. See Leo Rosten's definition (in Guggenheim n.d.).

References

Azulai, Y. 2016. "Israel Seeks Larger Slice of Security Market." *Globes*, 16 November 2016. Accessed 20 December 2016, https://en.globes.co.il/en/article-israel-seeks-larger-slice-of-cyber-market-1001161235.

Ben-Ari, E. 1998. *Mastering Soldiers: Conflict, Emotions, and the Enemy in an Israeli Military Unit.* Oxford: Berghahn Books.

Berda, Y. 2011. "The 'Security Risk' as a Security Risk: Notes on the Classification Practices of the Israeli Security Services." In A. Matar and A. Baker (eds.), *Threat: The Palestinian Prisoners in Israeli Jails.* London: Pluto Press. Available in SSRN papers.

———. 2013. "Managing Dangerous Populations: Colonial Legacies of Security and Surveillance." *Sociological Forum* 28 (30): 627–30.

Berndtsson, J. 2012. "Security Professionals for Hire: Exploring the Many Faces of Private Security Expertise." *Millennium-Journal of International Studies* 40 (2): 303–20.

Boyer, D. 2008. "Thinking through the Anthropology of Experts." *Anthropology in Action* 15 (2): 38–46.

Carr, E. S. 2010. "Enactments of Expertise" *Annual Review of Anthropology* 39: 17–32.

Chisholm, A. 2015. "Postcoloniality and Race in Global Private Security Markets." In R. Abrahamsen and A. Leander (eds.), *Routledge Handbook of Private Security Studies*, 177–86. London: Routledge.

Christensen Mynster, M. 2017. "Shadow Soldering: Shifting Constellations and Permeable Boundaries in 'Private Security' Contracting." *Conflict and Society: Advances in Research* 3: 24–41.

DPPS. 2015. "Deal Ruthlessly with Terrorists, Netanyahu Advises, Assures Kenya of Support." *Star*, 12 October 2015. Accessed 13 October 2015, http://www.the-star.co.ke/news/deal-ruthlessly-terrorists-netanyahu-advises-assures-kenya-support.

Forbes, Steve. 2015. "How the Small State of Israel Is Becoming a High-Tech Superpower." *Forbes*, 22 July 2015. Accessed 29 July 2016, http://www.forbes.com/sites/steveforbes/2015/07/22/how-the-small-state-of-israel-is-becoming-a-high-tech-superpower/#39df24116f9c.

Glick Schiller, N., and N. B. Salazar. 2013. "Regimes of Mobility across the Globe." *Journal of Ethnic and Migration Studies* 39 (2): 183–200.

Goldstein, D. M. 2010. "Toward a Critical Anthropology of Security." *Current Anthropology* 51 (4): 487–517.

Graham, S. 2010. "Laboratories of War: United States-Israeli Collaboration in Urban War and Securitization." *Brown J. World Aff.* 17: 35.

Grassiani, E. 2013. *Soldiering under Occupation: Processes of Numbing among Israeli Soldiers in the Al-Aqsa Intifada.* Oxford: Berghahn Books.

———. 2017. "Commercialized Occupation Skills: Israeli Security Experience as an International Brand." In M. Leese and S. Wittendorp (eds.), *Security/Mobility: Politics of Movement,* 57–73. Manchester: Manchester University Press.

Gregory, D. 2004. *The Colonial Present: Afghanistan, Palestine, Iraq.* Oxford: Blackwell Publishing.

Guggenheim, J. A. n.d. "The Supreme Chutzpah." *Jewish Law Commentary.* Accessed 1 August 2016, http://www.jlaw.com/Commentary/SupremeChutzpah.html.

Halper, J. 2015. *War against the People: Israel, the Palestinians and Global Pacification.* London: Pluto Press.

Joachim, J., and A. Schneiker. 2014. "All for One and One in All: Private Military Security Companies as Soldiers, Business Managers and Humanitarians." *Cambridge Review of International Affairs* 27 (2): 246–67.

Katriel, T. 1986. *Talking Straight: Dugri Speech in Israeli Sabra Culture.* Cambridge: Cambridge University Press.

Kimmerling, B. 1993. "Patterns of Militarism in Israel." *European Journal of Sociology / Archives Européennes De Sociologie* 34 (2): 196–223.

Klein, N. 2007. "Laboratory for a Fortressed World." *The Nation,* 2 July 2007.

Kondo, V. 2018. "Kenya, Israel Sign Pact That Will Promote Trade between States." *Standard Digital,* 29 November 2018. Accessed 29 November 2018, https://www.standardmedia.co.ke/business/article/2001304472/kenya-israel-sign-trade-deal.

Leander, A. 2005. "The Market for Force and Public Security: The Destabilizing Consequences of Private Military Companies." *Journal of Peace Research* 42 (5): 605–22.

Levy, Y. 1998. "Militarizing Inequality: A Conceptual Framework." *Theory and Society* 27 (6): 873–904.

Lomsky-Feder, E., and E. Ben-Ari. 1999. *The Military and Militarism in Israeli Society.* Albany: SUNY Press.

Melman, Y. 2009. "Why Did Lieberman Really Go to Africa?" *Haaretz,* 9 September 2009. Accessed 29 July 2015, http://www.haaretz.com/news/yossi-melman-why-did-lieberman-really-go-to-africa-1.8190.

"Mossad Hunts Terror Leaders." 2002. CNN.com, 29 November 2002. Accessed 1 August 2016, http://edition.cnn.com/2002/WORLD/africa/11/29/kenya.mossad/.

Namunane, B. "Uhuru, Netanyahu Agree Deals in Security, Health, Agriculture." *Daily Nation,* 6 July 2016. Accessed 28 July 2016, http://www.nation.co.ke/news/-/1056/3281800/-/pf9c9iz/-/index.html.

Neocleous, M. 2007. "Security, Commodity, Fetishism." *Critique* 35 (3): 339–55.

Neocleous, M., and G. S. Rigakos. 2011. *Anti-Security.* Ottawa: Red Quill Books.

Ochs, J. 2011. *Security and Suspicion: An Ethnography of Everyday Life in Israel.* Philadelphia: University of Pennsylvania Press.

Otenyo, E. E. 2004. "New Terrorism: Toward an Explanation of Cases in Kenya." *African Security Studies* 13 (3): 75–84.

Rigakos, G. S. 2011. "To Extend the Scope of Productive Labour: Pacification as a Police Project." In M. Neocleous and G. S. Rigakos (eds.), *Anti-Security,* 85–105. Ottawa: Red Quill Books.

Sadeh, S. 2016. "From Homeland Security to Water, with Netanyahu's Visit, Israeli Businesses Rediscover Africa." *Haaretz,* 21 July 2016. Accessed 29 July 2015, http://www.haaretz.com/israel-news/business/.premium-1.732681.

Senor, D., and S. Singer. 2009. *Start-Up Nation: The Story of Israel's Economic Miracle.* Toronto: McClelland & Stewart.

Sheffer, G., and O. Barak. 2013. *Israel's Security Networks: A Theoretical and Comparative Perspective.* Cambridge: Cambridge University Press.

Sheller, M., and J. Urry. 2006. "The New Mobilities Paradigm." *Environment and Planning A: Economy and Space* 38 (2): 207–26.

Singer, P. W. 2003. *Corporate Warriors: The Rise of the Privatized Military Industry.* New York: Cornell University Press.

Swed, O., and J. S. Butler. 2015. "Military Capital in the Israeli Hi-Tech Industry." *Armed Forces & Society* 41 (1): 123–41.

Zirulnick, A. 2015. "Kenyan Consumers Win This Round against Al Shabaab as Westgate Mall Reopens." *Quartz Africa,* 18 July 2015. Accessed 19 July 2015, https://qz.com/africa/457 808/kenyan-consumers-win-this-round-against-al-shabaab-as-westgate-mall-reopens/.

Zureik, E. 1979. *The Palestinians in Israel: A Study in Internal Colonialism.* London: Routledge.

Zureik, E, D. Lyon, and Y. Abu-Laban. 2010. *Surveillance and Control in Israel/Palestine: Population, Territory and Power.* London: Routledge.

Chapter 10

Explaining Efficiency, Seeking Recognition

Experiences of Argentine Peacekeepers in Haiti

Sabina Frederic

Introduction

What do the stories of members of the Argentine military say about their experience as peacekeepers in Haiti? How do they account for the effectiveness of this military operation, probably the most significant of their careers? Why is it considered a military operation if its success is attributed to the variety of civic tasks that established links of trust and cooperation with the Haitian population? What has been the role of the domestic and regional political scene in the construction of the operational environment of the peacekeeping mission? In this chapter, I answer these questions and show how commanders and soldiers sought to reestablish their reputation in the eyes of Argentine society through the peacekeeping operation, and argue that this way of rectifying their reputation is based on a paradox. Members of the military claim to be warriors, but neither the government, which despised militarism, nor their social tasks in Haiti underline this category of self-understanding (Brubaker and Cooper 2000). Their stories emphasize over and over the empathy and sensitivity toward Haitian people's suffering that they felt through carrying out civic or humanitarian tasks. Nevertheless, their wish to reaffirm their professional role as warriors involved a process of "identification as a complex (and often ambivalent) process" (Brubaker and Cooper 2000: 14). Thus this chapter will argue that their stories move from the entanglements of civil–military tasks to things that tend to disentangle or moderate the civilianization that the humane role of the peacekeeper involved.

Between 2004 and 2015, the Argentine armed forces deployed three military units in Haiti: an Argentine Joint Battalion (BAC is its acronym in Spanish) stationed in Gonaives, and the Air Force Mobile Hospital and the Argentine Air Force Unit in Port-au-Prince. Gonaives (Arbonite), the second largest city in Haiti, was assigned as the area of responsibility of the Argentine battalion, with a UN mandate to stabilize and secure the region. Over ten years, Argentina contributed to the UN mission in Haiti a total number of thirteen thousand troops in contingents comprising five hundred soldiers.[1] The troops were stationed at the base camp in Gonaives.

During those ten years, the specific nature of the mission changed from "imposition of peace" to "maintenance of peace." The commanders of the first Argentine contingents, who had to deal with the most difficult conditions, and faced enormous challenges, particularly valued the autonomy they had in such a critical and challenging scenario. Broadly, all the former members of BACs regarded the Haitian peace mission as the most important military operation in their careers.[2] "Extreme poverty," "criminal violence," "collapsed state institutions," "disbanded armed forces," "weak justice system," and a "weak and corrupt national police force," were the categories most frequently used by the troops when they described the Haitian scene. Although they knew almost nothing of the culture and the national language, French Creole, they realized immediately that they had to reach out to the local population, stressing their social abilities, to earn their acceptance and cooperation.

The plight of the Haitian people touched soldiers and officers deeply, and their stories evoked the abject misery that engulfed Gonaives and its inhabitants. But what most moved the Argentine troops was the hopelessness of the lives of the children, malnourished and neglected. The commanders of the Argentine contingent believed that an approach based on establishing close relations with the people was the key reason for the success of a mission in such a hostile and harsh environment. Using persuasion and negotiation, not force, was essential to preserving the legitimacy of the operation, and gaining the recognition of the Haitian people, the international community, and, above all, Argentine society.

Thus, providing "humanitarian assistance" to the Haitian people implied carrying out a multitude of nonmilitary tasks such as "civic actions," "assistance," "negotiations," or "psychological operations." The BAC members point out how the margin of operational autonomy (granted or earned) allowed them to adjust these tasks flexibly to meet the needs of the local population. Therefore, as we will show, the narratives of the members of the first two BACs constructed the operational environment in a way that explained mission effectiveness through the value given to the civic actions and the avoidance of the use of force. The former peacekeepers claimed their identity by situating themselves in that narrative (Brubaker and Cooper 2000). Nonetheless, officers partially tolerated that priority of civic tasks. The entanglement produced by the blend of patrols and civic action troubled commanders in different ways, ranging from its rejection to a particular acceptance of a civilian side of military performance.

The perspective that the former Argentine peacekeepers hold does not represent the traditional approach to civil–military relations, which encapsulates the military sphere as opposed to the civilian one, assuming a sharp distinction between them, and challenging any sort of military intervention in the civil domain.[3] The stories of the Argentine soldiers reveal situations where the boundaries between the civil and military spheres became blurred (Luckham 1971). Some of them show how the former peacekeepers try to make sense of a past experience where civic actions belong to the military through contra-insurgency strategies to combat guerrilla efforts—for example, in the early 1970s in Argentina. However, as the strategies were rejected as state terrorism methods, Argentinean peacekeepers struggle to hide, silence, or soften them. Birgitte Sørensen (2015) similarly examines Danish veterans' struggle with "secrecy work" in their postdeployment narratives. In other stories, soldiers express emotions they attributed to civilians but that actually permeated them as members of the military, such as the concept of masculinity among Israeli combatants (Ben-Ari 1998). Those civilian feelings and tasks were categories their narratives processed to combine with the military ones, searching for their self-understanding. In this process, as it is remarked by Sørensen and Ben Ari in the introduction to this book, civil–military entanglement potentially destabilizes and reconfigures the constituent parts. "It is not that there are no such divisions, but that the distinctions are effects or outcomes" (Hodder 2012: 91). Thus "military" feelings, actions, and traditions were also altered, incorporating some civilian parts, in the process of identification as majority world warriors, mainly once peacekeepers left Haiti and continued their careers in Argentina.

Ten years after the withdrawal of the Argentine troops from Haiti, the stories that the military shared with us were mostly accounts of the civic tasks driven by the UN mission and BACs' initiatives carried out during the operation. Although the interviewees had already been reabsorbed into military life and its duties, the civil aspect reemerged again and again, offering a sharp contrast to other situations in military life where a clear distinction is made between the military and the civilian spheres. This distinction is socialized in the military academies, as the ethnographic research has shown (Castro 1991; Badaró 2009).

However, the civic actions induced a degree of ambiguity in soldiers' military status. The members of the first two BACs used different strategies to resolve this ambiguity, reinterpreting differently the civil aspect of their professional performance.[4] Therefore, while in the first BAC civic actions seemed incompatible with the strictly military duties, in the second BAC they became part of the military tactical doctrine. A comparison of the later military careers of the first BAC commanders allows us to understand that their promotions depended on their ability to explain how those civic actions were promoted by Argentine military doctrine. Therefore, civic actions were used to explain the efficiency of the mission, as well as to reinforce the idea of the Argentine soldier as flexible, warm, generous, and caring, thereby strengthening the military.

This chapter will look into the stories of some former members of the first two BACs deployed between 2004 and 2005. The accounts were given during interviews and informal talks, which I held between 2014 and 2015 in their military units in Argentina: the Airborne Brigade, the Special Operation Force, and an Infantry Regiment. Although for the purpose of this article we will focus mainly on the accounts of those military deployed during the first year, the fieldwork subjects comprised members of ten of the twenty BACs stationed in Haiti. I analyze these accounts as narratives through which the soldiers recount the critical events that marked the operation and posed the most significant challenges. I interviewed a total of forty-three officers, NCOs, and soldiers, most of whom were still on active duty.[5]

These stories constitute narratives. As Edward Bruner (1984) points out, the narrative order highlights the difference between a "life-as-lived" (what actually happened), a "life-as-experienced" (the images, feelings, desires, thoughts, and meaning known to the person whose life it is), and a "life-as-told." Thus, the stories suppose a discontinuity with past experience, but they speak about "experiences." The narrative analysis shows how those stories introduce the actor in a social world, and through them the actors give meaning to their past and present existence, confirming or reconfiguring social identities and relations (Ricoeur 1991). Thus, through the lens of narrative, we have access to an identification process by which the former peacekeepers rebuild their experiences and try to articulate "doing civic tasks" while being military. Like Marilyn Strathern (1992) or Roger Brubaker and Frederick Cooper (2000), we are interested in the situational process by which identification combines parts or social categories. Thus how they moved from a supposed single socialization and cultural acquisition to a peacekeeping role was problematic since, as they see it, being military was a diverging and even conflicting entanglement of parts that coexisted or expressed themselves successively differently.

Arturo Sotomayor in *The Myth of the Democratic Peacekeeper* (2013) demonstrated that the deployment of the armed forces of Chile, Brazil, Argentina, and Uruguay in peace missions did not have the impact on the announced military democratization. Peacekeeping did not reconvert the military identity into a democratic one, such as Katherine Worboys (2007) argued. In support of Sotomayor, Philip Cunliffe (2017) demonstrated that peacekeeping operations do not necessarily stimulate democracy at home either (in Bangladesh, Fiji, or Gambia, where there was a coup d'état). For that reason, our objective is to analyze some of the devices that outlined the effects of the missions on former peacekeepers. Our ethnographic study aims to be a contribution in this sense, by exploring how, when narrated, the experience of the military presents continuities or discontinuities between past, present, and future, and alternative or competing categories of self-understanding.

Peace missions are particularly relevant to the armed forces of Latin America, because unlike other Western nations, "Latin America is among the most pacific regions on earth" (Pion Berlín 2016: 1). These operations contributed to an unprecedented international cooperation between Argentina, Chile, and Brazil, dissolving the old hypotheses of conflict (Pion Berlín 2016: 56). Until the end of the twentieth century, Argentina saw Chile and Brazil as potential enemies, especially Chile, which was an ally of the United Kingdom during the Malvinas/Falklands War. But for Pion-Berlin (2016), there is a limit to how much militaries can "stretch" beyond their conventional role during peacetime.

Our study moves in another direction. Far from presupposing a limit, an analysis of the Argentine case can contribute to an understanding of the logic governing the rigidity with which soldiers incorporate the experience as peacekeepers into military identities. Thus, I hope to contribute to some of the debates currently taking place. My aims are these: first, to understand the extent of the supposed flexibility of the Western armed forces to respond and manage the conflicts of the post–Cold War period (Dandeker 2006); second, to show how the Argentinean military answered demands for humanitarian or civic actions once they deployed, while insisting on their condition of warriors (Miller and Moskos 1995) and coping with the ambivalence of the new situation; third, to show how former Argentinian peacekeepers' narratives of their experience, to follow Chiara Ruffa (2014: 211), are linked to the context and experience of their home country. Ruffa (2014) demonstrates how the operational environment of the same peace operation changes according to the nationality of the military unit. She carried out a project examining how four military units of different countries interpret or construct the operational environment differently in the same UN mission. I also found in the stories of the Argentine military a sharp prevalence of their past experience before deploying, both personally and institutionally, in the way they built the operational environment in Gonaives, Haiti. That experience deplored the loss of prestige and reputation of the armed forces, the wave of civilianization, and the search for social and political recognition as militaries. Therefore, this is what introduced the strongest limit to flexibility in military self-understanding, and what can contribute to explain how they worked either to disentangle the civic aspects of their mission or to show how those tasks had to do with traditional military intelligence doctrine.

The Argentine Scenario: Democratization, Demilitarization, and Parliamentary Debate

Intense parliamentary debate marked the government's political decision to contribute to the UN Stabilization Mission in Haiti (MINUSTAH) with the largest contingent of troops ever deployed in a peacekeeping operation in Argentina's contemporary history. According to a law passed in March 2004, the departure of troops from the national territory had to be authorized by the National Congress. Moreover, the MINUSTAH was launched initially under Chapter 7 of the UN Charter. This chapter on "peace enforcement" authorized the use of restrictive measures, or use of force, under the limitations established by the Rules of Engagement (ROE).[6] Unlike the peace operation in Cyprus, launched under Chapter 6 of the UN Charter, the current Haitian scene called for a more forceful intervention.

The parliamentary debate in Argentina framed the country's policy for the military operation in Haiti, particularly in the case of the first contingents. It indicated that in no case must the blue helmets become a military occupation force at the service of the United States, or participate in civil conflict resolution, policing, and public security, all banned to Argentine military by law. Undoubtedly, the parliamentary authorization for deployment of troops in Haiti was supported by the fact that this was the first peace operation led by Latin American forces in the context of a regional approach as part of the policies of the Union of South American Nations (UNASUR) (Hirst 2016).[7] Brazil was assigned the role of leader of the operation, and the Force Commander of the MINUSTAH was always a Brazilian officer. In 2004, the Latin American troops comprised 70 percent of the total number of soldiers in Haiti; this number decreased to 60 percent in 2010, and later rose again to 79 percent in 2014. The process of regional integration committed Argentina to participate actively in MINUSTAH with Brazil and Chile, leaders in the region.

Moreover, all three countries were examples of successful democratization processes initiated during the 1980s, and saw themselves as capable of encouraging and imparting democratic principles in Haiti. Argentina was at the forefront of the human rights policy in the region, investigating and prosecuting those responsible for the crimes committed during the last dictatorship (1976–1983).

Although the Argentine military on active duty today were not involved in the last military dictatorship, they still feel they carry the weight of the crimes perpetrated by the armed forces during the state terror in the 1970s that brought such discredit to the armed forces in Argentina. They refer to it as "carrying a backpack" (Frederic, Masson, and Soprano 2015).

The democratization of the Argentine armed forces started immediately after the collapse of the military regime in Argentina (1976–1983), and was brought about by the defeat in the Malvinas/Falklands War. Two key laws prohibited military intervention in domestic security activities, limiting their participation in matters of external security or foreign affairs.[8] All other matters of internal security remained under the responsibility of the security and police forces.

These two flagship laws became state policy and served as the basis for reforming and reverting the process of militarization of the political field in Argentina that so strongly had defined the nineteenth century (Halperin Donghi 1978) and the twentieth century (Potash 1981; Rouquié 1981, 1982). This legislation was enacted to prevent the atrocities of the 1970s that left thirty thousand missing persons and an unknown number of dead people, torture survivors, exiles, and thousands of other victims from ever occurring again.[9] A drastic reduction of the defense budget was also endorsed. Additionally, in 2004, members of the military started being prosecuted for crimes against humanity during the last dictatorship. In a decade, almost a thousand troops were imprisoned.

With the demilitarization/civilianization/democratization, an element of uncertainty surrounded the function of the armed forces. In this context, the government decided in 1992 to increase significantly its UN peacekeeping contributions. Even though part of the armed forces actively resisted military intervention in external defense and security matters, the initiative gradually gained acceptance.

At the institutional level, the army considers war and the defense of the national territory as the military operation par excellence, and peace operations as subsidiary or secondary tasks. However, as the armed forces' participation in peacekeeping activities become increasingly common, the stories of former Argentine blue helmets that we interviewed questioned and reshaped that idea. The national pacification that followed the demilitarization of the political field since 1983 has left the military stranded in a sort of no-man's-land, without a clearly defined role. Among their new functions and duties are the provision of logistics, the recruitment and training of troops, the provision of assistance in emergencies, the support of community actions such as the distribution of resources (books, computers, food, or drinking water), supporting the population in regions of difficult access, and in marginal neighborhoods, or *villas*. However, the performance of these tasks has landed them in a sort of indeterminate space with lack of clarity about their specific professional functions as warriors. Only a minority of the military were in favor of a more "social" function of the armed forces, and they justified the performance of these tasks as an exercise of national sovereignty, instrumental in building the nation. Those actions were the ones carried out in Haiti—the ones called humanitarian by the UN. The problem with publically defending them was that they were part of military intelligence used against the guerrilla in the 1970s, subsequently condemned as the origin of state terrorism, and illegal since 2006.

The military performance of actions where the use of force is not the main tool has a deep history. At the height of the Cold War (1960–1970), these initiatives were known as "civic actions," a key concept of the French and American counterinsurgency doctrine supported by the U.S. government in Latin America, and carried out by the armed forces of the region. They were a part of "psychological operations" conducted by the military, implemented together with other strategies, such as torture and interrogations, to terrorize the population and undermine their morale (Robin 2005). The aim was to prevent the spread of communism in Latin America, or of the liberation movements in Algeria and Indochina, among local populations that generally supported the guerrillas. These activities included military participation in community activities like healthcare, education, and recreation to improve the relations with the local population and increase their cooperation. As Davis Bobrow (1966: 102) pointed out,

> The civic role of the military has become a principal American instrument to cope with communist revolution, political instability, and economic backwardness. Expressed in the doctrine of civic action, the civic role refers to the use of military forces on projects useful to the local population at all levels in such fields as education, training, public works, agriculture, transportation, communications, health, sanitation, and others contributing to economic and social development, which would also serve to improve the standing of the military forces with the population.

Although the political context changed radically in the post–Cold War scene, and the fight against communism was not one of the aims of MINUSTAH, in their stories the military underline a continuity. As the former commander of the second BAC, General Jorge Barcio stated, "To gain the cooperation and recognition of the local population, and to isolate the 'armed gangs' without using excessive force, we needed to carry out both civic actions and 'psychological operations.'" However, psychological operations had been banned in Argentina in 2006 when marines from a military base in Patagonia had been found conducting intelligence activity against political sectors. Because this kind of operation could no longer be performed, nor was it a part of military intelligence strategies, during fieldwork we were asked to treat this information confidentially.

Since then, instead of "psychological operations," the Argentine military speak of *civic actions*, what the UN called "humanitarian assistance." They described them as initiatives carried out by soldiers aimed at gaining the support and trust of the local population, making them more dependent on the Argentine troops and less susceptible to the influence of the local gangs. Conversely, in the view of the United Nations, these initiatives were basically performed by civilian organizations (the White Helmets in Argentina) or nongovernmental organizations. Nevertheless, as the *Handbook of Peace Operations* (published after Brahimi's [UN General Assembly Security Council 2000] report on the UN's study of peacekeeping operations) states,

> Humanitarian projects undertaken by the military can contribute significantly to improving relations with the local population and the parties to the conflict, thereby increasing security and building consent. These activities should be based on the international humanitarian objectives and policy framework in the mission area and avoid duplication of effort with humanitarian agencies. It is vital that the initiatives help build local capacity and be sustainable in the long term. (DPKO 2003: 64)

The level of autonomy that the Argentine troops had in Haiti allowed them to engage in a broad variety of projects and activities aimed at strengthening the ties of friendship and cooperation with the local population. They describe the white helmets as incompetent, with a limited recognition of the logistical and security requirements, and called them "improvisers."

To the Argentine military, Haiti was the chance to prove to themselves and to Argentine society that they could be effective, sensitive, and committed professionals. Their stories show how the progressive and continuous engagement in initiatives and actions to assist the Haitian people added to the military character traits such as sensibility, efficiency, pragmatism, and compassion. As a noncommissioned officer from the first BAC said with anguish, on the verge of tears, and with difficulty in continuing his story, "It hurts to see those barefooted and abandoned children; we tried to make time to help the orphanage even if it was not our main task. We gave them food, rebuilt the place . . . Apologies, but it hurts. We are supposed to be strong and cold as militaries." I encountered this scenario repeatedly during my fieldwork. It was awkward for me and for them: improper emotions for military men, a civilian penetration of their emotional socialization as warriors.

The Operational Environment in Gonaives: Suffering, Armed Violence, and Autonomy

Undoubtedly, the Argentine scene that I have already described played a significant part in the construction of the operational environment in Gonaives; the interviewees mention the challenge of appeasing both the Haitian and domestic fronts. Consequently, the commanders of the BACs took the necessary steps to minimize and limit the use of force, as they needed to create a favorable opinion of the mission at the local and national level. The then President Néstor Kirchner specifically warned them of the potential risks of overstepping those limits as the mission—and he himself—would remain under close scrutiny. Gonaives was one of the conflict's hotspots, where opposing political groups, former military personnel of the Haitian armed forces, armed political gangs, and bandits fought each other for political control of the territory.

The leaders of first two BACs were faced with a dangerous and volatile situation, and deliberately sought to avoid repression and confrontation. The first Argentine contingent arrived in August 2004 with around four hundred troops (70 percent army, 29 percent navy, and one air force soldier). Following a decision of the UN authorities, the BAC was stationed on the fringes of Gonaives, an abandoned terrain on a hillside. They had been able to take only some tents and the few personal belongings they had traveled with. The remaining equipment was due to arrive by ship in two months.

Living and working in a context of such poverty and misery deeply touched the Argentinians; their narratives evoked the abject misery that engulfed the city of Gonaives and its inhabitants. "There is nothing like that in Argentina," they said. Repeatedly, Gonaives was described as a "huge shanty town": the poor housing, the lack of urban planning and garbage collection service, the intolerable heat, and the appalling smells gave the town an air of wretchedness and misery.

What most shocked the Argentine military was, in fact, the misery, and not the armed violence. The vulnerability of the Haitian children, undernourished, emaciated, and often abandoned, was consistently brought up during the interviews; the memories sometimes visibly touched them, and they were forced to interrupt their accounts (Frederic 2016). This context was singled out as the ugliest and toughest side of their Haitian experience, and gradually gained precedence over the issue of armed violence, previously the main focus of the peace operation.

Still, during the first year of the MINUSTAH, the primary concern of the BAC was to disarm the "criminal gangs" rampant in the region, especially the armed groups of the disbanded former Haitian forces. The Haitian police force was by then thoroughly discredited. Prior to the arrival of the troops, the police station had been attacked with machetes by sectors of the population, who then freed the prisoners.

In the absence of legitimate state institutions to guarantee peace and security, the Argentine troops were forced to take on the role of maintaining law and order in their jurisdiction. Broadly, the UN mandate in Haiti was "to create and maintain a safe and secure environment," and no further details had been provided by the force commander in this regard, outside of those established by the "rules of engagement" for a rational and proportionate use of force. The communication and infrastructure problems added to the geographical isolation of the BACs, granting the Argentine commanders a considerable degree of operational autonomy. Although no more than a hundred kilometers separated Gonaives and Port-au-Prince, the critical condition of the roads, as well as the continuous threat of the armed gangs, made traveling between the two cities difficult and dangerous. Consequently, the commanders first resolved and then communicated. Thus the operational autonomy was constructed.

This level of discretion and freedom of action was highly valued. It was, in fact, one of the assets of the mission, as they were free to stamp the military operation with a distinctive Argentine character. Soon it became obvious that the use of force would not endear them to the local people. The relationship with the Haitian population could not be built on the use or threat of force. Local acceptance and recognition had to be earned by different means. Furthermore, it was a well-known fact that some of the Haitian people saw the MINUSTAH as an occupation force, a renewed version of the U.S. military occupation of the early twentieth century.

Therefore, regarding their ordinary, day-to-day dealings with the Haitian people, the former peacekeepers developed a way of self-understanding that was widespread, as we found in several conversations with them. "We were different. As Argentineans we are generous, supportive, and warm," said the former commander of the first BAC. Ultimately, their goal was being perceived not as an occupation force but simply as the Argentine troops. To this end, they carried out a series of different credit-deserving initiatives, many of which involved actions to deal with the aftermath of Hurricane Jeanne in Gonaives. As former peacekeepers argued, their behavior changed the perceptions of the population, secured them the acceptance of the local people, and won them recognition and legitimacy at the local and domestic level in Argentina.

Reaching Out to the Local Population: Flexibility and Ambiguity in the Military Role

To the first BAC leaders, the main question was "how to reach out to the people." Acceptance, recognition, and cooperation were in fact the tactical means to ensure the effectiveness of the operation without resorting to physical coercion. What was at stake was the opportunity to reestablish the prestige of the armed forces, and a chance to come to terms with their much-discredited profession. Reclaiming the more humane side of themselves added to their self-perception as warriors, even if it rendered it ambiguous. For this reason, it is not possible to talk here of identity changes—that is, from warriors to peacekeepers or diplomats; in fact, their stories ascribe the effectiveness of the civic actions to their flexibility and reassertion as soldiers, however ambiguous this remained.

According to the stories, the different civic actions and projects can be grouped into categories of ordinary, extraordinary, complementary to a military operation, or integrated in a military operation. Among the ordinary actions were arranging friendly football matches and competitions, assisting in the construction or reconstruction of schools or orphanages, and distributing potable drinking water every day. The extraordinary actions were emergency actions or relief activities carried out to deal with the aftermath of Hurricane Jeanne, as well as recreational activities like the organization of popular festivals in Gonaives. As part of a military operation, we will describe the negotiations conducted by the commanders of the BACs on two occasions.

In July 2004, when the first Argentine contingent arrived in Haiti, the overall situation was chaotic. First, the commander and the adjutant of the first BAC met a few of the community's leaders: the bishop, several priests, and members of a local club among others. Also, finding the background information on the predeployment course insufficient, some of the senior NCOs set themselves the task of learning about Haitian culture. Even if Haiti is part of the Latin American and the Caribbean region, this nation has generally remained outside Argentina's sphere of interest. The cultural and language differences have without doubt contributed to the country's isolation from the rest of the Spanish-speaking Latin American countries.

In Haiti, the majority of the population practices voodoo, a syncretic religion that blends Roman Catholic and African elements. The Argentine troops, conversant with the Catholic tradition, were mostly disconcerted by the voodoo practices and rituals. "To understand the Haitian people, one must learn about voodoo," explained Florencio Gomez, a retired army noncommissioned officer and former peacekeeper. He believed that voodoo lay at the root of the Haitian national character, and that it explained the "strangeness" of their conduct and their peculiar considerations of life and death, as well as the violence and poverty devastating most of the country.[10]Information about voodoo had helped the troops in their approach to the inhabitants of Gonaives.

Still, the Argentine contingent found the Haitian environment uncertain and hostile. As supplies from Argentina were delayed, food and toiletries were scarce, forcing them to exist on combat rations for a month. There was the ever-present danger of armed groups, plus the devastation that followed Hurricane Jeanne and the floods that caused over two thousand deaths. After this tragedy, the priorities changed, and the stories of the senior leadership of the BAC speak of a dilemma: having to choose between providing humanitarian assistance and security.

The floods that followed Hurricane Jeanne also hit the Argentine military base, washing away personal belongings, military equipment, and vehicles. Nevertheless, the troops mobilized to respond to the most pressing needs of the population. The medical staff of the BAC treated hundreds of victims who approached the base camp desperately looking for help. The troops redeployed to places in the city where the floods had already subsided. From there, the battalion's command, logistics, and health elements set out to assist the thousands of injured and displaced victims.

While they struggled to bring humanitarian assistance to the survivors, the Argentine troops also had to dispose of the hundreds of dead bodies left by the catastrophe. People dumped the dead bodies outside the military camps. All of these were tasks that moved them profoundly, especially the sight of dead children.

To the commander of the first BAC, Pedro Gimenez,[11] by then lieutenant colonel, the ensuing famine that ravaged the city of Gonaives was much worse. The survivors were in dire need of potable water and food, so the military had to turn the BAC into a center for storage and distribution of relief supplies. Even if this initiative brought them closer to the local population, it also increased the risk of looting, endangering the lives of the most vulnerable. Moreover, the increasing attacks from armed gangs on the distribution centers forced the commanding officers to change their distribution tactics so that the supplies reached the most vulnerable groups, the women and the children.

Shortly after the devastating floods hit Gonaives, about half of the soldiers there were suffering from severe stomach disorders, due to the lack of clean drinking water, and symptoms of physical and mental exhaustion. Still, every day they struggled to cope with new challenges and demands. As the former commander Gimenez said,

> The nature of our tasks changed on a daily basis, according to the emerging needs. We were confronted by pressing problems that demanded higher levels of flexibility as a commander. Security stopped being our priority. The main priority was given to ensuring that the women and the children received relief supplies. I ordered different initiatives toward this end: the use of concertina wire to protect the supplies from looting and plundering, lining people up in orderly queues to restrict and supervise access to the distribution center, or protecting the women and children from having their goods stolen. But, in the face of the desperation—and greed—all these actions proved useless, so, to put an end to the abuses we placed the area surrounding the warehouses under constant surveillance.

As soon as the distribution of the relief supplies was seen to, a group of former Haitian military, armed with guns and shovels, and using women and children as shields, appeared at the camp, attempting to recover the control of Gonaives by taking over control of the supplies. The leader of the band, a former general of the Haitian forces, was dressed in his old uniform and carried a scimitar. One of his advisors was a "hardliner," the other appeared more conciliatory. The chief of the BAC entered into a lengthy and difficult negotiation, determined to preserve control of the distribution center, while the French police currently on duty wanted to give in to their demands. Finally, the former Haitian military men gave in and agreed to leave in exchange for food; the BAC patrols regained control of security, having forced them to leave the area.

Such successful negotiation emphasizes again the use of capabilities outside the military sphere for those who were never prepared, as Marina Nuciari (2006) found in general for peacekeeping. Most important, as Gimenez said, "We could keep control of the distribution sites, the BAC gave the local population a clear and forceful demonstration of our authority, the Argentine troops gained recognition and legitimacy among the Haitian people. In their eyes the Battalion became a sort of surrogate state, guarantor of law and order."

In fact, the first BAC effectively countered the threat of the disbanded Haitian former military so that they no longer posed a problem when the second BAC deployed. Additionally, they engaged in recreational activities as part of the policy of developing relations of trust and cooperation with the population as in football matches between the Argentine troops and local people. The NCOs and the soldiers made sure that the popular rites and practices of the Haitian people to ward off the victory of the Argentine team were accepted and respected as part of the spectacle.

Just before the Argentine troops left Haiti, two months after the floods, a Sri Lankan battalion was stationed in Gonaives. According to Roberto Hernandez, operational officer in Haiti, "Sri Lankan soldiers lacked discipline, command and control. They were quite 'trigger happy'; for them, it was just a question of shooting. They caused problems instead of solving them. Now, a reinforcement of Brazilian troops would have been better, they have discipline and self-control." During the ten years that followed the withdrawal of Argentine troops from Haiti, the Argentine Centre for Joint Training in Peace Operations (CAECOPAZ, its acronym in Spanish), under the joint chief of staff, twice invited the former chief of this BAC to share his experience as a negotiator in Gonaives.[12] To the Argentine army, the demonstration of negotiation skills showed the professional competence of the commander and his leadership qualities. Therefore, over the years, he was placed in command of different elite combat units, a "number one"[13] until he eventually reached the rank of major general in the Argentine forces.

To the former members of this first Argentine contingent that I interviewed, the negotiations and activities such as food distribution, football matches, and other nonmilitary actions describe and explain the effectiveness of the peace operation and the recognition gained at the different levels. But the chief of this BAC admits that he faced "the leader's dilemma" when the floods hit Gonaives so badly and he was forced to choose between security and humanitarian assistance. He chose the second alternative and capitalized on the experience by considering it an experience of "command," while the "civic actions" remained to him something outside the military doctrine, only performed in Haiti.

From January to July 2005, a second BAC of around five hundred troops replaced BAC 1 and continued the mission at Gonaives. For a week, BAC 1 and BAC 2 shared the military base and exchanged all the relevant information pertaining to the operation.

In his narrative about the effectiveness of the operations, the former chief of the BAC 2, Fabio Retamoso, at that time lieutenant colonel, marks "a turning point":

> The turning point was for us the moment when the Haitian people no longer saw us as an occupation force, but as the Argentine troops. This had been one of the goals we had set ourselves once we arrived at Gonaives. We knew that it had been achieved when we organized a farewell party. It was a cultural encounter between Argentina and Haiti. There were Haitian and Argentinean musicians performing their songs. We publicized the party distributing pamphlets in Creole. It was a success. The main square of Gonaives was crowded. More than any political party. The local authorities, civil servants, judiciary members, religious officials, politicians and personnel of the MINUSTAH had

attended it. The Bishop had never spoken to so many people. The festival was a huge success, almost without money. The total cost of the festival was 140 dollars for the rental of the sound equipment.

However, what we highlight here are the reasons given by the former peacekeepers for this success, and how the ambiguity of the increasing participation of the military in civic actions was solved, not only by experience of command, but also through integration with the military doctrine. According to the chief of BAC 2, who was promoted to general ten years later and appointed operational commander of the joint chiefs of staff in 2016, the key to the mission's effectiveness was precisely *civic actions*. What emerges when he speaks about them is a certain paradox and ambivalence, between what was entailed by being a military and BAC 2's entanglement with civilian tasks. He said, "I am proud we never had to fire a single shotgun during my command. But we are warriors, although there are those who dislike it in the current government. Thus from time to time we showed our teeth . . . we exhibited we had the force."

How does this Argentine military commander explain the ambiguities and inconsistencies in being a soldier and acting like a civilian? In his opinion, the former staff of the intelligence section of the BAC (two officers, two NCOs, and two soldiers) were the ones who could best explain this. I interviewed one of the officers still on active duty, currently doing a master's degree in human rights, Ernesto Reboredo. He was a major in Haiti and a lieutenant colonel in 2015 when I interviewed him. After Haiti, Reboredo had become part of the Army Special Operations Force (FOE, its acronym in Spanish). He noted,

> I used one single concept to explain the connection between this assignment in Haiti and the actions of the FOE. Armies of third-world countries can only win a war if they follow Clausewitz, that is, if they undermine the enemy morale. To do this, they need to ensure local cooperation. In national territory, the FOE is the tool to carry out psychological operations, currently known as COSACO operations (Social Communication Applied to Combat), that are used to give assistance to the local populations. In the end, the psychological operations are a form of communication. The army is not there to kill, but to help, to give the people what they need. . . . Nowadays, the local populations are a part of the problem, and you need to isolate them from the enemy by giving them what they need.

For him and the second BAC, the ambiguity of the professional soldier performing civic tasks was not contradictory. The military tradition had situated the entanglements of civic and military. The military performance of civic actions is a key element in the resolution of the majority-world countries' conflicts, subsumed in the military doctrine. And even though the psychological operations were no longer allowed from the time the BAC 2 deployed, the COSACO operations achieve similar ends.[14]

What follows is the description of a military operation carried out by the Argentine troops in a small village about fifty kilometers from Go-naives, aimed at isolating the enemy. I recreate the situation that was de-scribed to me by Lieutenant Colonel Reboredo and General Barcino. At Gonaives, they had learned that the village sheltered an armed gang. Sev-eral murders had taken place in the area, and they set out to analyze and reconstruct the different crime scenes. In the meantime, they heard about the possible lynching of three people. When the military patrol arrived at the place, they found a dead body, a shovel, and a hole in the ground at the side of the road. They asked around and found out that another mur-der was about to be committed, of a man accused of sorcery. The patrol approached the targeted family and advised them to leave the village.

There was another story of that same village. Without explaining why, a local judge had ordered the Argentine troops to arrest one of the vil-lage's inhabitants. A few days later, a heavily pregnant woman appeared at the military base in tears. She told them her husband had been impris-oned just for picking some mangoes off the neighbor's tree, who had de-nounced him to the authorities. The Argentine peacekeepers spoke to the judge, and the man was released. To express his gratitude, the man gave them a bar of ice. The military later learned that the former leader of the disbanded Haitian military band came from this same village.

These situations and the relations that they established with the local population provided the Argentine forces with information, contacts, and the support and trust of the villagers. The commander of BAC then de-cided to send a unit of twenty soldiers to the village, including the medical staff of the battalion. About half of the troops fast-roped from a helicopter, dropping flyers in French Creole discrediting the leaders of the local armed band, saying they were "mercenaries in the pay of the United States." As General Barcino argued, "This was in fact a show of strength aimed at conveying a message: 'See, we can get anywhere.'"

They set up camp in the village, and approached the local people, find-ing out their most urgent needs and offering assistance. Argentine ex-in-telligence officer Reboredo explained, "Our goal here was that the villag-ers saw the armed bands as a threat, and refused to cooperate with them." Communication was the key element: "find out what the people need, and provide it." He described what they did to achieve it:

> We took a dentist and a doctor to examine the people of the village. The dentist was shocked by the condition of villagers' teeth; he said that most of them had never received proper dental care. In exchange, the villagers offered what they

had, mostly mangoes—we stuffed ourselves with mangoes. Still, we paid for everything they gave us. We also built a bridge, so that they could cross a small river with their animals. The villagers helped us, but again, we paid them. It's not true that the Haitian people are lazy, that they don't like to work. We finally succeeded in disarming and dismantling the band, with the cooperation of the locals. So, this is what it is all about: talking with the local people and helping them.

These achievements were the result of a constant daily effort to earn the villagers' trust, to "reach out to them." To understand them, members of the military intelligence unit, who carried loudspeakers to speak to the villagers, accompanied the patrols that scouted the village. With the help of a local interpreter, they communicated with the locals in French Creole, although when they found out that his translations were not always accurate, they were forced to keep an eye on him.

On another occasion, Barcino as the commander of the BAC 2 had to negotiate with the residents of a nearby village who had set up a roadblock. Due to the poor state of the local road, the vehicles had started using a rural track, covering the village in a huge cloud of dust, which in turn affected the villagers' health. When the troops arrived at the place, a man introduced himself as the leader, assuming the role of negotiator. They soon found out that the man was lying, and that he had not been chosen for this role. With the help of the intelligence staff, a local interpreter, and a loudspeaker, they went in search of the real leader. It turned out that he was also a bandit. Therefore, the commander of BAC 2 consulted the Argentine general who was second in command of the MINUSTAH, and, with his approval, entered into a negotiation with the "true leader," who in the end consented to lift the roadblock in exchange for the road being repaired. The military had to find the machines to repair that stretch of road, which was not an easy task.

In short, the stories of the BAC 2 linked the capacity for mobilization to the initiatives and tasks performed to establish and develop relations with the Haitian population. These relations required the sensitivity and empathy of the Argentine military to communicate and to understand the people. They attributed those virtues to an Argentinean way of being—their civilian side. Those who had the role of exploiting those virtues and being aware of who needed assistance, and how to provide it, were the military intelligence unit. The Brahimi Report (UN General Assembly Security Council 2000), written in the year 2000, had already highlighted the value of military intelligence. As General Barcino told me, they rested in that report, which was a result of the then UN secretary general's decision to improve the performance and efficacy of peace operations and avoid the failures, shortcomings, and human rights violations of previous experiences, such as in Rwanda.[15] The particular Argentinean civic–military entanglement was already established in a broader sense by the UN.

The positive image of the Argentine troops in Haiti was highlighted in the "lessons learned" reports written just after finishing the mission by each of the leaders of the BAC. At the time we did fieldwork in 2015, General Barcino, operational command of the joint staff, ordered a small team of four officers, ex-peacekeepers in Haiti, to analyze and systematize those reports. They underlined the relevance of the relations of cooperation and trust established with the Haitian population to ensure the efficient and effective implementation of the planned activities. These activities were denominated CIMIC (Civil–Military Co-operation) by the UN, and they constituted a decisive element in the forging of these links. One of the aforementioned reports states,

> The close relations between the BAC and the local population resulted in: (a) Improved patrol efficiency and access to information, (b) valuable knowledge of the respective areas of responsibility (practices and routines), (c) efficient anticipation of conflict and positive implementation of countermeasures, (d) added prestige for the BAC and the armed forces in general. To maintain the positive image, it is necessary to promote CIMIC (civil–military co-operation) and to carry out CIMIC activities designed to build and strengthen the links with the population. Recreational activities such as the organization of a festival to promote a cultural exchange of Haitian and Argentine music are very successful. Festivals have the capacity of attracting large audiences, so the "message" is conveyed efficiently and immediately.

What the BAC officer described as CIMIC activities were actions and initiatives where the civil and the military interweaved and became entangled. But those activities were ones they carried out only during a short period of their professional career. Former peacekeepers' narratives frame this time as an opportunity to demonstrate their capacity to assume the responsibilities assigned to them by the Argentine government. At the same time, they express their limits in stretching their self-understanding as warriors, or their objection to making flexible that role.

The former peacekeepers' narratives were strong instruments showing, in the time after they came back from Haiti, how they entangled civilian tasks, sentiments, or virtues with their self-understanding as warriors, the military condition par excellence for most of them. Nevertheless, during fieldwork it was the domestic front that constructed the operational environment in Haiti, and pushed them to enforce their civilian roles. The Argentine military want to be recognized as professionals controlling the use of force but without civilianizing their condition as military. Thus to accept and address the ambivalence in the military performance of civic actions, military intelligence was crucial. Moreover, it allowed tracing a continuity between present and past, and between Argentinean and international military doctrine.

Conclusions

When they recount their experience in Haiti, the Argentine military who were part of the first two BACs built an operational environment in which the patrolling activities to impose peace and provide security merged with the sensitivity and compassion they felt over the suffering of the Haitian people. Their stories clearly show how efficiently performing their role as blue helmets implied an ambiguity between the soldier role and the variety of civic actions they carried out to avoid the use of force. The military were seeking professional recognition in a complex domestic scenario marked by the processes of democratization and civilianization that were seen by the majority of Argentinians as demilitarization. Although the civic actions gave them a positive self-image more in keeping with the "Argentine" way of being—that is, kind, generous, and compassionate—it also reinforced the image of the "civilian" soldier, which they saw as a threat to their self-image. Therefore, operational flexibility was limited when the traditional warrior role became entangled with civilian tasks. They could adopt and defend civilian capabilities, emotions, and tasks as long as their self-understanding did not conclude with a kind of civilianization that neglects their warrior side—that is, the potential use of force.

Ten years after Haiti, the accounts of the former Argentine blue helmets show the need to clarify and resolve the ambiguities of what they perceive as an invasion of civic traits into military performance, linking the Haitian experience to their past and future performance. We see that there are considerable variations in the way the military reconnect their past and present experience with their expectations about their future professional lives in dealing with these inconsistencies. In one case, the self-understanding of the first BAC's officers emphasized the value of leadership and later transferred what they had learned to their careers. Both the chief and his staff in Gonaives explain their promotion to the highest ranks of the army because of that deployment. Although the extent of the civic actions that the Argentine contingents carried out in Haiti exceeded the UN mandate, what prevailed was being recognized as a military commander. This is why, when this chief tells us about the floods in Gonaives, the story exposes the commander's dilemma between priorities (security or assistance, in this case).

BAC 2 dealt with the ambiguity differently. In their case, the civic actions were seen as crucial to the effectiveness of the mission and included in the doctrine of military intelligence within COSACO operations. This psychological operation belongs to international and national experience in applying knowledge from disciplines such as communication and psychology to "reach out" to the local population, balancing the use of force. Therefore, in their accounts, peacekeeping is interpreted as a military operation and seen as an opportunity to prove how they can be effective as majority world soldiers even though as a rule they use more words than weapons.

From time to time, the joint chiefs of staff responsible for peace missions ensures that interventions in cases of floods in Argentina, which can be quite dramatic, must be carried out following this method of aiding the civilian population. Thus they reaffirm their self-understanding as a sensitive military, willing to come closer to help the population. While they do not abandon their role as warriors, this condition has been permeated by an identification process characterized by elements previously condemned as being "civilian."

The Argentine troops withdrew from MINUSTAH in May 2015. To members of the last Argentine BACs, the everyday activities had become tedious, routine, and posed no challenges. Apparently, the goal of reorganizing the collapsed Haitian state had been met by the first two BACs. Also, the image of the blue helmets at the national and international levels was positive, as they had not been implicated in any scandal. The number of videos uploaded to YouTube, some talk shows on state television, and even photographs of the then President Cristina F. de Kirchner wearing a blue helmet and surrounded by Argentine soldiers express this change. In terms of this volume, the implication of this case is to underline how the history of a nation deploying troops abroad within UN missions is entangled in the very relationships that its troops form and the actions that they carry out.

Acknowledgments

I would like to express my gratitude to Eyal Ben-Ari and Birgitte Sørensen for the valuable comments on previous versions of this chapter. The work also benefited from the suggestions that Dirk Kruijt, Sabrina Calandrón, Laura Masson, Ivan Poczynok, Samuel Rivera, and Omar Gutierrez Valdebenito gave to my presentation at the ISA Conference-RC01 in Rio de Janeiro.

Sabina Frederic holds a Ph.D. in social anthropology from the University of Utrecht, the Netherlands, is a professor at the National University of Quilmes (UNQ), and an independent researcher of CONICET. She was director of the Department of Social Sciences UNQ (2005-2008), undersecretary of training at the Ministry of Defense of the Argentine Republic (2009-2011), and director of the Doctorate in Social and Human Sciences at UNQ (2012-2015). She received the First National Prize for Culture in 2014 for *Las Trampas del Pasado. Las Fuerzas Armadas y su Integración al Estado democrático* (Fondo de Cultura Económica, 2013).

Notes

1. The Armed Forces of the Argentine Republic had an average of eighty thousand active members between 2004 and 2015.
2. Only one of the interviewees, an NCO of the first BAC, had fought in the Malvinas/Falklands War (1982). He told us that the pain and distress that followed the death of a comrade were still fresh. The controversies about the performance of the military during that war were such that no lessons were drawn out of this painful experience, only a highly critical report of Argentina's military leadership known as the Rattenbach report and some scattered information.
3. In Argentina and Latin America, David Pion Berlín (2001), Alfred Stepan (1988), and Ernesto López (1994) represented this line of thought until the end of the twentieth century. They offered helpful guidelines on how to demilitarize the political field and restrict military autonomy, deferring the control of the armed forces to the civilian authorities, contributing to the transition toward democracy after the military dictatorship in the 1970s.
4. We agree with Marilyn Strathern (1992) that a person's identity is not whole and final, nor a result of an early and single socialization and "cultural" acquisition. Therefore, we conceive the military as people with diverging and even conflicting dimensions, simultaneously or successively.
5. The project started individually, and was funded by the National University of Quilmes. Later, it received the support of the Ministry of Defense, and involved the participation of the following researchers: Mónica Hirst, Sabrina Calandrón, Bernabe Malacalza, Mariano Melotto, Guadalupe Gallo, Marina Martinez Acosta, and Emanuel Fariña. Nevertheless, I alone gathered the data that is displayed in this chapter.
6. The Rules of Engagement (ROE) are the rules or directives for the use of force. According to Rear Admiral Gustavo Trama (2013) of the Joint War School of the Argentine Armed Forces, they are "rules or directives that are forced on the commanders of the operational theatres by the military strategy level to regulate the use of force." The UN defines them as "directives for the operational commanders that describe the circumstances under which the use of force may be applied by the UN military personnel in a peace operation. They are the commanders' rules for the use of force, and describe the kind of appropriate action that commanders may or may not authorize. They also allow for the use of force in self-defense" (Trama 2013).

7. The Argentine contingent was the region's third largest troop deployment; out of 3,134 troops deployed in 2004, Argentina contributed 559—that is, 17 percent of the total number of troops (Frederic and Hirst 2016).
8. Namely, the National Defense Act (1987) and the Domestic Security Act (1992).
9. For further reading on the violence and political upheaval of the 1960s and 1970s in Argentina, the Revolutionary War, and the reaction of the military government during the Cold War, see Antonius Robben 2005.
10. Voodoo cult is a traditional widespread practice in Haiti. It originates in Africa and intermingles with elements of the Catholic religion. Although the latter formally prohibited its practice in Haiti, it is still a vital part of the Haitian culture.
11. Names are changed to protect anonymity.
12. CAECOPAZ is a training center created in 1995 as a response to an increased Argentine participation in peacekeeping operations. It is recognized by the UN Peace Operations Training Institute.
13. As those who achieve the highest ranks among the graduates of the same class are familiarly known.
14. The psychological operations were banned by the Ministry of Defense in 2006, after the scandal of the Almirante Zar Base in Trelew. Since then, they have been included in the military doctrine under COSACO operations, or *civic actions*.
15. The text states, "In particular, UN forces employed in complex operations must be aided by timely and adequate field intelligence and other necessary resources in order to build up an effective defence against violent opposition" (UN General Assembly Security Council 2000: x).

References

Badaró, Máximo. 2009. *Militares o Ciudadanos. La formación de los oficiales del Ejército Argentino*. Buenos Aires: Prometeo.

Ben-Ari, Eyal. 1998. "Civilian Lives: Emotions, Control, and Manhood." In Eyal Ben-Ari, *Mastering Soldiers. Conflict, Emotions, and the Enemy in an Israeli Military Unit*, 106–19. New York: Berghahn Books.

Bobrow, Davis. 1966. "The Civic Role of the Military: Some Critical Hypotheses." *Western Political Quarterly* 19 (1): 101–11.

Brubaker, Rogers, and Frederick Cooper. 2000. "Beyond 'Identity.'" *Theory and Society* 29: 1–47.

Bruner, Edward. 1984. "Introduction: The Opening Up of Anthropology." In E. Bruner, *Text, Play and Story: The Construction and Reconstruction of Self and Society*, 1–16. Washington, DC: American Ethnological Society.

Castro, Celso. 1991. *O Espírito Militar. Um antropólogo na caserna*. Rio de Janeiro: Jorge Zahar Editor.

Cunliffe, Philip. 2017. "From Peacekeepers to Praetorians: How Participating in Peacekeeping Operations May Subvert Democracy." *International Relations* 32 (2): 218–39.

Dandeker, Christopher. 2006. "Building Flexible Forces for the 21st Century: Key Challenges for the Contemporary Armed Services." In Giuseppe Caforio (ed.), *Handbook of the Sociology of the Military*, 405–16. New York: Springer.

DPKO, Department of Peacekeeping Operation. 2003. *Handbook_on United Nations Multidimensional Peacekeeping Operations*. New York: United Nations Peacekeeping Best Practices Unit. Available at https://peacekeeping.un.org/sites/default/files/peacekeeping-handbook_un_dec2003_0.pdf.

Frederic, Sabina. 2016. "Distancia, encierro y tiempo libre: la dimensión familiar y personal."

In S. Frederic and M. Hirst (eds.), *La presencia de Argentina en Haití: contexto global, regional y experiencia militar (2004–2015)*. Buenos Aires: Editorial Teseo.

Frederic, Sabina, and Mónica Hirst. 2016. "Introducción." In. S. Frederic and M. Hirst (eds.) *La presencia de Argentina en Haití: contexto global, regional y experiencia militar (2004–2015)*. Buenos Aires: Editorial Teseo.

Frederic, Sabina, Laura Masson, and Germán Soprano. 2015. *Fuerzas Armadas en Democracia. Percepciones de los militares argentinos sobre su reconocimiento*. Rosario: Prohistoria.

Halperin Donghi, Tulio. 1978. "Militarización revolucionaria en Buenos Aires, 1806–1815." In Tulio Halperin Donghi (ed.), *El ocaso del orden colonial en Hispanoamerica*. Buenos Aires: Sudamericana.

Hirst, Mónica. 2016. "El Marco Multilateral y la Presencia Regional en Haití." In S. Frederic and M. Hirst (eds.), *La presencia de Argentina en Haití: contexto global, regional y experiencia militar (2004–2015)*. Buenos Aires: Editorial Teseo.

Hodder, Ian. 2012. *Entangled: An Archaeology of the Relationships between Humans and Things*. Oxford: Wiley-Blackwell.

López, Ernesto. 1994. *Ni la Ceniza, Ni la Gloria: actores, sistema político y cuestión militar en los años de Alfonsín*. Buenos Aires: Editorial de la Universidad Nacional de Quilmes.

Luckham, Robin A. 1971. "A Comparative Typology of Civil–Military Relations." *Government and Opposition* 6 (1): 5–35.

Miller, Laura, and Charles Moskos. 1999. "Humanitarians or Warriors?: Race, Gender, and Combat Status in Operation Restore Hope." *Armed Forces and Society* 21 (4): 615–37.

Nuciari, Marina. 2006. "Models and Explanations for Military Organization: An Updated Reconsideration." In Caforio Giuseppe (ed.), *Handbook of the Sociology of the Military*, 61–85. New York: Springer.

Pion-Berlin, David. 2016. *Military Missions in Democratic Latin America*. New York: Palgrave Macmillan.

——— (ed.). 2001. *Civil–Military Relations in Latin America: New Analytical Perspectives*. Chapel Hill: University of North Carolina Press.

Potash, Robert. 1981. *El ejército y la política en la Argentina*, 2 vols. Buenos Aires: Sudamericana.

Ricoeur, Paul. 1991. "Narrative Identity." *Philosophy Today* 35 (1): 73.

Robben, Antonius. 2005. *Political Violence and Trauma in Argentina*. Philadelphia: University of Pennsylvania Press.

Robin, Marie-Monique. 2005. *Escuadrones de la muerte. La escuela francesa*. Buenos Aires: Sudamericana.

Rouquié, Alain. 1981. *Poder militar y sociedad política en la Argentina, t. I: Hasta 1943*. Buenos Aires, Emecé.

———. 1982. *Poder militar y sociedad política en la Argentina, t. II: 1943–1973*. Buenos Aires: Emecé.

Ruffa, Chiara. 2014. "What Peacekeepers Think and Do: An Exploratory Study of French, Ghanaian, Italian, and South Korean Armies in the United Nations Interim Force in Lebanon." *Armed Forces & Society* 40 (2): 199–225.

Sørensen, Birgitte. 2015. "Veterans' Homecomings: Secrecy and Post-deployment Social Becoming." *Current Anthropology* 56 (12): 231–40.

Sotomayor, Arturo. 2014. *The Myth of the Democratic Peacekeeper: Civil–Military Relations and the United Nations*. Baltimore: John Hopkins University Press.

Stepan, Alfred. 1988. "Las prerrogativas de los militares en los nuevos regímenes militares." *Desarrollo Económico* 27 (108): 479–504.

Strathern, Marilyn. 1992. "Parts and Wholes: Refiguring Relationships in a Post-plural World." In A. Kuper (ed.), *Conceptualizing Society*, 75–104. London: Routledge.

Trama, Gustavo. 2013. *Reglas de empeñamiento: historia definición y objetivos*. Buenos Aires: Escuela Superior de Guerra Conjunta de las Fuerzas Armadas. Available at http://www.cefadigital.edu.ar/bitstream/123456789/74/4/RE%201%20TRAMA.pdf.

UN General Assembly Security Council. 2000. *General Assembly Fifty-fifth Session: Item 87 of the Provisional Agenda; Comprehensive Review of the Whole Question of Peacekeeping Operations in All Their Aspects*. (Brahimi Report). United Nations. Available at http://www .un.org/en/ga/search/view_doc.asp?symbol=A/55/305.

Worboys, Katherine. 2007. "The Traumatic Journey from Dictatorship to Democracy. Peacekeeping Operations and Civil–Military Relations in Argentina, 1989–1999." *Armed Forces and Society* 33 (2): 149–68.

Chapter 11

Crossing over Barbed-Wire Entanglements of U.S. Military Bases

On Environmental Issues around MCAS Futenma in Okinawa, Japan

Masakazu Tanaka

Introduction

This chapter aims to analyze military environmental issues as major elements of entanglements between civil or local communities and the military. A case is taken from the U.S. military base in Okinawa.

According to Ian Hodder (2012: 17–18), the nature of entanglements is characterized as dependence and dependency. He criticizes scholars, such as Bruno Latour, who try to understand human–thing relationships as symmetrical networks, as they fail to consider asymmetrical power relationships of dependency (2012: 94). The former means reliable and contingent relationships for production and creation, while in the latter, "constraint" and "entrapment" are key words. I prefer the term "positive" to "dependence," and "negative" to "dependency." Thus, positive entanglements are a sum of human–thing, human–human, or thing–thing relationships which have creative effects, while negative entanglements constrain those depending on the other humans or things.

In the case of Okinawa, U.S. military bases and local communities present a typical example of dependency, or negative entanglements. The former may depend on the latter for some human and material resources, but their presence is made possible originally by military forces and later

---

Note for this chapter begin on page 250.

legitimatized by laws, such as the Japan–U.S. Status of Forces Agreement (SOFA), and changing international politics, never by the requests or consensus of local communities. Because of military environmental hazards, including crimes committed by U.S. military soldiers, anti–U.S. base movements have been active in Okinawa. A typical counter-discourse against the anti-base movements sounds like this: we Okinawans need the bases for economic stability and prosperity. Okinawa consists of small islands without natural resources or big factories and is too far from mainland Japan to ask big manufacturing companies for investments. Many young Okinawans migrate to the mainland for higher education and better job opportunities. Thus, except for the public sector, the military bases have become major places to provide local people with job opportunities and other economic resources.

This argument certainly reminds us of dependency theory debates in South America and Africa. While it is true that bases provide job opportunities, it does not mean that Okinawa would financially collapse without the U.S. military bases. Some insist that by replacing them with other nonmilitary facilities, such as amusement parks and museums, Okinawa will develop in a healthier way.

Many Japanese locals work on a base and in related jobs, such as in restaurants and bars around the bases. Their working conditions vary, but these regular employees, numbering over 8,500, are equivalent to civil servants in Okinawa. They are not, however, docile workers, and sometimes are very active in collaboration with local anti-base movements.

The military bases are not completely closed off from the local communities in Okinawa. It is true that they are heavily guarded and fenced with barbed wire *entanglements*, but the boundaries between the bases and surrounding communities are not so clearly marked. As mentioned above, many locals visit the bases for several reasons, such as working, meeting friends, studying the Bible, attending religious services, and learning English.

U.S. military personnel, on the other hand, are free to go out to shop, eat, sightsee, and date. Some marry local women and remain in Okinawa after retirement.

This chapter first focuses on nonhuman elements (things) in military environmental issues, such as roaring sounds, bad industrial smells, chemical pollutions, and the very presence of the occupying bases. To use Hodder's three classifications of entanglements (2012: 88), they are typical examples of human–thing entanglements. Second, regarding human–human entanglements, this chapter analyzes intergenerational relationships—the relationships between parents and children in the context of the military environmental issues.

Based on documented interviews carried out with people living in the vicinity of the U.S. Marine Corps Air Station Futenma, located in the Japanese city of Ginowan on Okinawa Island, this chapter seeks to present the entangled realities of life around the base for local residents. The issues associated with the base are the subject of what has become a considerable literature of academic texts and journalistic reportage. Even so, as I discuss below, few of these accounts communicate the voices of local residents in any real way. In this chapter, I hope to foreground these voices as much as I can in order to not only get at the realities of the base problem, but also to show evidence of entangled life in the vicinity of the military bases.

Military Environmental Issues in Okinawa

Hayashi (2011; cf. Gleditsch 1998) compares environmental pollution generated by the military with industrial pollution produced by the private sector, and notes four main features of the former as follows: (1) the state's culpability for environmental destruction, (2) the information confidentiality to which damages are subject, (3) the discriminatory treatment of victims, and (4) the severity of the damages. In his book, Hayashi discusses military environmental issues by dividing these into the four broad categories of base construction, on-base military activities, preparations for war (e.g., drills), and actual practices. In addition to these, the scope of "environmental issues" may also be understood more broadly to encompass other eventualities, such as chemical weapons experiments, accidents at manufacturing facilities, and crimes committed by military personnel.

It is true that military environmental issues have been discussed from a variety of perspectives, including those relating to international politics, environmental problems, judicial perspectives, and historical research. Nevertheless, this is not necessarily to say that the voices of residents living around the base have been sufficiently recorded, communicated, or considered (cf. Yoichi 2010; Hayashi 2011; Fukuchi 1996; Saitō 2010; and Yamauchi 2012). They remain silent victims.

Of course, this is not to deny the court testimonies that have been given in the context of legal struggles or questionnaires conducted during environmental studies or the claims that have been made by concerned activists. However, the ideas of the people concerned are by no means uniform. For this reason, I have eschewed synthesis, endeavoring as much as possible to have those concerned to tell their stories freely.

Through their accounts of various environmental issues, it becomes obvious that people do not always suffer and feel helpless. They get accustomed to the constantly occurring environmental hazards, an entangled situation called "fittingness" (or "adaptive fitness") (Hodder 2012: 113). Such fittingness is sometimes disturbed by their children's reactions to, say, roaring sounds. They are reminded of their own childhood. They depend on their children. Thus, intergenerational relationships are entangled through environmental issues. In addition, I present some childhood memories of the bases in order to show other aspects of civilian–military entanglements.

MCAS Futenma

The U.S. Marine Corps Air Station Futenma (hereafter MCAS Futenma) is situated in the city of Ginowan, which is approximately twelve kilometers north of the Okinawan prefectural capital of Naha. The base covers an area of 480 hectares, the equivalent of about 103 Tokyo Domes. The central feature of the base is a runway 2,750 meters long and 45 meters wide. MCAS Futenma occupies approximately 24 percent of Ginowan's urban territory, and with the inclusion of Camp Foster, more or less adjacent to the northern section of the base, the proportion rises to about 32.4 percent. Three-quarters of U.S. base facilities in Japan are concentrated on Okinawa Island, where they reportedly occupy 20 percent of the island's total land area. From this, we can see that the proportion occupied by the U.S. base in Ginowan is considerably higher than for the island as a whole (Uemura 2015; Miyamoto et al. n.d.; see also "About US Military Bases" n.d.; "Welcome to 'Futenma Base'" n.d.).

Because MCAS Futenma is situated in such a densely populated area, it has gained a reputation as the most dangerous airfield in the world. Moreover, the fact that the air station has been constructed so as to transect the center of the city means that urban residents are forced to take detours, especially when attempting to move between the eastern and western sections.

More severe problems, however, include the roar of noise that accompanies the takeoff and landing of aircraft and the physical and psychological effects of the attendant noise and vibration, as well as pollution around the base and even aircraft-related accidents. While as many as nineteen separate air crash incidents involving aircraft associated with Futenma have been recorded since Okinawa's return to Japan (Uemura 2015: 105), the crash of a CH-53D helicopter onto the campus of Okinawa International University (OIU) on 13 August 2004 remains fresh in people's minds. Furthermore, the deployment of the Osprey, a model of aircraft that has been involved in a string of crashes possibly owing to structural problems, was pushed through despite fierce opposition by local residents.

Crimes committed by U.S. soldiers stationed in Okinawa, especially crimes of a sexual nature, have frequently been featured in mass media. According to statistics covering the period from the return of Okinawa to Japan in 1972 until 2009, military personnel were responsible for a total of 5,634 crimes. The recorded infractions include 25 counts of murder, 385 robberies, 25 incidents of arson, 127 cases of rape, 306 assaults, and 2,827 thefts. Of these, the crime that had the most serious political repercussions was the sexual assault of a sixth-grade elementary school student by three marines, which took place in September 1995. This incident, which became an international issue, triggered the series of events that led to the agreement signed the following year between Japan and the U.S. for the return of the land occupied by MCAS Futenma and the relocation of base facilities. However, although plans were floated for the relocation of base facilities outside the prefecture at the time of the Democratic Party of Japan government from the summer of 2009 through the end of 2012, it was decided (in the face of a fierce opposition movement) that military operations would be moved to Henoko in northern Okinawa, where the preparation of base facilities is now underway.

Interview Sources

For the interviews, I relied for the most part on the assistance of Mr. O (a former junior high school teacher in his late fifties), an Okinawan resident originally from the Japanese mainland. After meeting with him and explaining my intention, we exchanged emails and eventually settled on questions to ask in the subsequent study after a process of trial and error. The interviews were conducted over the autumn of 2014. I met in person with two informants in 2015 and three in 2016, conducting interviews that Mr. O also sat in on. The interviews lasted about two hours for each informant.

We interviewed a total of thirty-two people (nineteen men and thirteen women). However, although their wives occasionally provided supplementary explanations for the men, and sons for the women, these individuals are not reflected in the numbers here. In terms of experience and age, the oldest informant was eighty years old, while the youngest was twenty-six. However, about half of the total number was comprised of sixteen informants in their sixties. The average age of informants was 53.4 years. In terms of background, twelve individuals were originally from other prefectures, while one resident had been born in the Philippines. In terms of the number of years they had been living near MCAS Futenma, the longest was sixty years and the shortest was four months, with an average length of 20.4 years. Taking into account the age distribution and related factors, while I focus on the oral accounts of the ten individuals listed here, I also describe the accounts of other individuals where I feel it necessary.

No. 2 male. Born in Okinawa in 1930s. He moved into Futenma at the end of the 1960s.

No. 3 male. Born in Okinawa in the 1940s. Living in mainland but came back home in the 1960s.

No. 4 female. Born in Okinawa in the 1940s. She moved to Futenma in 1972.

No. 5 female. Born in Okinawa in the 1930s. She moved to Futenma after marriage.

No. 8 female Born in Okinawa in the 1930s. She moved to Okinawa after marriage. She rented a house to white American soldiers.

No. 10 female. Born in Henoko, Okinawa, in the 1950s. She has been living in Futenma since the 1990s.

No. 14 male. Born in Okinawa in the 1970s. He has been living in Futenma for the last fifteen years.

No. 17 male. Born in Okinawa in the 1970s. He was born in Futenma.

No. 20 male. Born in Okinawa in the 1980s. He is scared of many items related to the military.

No. 24 male. Born in Okinawa in the 1950s. Very active in anti–military base movements.

In the next section, I introduce interview materials from ten informants along separate themes. Although these have been edited to avoid repetition and improve readability, I have not changed or added any of the terms used. My own editorial remarks and insertions are indicated by square brackets [ ]. Finally, it should also be noted that personal information has been kept to a minimum so as to preserve anonymity.

Futenma's Military Environmental Issues

In this section, I would like to present the contents of informants' oral accounts in turn as they touch on the respective issues of noise, air crashes, fears of war and the military, environmental pollution, and political awareness.

Noise

Noise does more than just cause physical damage to people's bodies and houses; it also reminds people of the possibility of a helicopter or jet plane crashing, an anxiety and uncertainty that contributes to mental anguish.

The validity of these anxieties was confirmed when a helicopter crashed on the OIU campus in 2004. Additionally, for residents who lived through the Battle of Okinawa in 1945, noises from the base can conjure up the memory of wartime experiences.

Houses around the base have been equipped with soundproofing with the support of the local government. Residents must therefore use air conditioning in summer, keeping their windows closed. However, the absence of any assistance with electricity bills means that residents face an increased economic burden, and some have also pointed out that tightly sealed rooms are more prone to vibration.

Noise pollution grew even worse following the deployment of the Osprey aircraft in 2012. While quieter than conventional helicopters, the harm to human bodies and houses caused by the rumbling bass of the aircraft was greater than anticipated. Although the main reason for the opposition to the deployment of the Osprey aircraft was the frequency with which they had crashed in other areas, once they had actually been deployed, it was the day-to-day noise caused by the Osprey flights that was found to be intolerable.

To begin, I present an account by an Okinawan-born man on the ferocity of the noise produced by the jet planes:

> It really shocked me when I was in university. I was at the local convenience store when I heard some kind of rumbling. It was the sound of a jet [makes roaring sound]. It really made a strong impression. Just outside the store. It was unique, like something I'd never experienced before. I couldn't see the aircraft—that was the scariest thing about the experience. It was probably the sound of the jet taking off. Even the surrounding buildings were shaking a little. (No. 20)

With the helicopters, it is not only the sounds, but also the low-altitude flights that take place in such close proximity, that informants found difficult. Additionally, the absence of any time restrictions for engine adjustments on the ground meant that, even more than the flight sounds, residents would grow frustrated by the sounds of engine adjustment late at night or early in the morning:

> The sound of engine adjustments at dawn is awful. It's not clear where it comes from, maybe somewhere on the east side of the airfield, near the city office I think. The noise is awful when they take off, but then after a little while, they come back again! It's awful. So noisy. They do maneuvers all the time, and the noise goes on and on. (No. 8)

> The worst are the engine adjustment sounds. When you have a heart condition or arrhythmia, you get a pacemaker that automatically kicks in to adjust [your heart rate]. The standard is about sixty beats a minute. With the engine adjustment sounds, the north wall trembles, making a low sound [makes vibrating

noise]. When that happens, I start to feel worse. That kind of thing makes me think that those engine adjustment sounds must have some effect on pacemakers. (No. 3)

In some cases, people become habituated to the noise:

We're used to it, I suppose. It's routine. When friends come to visit from around Naha, it really surprises them. (No. 8)

Those who are thinking of moving away probably weren't born on the island. They're different from those who are originally from here, I think. People originally from the island wouldn't consider moving away. It's strange to say, but I think we're kind of used to it. We're used to the noise. (No. 17)

Residents' realization of such habituation stems from the accidents that I discuss next, as well as the reactions of children, which will be introduced later.

The U.S. Marine Helicopter Crash at Okinawa International University

The noise issue is closely linked with anxiety about accidents. Here I present a sampling of remarks by people who gave typical responses to questions about the air crash that took place on the campus of OIU in 2004.

For me, getting some release from the mental anguish of the noise problem can't happen soon enough. Accidents happen when you don't expect them. Ten years ago [the helicopter crash at OIU] was like that, too. It was an accident out of the blue. Our feelings are that this situation [the relocation of MCAS Futenma] should be addressed as quickly as possible. (No. 2)

It really brought home to me the fact that this is a dangerous place, the danger we face living under a runway. Although when the crash happened, it happened way over there. Even more than the noise, the mental anguish and distress are huge. Aside from specific noises. It's a lifestyle problem. A life-threatening problem. Obviously it would be better if the relocation happened as soon as possible. (No. 2)

Some older residents also remember another major accident that took place before the return of Okinawa, on 30 June 1959, when an F-100 jet crashed into Miyamori Elementary School, killing twelve schoolchildren and six others, and causing serious or slight injury to another 210 people, including 156 schoolchildren.

Next, let us turn to the following account of a married couple who spoke in concrete terms about what they were doing on the day of the air crash at OIU:

I'd just passed through that area when the crash happened. It was near our house, at a spot that I often pass through on my way to work. At the time, I was driving from Samashita to Nagata [neighborhoods in Ginowan]. Two car-lengths in front of me, the road became impassable beside the accident site. Before then, traffic had been getting through by taking turns squeezing through on the right side of the road. I was forced to stop and pull a U-turn.

... For the first 100 meters or so, I noticed thick smoke rising up ahead of me.

... After pulling a U-turn, I backtracked a little to take a back road [on the other side of the university]. When I did, I saw that helicopter parts on the road—about 2 or 3 meters long, what I guessed was part of the rotor—was blocking the lane. Since cars were lining up behind me, I just pulled around on the left so that I could get through more easily. My feeling was that I just wanted to get out of there quickly. Then, too, thick smoke was still billowing up from the university side. In some ways, it was kind of a surreal experience. (No. 14)

I thought war had broken out and the bombs were falling. (Wife of No. 14)

As well as the accident itself, many accounts also discussed being affected by the shock of the field blockade that was implemented by the marines in the immediate wake of the disaster.

When the helicopter crashed, the fire engines, emergency vehicles, and police arrived, but they were kept away [from the scene of the accident]. I found it really frustrating that [the Americans] would close ranks like that even off the base, even though they were the ones causing trouble for us. Since then, dissatisfaction among the citizenry has grown more intense. (No. 3)

At the time of the helicopter crash, not being allowed to deal with the incident and being barred from the accident site presented a big problem for the U.S.–Japan Status of Forces Agreement (SOFA). I find it very frustrating. It's a question of who has sovereignty. (No. 4)

Fears Relating to War and the Military

To live near the base is to be constantly aware of war:

When the world situation grows tense—whenever there's a Vietnam, a Gulf War, or war on the Korean Peninsula with North Korea—the aircraft [noise] ramps up. We might not know what's going on with the base, but we know right away when the noise gets worse. When that happens, you'll read in the paper the next day about the start of some new war in the Gulf. (No. 2)

The informant who spoke most eloquently about his fears about war was No. 20:

It seems to me that most of the helicopters I can see from my house are bristling with machine gun barrels. Every time the helicopters do maneuvers, they're pointed in a different direction. Misfires are not unthinkable. And don't operational errors and the like also happen on occasion? Sometimes, they are pointed at me, too. It's terrifying.

 . . . In the early hours, at dawn, around 0600, the soldiers are running about, raising their voices as they carry out their drills. Sometimes I can hear them, sometimes I can't. It's not a good feeling. It's redolent of war. Even the slightest sound makes me uncomfortable. (No. 20)

While No. 20 lists specific examples that evoke his fears, all of these are fears that relate to the aggression shown by the army and the specter of war that these evoke. No. 20 expresses these with words such as "not a good feeling", "uncomfortable" (*fukai*), "anxiety" (*fuan*), and "unnatural" (*fushizen*).

No. 8, born in the 1930s, is reminded by the noise of her experience of the Battle of Okinawa in 1945:

For me, the sound of the maneuvers brings back memories of the battlefield. Not just the noise, but wartime itself. Because we fled to Shimajiri, because we came to such terrible grief. It makes me want to scream, truly, "We are the victims who have suffered the most." (No. 8)

Recall that at the time of the helicopter crash at OIU, the wife of No. 14 stated that she "thought war had broken out and the bombs were falling." The experience of living near the base is a constant reminder not only of wartime experiences, but of war's very possibility.

Environmental Pollution

Noise and accidents are not the only sources of anxiety. Other environmental problems also exist in the vicinity of the base. However, the fact that it is not entirely clear what these are only adds to people's anxieties.

Regarding pollution from harmful substances, like in the soil on the site occupied by the base—the base was built around 1950, I think, but that was a time when we didn't have any concept of "pollution." That was before we knew anything about either Yokkaichi or Minamata [references to two of the "Big Four" pollution-related diseases in Japan]. So I have no doubt that a variety of harmful substances would probably have been buried [in the soil on the base]. (No. 14)

Political Awareness

While we did not ask many questions about political activities or opinions during the interviews, some informants spoke incidentally of topics such as the relocation, the U.S. military, and anti-base sentiment in their responses to other questions. In response to our question "Do you have any plans to move away from Futenma?," informants' consciousness that they "had to remain" came across vividly. Here are some specific accounts:

> Since coming here, rather than move away, we've come to feel rather that we need to protest—to make our voices heard. (Wife of No. 17)

> It's hard to explain. First of all, it's not so easy to just pick up and move. Particularly because we own the property and the house we live in now. It's the bedrock of our lives. I don't think we're in a situation where we can easily sell and buy some new place to live in. The thing is, I'm always saying that they [the powers that be] need to stop infringing our property rights! (No. 2)

The air crash also proved to be strong motivation for political activity:

> A few hours earlier [in the morning], the crash had happened along my usual [car] commuting route. I knew about that from media coverage from NHK, maybe, or else the broadcast office in Fukuoka [of Kyusyu Island, not Okinawa]. At the time, my father was on the front line putting out the fires. When I learned that there was a possibility that [the helicopter] had been loaded with radioactive materials, I worried whether there might be some adverse effect on the firefighters or local residents. I grew anxious. I wondered why we hadn't been more active, and thought we should take more actions, like sit-ins or demonstrations. I'm involved in a prefecture-wide gathering now. I take the kids. (No. 17)

Informants are also unable to agree entirely with the relocation to Henoko. This is because they know how difficult it will be to take over the air station once the U.S. forces leave.

> For example, we're overjoyed that the base is going to Henoko. Because our suffering will end. But then, it will be the people of Henoko who will suffer. That's what we Okinawans are clamoring about. We suffer either way. The government should decide after listening to the opinions of the people, but . . . the government is being high handed, you know? Trying to force the issue. Isn't there any space in the prefectures on the mainland? But . . . we agree with the plan in general, but are against how it's being carried out. And so we get fixated, and the status quo continues. In the end, our suffering will simply continue.
> . . . Even the Americans are saying it's dangerous, but for things to continue as they are now, that's a question of the government's responsibility. The national government is telling us that if it's not the best option, then Henoko is at least better for now. As residents of Ginowan, it's not our concern either way [i.e., whether Henoko is decided as the base's new location, or somewhere else]. I'm not saying Henoko is a bad idea. Because it's too dangerous [here]; having the base in Henoko would only be about a tenth as dangerous [as now]. The only thing I can say is that I want the base relocated as quickly as possible. It doesn't matter where. Obviously, the mainland would be best. (No. 2)

No. 2, even while hoping that the base is moved as soon as possible and pointing out the fact that the dangers associated with the base would be lessened in Henoko compared with Futenma, states that "It doesn't matter where. Obviously, the mainland would be best," thereby offering us a glimpse into inner thoughts that he is otherwise unable to state decisively. No. 10, who is originally from Henoko, offers thoughts that are even more complex:

> Those Henoko grandmothers you see on television—I know all of them. Some are the mothers of my classmates. The mothers of friends I walked to school with every day. Since so many years had passed, I didn't even realize until a friend told me who they were, and then I finally twigged. Some people are in favor of it [the relocation to Henoko], you know. But I know full well that so many people back in Henoko—back in my hometown—are howling about it, devastated. I don't live there anymore, but I guess Henoko really is my hometown. I know so many people there.
> . . . I know people from Henoko. Even my own relatives are divided over the relocation to Henoko. I'm usually . . . since I've moved away from Henoko, it's on my mind that much more. In some ways, part of me really misses it. (No. 10)

Finally, let me present the words of No. 3, in which may be found a certain kind of resignation and doubts about activism:

> At that time, my friends [fellow contractors] and I were in agreement with the proposed merger with Kadena. First of all, that was, after merging with Kadena, we needed to think carefully about what came next. The sooner the move happened, the sooner we could start making use of the site. That would have meant more work for us contractors. A fair number of the contractors had moved their main offices from around Naha up here to Ginowan. That was about twenty years ago. When there was talk of moving [MCAS Futenma] to Henoko, then the Democratic Party Japan got in and there was talk of moving the base outside of the prefecture or even overseas. We got on board (*sono ki ni natta*). But the proposals have been overturned again and again by the mayor up in Nago. This is an issue between one country and another, and kicking up a fuss is not going to accomplish anything. By which I mean activism is fine for folks with a lot of time, but we don't have that luxury. (No. 3)

Above, I have presented oral accounts touching on military environmental issues. These materials reveal more than just the easily supposed fears of air crashes and anxieties over noise and pollution. Rather, I would like to focus on how residents' fears are engendered precisely by the proximity of seeing the faces of the pilots as they maneuver the helicopters, of being under the muzzles of the helicopters' guns, and of hearing the marines forming ranks and training hard from early in the morning. To live alongside the base is to have to live with the feeling of such fears on a daily basis. Also clearly evident, it would seem, is the presence of an underlying distrust of the U.S. military. Such fear and distrust are stoked even more when accidents actually happen. At the time of the OIU helicopter crash in 2004, even more than fears of an accident, what was felt most problematic was the fact that the U.S. forces cordoned off the scene of the accident, keeping out Japanese police, emergency personnel, and even university officials.

In order to eliminate such fears, most interviewees hoped that MCAS Futenma would be relocated. However, the fact that the proposed location, Henoko, was also in Okinawa proved to be a troubling matter. For No. 10, a woman who, although originally a native of Henoko, was now living in Futenma, the relocation problem was a particularly thorny issue. Even among the others, who had no personal connections to Henoko, none were wild with joy about the idea of relocation there.

In such circumstances, proximity brings a deadening of the senses. Local residents call this "habituation" (*nare*). Such habituation, at the same time as being a kind of adaptation or fittingness (one form of entanglements) for living alongside the base, desensitizes inhabitants to anxiety and fear, encouraging an attenuated awareness of the problems that arise as a result of living in a community that adjoins the base. As the proverb says, "There is no place like home." So how can we confront the problem presented by the base without relinquishing mind and body to be subject to such habituation? If habituation is to be considered a way of surviving everyday life around the base, then its rejection is made by some external source like a casual visitor. Of course, this is not to advise some injunction against habituation by people living in communities without bases. Rather, it is none other than children who would play the most valuable role in such an enterprise. This is because children encourage the realization of such habituation; they suggest an alternate perspective on the base and elicit the memories of an even more distant past.

Accounts Involving Children

In this section, I would like to refine my focus to consider how children have appeared in the accounts of civilian–military entanglements that have been presented so far. First, I show some cases where adults' "habituation" is disturbed by their children. Entanglements imply not only children's dependency (negative entanglements) on their parents for security, but the latter's dependence (positive entanglements) on the former for their understanding of the nature of habituation and the seriousness of the military environmental issues. Second, I give examples in which childhood memories reveal various ways of interaction, some regrettable, the others adventurous, with the military base.

Interactions between Children and Adults: Disturbing Fittingness

Regarding the Noise Issue

First, I introduce the case of someone who decided to move after noticing that noise [from the base] was prompting reactions from her unborn child:

> A woman living in a nearby apartment, before the Ospreys were stationed, moved to Nakagusuku when she couldn't stand the noise of the helicopters. While pregnant with her first child, she had experienced movement in her womb. She initially thought her baby was just active, but then she noticed that her baby moved whenever the helicopters flew by. Since her second child was the same, she thought "this might not be the best place to raise children" and moved away [from Nodake, northeast of the base, to somewhere helicopters would be unlikely to fly]. (No. 24)

Those able to move may still be happy. Those remaining around the base, however, can only look squarely at the changes and reactions of their children. Moreover, while we will see in the account of No. 17 that "the children of Futenma are always restless," as well as No. 14's statement that "there are drawbacks for the children," behind both sentiments are thoughts about their own children and grandchildren:

> For myself, I'm used to all this [*nare ga aru*]. However, the children are terrified by the noises. They get scared and run to me for a cuddle. When I see that, I think we can't go on like this. I want to protect them. When I was in high school, the base, the noises, I had the sense that all that was commonplace (*atarimae*). My feelings have changed since I became a parent. At the elementary school, they're always saying that "the children of Futenma are always restless" and the like. (No. 17)

> Since the house we're living in now is also property I built with my husband, I have no desire to move. That said, there's also the aspect that I don't want the little ones [her grandchildren] exposed to that awful noise. Compared to children who can live their lives free of noises and such, there are drawbacks for children living here, aren't there? (No. 4)

However, these children, too, slowly grow habituated to the noise. For their part, the adults have also become accustomed to seeing the children startle:

> The kids have lived there since they were born. Before, while they were still young, they'd cower and cry when there were loud noises, but now, whenever there's noise, I've begun comforting them by telling them how it's not all that

scary . . . growing accustomed to the sound is scary in itself, isn't it? The children don't seem to mind the noise anymore either. (No. 4)

And then there's the danger of crashes. When the children are playing in the yard and hear the aircraft sounds of a helicopter, they coming running in to find me, you know? Even so, living here, I've grown accustomed to that kind of thing. Maybe I don't really feel it at all. (No. 5)

Regarding the Crash

In accounts of the air crash, as well, the topic of children came up several times. These included a father who was unable to contact his son, an OIU student, in the immediate wake of the accident, and a panic-stricken mother who rushed to pick up her eldest daughter from the neighborhood daycare center (the wife of No. 4). Here, I would like to go into two accounts in some detail:

My granddaughter was here at the time of the OIU crash. At the time, my husband had been in the hospital for about a year, and I was visiting the hospital quite a bit. Our eldest son's family lives with us, and our granddaughter was two years old. The crash happened while she was playing outside, and she ended up seeing it [i.e., witnessing the crash]. The explosion was terrible, the smoke was terrible, and she saw it. She was horribly frightened, running into the house and clinging to her parents [as the interviewee was not herself present for these events, this seems to be hearsay]. Her trembling wouldn't stop. As a result, she got terrified of fireworks, and wouldn't watch them. She really was terrified, just terrified. She got frightened just by hearing the odd sounds Oki-chan made at the aquarium [Oki-chan is a dolphin at the Ocean Expo Park, in Motobu on the northern part of the island]. She was afraid when she heard unfamiliar sounds, though she can stand to watch fireworks now that she's in the sixth grade. We had a dog, but after the accident, the dog also started running into the house whenever the helicopters flew by. That was a CH [the CH-53 Sea Stallion], rather than an Osprey like they have now, but the dog was frightened by the sound of the rotor whirring. I felt so sorry that that my granddaughter had to experience something like that. (Wife of No. 4)

In the next account, No. 5 states that while *she* did not observe the accident directly, she nevertheless found the event to be one that shook her out of her "habituation." She describes her thoughts at the time as follows:

What I thought was, how sorry I was for my daughter. [It used to be that at the sound of helicopters] my own children were startled. But I didn't feel that this would become a chronic issue. Now that my daughter has married, when my grandchildren come to play, now they're the ones who are startled. I was reminded again that children being startled by the noise is something that hasn't changed. I realized once again that there was nothing I could do for them. That is, since the helicopter came down, we've all realized what a terrible thing it is. [Until then] we weren't really interested. (No. 5)

If we consider the accounts in this section as a whole, we find that children signal the exceptional nature of Futenma as a community to its adult population. These children gradually grow accustomed to the noises. It was the air crash that forced the awareness of this habituation, leaving one child suffering from post-traumatic stress disorder (PTSD). The word "sorry" (*sumanai*) appears in the accounts of both No. 4 and No. 5. How should we interpret this? In the case of No. 4, this is used in direct reference to her granddaughter, and expresses a regret that she was made to witness the accident. No. 5, in saying that she realized once again that "there was nothing I could do for them," expresses her sense that a parental generation has bequeathed circumstances that evoke fear and anxiety to the future generation to which their children belong. However, it remains unclear whether such remarks could lead to concrete political action.

Memories of Childhood

The next topic I would like to discuss, rather than informants' relationships with their own children, is their accounts of childhood. These include painful experiences as well as anecdotes full of adventure. To start, let me present No. 10's account of a hit-and-run accident.

> In fact, I've been in a traffic accident myself—I was run over by a foreigner. I've still got the scars, right here. At the time, I was in the fourth year of elementary school [living in Henoko], and I got nothing in the way of compensation. In those days, we didn't make a fuss about it either. It was a lot different than it is today. But then I guess times have really changed quite a bit. In those days, things were [so bad] that even if the police stepped in, you'd still be crying yourself to sleep, so to speak.
>
> It was a weekend, and it seems the car was overcrowded with five young fellows. The story was that the brakes failed. According to my parents, by the time the police came to the scene, the offenders had bolted. That's why they didn't collect any witness statements. In those days, our police [i.e., the Japanese police] didn't have jurisdiction in such cases—it was the other side [i.e., the U.S. forces].
>
> . . . There was no compensation at all. Not even an expression of concern. It was like that, back then. A time when you couldn't say anything. (No. 10)

Although No. 10 recovered sufficiently from her experience to be able to enjoy a happy and normal life, in junior high school, she suffered attacks of pain that may have been the result of residual damage.

No. 20 worries about the damage he might have suffered as a child due to pollution. From there, his thoughts come to dwell on the behavior of children today. Herein, through such imaginary traces (damages to the body), we may recognize the association from one child to another child:

I feel frightened about things like pollution in the soil. I'm sure there must be a lot of other things that are also hidden. I played in the parks and other places outdoors when I was a kid, drinking the water, and now I'm worried about that sort of thing. Although kids today might not drink the water in the park. (No. 20)

In contrast to No. 20, No. 17 spoke a little more positively of his days attending Futenma Second Elementary School:

At Halloween, we got in through a hole in the fence. This story takes place at Camp Zukeran [i.e., Camp Foster, located on the north side of Futenma]. [Visiting the houses of U.S. military personnel] we would receive candy and then go home. We didn't tell our parents, and we didn't tell our teachers. Although, some kids did get caught by the MPs [for going onto the base without permission] and such as well. In those days, costumes didn't matter. You'd say, "Trick or treat," and then you'd get a toy. When we were at Futenma Second Elementary, [we'd yell] "Trick or treat" at the Americans running on the other side of the fence. Then they'd throw the candies they were carrying back over the fence at us.

... Sometimes, when our balls went over the fence, we'd plead with the Americans passing by on the other side to throw them back. Then again, we also heard about an elementary student who had a gun pointed at him when he went to get his ball back. So, going through the fence also had the sense of being a test of courage. (No. 17)

A Place of Memory

The final topic I would like to introduce is exemplified by an account by No. 10, the woman from Henoko. She recounts her memories of a place where she lived together with her children and some relatives, and indicates Henoko as a place of importance. However, considering that Henoko is also her hometown, this account must have brought back memories of her own childhood. At the intersection of her own childhood and that of her own children, now grown, the "place of memory" mentioned in this account is revealed to be fraught with emotion:

Some places filled with important memories from when my children were little are Ōura Bay in Henoko, as well as the islands of Hirashima and Nagashima. These were places that we'd get to by chartering a boat ... getting all of the relatives together for a pleasure outing. My sister would come back to town, and we'd also have relatives [adults and children] visiting from Osaka, so it also had the sense of being a welcome party for these folks. We'd spend the whole day enjoying ourselves. These places were rich with nature's bounty, a home to sea urchins, giant clams, and wild rabbits. Massive schools of tropical fish. We'd enjoy barbecues there. We'd take photographs, make home videos. I show the kids the photos, telling them that this is the kind of place where the base will be built. We used to go there all the time when the kids were little. My kids also remember spending time having fun with all their relatives. It was such a place. (No. 10)

Children, just as with endangered wild animals and female high school students, tend to be represented in the context of anti-base activism as iconic and innocent victims: children who leap into their parents' arms at the noise of helicopters. Such images would certainly support the idea of children as helpless victims, depending on their parents. In bodily fashion (leaping, weeping), the children of Futenma indict the exceptional nature of life on the base to the adults around them. Here, while passive, the children at the same time constitute an active presence. In response to this indictment, their parents might at times engage in political activism, at other times feel sorry, and even become aware of their own desensitization. Children are a kind of "alter ego" (Kohama 1987) that simultaneously represents their past, present, and future. In this, they differ from a notional visitor from Naha. Children are regarded as victims of the base, and it is no great stretch to see them as being in need of salvation. However, in so doing, we end up overlooking far more complicated entanglements between adults and children.

In the vicinity of MCAS Futenma, particularly at Futenma Second Elementary School, it might be said that a unique childhood culture has been passed down in relation to the base. Their relationships with the military base suggest that the nature of civilian–military entanglements in Okinawa is not always of dependency. Similar to the protagonist in J. G. Ballard's autobiographical novel *Empire of the Sun* (1984), the image of childhood here is not one that requires rescue from some external source. These children are not helpless.[1] Of course, by this I do not mean to portray these children's world as some dimension of freewheeling excess and independence. Whether victims or hellions, we need to avoid any fixed representation of childhood so that we might maintain continuity along the path to adulthood.

Conclusion

This chapter has shown that military environmental issues are a rich field to understand civilian–military entanglements, where victims do not remain helpless in the face of the intrusion of environmental hazards into their life-world. One of the ways to cope with the noise of aircrafts is habituation. Habituation is a sensory shelter against the overwhelming power of the U.S. military. It is a case of fittingness of the local dependency on the military to the point of indifference. However, habituation is occasionally disturbed by the reactions of children.

The MCAS Futenma, like other U.S. military bases, was built after the Battle of Okinawa, which started in April 1945, destroying the local eco-system of farming. It was gradually expanded. It has been well fenced off from local communities, but few remain confined on base. Aircrafts, including helicopters and Ospreys, are busy taking off and landing, sol-diers—some with criminal intent—sneak out of the base, looking for lo-cal girls, and unidentified pollutant substances leak out of bases without being noticed by anyone. Using various devices, activists, local people, academics, and civil servants identify the source of environmental issues; thus, for example, aircraft traces are visualized, their noise measured, and complaints of the locals recorded. The noise-centered network is well ex-tended to the degree that we can include not only local people, but also their house structures, aircrafts, airbases, pilots, flight schedules, and the Pentagon. Their networking relationships are, however, not symmetrical or flat. They suggest a series of entanglements of dependencies. The same is true of environmental issues other than noise. This chapter dealt with only a tiny part of such entanglements and shows that adults "depend" on children to break their habituation to the roaring sound, not vice versa. In this sense, their relationships are entangled. We also came to know that although the fenced base is difficult to enter, children sneak into the base as a part of their adventurous activities. This kind of childhood memory may affect the local people. They are certainly dependent on the base, but it becomes a source of creative activities rather than dependency.

Acknowledgments

I thank my assistant, who arranged interviews and collected most of the interview data for this chapter. This research was financially supported by the Research Institute for Humanity and Nature and the Mitsubishi Foundation.

Masakazu Tanaka is professor of social anthropology at Kyoto University. His books include, in English, *Patrons, Devotees and Goddesses: Ritual and Power among the Tamil Fishermen of Sri Lanka* (Manohar, 1997) and (coedi-tor) *Living with Śakti: Gender, Sexuality and Religion in South Asia* (National Museum of Ethnology, Osaka, 1998); and in Japanese, *Anthropology of Se-duction* (Sekaisyoin, 2018), *Anthropology of Erotics* (Chikumashobo, 2010),

Transformation of the Sacrificial World (Hozoukan, 2002), (editor) *Cultural Anthropology of Military* (Fukyosha, 2015), (editor) *Fetishism Studies*, 3 vols (Kyoto UP 2010–16), and (coeditor) *Humanities of Contact Zone*, 4 vols (Koyosya, 2012–14).

Note

1. See also Kulka 2013 for experiences of children at the Auschwitz concentration camp.

References

Fukuchi Hiroaki. 1996. *Kichi to kankyō hakai: Okinawa ni okeru fukugō osen* [Bases and environmental destruction: Complex pollution in Okinawa]. Tokyo: Doujidaisya.
"About US Military Bases." n.d. Ginowan City website. Accessed 16 October 2016, http://www.city.ginowan.okinawa.jp/organization/kichisyougaika/archives/1004.
Gleditsch, Nils Petter. 1998. "Armed Conflict and the Environment: A Critique of the Literature." *Journal of Peace Research* 35 (3): 381–400.
Hayashi Kiminori. 2011. *Gunji kankyō mondai no seiji keizaigaku* [The political economy of military–environmental issues]. Tokyo: Nihon Keizai Hyouronsha.
Hodder, Ian. 2012. *Entangled: An Archaeology of the Relationships between Humans and Things.* Chichester: Wiley-Blackwell.
Kulka, Otto Dov. 2013. *Landscapes of the Metropolis of Death: Reflections on Memory and Imagination* (Trans. by Ralph Mandel, originally *Landschaften der Metropole des Todes: Auschwitz und die Grenzen der Erinnerung und der Vorstellungskraft*). Cambridge, MA: Belknap.
Miyamoto, Kenichi, Osamu Nishitani, and Seiji Endou (eds.). n.d. *What Have We Seen from Futenma Military Base Issues.* Tokyo: Iwanami.
Saitō Mitsumasa. 2010. "Kakusareta Jiko" [Hidden incidents]. In *Zainichi beigun saizensen* [On the front lines with U.S. forces stationed in Japan], 201–48. Tokyo: Shinjinbutsu Ōraisha.
Uemura Hideki. 2015. *Kurashite mita Futenma: Okinawa Beigun kichi mondai o kangaeru* [My Futenma: Thoughts on Okinawa's U.S. base problem]. Tokyo: Yoshida Shoten.
Yamauchi Shigeo. 2012. "Ginowan: Futenma kichi no sōon mondai to kiken-sei" [Ginowan: Risk and the Noise Pollution Problem at Futenma Base]. In *Ryūkyū rettō no kankyō mondai: "Fukki" 40-nen jizoku kanō na shima shakai e* [Environmental problems in the Ryūkyū Archipelago: Toward a sustainable island society on the 40th anniversary of the return], edited by Okinawa University, 90–97. Tokyo: Koubunken. Available at http://honto.jp/netstore/pd-worklist_0625413869.html.
Yoichi Yoshiyuki. 2010. *Beigun kichi to kankyō mondai* [U.S. base and environmental issues]. Tokyo: Gentosha Renaiss.
"Welcome to 'Futenma Base & Living with US Military Airfield!'" n.d. Futenma Base & Living with US Military Airfield website. Accessed 16 October 2016, http://futenma.info/.

Chapter 12

The Entanglements of Military Research at Home and Abroad

An Experience of an Israeli Anthropologist

Nir Gazit

Introduction

Studying the military is a processual endeavor that involves issues of negotiations with gatekeepers and informants over the process of gaining access, knowledge production, and postfieldwork dilemmas about writing and publication. Although such complexities exist in many fields, they are especially significant in studying military and war, given the ideological and political controversies surrounding these domains. Furthermore, the common social construction of the civil–military dichotomy, which stands at the base of the prevalent political culture of liberal industrial democracies, has only complicated things further for military anthropologists. Since many anthropologists who study the military are civilians, the research process itself becomes an interesting example of a civil–military entanglement. From this perspective, the ways in which the relationships in the field unfold, and the methodological entanglements that characterize the research process, determine what we can (and cannot) know about the military.

The following chapter is an extension of a previous article (Gazit and Maoz-Shai 2010) that discussed the intricacies of studying the military "at-home"—literally in the researcher's own country. The original paper proposed a dynamic conceptualization of the subject–object relationship.

The present chapter broadens this discussion by offering a comparison between studying the military at home and abroad. Instead of offering a general analysis of the methodologies used by anthropologists to study the military and a comprehensive review of existing research, the chapter draws on my personal experience as an Israeli anthropologist who has studied the military in his own country as well as abroad. My goal is to use my personal experience to illuminate the process of anthropological knowledge production when researching the military, and to discuss the entanglements associated with it.

I posit that when the research takes place in the researcher's own country, the (perceived) dichotomy between the researcher and the respondents breaks down and gives way to a dense web of interactions, expectations, and negotiations. As a result, it conditions the sort of knowledge produced. While the researcher's background continuously shapes the research process, the structural components of his or her background are ephemeral elements, humming and screeching as the research develops, and the level of their impact varies. In addition, the dominant political culture in the country and society in which the research takes place, which determines the attitude toward the military, also conditions the way the researcher will be accepted in the field and may put limits on what she or he can study. Thus the following analysis portrays the (civilian) anthropological research of the military as an ongoing process of knowledge production, resulting from enmeshing dynamics in the field.

I begin with a short introduction that presents my main research projects and my background. Consequently, I discuss the theoretical conceptualization of "entanglements" and its relevance to the anthropological research of the military, as I have experienced it. Subsequently, I discuss the impact of the structural elements and their meshing with the military by breaking down the research process into three phases: "entering the field," "while in the field," and "postfield dilemmas." Although in anthropology such a clear-cut distinction is uncommon, I am doing it for an analytical purpose since I believe it would help elucidate the various complexities of studying the military from an anthropological perspective.

Personal Background

I am an Israeli researcher who has mainly studied the Israeli military. In recent years, I also studied military issues in Canada and Spain. I am an Israeli-born citizen and, as most Jewish citizens in Israel, I was enlisted to the IDF (Israel Defense Forces) when I was eighteen years old.[1] For two years, I served as a combatant in an armory unit. After finishing Officer

Cadet School (OCS), I joined the IDF Southern Command as a logistics officer for two years. Today, I am a captain in the Israeli military reserves.

As an anthropologist, my research in Israel mainly explores the conduct of Israeli military forces in the Occupied Palestinian Territories (Ben-Ari, Lomsky-Feder, and Gazit 2004; Ben-Ari et al. 2005; Lomsky-Feder, Ben-Ari, and Gazit 2009; Gazit and Brym 2011; Gazit 2015). In these research projects, I examine the patterns of Israeli military violence and evaluate its political significance. More recently, I started a new research project on the Israeli soldiers deployed along the Israeli–Egyptian border. This project investigates the perceptions and practices of the soldiers vis-à-vis the irregular migration from Africa to Israel and the threat of terror in this region. In both projects, my methodology has consisted of participant observations, interviews (in and out of the field), and analysis of unclassified documents.

In 2009–2010, I conducted fieldwork in Canada that dealt with civil–military cooperation between transnational humanitarian nongovernmental organizations and the Canadian military forces in Afghanistan. In this study, I examined the relationships between agencies and actors, both on the institutional and the individual levels. I conducted interviews with Canadian key informants at varying levels in civilian and military agencies (e.g., government officials, high-ranking military officers, field commanders, and NGO officials). The interviews were conducted in military headquarters and NGO offices in Canada. Hence, both for me and for my respondents, it was an off-site research project, far away from the "real field" in Afghanistan. Yet, for the respondents, it was very much at home, in Canada, while for me it was a foreign territory.

In the case of my fieldwork in Spain, it was just the opposite. As part of a German-Israel research team who studies irregular migration in the Mediterranean, in 2014, I joined German colleagues in their fieldwork in Melilla, the Spanish enclave in North Africa. In this joint project, we compared the conduct of border-control forces in different countries and identified similarities and dissimilarities in their on-ground practices toward irregular migrants. In Melilla, we interviewed personnel of the Spanish paramilitary organization Guardia Civil. Although I was not the leading researcher in the field, my Israeli identity turned out to be a significant methodological asset, as well as an ethical burden, for me and for my German colleagues.

Israel, Canada, and Spain differ in their political cultures and in the social status of their military establishments. Both Israel and Spain have militaristic traditions, although the two countries have very different historical and geopolitical backgrounds (Ben-Eliezer 1998; Ehrlich 1987; Kimmerling 1993; Martínez and Barker 1988; Morn and Toro 1989). Canada, on the other hand, has a much more liberal political culture and thus tends to avert military actions unless they are framed as "humanitarian" or "peace" missions. As I shall demonstrate, these differences have had a great impact on the dynamic of studying the military in each country.

The Meshwork of Studying the Military

The seminal works of Samuel Huntington (1957) and Morris Janowitz (1960) portrayed the military and the civilian worlds as two separated social spheres. Although the two theorists were in dispute about the appropriate relations between the two worlds, they agreed that essentially there are fundamental differences between them. This perspective has led civilian social scientists to claim an objective epistemological positionality vis-à-vis the military that enables them to research the military objectively. Later, theorists such as James Burk (2002; see also Feaver 1999) challenged this view and emphasized the fluid boundaries and diffusion that exist between the military and civilian society. It is now widely acknowledged that the civilian sphere and the military sphere intertwine in a multifaceted manner. But how do their interrelations influence our ability to research the military? What sort of entanglements evolve when a civilian anthropologist penetrates the military in order to study it? To what degree does the social and personal background of the researcher expend into the field of study, the military, mingle with it, and influence the knowledge production?

Recently, several publications discussed methodological issues in military studies. Carreiras and Castro's (2013) edited volume, for example, have offered a collection of anthropological accounts on the hurdle of gaining access to the field and positionality of researchers vis-à-vis the military. These accounts exemplify the complexities of studying the military in different countries and the strategies researchers adopt to mitigate them; contributors highlight cognizant reflexivity (Castro 2013), methods of auto-ethnography (Liebengerg 2013), and gender management (Carreiras and Alexandre 2013). Soeters, Shields, and Rietjens's (2014) book also reviews the various methods scholars use when studying the military. Qualitative researchers who contributed to this volume mainly focus on issues of access, data collection, and, more specifically, on the method of participant observation. While both collections offer important insights on what it means to study the military, they seem to neglect the overall process of researching the military and the entanglements and trajectories associated with it. Furthermore, most of the studies presented are of scholars who research the military in their own country and ignore the unique challenge of studying foreign militaries.

An anthropological study of the military, whether at home or abroad, involves not only the challenge of the scholarly entrance of the researcher into a (potentially) foreign territory, which exists in any anthropological endeavor, but also a potential clash between the civilian world and the military world, in which the researcher's personal and social traits are always an issue. The researcher is not just a mediator of knowledge between the military and the civilian society, but also becomes an extension of the two domains, a medium that is entangled between them and takes an active part in the process of interweaving knowledge. This is why it is crucial to discuss how the researcher's background shapes the positionality vis-à-vis the military and civil society alike. The theoretical writings of Hodder (2014) and Ingold (2010) seem useful in explaining the nature of this entanglement.

The anthropologist Ian Hodder (2014: 20) defines "entanglement" as a form of mutual dependencies that on the one hand are enabling, and on the other hand involve some sort of constraint. Although Hodder uses the term "entanglement" to theorize the dialectical relations between humans and *things*, his analysis seems useful to shed light on the way people and *groups* are entrapped in complex systems from which it becomes difficult to become detached. The continuous tensions and complexities between the military and the civilian world (see Sørensen and Ben-Ari, this volume) do not leave the researcher immune from the entanglements and entrapments they produce. Moreover, the scholarly act itself is an entanglement that deserves our attention. To paraphrase Tim Ingold's (2010: 6) assertion, there could be no knowledge about the military in a world where the military and civilian life do not mix and mingle.

It has long been recognized that social research, especially in anthropology, is strongly affected by the researcher's personal and social identity. Not only does the researcher carry her or his identity (and world view) from the civilian world into the field of the military, these often mingle with the fundamental traits of the military domain and create methodological and ethical entanglements.

When studying the military, whether at home or abroad, various components of the researcher's background affect his or her access to the field and become dominant in shaping the interaction with the respondents (Gazit and Maoz-Shai 2010). These components may include the researcher's ethnonational and citizenship affiliations, military experience, academic affiliation, gender, and his or her political stance. The impact of these structural components, and especially their combination, mainly depends on the (perceived) social distance between the researcher and the field of study. The researcher's social background shapes not only his or her epistemological positionality, but even more so the willingness of the respondents to cooperate with the research, and the kind of knowledge produced.

Equally important is the dominant local political culture, which influences the ability to study the military. The relation to the military and war varies across societies. Militaries have different social status in different countries, and the legitimacy of using military force to advance political goals also differs significantly, and thus different methodological and ethical entrapments develop. Different political cultures may not only initiate different frames of analysis, but also influence the impact of the social background of the researcher on the research process.

Hence, in order to reveal the complexity of studying the military from a civilian perspective, one should map the congruities and incongruities between the researcher's social traits and the military. In other words, the conceptualization of "civil–military entanglements" opens a new avenue to explore the dense web of relationships between the researcher and the respondents and how these relationships are embedded within a wider set of entanglements between the military and civilian world. This perspective not only rejects the binary view of military and society, but also point to the active and dynamic influence of the civilian scholar on the research process.

Ingold (2010) concurs with Klee's (1961, 1973) argument that "the role of the artist is not to reproduce a preconceived idea, novel or not, but to join with and follow the forces and flows of material that bring the form of work into being" (Ingold 2010: 10). He emphasizes the power of itineration of the artist when his work is consubstantial with the trajectory of his or her life. Similarly, one should not ignore the dynamics of entering the field of the military, of being in the field, and after leaving it. As I shall demonstrate, the mingling of the structural elements of the researcher's background and the traits of the military sphere constantly changes and yet is constantly powerful in shaping the whole scholarly conduct.

In what follows, I present my personal experiences in studying the military in my home country, Israel, and abroad. I relate to three structural elements in my identity that I have found most influential—ethnonational affiliation and citizenship, past military service or lack thereof, and academic affiliation. It is important to note that since the analysis is mainly based on personal experience, some of the dynamics I discuss may seem less relevant to other anthropologists that have different backgrounds or may study different cases. In such cases, other structural elements in the researchers' background may become more relevant and therefore would produce different methodological and ethical entanglements.

Entering the Field

Gaining access is always a precarious, ongoing, and constantly renegotiable process (Johnson 1975). It is one of the main challenges every researcher faces when studying institutionalized organizations such as the military (Sion 2006: 458). Because the military represents the state's sovereignty and core national interests, it holds an important position within the realm of state bureaucracy. Consequently, the military, similarly to other state bureaucracies, is hierarchical, confidential, and sensitive to public criticism. As such it tends to control outsiders' interventions (Gerth [1946] 2003).

Entering the field of the military often begins with the need to acquire formal authorization to conduct the research. Since it is exposed to public scrutiny, particularly in times of a controversial conflict, the military aims to screen any penetration by outsiders who represent a potential threat to the organization and to what is defined as "national security." Many militaries have a public relations office or spokesperson department that monitors all connections with external researchers and journalists. Passing the organization's gatekeepers often requires being subjected to formal as well as informal criteria. A highly crucial factor affecting access is the researcher's ethnonational descent, his or her civil status, and a military background or lack thereof.

Because the military has a critical role in the creation of states and symbolizes the nation (Tilly 1992; Giddens 1985), studying the military at home raises questions of loyalty and patriotism. Thus an affiliation with the ethnonational group considered dominant by the state indicates that the researcher can be trusted. In the case of Israel and Spain, for example, citizenship and ethnonational affiliations are interrelated properties: ethnonationalist and republican discourses combine to produce a stratified sociopolitical hierarchy (Shafir and Peled 1998; Yiftachel 1999).[2] In Israel, this inextricable connection reproduces the Jewish dominance and maintains equivalence between Jewish nationality and what is considered as "full" citizenship. Belonging to the "favorite" ethnonational community increases one's array of social, economic, and political possibilities, as well as research opportunities.

A non-Jewish scholar would find it almost impossible to carry out fieldwork within the Israeli army. Although Palestinians make up about 20 percent of the Israeli citizenry, the field of security in Israel is very restricted, and it is practically inaccessible to Palestinian researchers, mainly because the common perception among Israeli security officials is that "security is for Jews only." Exacerbating this is the fact that the entire Palestinian collective is considered a rival ethnonational community.

Therefore, before agreeing to participate in a study, key informants, usually officers in the Military Spokesperson Department or the Information Security Department, carry out an informal "friendly clearance investigation" to guarantee that the researcher belongs to their "in group" and thus can be trusted. Israeli-Jewish surnames and family names, the lack of a foreign accent, native Israeli figures of speech, and even physical appearance (Hajjar 2005) are all important informal criteria proving the appropriate ethnonational affiliation.

Before conducting research in army bases and carrying interviews with active officers and rank-and-file soldiers, I needed to go through such a formal and more comprehensive clearance in order to get permission to do the research. During this process, I was asked to provide details on my biography, family members, and friends. Any relationships, whether professional or personal, with foreign colleagues (particularly from Arab descent) might have jeopardized the research.

During such formal and informal clearance procedures, another structural element in my background came into play, affecting the entrance to the field—my past military service. Both in militaristic and nonmilitaristic societies, researchers who wish to study the military benefit from having a military chapter in their biography, although it is not always be a precondition (see, for example, Kirke 2005; Castro 2013). This is particularly salient in militaristic societies. In Israel, for example, the military is considered the (Jewish) "people's army," and common sentiments are that "everybody knows the army," and "everybody served in the army." Military service is a crucial component in the normative Jewish Israeli communal and personal narrative (Lieblich 1989). Hence, belonging to a community of warriors is experienced in terms of embeddedness in society, as a creation of normalcy, and as an entitlement that legitimizes participation in civil society (Helman 1997, 1999). This imagined community is stratified, and becoming a legitimate and full member of it depends upon military service. Consequently, even when the researcher is no longer a member of the military establishment, it can transform him or her from a potential intruder to a "familiar alien." As I shall demonstrate later, I have found that this position has significant methodological and ethical implications.

Specific past positions within the military hierarchy are even more crucial in paving the researcher's way in. For example, my past service as a soldier in a combat unit and as an officer in the IDF enabled me to use my personal social circle to contact potential respondents and gain their trust. Moreover, my service in reserve forces enabled me to maintain these personal ties and create new ones. I was consistently perceived as having a hybrid identity of a member in the imagined community of soldiers and as an anthropologist.

Having a military or other security background also helps the researcher develop informal access to the organization and reduce social distance from the respondents. Being classified as "friendly" to the institution under study thus helps the researcher overcome these barriers. In all my research on the Israeli military, I was primarily evaluated by my informants according to past military service as a former combatant in the military armored corps. In many instances, the respondents told me that my past military experience in a combat unit was not only important for gaining their initial trust but also made them confident that I would not misinterpret their explanations.

When researching foreign militaries, the researcher's prime identity is "foreigner." Thus his or her scholarly access to the military is significantly limited compared to a local researcher, since the foreign researcher's loyalty to the national security interests of the host country is, at the very least, questionable. I have found that having a military chapter in my biography turned out to be the most important factor in overcoming the barrier of being a foreign scholar.

During my initial contacts with gatekeepers in the Canadian army, for example, the very first question I was asked was about my nationality. When I answered that I am an Israeli scholar, the immediate following questions were whether I served in the Israeli army, in what unit, and what my military rank was. In a way, these questions resemble questions a prisoner of war might be asked immediately after being taken into captivity. However, it turned out to be an informal procedure of clearance, and my past military service in the IDF and being a veteran, even of a foreign military, increased my access to the field. The officer interviewed me started to ask me informal questions about my military service, and surprisingly started to share his own military experiences. The formal clearance procedure very quickly turned into a friendly chat between a veteran and an active officer.

A similar scenario took place before I started my fieldwork in Melilla, Spain. One of my German colleagues tried to coordinate interviews with a senior *Guardia Civil* officer before I arrived in Melilla. Although she holds an EU passport, speaks Spanish, and lived in Spain for several years, she felt that the gatekeeper she contacted was willing to cooperate more freely when he heard that her Israeli colleague, a veteran of the IDF, would join the interviews. She was asked to provide details about my military service. The informal inquiry seemed equally important as the formal authorization, as access to the field very much depends on the goodwill of gatekeepers. Although a foreign scholar with a military background might raise suspicion, it also raises curiosity among the respondents and thus encourages their willingness to cooperate.

Hence, to a certain extent, the imagined community of soldiers is trans-national. It is not surprising, therefore, that many researchers in this field are scholars affiliated with military academies or who have served in the military (Sion 2006: 458).

In the Field

Long after the researcher enters the field, the sociostructural components of the researcher's identity continue to influence the research and force the researcher to balance between sets of ambivalent epistemological po-sitions. In at-home research, there is an inextricable link between the field of study and the researcher's *lebenswelt* that often encapsulates ideologi-cal, social, and professional sentiments. In this sense, the researcher has a significant social investment, either direct or indirect, in the institutions under study. Hence, the researcher's background creates an ambivalent and dynamic positioning while he or she is in the field, influencing the point of view and creating particular expectations.

In Israel, belonging to the Jewish hegemonic community comes with a set of expectations that a Jewish civilian must follow, which is encapsu-lated in what could be called "ethnoloyalty" (Gazit and Maoz-Shai 2010). Because rights and duties are bestowed and demanded according to one's ethnic origin and communal contribution, the researcher's citizenship and ethnonational affiliations become an integral part of the research endeavor, thus factoring into the researcher's conduct in the field. To a certain extent, during at-home research, civilian affiliation in terms of ethnonationalism becomes the researcher's master status while studying the military, since this is the main structural element that the researcher and the informants share, and conditions the trust of the latter.

Ethnonationalism and national security combine to create a set of prem-ises. Considered by the respondents as part of the system, the researcher is perceived by the organization not only as trustworthy but also as rela-tively more controllable. In my research projects in Israel, the informants translated my social and military background into a perceived status of comrade and "secret keeper" [*Shomer-Sod* in Hebrew]. They perceived me as belonging to an inner-circle community of those familiar with the sensi-tivity of security information and committed to protect it. This status gave me an "informal clearance" while collecting data, but it came with the expectation that I would not misuse it and endanger national security in-terests or slander the military. In many instances, they voluntarily shared classified information, trusting that I would understand its sensitivity and therefore would not publish it.

Kirke (2005) suggests that when the researcher is a full-time member of the social group he or she studies, in his case the British army, it may become a burden impeding the creation of a degree of detachment and "stranger value." However, when studying the military at home, researchers may develop a special kind of "multilayered vision." Phenomenologically, they experience a particular tension of being both a "stranger" in the Simmelian sense (Simmel 1950) and a "marginal informant" (Freilich 1970). Let me illuminate this complex scholarly positioning by mentioning a similar structural complexity. Lomsky-Feder, Gazit, and Ben-Ari (2008) conceptualize reserves soldiers as transmigrants to explain their special character and dynamics. Like transmigrants, reserves constantly "travel" between, and mediate among, the army and wider civilian society. Many of them bring into the military the resources, skills, and abilities of their civilian occupations and specializations. More importantly, this constant movement—like the shifting of transmigrants between different homes— may bring about critical thinking about "what is going on" within the military. Lomsky-Feder, Gazit, and Ben-Ari (2008) propose that reservists have a special kind of "double-vision" (or double-consciousness): they see things *in* and *about* the military that people from inside or outside do not see (or do not want to see). Similarly, civilian researchers with military background also enjoy multiple prisms. Simultaneously and consequentially they experience a parallel consciousness.

This, of course, also depends on the researcher's biography. Sasson-Levy (2006), for example, argues that although she conducted her research of the Israeli military at home, it did not feel "at home" during her fieldwork, mainly because the informants considered her past military service marginal. Nevertheless, she did turn what might have been an obstacle into a methodological asset by using her relative "strangeness" to justify asking detailed questions and demanding "thick description" from her respondents (see also Lomsky-Feder 1996). Ben-Ari (1989), on the other hand, explains that when he studied his platoon during his service in the reserves, his social similarity with his comrades enabled him to adopt the "natives' point of view." Yet, at the same time, his academic background led him to critically analyze their mutual experiences. Thus, Ben-Ari's position gave him the advantage of holding a dual perspective of both marginal informant and critical observer.[3]

Ben-Ari's experience echoes the expectation raised by the academic community that researchers will analyze material rigorously, particularly if they are affiliated with their research objects. Traditionally, the field of anthropology urged scholars to "immerse in the field" and to reduce distance from their subjects. However, when studying the military, the possibility of "going native" can be threatening. In social sciences, particularly in anthropology, studying violence from the perpetrators' perspective is frowned upon. Further, critical circles in the academic community would most likely not tolerate an empathetic representation of this perspective (Huggins, Haritos-Fatouros, and Zimbardo 2002). This normative framing of the research compels researchers to guarantee a secured position toward the informants that would enable them to preserve a space of relative objectivity. On the other hand, and as mentioned above, the researcher's background could oblige him or her to embrace an insider perspective, and consequently position himself or herself as a marginal native. Experiencing this dual position often creates ambivalence and is confusing. While it is relatively easier to maintain a more neutral stance toward the object of study when the research is conducted overseas, it is much harder when it is conducted at home, especially in times of conflict and when there are political controversies about it. Since the researcher is personally participating in the everyday reality under study, it is very difficult not to hold a political opinion about it. Often, the immediate interaction with soldiers in the field summons incidents in which the researcher faces two alternatives: either to express political and/or moral viewpoints or to remain silent.

This entanglement is both methodologically enabling and limiting. Being an Israeli soldier during the first Palestinian uprising (1987–1993), I often participated in military missions in the Occupied Palestinian Territories. My respondents, who were familiar with this fact, tried to lean on my personal experience to legitimize their current actions. In one occasion, my informant described his service in one of the Israeli army checkpoints in the West Bank. As he elaborated on the surveillance mechanisms and collective punishment measures he and his soldiers implemented toward Palestinian civilians in the checkpoint, he asked me, *"You* know how it is? You stand in the sun for hours. Thousands of people going by and you must check each and every one of them. . . . They drive you crazy and you do things that afterwards you're not always comfortable with. . . . *You* know how it is, *don't you?!"* The interviewee felt free to disclose sensitive information. Yet, he expected me to empathize and share his rationalization of acts that he himself perceived as morally problematic. What enabled him to do it was the combination of my external position, as civilian scholar, and my perceived belonging to the large imagined community of Israeli soldiers. The interviewee's effort led me to stand at an epistemological and moral crossroads: cooperating with his reminiscence would enhance the rapport established in the interview and probably help the respondent to reveal more details; however, embracing "the native point of view" would risk wiping out any ontological distance between us, which was already quite blurry. This situation might be interpreted as a methodological manipulation, in which the interviewer seeks to gain deeper and richer information by "faking empathy" (Campbell 2003). Moreover, the diminishing ontological gap with the respondent could prevent the researcher from adopting a critical point of view, which might bias the entire analysis. Yet it also demonstrates how the researcher's social and personal identity does not remain in the background. Rather, it enmeshes him or her, and turns into an active ingredient in the production of knowledge. The anthropologist becomes dependent in epistemological relations that he or she knows are entrapping them.

During my fieldwork in Melilla, I encountered a similar experience. It was during an escorted field trip to the separation fence on the border between Melilla and Morocco. One of the respondents, a senior officer of the *Guardia Civil*, wished to legitimize the violent practices he and his soldiers have used toward the African migrants crossing from Morocco and compared the situation in Melilla to the West Bank. Familiar with my Israeli identity and my past military experience, he approached me and asked, "You Israelis know what the risk of terror is. You built a separation wall (in the West Bank) and you know how difficult it is to deal with terrorists infiltrating your country. It is a dirty job that must be done by someone. Explain it to them. . . ." By "them," the Spanish officer was referring to German researchers who had asked him about any violent events that took place along the fence. The officer interpreted their question as a blunt critique and expression of their lack of appreciation of the Spanish forces' efforts to "protect Europe from the illegal migrants." Under these circumstances, I, an Israeli ex-military man, was turned by the respondent into an imagined comrade, who was asked to explain to the ignorant scholars from Germany how difficult it is to fight "foreign infiltrators." His comment put me in a delicate epistemological position in which I had to decide whether to criticize his comparison between African migrants and terrorists, or stifle my criticism and allow him to tell his story. Interestingly, when I continued asking him questions about using violence along the fence, he seemed more tolerant of my questions and interpret them as more legitimate "professional" questions in contrast to my colleagues' "political" questions. Hence, my dual status in the field as foreign scholar and as an imagined comrade was helpful to gain the cooperation of the interviewee. Yet, I felt that he also manipulated me in order to challenge my colleagues' epistemological stance.

At the same time, when research takes place in a foreign country, it may touch issues that might be interpreted as too sensitive or risky. As this is often the case when studying the military, the researcher might be tagged as a potential infiltrator or even a spy. Consequently, the researcher should be aware to how his or her national identity might be interpreted in the field. Hiding it or remaining vague about it might complicate the dynamic in the field and even endanger his or her personal freedom, as the research might be considered an act of subversion. In terms of knowledge production, it would limit the sort and quality of information that the informants disclose.[4]

The effect of these entanglements might lead to uneasy situations and unintended confrontations that may affect the entire network. During one of my interviews in Canada, I asked a senior Canadian general about the potential tension between what is termed the "war on terror" and humanitarian considerations of the Canadian army in Afghanistan. My interviewee interpreted my questions as an inappropriate criticism of the Canadian army conduct in Afghanistan. Furthermore, the fact that I was a foreign researcher amplified his irritation. When I made a comparison between the moral dilemmas of Israeli soldiers in the occupied territories and potentially similar dilemmas of Canadian soldiers in Afghanistan, he quickly asked to shorten the interview, muttering angrily that this was an improper comparison. He also abstained from referring me to other potential respondents from his unit.

These examples illustrate entanglement of the "politics of methodology" and the realpolitik per se, which is common in studying the military at home, as well as abroad. From this perspective, entering the field of the military is not a mere technical act; rather, it encapsulates a dense network of expectations. To a certain extent, researchers and their informants formulate an implicit contract, according to which the informants will share their experiences with the researcher in exchange for, at the very least, some compliance with their expectations. These expectations are also based on the researcher's structural positioning. If researchers are veterans, they are expected to "do no harm to their comrades" and to appropriately represent the security system and its agents, even if it is foreign. Being a citizen and a military researcher, the researcher is coerced into dealing with the demand to "do no harm to your country." The researcher's ethnonational community expects him or her to be a patriot—to represent its side in the conflict and its security constraints. While in the field, and once the fieldwork is accomplished, one cannot escape the attempt to try to do both: to "be native" and to criticize the "natives' point of view." The problem with doing research overseas is that one is not always aware of the political sensitivities associated with the research.

Postfieldwork Entanglements

When undertaking at-home research, researchers can never be "out of the field" because they are socially and personally embodied in it. Studying the military in militaristic societies or in antimilitaristic societies takes this assertion to its extreme.

Postfieldwork does not entail the suspension of the above-mentioned structural dilemmas. On the contrary, the trajectories established by the civil–military entanglements in the field linger and continue to influence the research during the postfield phase; however, the direct intricacies with the respondents give way to dilemmas the researcher faces when "returning" to the civilian world. After concluding the fieldwork, researchers must confront the implications of their decisions and the relations they established. Analytically, it is important to distinguish between two sets of dilemmas: the writing process and publishing. Both have significant implications for maintaining a future relationship with the field of study.

Like the classic transmigrants (Glick-Schiller, Basch, and Szanton-Blanc 1995), the researchers return to their native home community—academia— and should perform according to its norms and values. Yet the experiences and relationships from the fieldwork develop new complexities. The political atmosphere of the university and the status of the researcher often have a meaningful impact on the research and publication. Critical academic scholars may also feel that when it comes to writing, it is necessary to create an epistemological gap between their ethnonational and military "homes" and themselves. Alternatively, affiliation with a politically conservative or military academic institution might discourage a critical stance. Researchers might be worried about their career, and would therefore be more critical or less critical in the writing according to their institution's leanings. Thus, when the research is politically charged, academic status might be crucial. The author must decide how far to go when analyzing and theorizing the data accumulated, particularly in cases that deal with real (or alleged) national security issues.

Similarly, the extent of cooperation the researcher received while in the field might become a honey trap. As cooperation increases, so might the official demand for censorship under the terms "do no harm to your country," as well as the informal expectation to "do no harm to your fellow comrades." These expectations might increase military involvement and inspection, thus limiting the researcher's freedom in terms of the issues investigated, the research outcomes, and publications. The negotiations between the researcher and the military often start before the research begins. For example, a Japanese colleague who studies the Japan Self-Defense Forces and belongs to the department of economics, was asked by the senior officers she contacted to give the soldiers and their families financial advisement. They also used these prestudy negotiations to verify no confidential information would be disclosed in the research. When I asked to enter a military base in order to study a new project of the IDF with environmental implications, the precondition was that I would not criticize the project. The fact that I cannot surrender any details about the nature of this research here also exemplifies the power of the military in forcing censorship on civilian researchers of the military.

Criticizing the military—for example, by uncovering acts of atrocity against civilians or even discrimination against women soldiers—might stigmatize the researcher as "disloyal to the system and to the country." Further, the military wields considerable power over the research by controlling the sort and amount of data released for analysis and publication. Therefore, researchers may have no alternative but to base their conclusions on partial and incomplete security-sensitive (and occasionally partially classified) empirical data. This might raise doubts regarding the validity of the findings. When conducting research in a foreign military, access to such classified materials is often impossible, and thus the dependency of the researcher on local informants increases.

Every study that aims to understand the logic and conduct of militaries and the phenomenology of agents of violence requires a certain level of interaction with these institutions and their officials. But Huggins, Haritos-Fatouros, and Zimbardo (2002) wonder, "How are researchers to listen to the powerful and the violent?" From what intellectual and moral stance should researchers analyze their accounts? As Robben (1995) argues, the traditional academic expectation, specifically in anthropology, is to unveil those who abuse power rather than to try and understand their reasoning. The growing involvement of militaries of the industrial democracies in a whole array of violent (or potentially violent) conflicts and the friction between soldiers and civilians intensify the ethical intricacy of studying the military.

In Israel, studying the military is greatly influenced by ideological and political controversies regarding the Arab–Israeli conflict, the dominance of the military in Israeli society, and of politics in the Israeli academy (Kimmerling 2005). However, only a handful of social scientists have acknowledged these complexities. Further, the literature rarely discusses the connections among the military establishment, militaristic culture, and academic research (but see Ben-Ari and Levy 2014 and Kimmerling 2005 for exceptions).

The researcher's academic affiliation may influence the research in several ways. First, the academic position structures the researcher's position vis-à-vis the domain of security. This is evident, for example, in the military personnel's common perspective of civilian researchers as outsiders and a potential external threat. Second, academia has its own expectations about how scholars should analyze and theorize their materials. In cases

where the academic institution has a definite political or ideological inclination—for example a religious or conservative university that promotes
patriotism—the researcher might refrain from criticizing the military according to his or her institutional stance. Alternatively, if affiliated with
a liberal and critical research institute or with a private university that
is not dependent on governmental funding, the researcher might adopt,
or be expected to adopt, a more radical perspective when studying the
military. Thus, such expectations are part and parcel of academic study of
the military. For example, when I was writing my doctorate dissertation
on Israeli soldiers in the Occupied Territories, I had doubts about whether
I was critical enough when describing and analyzing the data. The informal yet tangible expectation in the academic circle around me was that I
should produce a (political and) critical account of the Israeli occupation.
Yet, although I could politically identify with this expectation, I also felt
equally committed to represent the narratives of my respondents without
subjecting them to political criticism.

While such dynamics might be relevant in other fields, I have found
that their impact tends to increase when studying military issues, as they
are often coupled with expectations raised by the ethnonational community of reference. This is why the academic affiliation of the researcher,
particularly if he or she comes from a nonmilitary educational establishment, becomes less salient when studying foreign militaries abroad. Since
the ethnonational identity of the researcher is the most dominant one
when conducting such research, his or her academic affiliation is usually
less important for the respondents.

During at-home research, the major governing force is not official censorship but rather informal expectations of loyalty and patriotism due to
the researcher's background. The respondents assume that the researcher
will impose self-censorship, and this may paradoxically increase the researcher's flexibility in the field, yet create a burden after leaving the field.

Such complexities can get even more severe when studying foreign
militaries. While gaining access is often based on informal procedure,
publishing is often subjected to formal authorization by the local censorship office or spokesperson, who may put limits on what can be published
or even jeopardize the publication altogether. In a way, being a foreign
researcher may make it easier to bypass such restrictions if one publishes
his or her findings outside the country; however, this might endanger the
respondents and the researcher's future contacts in the field.

I faced this problem in my research in Canada. Although I did receive a
formal authorization to conduct the research, I apparently did not receive
the permission to publish the findings without an institutional review of
the Canadian army spokesperson. Here my Israeli identity turned into

an obstacle, since they were willing to talk only with Canadian citizens. These bureaucratic difficulties jeopardized the publication of the findings altogether.

To prevent such situations, anthropologists of the military can chose among several alternative routes. First, they may decide to avoid controversial or sensitive issues in their research to minimize any institutional restriction on using the data. Second, they may choose to act in accordance with the military expectation, and pay the price of censorship so that they may have access to sensitive materials. Third, researchers may decide to use only secondary data (i.e., media publications and old materials collected by others). None of these alternatives is ideal as all of them would limit the researcher's scholarly freedom and, more importantly, would weaken the validity of the findings. A partial solution is to use, if possible, original materials gathered though unofficial channels; for example, to interview soldiers in reserves or recently released veterans, who are less committed to formal censorship. As presented in the last example, such a solution might not be enough when studying foreign militaries.

Conclusion

In this chapter, I have traced the methodological and ethical intricacies of researching the military at home and abroad. My argument has been that whenever a researcher studies the military, the structural components of his or her personal and social background become fundamental variables that intervene in the research process. Obviously, personal and social backgrounds are always significant; yet previous writing on the subject has tended to present these variables in a rather static manner. The analysis here suggested that researchers are structurally positioned vis-à-vis several corresponding and dynamic communities of reference, driven by their multilayered background: ethnonational and citizenship affiliation, military past, and their relationship with the academic community. The actual influence of these components is dynamic and changes throughout the research process, varying according to the personal biography, object of study, and, more importantly, the local political culture that determines the attitude to military forces and the study of them. Thus, the epistemological positioning of researchers becomes multifaceted, as researchers constantly change positions in relation to each—fields, their respondents, and fellow scholars. As the salience of each of the above-mentioned structural components shifts throughout the research process, researchers are compelled to alter their epistemological stance.

I find that the primary factor that shapes these negotiations is the re-searcher's ethnonational identity, mainly because the military is the most associated organization with the nation-state. When the research is con-ducted overseas, the researcher seems to carry abroad his or her structural components. However, the significance and magnitude of these structural components may change in response to the local political culture that frames the social status of the military, and impacts the ability to study it ethnographically.

To overcome the complexities presented above, a researcher may take a number of paths:

First, researchers should coordinate research expectations with the or-ganization under study in advance, regarding both research design and future publication of the results. This is particularly important in cases of research that involved direct cooperation with the military. This cooper-ation may increase access to valuable data and improve rapport with the respondents. At the same time, however, it might also increase pressures and impose scholarly limitations that nonmilitary researchers would like to avoid. Therefore, it is important that researchers determine the extent of organizational intervention in the research process and clarify that the re-search products will be published in academic venues. It is often difficult to achieve such coordination when researching foreign militaries, which often do not tolerate nonlocal researchers.

Second, and following the last point, it is recommended to include na-tive researchers when studying foreign militaries. This will increase access and cooperation. By the same token, it is also advised to include nonnative researchers in the research team during at-home research. Even though it might limit the organization's willingness to cooperate, it may neverthe-less enrich the research perspective and its theorization. Hence, collabo-ration between local and foreign researchers may alleviate some scholarly restrictions driven by the researchers' structural positions.

Finally, it is important to note in this context that the magnitude and interrelations of these components might differ from society to society. In any given society, other components of the researcher's background might become relevant. For example, in theocratic regimes, such as in Iran and Saudi Arabia, religious affiliation would probably become a most crucial variable when studying the state apparatus. In Turkey, on the other hand, being secular is probably an important asset in gaining access to the military. Hence, the influence of political culture, social com-position, and historical circumstances are key ingredients in research, as they mediate the effects of structural variables on scholarly access and research dynamics.

To summarize: researchers can, at least to a certain extent, choose what would be the master status from the status set, and use it as a methodological advantage. Yet, as demonstrated above, it is very difficult for the researcher to control and manage his or her identity since from very early stages of the research to its aftermath, they are intertwined with the field and become an integral part of the meshwork of studying it.

Nir Gazit is a senior lecturer at the Department of Behavioral Sciences at the Ruppin Academic Center and a research fellow at the Harry S. Truman Research Institute for the Advancement of Peace at the Hebrew University of Jerusalem. His research interests include transnational civil–military relations, governance and sovereignty, and political violence. His recent articles have appeared in the *International Journal of Politics, Culture and Society, City and Community, Qualitative Sociology, International Sociology, International Political Sociology, Sociology,* and *Journal of Contemporary Ethnography.*

Notes

This chapter is an extension of a previous article: N. Gazit and Y. Maoz-Shai, 2010, "Studying-Up and Studying-Across: Researching Governmental Violence Organizations at Home." Qualitative Sociology 33 (3) 275–95, https://doi.org/10.1007/s11133-010-9156-y, portions reprinted with permission.

 1. According to Israeli law, all Jewish men and women at the age of eighteen years are obliged to take part in military service. Upon their release, all Jewish Israeli men and some of the women are enlisted in a reserve service, which is the primary military component of Israeli defense forces in times of national emergency (Horowitz and Kimmerling 1974; Lomsky-Feder, Gazit, and Ben-Ari 2008). While most Israeli Jewish female soldiers do not serve in combat units, their participation in the military includes them as legitimate members of the ethnonational community. At the same time, it is important to note that though military service is obligatory for both men and women in Israel, only 75 percent of men and 60 percent of women actually do military service (Levy 2007).
 2. Shafir and Peled (1998) identify three discourses of citizenship in Western political thought— liberal, republican, and ethnonationalist—that define the relationship between the nation and its members. Liberal and republican discourses mostly refer to the question of what should come first—civil rights or the state's responsibilities, but the ethnonationalist discourse of citizenship creates an inextricable link between civilian status and ethnic descent.
 3. On the advantage of conducting an auto-ethnography in the field of military studies, see Higate and Cameron 2006.

4. At the same time, however, in countries, such as Japan for example, where the military strives to restore its legitimacy, even foreign researchers may enter the field and conduct research within the military (see Frühstück and Ben-Ari 2002; Ben-Ari, this volume).

References

Ben-Ari, E. 1989. "Masks and Soldiering: The Israeli Army and the Palestinian Uprising." *Cultural Anthropology* 4 (4): 372–89.

Ben-Ari, E., and Y. Levy. 2014. "Getting Access to the Field." In J. Sorters, P. M. Shields, and S. Rietjens (eds.), *Routledge Handbook of Research Methods in Military Studies*, 9–18. London: Routledge.

Ben-Ari, E., E. Lomsky-Feder, and N. Gazit. 2004. "Notes on the Study of Military Reserves: Between the Military and Civilian Spheres." In K. Spohr-Readman (ed.), *Building Sustainable and Effective Military Capabilities: A Systematic Comparison of Professional and Conscript Forces*, 64–78. Amsterdam: IOS Press.

Ben-Ari, E., M. Maymon., N. Gazit., and R. Shatzberg. 2005. *From Checkpoints to Flow-Points: Sites of Friction between the Israel Defense Forces and Palestinians*. A Gitelson Peace Publication, No. 31. Jerusalem: The Harry S. Truman Research Institute for the Advancement of Peace, The Hebrew University of Jerusalem.

Ben-Eliezer, U. 1998. *The Making of Israeli Militarism*. Bloomington: Indiana University Press.

Burk, J. 2002. Theories of Democratic Civil-Military Relations. *Armed Forces & Society* 29 (1): 7–29.

Campbell, E. 2003. "Interviewing Men in Uniform: A Feminist Approach." *Social Research Methodology* 6: 285–304.

Carreiras, H., and A. Alexandre. 2013. "Research Relations in Military Settings: How Does Gender Matter?" In H. Carreiras and C. Castro (eds.), *Qualitative Methods in Military Studies: Research Experiences and Challenges*, 97–115. Oxon: Routledge.

Carreiras, H., and C. Castro (eds.). 2012. *Qualitative Methods in Military Studies: Research Experiences and Challenges*. Oxon: Routledge.

Ehrlich, A. 1987. "Israel: Conflict, War and Social Change." In C. Creighton and M. Shaw (eds.), *The Sociology of War and Peace. Explorations in Sociology*, 121–42. London: Palgrave Macmillan.

Feaver, P. D. 1999. Civil–Military Relations. *Annual Review of Political Science* 2 (1): 211–41.

Freilich, M. 1970. "Field Work: An Introduction." In M. Freilich (ed.), *Marginal Natives: Anthropologists at Work*, 1–37. New York: Harper and Row.

Frühstück, S., and E. Ben-Ari. 2002. "'Now We Show It All!' Normalization and the Management of Violence in Japan's Armed Forces." *Journal of Japanese Studies* 28 (1): 1–39.

Gazit, N. 2009. "Social Agency, Spatial Practices and Power: The Micro-Foundations of Fragmented Sovereignty in the Occupied Territories." *International Journal of Politics, Culture, and Society* 22: 83–103.

———. 2015. "State-Sponsored Vigilantism: Jewish Settlers' Violence in the Occupied Palestinian Territories." *Sociology* 49 (3): 438–54.

Gazit, N., and B. Brym. 2011. "State-Directed Political Assassination in Israel: A Political Hypothesis." *International Sociology* 26 (6): 862–77.

Gazit, N., and Y. Maoz-Shai. 2010. "Studying-Up and Studying-Across: At-Home Research of Governmental Violence Organizations." *Qualitative Sociology* 33 (3): 275–95.

Gerth, H. H. (1946) 2003. *From Max Weber: Essays in Sociology*. New York: Oxford University Press.

Giddnes, A. 1985. *The Nation-State and Violence*. Cambridge: Polity.

Glick-Schiller, N., L. Basch, and C. Szanton-Blanc. 1995. "From Immigrant to Transmigrant: Theorizing Transnational Migration." *Anthropological Quarterly* 2: 48–63.

Hajjar, L. 2005. *Courting Conflict: The Israeli Military Court in Israel and Gaza.* Berkeley: California University Press.

Helman, S. 1997. "Militarism and the Construction of Community." *Journal of Political and Military Sociology* 25: 305–32.

Higate, P., and A. Cameron. 2006. "Reflexivity and Researching the Military." *Armed Forces and Society* 32 (2): 219–33.

Hodder, I., 2014. The Entanglements of Humans and Things: A Long-Term View. *New Literary History* 45 (1): 19–36.

Horowitz, D., and B. Kimmerling. 1974. Some Social Implications of Military Service and the Reserves System in Israel. *European Journal of Sociology* 15 (2): 262–76.

Huggins, M. K., M. Haritos-Fatouros, and P. Zimbardo. 2002. *Violence Workers: Police Torturers and Murderers Reconstruct Brazilian Atrocities.* Berkeley: University of California Press.

Huntington, S. P. 1957. *The Soldier and the State: The Theory and Politics of Civil–Military Relations.* Cambridge, MA: Harvard University Press.

Ingold, T. 2010. "Bringing Things Back to Life: Creative Entanglements in a World of Materials." ESRC National Centre for Research Methods Working Paper Series 05/10, Manchester.

Janowitz, M. 1960. *The Professional Soldier: A Social and Political Portrait.* New York: Simon and Schuster.

Johnson, J. 1975. *Doing Field Research.* New York: Free Press.

Kimmerling, B. 1993. "Patterns of Militarism in Israel." *European Journal of Sociology* 34: 196–223.

———. 2005. "The Failure of Israeli Academic and Public Sociologies: A Call for Discussion and Debate." *Israel Studies Forum* 20: 28–48.

Kirke, C. 2005. "Grappling with the Stereotype: British Army Culture and Perceptions, An Anthropology from Within." Paper presented at the conference *Recontextualising and Reconceptualising Delineations and Infusions of Militarization in Organizational Theory and Lives,* Cambridge, UK. Accessed 16 June 2017, http://www.mngt.waikato.ac.nz/ejrot/cmsconference/2005/proceedings/recontextualising/kirke.pdf.

Klee, P. 1961. *Notebooks.* Vol. 1: *The Thinking Eye.* Edited by J. Spiller. London: Lund Humphries.

———. 1973. *Notebooks.* Vol. 2: *The Nature of Nature.* Translated by H. Norden; edited by J. Spiller. London: Lund Humphries.

Levy, Y. 2007. *Israel's Materialist Militarism.* London: Lexington Books.

Liebenberg, J. C. R. 2013. "Evolving Experiences: Auto-Ethnography and Military Sociology; A South African Immersion." In H. Carreiras and C. Castro (eds.), *Qualitative Methods in Military Studies: Research Experiences and Challenges,* 50–6. New York: Routledge.

Lieblich, A. 1989. *Transition to Adulthood during Military Service: The Israeli Case.* Albany: State University of New York Press.

Lomsky-Feder, E. 1996. "A Woman Studies War: Stranger in a Man's World." In R. Josselson (ed.), *Ethics and Process in the Narrative Study of Lives,* 232–44. London: Sage.

Lomsky-Feder, E., N. Gazit, and E. Ben-Ari. 2008. "Reserve Soldiers as Transmigrants: Moving Between the Civilian and Military Worlds." *Armed Forces and Society* 34 (4): 593–614.

Martínez, R. B., and T. M. Barker (eds.). 1988. "Armed Forces and Society in Spain Past and Present." Boulder: Social Science Monographs.

Morn, F., and M. Toro. 1989. "From Dictatorship to Democracy: Crime and Policing in Contemporary Spain." *International Journal of Comparative and Applied Criminal Justice* 13 (1): 53–64.

Robben, A. 1995. "The Politics of Truth and Emotion among Victims and Perpetrators of Violence." In C. Nordstrom and A. Robben (eds.), *Fieldwork Under Fire: Contemporary Studies of Violence and Survival,* 81–104. Berkeley: University of California Press.

Sasson-Levy, O. 2006. *Identities in Uniform: Masculinity and Femininity in Israeli Army* (Hebrew). Jerusalem: Magnes Press.

Shafir, G., and Y. Peled. 1998. "Citizenship and Stratification in an Ethnic Democracy." *Ethnic and Racial Studies* 21 (3): 408–27.

Simmel, G. 1950. "The Stranger." In K. Wolff (ed. and trans.), *The Sociology of Georg Simmel*, 402–8. New York: Free Press.

Sion, L. 2006. "Too Sweet and Innocent for War?" *Armed Forces and Society* 32: 454–74.

Yiftachel, O. 1999. "Ethnocracy: The Politics of Judaizing Israel/Palestine." *Constellations* 6: 364–91.

Three Interpretations of Civil–Military Entanglements

Birgitte Refslund Sørensen and Eyal Ben-Ari

Introduction

In this afterword, we add another integrative voice to the volume by focusing on three distinct forms of entanglement and how the different chapters exemplify and unfold these. Our aim is integrative in the sense of bringing together the different empirical bases and analytical foci of the contributions so that a coherent set of contentions about the links between "things military" and "things civilian" can be stated. Our argument is that, looking at the scholarly literature on entanglements, we discern three types of (often overlapping) approaches that illuminate and underscore different aspects of social experiences. Accordingly, we reread the chapters through these three perspectives with the aim of further developing the idea of civil–military entanglements.

Entanglements as Entrapment

The first, and probably most used, approach to entanglements has been developed by Ian Hodder (2012, 2014) within archaeology with an analysis of how people and groups become entrapped in systems of material things and social relations. His emphasis here is looking at human systems along timelines where previous conditions (themselves emergent) not only precondition the next stage but actually entrap—that is restrain—actors within webs of ties and resources in ways that make getting out of such relations very difficult. His analysis goes beyond networks simply connecting separate entities because it underscores dialectic relationships between productive and enabling "dependence" and constraining and limiting "dependency" (Hodder 2012: 88; 2014: 20).

Hodder's idea of entrapment is important for our purposes since it guides us to investigate the power and the reproductive capacity of entanglements as is evident in a number of contributions. Take the contribution of Truusa and Kasearu centered on kinship and the armed forces. This essay illuminates how wives of professional Estonian military soldiers are constantly obliged by others to answer expectations and create identity claims as (military) partners and to situate themselves vis-à-vis the military ethos. In such cases, which are crucial for civil–military studies, entanglement as entrapment reaches beyond the institution down into the very lives of families where the civilian partners inevitably become entangled or entrapped in a military world whose boundaries they are constantly negotiating.

This idea of entrapment is especially productive for the study of the various ties linking "things military" and "things civilian" since it alerts us to explicitly deal with broader and longer-lasting implications. The first implication is that of unintended consequences or outcomes that are not foreseen or intended by a purposeful action. This is the argument made by Rubinstein and Zoli where the unintended consequences of civil–military cooperation made the boundaries between them more permeable and then led to such things as the militarization of the police, which gained a life of its own. The second implication is that once people are committed to, or find themselves within, a set of civil–military entanglements, it becomes very costly to leave since ongoing cognitive and emotional investments have been made (and are constantly remade). Tomforde's chapter shows how entrapped today's German forces are in the legacy of the Second World War. Indeed, whether they like it or not, many of their actions are embedded in the history and imagery of that war. And in an interesting way, Uesugi's analysis sheds light on how the very entanglements of Gurkha soldiers in both Nepal and the United Kingdom is related to multiple levels (one being in local British communities), and how Gurkha soldiers use these ties to negotiate with the national government over citizenship. Her chapter underscores a third implication that much of the classic civil–military relations theory missed (and still to an extent misses), namely the cross-national dimension or the global connectedness of civil–military entanglements. This point is also underscored by Grassiani's study of the Israeli security industry, and Rubinstein and Zoli echo and develop this point explicitly by showing how the "cultural turn" in U.S. warfighting first entangled and then trapped the country's forces into certain modes of action abroad. Their chapter also alerts us to a fourth implication, which is that entrapments often occur across different professional sectors or knowledge domains, as the military cooperate with civilians in and around humanitarian missions. Indeed, as they and Pedersen and Frederic all show, civilian, legal, humanitarian, and military entanglements have become a defining feature of all of today's conflicts. In fact, Pedersen's chapter on Danish soldiers negotiating morality in Afghanistan illuminates how entangled processes (not only ties) of the "civilianization of war" and the "warriorization of soldiering" are fundamentally implicated in their actions.

To summarize, civil–military entanglements may develop into entrapments that produce particular social lives. Entrapped institutional and individual actors may experience this as either enabling or constraining their particular ways of thinking, acting, relating, and being. Importantly, entrapments tend to reverberate into and influence or take hostage domains not immediately associated with civil–military relations and affairs. In other words, the sites and arenas of civil–military entanglements and entrapments can never be determined a priori, but always have to be identified empirically.

With the entrapment perspective in mind, let us now move to the second use of entanglement that inspired and was reinforced in our empirical cases and which we consider particularly fruitful for future analysis.

Entanglements and Materiality

The second, a Latourian-inspired (Latour and Woolgar 1986, 2013; Graham 2014) reading of the notion of entanglements, suggests—even more than Hodder—integrating the materiality of life into the realm of civil–military relations. The material world has not been entirely absent in previous studies of the military. However, focus has mainly been on the intentional use or conscious awareness by the armed forces of, say, weaponry, terrain, climate, and so on, and sometimes their unintended consequences (environmental impact). Material objects have also been examined anthropologically as important aspects of "military material culture" with deep social and symbolic value. The entanglement perspective does not disregard these, but allows scholars to trace out how both material objects and human actors are entangled actants, and parts of one system (Harman 2014: 39). This is a rather innovative way of thinking about the role of materiality in civil–military relations. We add to this a particular attention to the sensory affordances of materiality (Gibson 1977), and civilians' embodied perceptions, experiences, and memories of "things military."

As an example of this perspective, Ben-Ari's chapter suggests that we look at the very means—in his case products and productions of popular culture—by which an armed force's potential for violence is handled (managed, explained, legitimated) by being directed at the various senses. To put this by way of examples, the very materiality of animation images appeals to the visual and aural, the food served in Japanese Self-Defense Forces' open days at camps is directed toward smell and taste, and acts of climbing on tanks or handling weapons in exhibitions involve the sensual use of whole bodies. Tanaka's piece about noise pollution produced by American air bases in Okinawa traces out the way that the material manifestations of airplanes' take offs and landings are entangled with people's lives and experiences. His argument is that the very waves of noise in Okinawa (of American military planes using runways next to residential neighborhoods) cross the civilian–military divide to create one entangled entity that shapes people's ongoing sensual experiences and memories of the past. This point is important since the very mapping out of an entity (or entangled amalgam) includes material "things" (planes, airports, houses, window and door panels, and sound waves) and human systems in a way that cannot be reduced to any one of the constituent elements. Grassiani's study of Israeli security providers demonstrates how military knowledge and equipment developed to handle domestic security issues become reconceptualized, branded and recirculated in a global commercial security industry that is informed by contemporary politics as well as historical and colonial trajectories. The chapter by Sørensen and Heiselberg proposes that we look at the means of communication—the material manifestations, as in screens and computers—that have become part of many homes of soldiers deployed abroad and that are part of the entangled kin ties between soldiers and civilians today. Indeed new media affords a much closer and more intense material set of ties, which destabilizes the institutional boundaries between civil and military, and overcomes the spatial distances between battle front and home front, as well as the temporally asynchronous everyday lives, and at least momentarily collapses these into one experiential social world.

Analytical attention to materiality beyond simple functionality and intentionality and to human–things relationships has much to offer in terms of understanding the entangled nature of civil–military domains. As illustrated, it opens up new avenues for exploring spatial, temporal, embodied, and sensory constructions of civil–military entangled worlds.

The Dynamics of Entanglements

Third, turning to Ingold's (2008, 2010) use of the term "entanglements" allows us to understand not only how civil–military relations are experienced in terms of human senses and embodiment, materiality, or form sorts of entrapments of systems, but how these experiences are structured and what their dynamics are. Ingold's analysis looks at entanglements in a much more microdynamic way than both Hodder and Latour (although Latour does talk about processes), and invites into the analysis even the most ephemeral elements, such as sound waves, as immediately perceived into a system that is matter-in-flux. Attention to the field's dynamic, contingent, and emergent nature is a promising development of the more established and rigid civil–military binary.

The chapters in this volume demonstrate how the dynamics and ongoing construction of civil–military entanglements manifest themselves at different levels, from the global and international levels at one end, to the domestic and intimate domain at the other. Moreover, dynamics at one level often affect the dynamics at other levels, which direct our attention to the issue of power, actors' relative bargaining power, and efforts to negotiate boundaries and relationships. A second point relating to civil–military entanglements as always in the making concerns context and contingency. Recent critical scholarly literature has mainly been preoccupied with processes of militarization and militarism, and the entanglement perspective could be seen as just another manifestation of this. However, with a broad conceptualization of entanglement that aims at capturing diverse — both bold and more subtle — empirical manifestations of civil–military ties, we incorporate into our analysis dynamics that may point towards disentanglement, demilitarization, and civilianization.

Gustavsen and Laugen Haaland's chapter demonstrates that on a historic level, the shape and content of entanglements may change. As they show using the case of Norway, civil–military ties have transformed into being much more open, public, and formal — away from the Cold War period of being secret, private, and taken for granted. Their chapter hence highlights the large-scale transformation of one entangled system by another, and is echoed by Tomforde, who shows that entanglements are historically created entities and that major international events, such as deployment of German troops to Afghanistan, may change the way soldiers are seen by civilian publics as the "other."

On the issue of power, Uesugi's analysis of the domestication of entanglements proposes that we look at the power of the forces that are entangled. And, in an analytically similar way, Rubinstein and Zoli show how the power differences between the military and civilian partners in joint missions came to be dominated by one over the other.

Frederic's chapter on two Argentinian battalions in Haiti can be read this way for how it uncovers diverse interactions that take place in the entangled ties linking soldiers and locals abroad and how the officers constantly attempted to narratively disentangle the mix of civilian and military dimensions of the mission they undertook. Thus the very undertaking of civic activities is not only deeply related to the mission on site but also emerges back home upon reflection on differing emphases in military identity. On a more mezzo level, Gazit's chapter underscores how changeable and difficult are the ties linking social science scholars and armed forces. He traces out the different ways in which scholars are entangled while doing research on the military and with the military, and how their ties have to be constantly negotiated.

While the microdynamics of entanglements are less covered in the book, some chapters offer tantalizing hints and suggestions: for example, in and around new media links with deployed soldiers, the consumption and co-creation of popular cultural products, or the experiences of attending national rites or viewing them on television. Thus it is not only the interdependence—say of the public and the private spheres—around civil–military relations but, as Gustavsen and Laugen Haaland and Pedersen underscore, this is a dynamic, often powerful, interpenetration. Thus, while critical social scientists may emphasize the militarization of civilian life, we must also ask about the civilianization of military life. These become empirical questions.

At the same time, we suggest that our understanding of Hodder's approach offers a complementary set of observations to the emphasis on entrapment. First, as Grassiani points out in regard to Israeli officers selling their expertise in Kenya, civil–military entanglements work in two directions: the military background of security professionals helps them in their commercial efforts, while the global security industry, as part of the military industry complex, strengthens the reputation of Israeli military commanders. Moreover, as Rubinstein and Zoli and Gazit in their respective chapters underscore, we should not rush to assume entrapment since entanglements actually potentiate and enable change and action.

In Lieu of a Conclusion

Perhaps a good way to end is with a plea for more interactional ethnography or a rereading of previous ethnographies in terms of these three forms of entanglements. Such work would further destabilize the civil–military dichotomy by showing their coproduction through interaction. Accordingly, within this view "civilian" and "military" are categories that are constantly negotiated in military families, in consumption of popular cultural products, or in links between peacekeeping forces and "locals." It is these interactions that constantly create and recreate the boundaries between them and at times show how blurred and changeable they are. The anthropologists in this volume point to the astonishing diversity of places where "civilian" and "military" are produced and reproduced: from statespersons deciding about security alliances to the division of labor over who will change baby's diapers, from cross-national negotiations about citizenship to evocations of morality and self among soldiers in conflict, from Hollywood blockbusters depicting heroes to "marriage markets" in Japan, from national commemoration of fallen soldiers to the implicit contracts struck between researchers and military officials, from the Israeli security industry in Kenya to the production of animated cartoons in Japan, from the narratives of Argentinian commanders to the noise produced by American military planes in Okinawa, and from the artistic productions of German artists to the militarization of the police in the United States. To end with Gazit's paraphrase of Tim Ingold's (2010: 6) assertion, "there could be no knowledge about the military in a world where the military and civilian life do not mix and mingle."

Birgitte Refslund Sørensen is associate professor at the Department of Anthropology in Copenhagen. With her background in conflict studies and political anthropology, Sørensen has been both practitioner and researcher on issues of postconflict reconstruction for the United Nations Research Institute for Social Development and the Danish Refugee Council. She has also been a consultant on veterans' affairs in Denmark. Her latest publications include "Veterans' Homecomings" in *Current Anthropology*; "Public Commemorations of Danish Soldiers" in *Critical Military Studies*, and "Postconflict Reconstruction" in Palgrave MacMillan's interdisciplinary handbook series on gender.

Eyal Ben-Ari is director of the Center for Society, Security and Peace at Kinneret College on the Sea of Galilee. He has carried out research in Israel, Japan, Singapore, and Hong Kong. His main areas of research are the sociology of the armed forces, early childhood education, and popular culture in Asia. Among his recent books are (with Zev Lehrer, Uzi Ben-Shalom, and Ariel Vainer) *Rethinking the Sociology of Warfare: A Sociological View of the Al-Aqsa Intifada* (2010), (with Nissim Otmazgin) *The State and Popular Culture in East Asia* (2012), (with Jessica Glicken Turnley and Kobi Michael) *Social Science and Special Operations Forces* (2017), and *Japanese Encounters* (2018).

References

Gibson, J. J. 1977. "The Theory of Affordances." In R. Shaw and J. Bansford (eds.), *Perceiving, Acting, and Knowing: Toward an Ecological Psychology*, 67–82. New York: John Wiley and Sons.

Ingold, Tim. 2008. "When ANT meets SPIDER: Social Theory for Arthropods." In C. Knappett and L. Malafouris (eds.), *Material Agency: Towards a Non-anthropocentric Approach*, 209–15. New York: Springer.

———. 2010. "Bringing Things to Life: Creative Entanglements in a World of Materials." ESRC National Centre for Research Methods NCRM Working Paper Series 05/10, Manchester.

Hodder, Ian. 2012. *Entangled*. Oxford: Wiley-Blackwell.

———. 2014. "The Entanglements of Humans and Things: A Long-Term View." *New Literary History* 45 (1): 19–36.

Harman, Graham. 2014. "Entanglement and Relation: A Response to Brunot Latour and Ian Hodder." *New Literary History* 45 (1): 37–49.

Latour, Bruno. 2013. *An Inquiry into Modes of Existence: An Anthropology of the Moderns*. Cambridge, MA: Harvard University Press.

Latour, Bruno, and Steve Woolgar. 1986. *Laboratory Life: The Construction of Scientific Facts*. Princeton: Princeton University Press.

Index

Lightning Source UK Ltd.
Milton Keynes UK
UKHW010318041019
350962UK00003B/60/P